M. N. ROY'S MISSION TO CHINA

M. N. ROY'S MISSION TO CHINA

The Communist-Kuomintang Split of 1927

ROBERT C. NORTH

and XENIA J. EUDIN

Documents translated by Helen I. Powers

University of California Press, Berkeley and Los Angeles, 1963

University of California Press
Berkeley and Los Angeles, California
Cambridge University Press
London, England
© 1963 by The Regents of the University of California
Library of Congress Catalog Card Number: 62-21387
Printed in the United States of America

CONTENTS

INTRODUCTION.

THE DOCUMENTS:

ORIGIN AND SIGNIFICANCE

M. N. Roy was undoubtedly the most colorful of all non-Russian Communists in the era of Lenin and Stalin. A Hindu Brahmin by birth, an ardent Indian nationalist and revolutionary in his youth, and a convert to Marxism only after the Bolshevik revolution in Russia, he rose rapidly within the Comintern hierarchy to become the most prominent Asian exponent and theoretician of communism for Asia. As a member of the Executive Committee and Presidium of the Communist International, his influence was cleary identifiable in Comintern resolutions throughout most of the twenties, and his concepts of revolution for the colonies and so-called semicolonies were incorporated into many of the most important decisions of the Communist International.

In August, 1920, Roy's Supplementary Theses on the National and Colonial Questions complemented the Theses prepared by Lenin and provided a theoretical basis for Communist political strategy and tactics in the colonies and "semicolonies" which is still recognizable in Soviet and Chinese Communist practice. It is no exaggeration to state that Roy ranks with Lenin and Mao Tse-tung in the development of fundamental Communist policy for the underdeveloped, as contrasted with the industrialized, areas of the globe.

In 1927 the Communist International assigned Roy the task of troubleshooting the alliance between the Kuomintang and the Chinese Communist Party, which was suffering increasingly disruptive stress. As it turned out, his failure to achieve a satisfactory solution made him *persona non grata*—or more precisely, perhaps, a scapegoat—in the eyes of Stalin, and so it was that the China mission, which might have enhanced his already considerable prestige within the Comintern, actually brought about his political downfall.

Reaching China on the eve of the fatefully important Fifth Congress of the Chinese Communist Party, Roy carried with him the "Theses on the Chinese Situation," which had been adopted by the Seventh Extraordinary Plenum of the Executive Committee of the Communist International in December, 1926, and which he had helped to draft. In seeking to implement the Theses as he understood them, Roy found himself in sharp conflict with M. M. Borodin, who had been serving as Communist adviser to the Kuomintang and to the Chinese Communist Party since late 1923. Until this moment, Moscow had been guided in its support of the Kuomintang-Communist alliance mainly through reports dispatched by Borodin, G. N. Voitinsky, and others, but now Roy had come armed with his own radical viewpoint and with the Theses of the Seventh Plenum which emphasized the importance of strong Communist support of the agrarian revolution already surging over the Chinese countryside.

The flaw in the Comintern position was that support for the Kuomintang and support for the agrarian revolution were antagonistic, mutually exclusive policies. The Communists might have chosen one course or the other, but the attempt to do both could end only in trouble—as unfolding events were soon to demonstrate. The documents here presented in translation from the Russian language go a long way toward revealing how the Communist leadership both in Moscow and in China were "internally conflicted" and how these mutually incompatible tendencies moved the various actors in the complicated plot toward almost inevitable disaster.

Until now there have been virtually no documents available for reconstructing either the proceedings of the Fifth Congress of the Chinese Communist Party or the pertinent discussions and controversies immediately preceding and following its crucially significant sessions. Harold Isaacs, in his excellent and enduring volume *The Tragedy of the Chinese Revolution* records with considerable accuracy the course of events that distinguished the period, but it is clear that in attempting to present the viewpoints, the main lines of argument, and the nature of the clashes among the various protagonists, he did not have the advantage of access to these fundamental documents.

Similarly, in their standard work *A Documentary History of Chinese Communism,* Conrad Brandt, John K. Fairbank, and Benjamin Schwartz were forced to rely largely upon secondary sources for their treatment of the Fifth Congress. On page 89 of that volume the authors state: "The following document is a Japanese summary of the political and agrarian platforms adopted by the Fifth Congress of the CCP, which convened in Hankow in late April and early May 1927. Although far from complete, this summary is presented here as a substitute for the original text, which is apparently unavailable in the United States." The Fifth Congress is also discussed and quoted—and the most important resolutions given—in Mif, *Kitaiskaia Kommunisticheskaia Partiia v kritichenskie dni,* but the original speeches are not included.

Even the most reliable monographs dealing with the Chinese Communist movement and with analyses of the 1927 struggle between the Kuomintang and the Chinese Communists have been forced to rely upon substantially the same sources used by Isaacs and upon the Japanese summaries presented by Brandt, Schwartz, and Fairbank. Indeed, there was nowhere else to go for evidence.

It was known, however, that in the introduction to his book *Revolution and Counter-Revolution in China,* M. N. Roy had stated that upon his return to Moscow from China "all the documents (stenographic reports of the proceedings of the Fifth Congress of the Communist Party of China, of all the meetings of its Central Committee during the period of my stay in China, and so on) were published in a book called 'The Chinese Revolution.' It was published in Russian by the State Publishing Department." That book, according to Roy, was never published in any other language, while he himself, on request from Moscow, had sent the original manuscript back from his headquarters in Berlin to Russian Communist authorities. Until his death in 1954 Roy believed that no copy of the volume existed outside Communist archives in Moscow. Up to the time of this writing, morever, the present authors have no knowledge of a single Western monograph or other written analysis of the period which quotes from the Roy materials or directly cites them.

Some years ago, however, Professor Richard Park informed us that at least a part of Roy's report had been found in the University of California Library under a Moscow imprint. A second copy was found later in the rare-book collection of the Hoover Library at Stanford University. In view of the rarity of the book, the unique character of the documents, and the additional information they contain about the China situation in 1927, Professor Park felt—and the present authors agreed—that the text should be put into English and made more widely accessible.

How this volume, *Kitaiskaia revoliutsiia i Kommunisticheskii Internatsional,* came to be published in Moscow in 1929—at a time when Roy was no longer acceptable to Stalin and, indeed, was regularly referred to in Party literature as a renegade—remains a mystery. Bukharin was well-disposed toward Roy, however, and it is possible that the book was published under his aegis. A further question arises in that the volume, in contradiction to Roy's statement in *Revolution and Counter-Revolution in China,* does not contain stenographic reports of all the meetings of the Central Committee or even the full proceedings of the

Fifth Congress. What we find are speeches and articles by Roy and a collection of theses, manifesto, declarations, and proclamations of the Party. When he wrote his introduction to this later work Roy may have forgotten the precise contents of the earlier one, or someone in Moscow may have deleted the stenographic reports from the manuscript Roy submitted. At the time of this writing there are still no minutes of the congress available either in Russian or in Chinese.

Desirable as acquisition of the full proceedings would certainly be, we believe that this collection of documents, for all its inadequacies, provides material of extraordinary value not only to the history of Sino-Soviet relations and of Chinese Communist Party development, but also for delineating basic Communist theory concerning revolutionary politics and government and especially the concepts of "revolution from above" and "revolution from below" in the colonial and so-called semicolonial areas of Asia, Africa, and South America.

It is important to remember that in the course of his career Roy had already served revolutionary causes, not only in his native India but throughout much of the world. As a youngster still in his teens he had joined a terrorist cell, swearing life-time allegiance to the cause of expelling the British from India. During World War I he smuggled arms into India and in later years served the revolutionary cause in places as diverse as Batavia, Tokyo, Berlin, Paris, Amsterdam, San Francisco, and even the campuses of Stanford and Columbia universities. Apprehended in New York, just before the entry of the United States into World War I, Roy escaped to Mexico where, in collaboration with Borodin, he played a role in the establishment of the Mexican Communist movement.

It is against this almost incredible background of experience and in view of the powerful influence of his ideas about agrarian revolution and about the functioning of a Communist-dominated revolutionary government in the underdeveloped areas—an influence that persisted long after he had been denounced by the Stalinist leadership in Moscow —that we perceive the value of these documents as a source for better understanding the various Communist movements in underdeveloped areas of the globe today.

Our intent is not to present a monograph, but rather a source book centering on the report which Roy submitted to the Comintern. Toward this end the chapters from *Kitaiskaia revoliutsiia i Kommunisticheskii Internatsional* have been allowed to stand as translated from the original volume with the addition of only one document—a translation of the Theses on the Situation in China adopted by the Seventh Extraordinary Plenum of the Executive Committee of the Communist International, which figures again and again in the Chinese Communist resolutions and documents. Also, the foreword to the original volume has been transferred to the end of Roy's text.

In presenting the six chapters of commentary, the authors have not attempted a full analysis of the documents, but only a minimal historical context and a suggestion of the significance of the controversy and the main lines of argument. It should be clear that the section embodying the documents of *Kitaiskaia revoliutsiia i Kommunisticheskii Internatsional* contains significant historical and political data well beyond what is touched upon in the commentaries.

The basic contradiction revealed in these documents between the tactic of "revolution from above" and "revolution from below" has plagued Communist policy-makers since the debates between Roy and Lenin in 1920, and recent controversies between Moscow and Peking suggest that the issue has yet to be resolved. In 1926 the question was whether primary emphasis should be placed upon tactical collaboration with Chiang Kai-shek, "the bourgeois nationalist," or upon development of the Chinese Communist movement as an aggressive independent force. A few months later—during the period covered by this volume— the issue lay between emphasis on tactical collaboration with the "Left militarists" and the "petty-bourgeois leadership" of Wuhan on the one hand and large-scale agrarian revolution on the other. Today the problem facing leaders in Moscow and Peking is how much reliance should be placed upon men like Nasser, Nkrumah, and Sukarno at the expense of local Communist parties—and for how long.

From the viewpoint of Communist leaders today—as in the time of Roy's mission to China—the problem is not to decide whether to support national revolutionary movements, but to agree upon priorities of initiative and relative allocations of men, money, and other resources between the local Communist parties and the Nasser, Nkrumah, and Sukarno governments—or the parliamentary democratic government of India. The decision reached by a Soviet or Chinese Communist leader depends upon his assessment of the strength, potential strength, and popular support for the nationalist movement in comparison with the local Communist party and also upon his calculation of the point where the nationalist leaders will balk at Communist policies and pressures and "go over to the imperialists." In this connection it is worth comparing, over recent years, the Soviet and Chinese Communist attitudes toward the Indian Communist Party, on the one hand, and the government of India on the other.

There has been a tendency, in analyzing the controversy between the "revolution from above" and the "revolution from below" viewpoints to oversimplify the lines of cleavage and to dichotomize categorically between those who blindly followed Moscow and those who knew better but were frustrated by Stalin's stubbornness and inflexibility. On pages 77–78 of *Problems of the Chinese Revolution,* for example, Trotsky describes Ch'en Tu-hsiu as "bound hand and foot by the false leadership of the representatives of the Comintern."

Ch'en Tu-hsiu himself, in later years, regularly asserted that he had been opposed to collaboration with the Kuomintang all along. According to Benjamin Schwartz in *Chinese Communism and the Rise of Mao,* p. 60, "After Chiang Kai-shek's April [1927] *coup d'état* in Shanghai, Ch'en claims to have been just as averse to the alliance with the 'Left Kuomintang' as he had previously been to the alliance with Chiang Kai-shek." Similarly, in the *Biulleten Oppozitsii,* Nos. 15–16, September–October, 1930, pp. 19–23, Ch'en—in his "Letter to All Members of the Chinese Communist Party" dated December 10, 1929—declares that twice on the occasion of the Changsha *coup* of May 21, 1927, he proposed that the Chinese Communists break with the Kuomintang. "I approached Borodin for advice. He said: 'I fully agree with you, but I know that Moscow will never permit it.' "

The documents of Roy's report suggest, by contrast, that there was a sharp difference of opinion between the two Comintern representatives, Borodin and Roy, and also that Ch'en Tu-hsiu—at the time—may have been closer to the Borodin viewpoint than he subsequently led others to believe.

The further statement has been made that none of the Comintern representatives in China at the time—Borodin, Roy, Mif, Lozovsky, Browder, Doriot—questioned Comintern directives or "spoke up for any different course." According to Harold Isaacs (p. 218), "Roy later claimed that he had fought hard to get the Chinese Communist party to pursue a bolder revolutionary course even if it meant a break with the Kuomintang. His own reports published at the time, however, failed to back him up in this claim." Isaacs also quotes Ch'u Ch'iu-po (p. 218) to the effect that Roy failed, after the defection of Chiang Kai-shek, "to point out the possibility of new betrayals."

The allusion to Roy's reports refers, apparently, to the single article "Le V͏e Congrès du Parti Communiste de Chine" published in *International Press Correspondence* (French edition), July 13, 1927.

The documents of *Kitaiskaia revoliutsiia i Kommunisticheskii Internatsional* do not reveal Roy as more accurate or prophetic in his judgment than anyone else associated with the debacle. The truth of the matter seems to be that everyone—Trotsky not excluded—was a better prophet after the fact than beforehand. What the documents do suggest is that Roy argued consistently for agrarian revolution and a substantially "different course"—up to the point, during the Fifth Congress, where revolution "from above" clashed head-on with revolution "from below." Actually, Roy continued to argue in favor of agrarian revolution. Either he did not perceive that a single concession to the Left Kuomintang on the confiscation of land had placed effective support for the peasantry entirely out of the question [*Document 16*]; or he was overruled by Borodin, backed, in turn, by Stalin.

In all this confusion the essential fact was not that the Chinese Communists were forced to submit themselves—against their better judgment —to a single, dogmatic, and uniquely mistaken line from Moscow. Unquestionably the major responsibility was Stalin's. We must keep in mind, however, that he was thousands of miles away and dependent upon the undoubtedly conflicting information sent from China by Borodin, Roy, Voitinsky, and other Comintern representatives.

In view of these considerations, the essential and overwhelmingly disruptive fact seems to be precisely the opposite: that virtually everyone "spoke up for a different course," that virtually everyone "contended," that hardly anyone agreed with anyone else, and that the misperceptions, the errors, and the contradictory decisions were by no means attributable only to Stalin, but were widely shared by both the Chinese and the Russian Communists. Scarcely anyone of them really understood what was taking place; none foresaw clearly and sufficiently in advance the difficulties inherent in harmonizing revolution "from above" with revolution "from below."

Among even the bitterest critics of communism there is frequently an inclination to endow Communist leaders with a monolithic command of independent decision and power which, in fact, they may rarely enjoy. The appended documents suggest that the 1927 Communist debacle in China was not the outcome of "simple repetition of the [misguided] formula laid down in Moscow"—but the upshot of a proliferation of formulas, the consequence of a bewildering babble of proposals and counterproposals.

The wonder is that the Communists even succeeded in China at all. Indeed, one may rightfully question whether they could have succeeded if the Soviet Russians had not withdrawn sufficiently to allow Mao Tsetung—with his own army, his own police force and his own political institutions—to work out his own special mixture of so many revolutionary elements "from below" and so many others "from above." However that may be, the major importance of the presented documents is not for what they reveal about who was relatively more or less at fault. The documents are significant, rather, for their delineation of a central contradiction in Communist tactical theory, their exposure of a major weakness in the Communist system, and their revelation of the disruptive consequences that can emerge from uncertainties over how much of a revolution should be fought "from above" and how much "from below."

Generally, the documents reveal the essential cleavage between the Roy and Borodin points of view. To widen the context and to suggest in broad outline the arguments of other, in some cases more distant, participants such as Stalin and Trotsky, we have woven into the commentaries a considerable amount of material from Comintern and from Soviet and Chinese Communist Party sources.

The immediate broad objective—initially shared by the Comintern and by the Chinese Nationalists and Communists alike—was to overthrow the legal, so-called warlord regime in Peking and establish a revolutionary government. Since the Communists had no army of their own at that time, they either had to rely on the various forces associated with the Nationalists, or somehow develop an army of their own out of the dissatisfied peasantry.

Borodin maintained that the Communists could not posssibly establish a firm base in China without a dictatorship of the proletariat, and consequently it was necessary to rely upon Nationalist forces. Thus the Northern Expedition against Peking was initially undertaken by Chiang Kai-shek and the Communists in alliance, but later, after Chiang had broken away to form the Right Kuomintang, it became necessary to rely upon the forces of T'ang Sheng-chih, Fêng Yü-hsiang, Yen Hsi-shan, and other militarists associated with the Left Kuomintang or believed to be sympathetic to it. This policy required, of course, that the agrarian program should be deferred lest it antagonize the military officers and Nationalist leaders and thus destroy the "revolutionary bloc" before the Peking regime could be overthrown [Document 18].

Ch'en Tu-hsiu, whose attitudes paralleled those of Borodin, insisted that "the extension of the revolution must take place before it is deepened."

Roy argued, on the other hand, that an immediate campaign against the north was "fraught with grave danger" [Document 5]. Chiang Kai-shek already threatened the right flank of Wuhan forces, and so did the warlord forces of Peking. The rear was already vulnerable because Li Chi-shen, a Kwangtung militarist, had seized power in Canton during the Nationalist advance to Hankow. Borodin's whole plan was built on the assumption that T'ang Sheng-chih, Yen Hsi-shan, and Fêng Yü-hsiang were reliable. Yet it was quite possible that T'ang and Yen were cut from the same pattern as Chiang Kai-shek, and no one knew for certain what stand Feng would take.

"Borodin proposes that the revolution withdraw," Roy charged, "from the provinces where there exists an organized proletariat with political experience, where a partial success has been achieved already, and go to regions where the reaction is stronger" [*Document 5*]. In the circumstance of an immediate campaign in the North, Roy predicted, the petty bourgeois leadership in Wuhan—under pressure of militarists and others—would "turn to flight and abandon the masses." Under these circumstances the importance of the so-called Left militarists should not be overestimated.

"Comrade Borodin thinks that the principal factor in the revolution is not the masses," Roy complained, "but the Communist ability to maneuver with the petty bourgeoisie and with the various military elements" [*Document 5*]. The agrarian revolution, Roy insisted, must be pushed immediately.

Two courses lay before the Chinese Communist Party, as Roy saw the situation: either to support the peasant demands on land, or to retard the development of the agrarian revolution "for the sake of buying an alliance with the petty bourgeoisie" [*Document 11*]. Already the petty bourgeoisie was betraying the national revolution, according to Roy, and if the Chinese Communist Party were to support the plan for an immediate campaign against the North, it would, in effect, be supporting this betrayal.

Did Communist support for the agrarian revolution mean renouncing collaboration with Wuhan altogether? Roy thought not.

"The petty bourgeois Left, onto whose wagon Comrade Borodin wants to harness the Communist Party," Roy admitted, "has neither the daring nor, simply, the desire to start an agrarian revolution" [*Document 5*]. But it was also "a well-known fact" that the petty bourgeoisie "never represent an independent political force," but joins either the bourgeoisie or the proletariat. In China where the petty bourgeoisie was "an oppressed class," it could be counted upon, at the moment of crucial choice, to join with the proletariat—provided only that the location of its "true interests" could be revealed for them. The proletariat would gain the support of the petty bourgeois, Roy thought, in the course of "freeing it from feudal bourgeois elements." As the position of the peasantry improved, trade on the countryside would flourish and the petty bourgeoisie would gain. In the meantime—and here Roy was guilty of a grievous miscalculation—the petty-bourgeoisie Left Wing power in Wuhan could not "exist another day" without the support of the Communist Party and the working class of China.

Against this background of assumptions Roy urged the following program: the arming of the peasantry and encouragement of agrarian revolution in Hupeh and Hunan; the destruction of feudalism, the seizure of political power in the villages by the peasants, and the establishment of "rural self-government"; the creation of a revolutionary army (under Communist control) not by "converting the militarists" but "from below" by winning over the rank and file of peasant soldiery and turning them against their officers; organized political penetration into Kiangsi and Kwangtung reinforced by military action; the subjection of Kiangsi, Fukien, Kwangtung, and Kwangsi to the Wuhan government; energetic propaganda, organization and agitation in Shanghai; a maximum use of Communist power through the Wuhan ministries of Labor, Agriculture, and Foreign Affairs; and—from this central power base—the "improvement of relations" with Fêng Yü-hsiang and Yen Hsi-shan.

Such, in essence, was the program Roy took before the Fifth Congress of the Chinese Communist Party. In the course of these sessions the issue in its many phases was stubbornly debated—with Roy losing ground and eventually compromising his position. The Fifth Congress, he asserted after its decisions had been made, was an important event in the history of both the Chinese and the world revolution [*Document 19*].

Essentially, the Fifth Congress called for a "radical solution of the agrarian problem" through "a fundamental redistribution" and "nationalization" of land and the seizure of village political power by the peasantry [*Document 16*]. At the same time, however, the congress exempted from land confiscation the small owners and "officers of the revolutionary army."

This basic compromise unmistakably shaped the course of events to come. Communist tactics had renounced "revolution from below" in favor of "revolution from above," and henceforth the Chinese Communists were dependent upon—and at the mercy of—the "Left militarists." When the peasants began rising on their own initiative, the Communist Party found itself joining the Left Kuomintang in deploring the excesses. Power steadily accumulated in the hands of the "Left" militarists—until they no longer valued the Communists even for the Russian arms that Borodin was in a position to distribute. In short order both Roy and Borodin found themselves banished from Wuhan and on their way back to Soviet Russia.

Expelled from the Comintern in 1929 for alleged deviations, Roy returned to India, where he headed an anti-Stalinist Communist move-ment. Captured in 1931 by British authorities after a spectacular police search, he was convicted of inciting disobedience to the king-emperor and imprisoned for six years. Since material of political nature was de-nied him during this period of confinement, Roy turned to the natural and social sciences, and the books that found their way into his cell left a profound imprint upon his thinking. After his release in 1937 he moved away from doctrinaire materialism. The last years of his life were devoted to radical humanism, and at the time of his death in 1954 he was searching for ways of applying the social sciences more ef-fectively to problems of global conflict.

I

LENIN, ROY, AND THE
COMMUNIST-KUOMINTANG ALLIANCE

At the Second Congress of the Communist International meeting during July, 1920, which opened in Petrograd and continued in Moscow, a fundamental debate was joined between V. I. Lenin and M. N. Roy, a veteran Indian revolutionist who only recently had been converted to communism.

During the early years of World War I Roy had been part of a world-wide plot, financed by the Imperial Germans, to overthrow the British in India and in other colonial areas. Apprehended in the United States along with other plotters, Roy escaped from New York City with his American wife and took refuge in Mexico City where, in due course, he met M. M. Borodin, who had been engaged in an ill-fated attempt at selling a suitcase full of tsarist crown jewels in Western Hemisphere gem markets.

In the course of checkers sessions lasting into early morning hours, Borodin gradually converted Roy to communism and in 1920 arranged for him to attend the Second Congress of the Communist International.

Ironically, it was these two checkers cronies who, coming face to face in Hankow seven years later, argued over the meanings of Comintern policy, and, even more ironically, it was Roy, the disciple of Mexico City days, who was sent to check on the failures of Borodin. Later yet, and still more ironically—though the story will not be told in this volume—it was Borodin who, almost more than any other Russian except Bukharin, was responsible, probably at great risk to himself, for getting Roy safely out of Moscow—when the Indian had fallen into disfavor—and beyond the range of Stalin's wrath.

Delegates to the Second Congress discussed at considerable length the political strategy and tactics which the Communists ought to follow in the encouragement of revolution in the colonial and dependent—as distinct from the Western capitalist—nations. The problem in its many aspects was argued first of all in the Commission on the National and Colonial Questions and later at sessions of the congress itself. The outcome of these discussions was the adoption of the "Theses on the National and Colonial Questions," [1] which presented Lenin's views modified somewhat by proposals introduced by Roy in the "Supplementary Theses."

Lenin's most controversial contention—embodying the concept of "revolution from above"—was contained in Point 11 in a preliminary draft of the theses:

> The Communist International must enter into a temporary alliance [*soiuz*] with the bourgeois democracy of the colonial and backward countries. It must not, however, amalgamate with it. It must retain the independent character of the proletarian movement even though this movement be in the embryonic stage. [2]

In the final draft of the theses the first sentence of this passage was altered to read: "The Communist International must be ready to establish temporary relationships [*soglasheniia*] and even alliances [*soiuzy*] with the bourgeois democracy of the colonies and backward countries." [3]

Roy challenged some aspects of Lenin's argument:

> Two distinct movements which grow farther apart each day are to be found in the dependent countries. One is the bourgeois democratic nationalist movement, with a program of political independence under the bourgeois order. The other is the mass struggle of the poor and ignorant peasants and workers for their liberation from all forms of exploitation. [4]

In order to overthrow foreign capitalism, according to Roy, it would be profitable to make use of the coöperation of the bourgeois national revolutionary elements—but only in initial stages and with circumspection. The foremost task was to form Communist parties which would organize the peasants and workers and lead them to the revolution "from below," so to speak, and to the establishment of soviet republics.

Beyond this, Roy contended also that the revolutionary movement in Europe was absolutely dependent upon the course of the revolution in Asia. Superprofit extracted from the colonies was the mainstay of

---

[1] Communist International, "Theses on the National and Colonial Questions," *Vtoroi Kongress Kominterna*, pp. 490–496.

[2] Lenin, *Sochineniia*, XXV, 290.

[3] Communist International, *Vtoroi Kongress Kominterna*, p. 495.

[4] Communist International, "Supplementary Theses," *Vtoroi Kongress Kominterna*, pp. 496–499.

modern capitalism. "Without control of the extensive markets and vast areas for exploitation in the colonies," he declared, "the capitalist powers of Europe could not maintain their existence even for a short time." [5]

Lenin took strong exception to parts of Roy's thesis. Drawing on his own experience, he reminded the delegates that Russian Bolsheviks had supported liberal liberation movements against tsarism. Similarly, the Indian Communists were "duty bound" to support "bourgeois liberation movements" without in any sense merging with them. Roy, moreover, had gone too far in declaring that the destiny of revolutionary forces in the West would depend decisively upon the strength of the mass revolutionary movement in Asia. [6]

In any case, the class structure of the colonies and semicolonies, as revealed in the theses of the Second Congress and by the debates, was perceived by the Communists to be something like this:

> imperialists
> feudal remnants; militarists
> compradores
>
> national bourgeoisie
>
> petty bourgeoisie
>
> rich peasants
>
> middle peasants
>
> poor peasants
> proletariat

The hopelessly "reactionary" classes within this scheme were the imperialists and their "natural allies" the feudal remnants, militarists, and treaty-port compradores. The national bourgeoisie was perceived as opposed to imperialism and therefore revolutionary at first—though for how long was a question of serious debate. The petty bourgeoisie remained essentially "wavering," but in the colonies and semicolonies this class could be counted on to support the revolution. In a country like China the vast revolutionary masses, of course, would consist largely of peasantry, while leadership would fall to the proletariat.

---

[5] *Ibid.*

[6] M. N. Roy in an interview with Robert C. North at Dehra Dun, India, October 15, 1951.

Against this class analysis the fundamental question was to what degree and for how long should the Communist Party, as the vanguard of the proletariat, ally itself—"from above"—with the anti-imperialist and non-Communist national and petty bourgeoisie, and how much of its energies should be devoted to enhancing the power of the proletariat and the peasantry—"from below."

After considerable debate the Second Congress sought to resolve the argument by approving both theses. While collaborating with middle-class nationalists in the colonies and semicolonies, Communist leaders were expected to make every effort to arouse and organize the working masses and to penetrate and gain leadership over existing revolutionary movements. Revolution, in short, must embody a subtle balance of tactics "from above" and "from below."

Over the ensuing years, headquartering first in Berlin and later in Paris, Roy developed his concepts for revolution in the colonies and semicolonies around four central themes: (1) the absolute necessity for insuring that leadership for all stages of the revolution should rest at all times with a Communist vanguard; (2) the usefulness of limited, tactical, and strictly controlled Communist coöperation with essentially hostile bourgeois democratic elements during early stages; (3) recognition of the wavering tendencies within the petty bourgeoisie who, as an exploited class in the colonies and semicolonies, shares with the peasantry and the proletariat certain interests which it does not at first perceive—but which, under Communist leadership, it can be brought to see; and (4) the function, during initial revolutionary stages, of a Communist-led program encompassing many petty-bourgeois capitalist reforms such as the division of land, the nationalization of transport and key industries, and so forth.

Roy's Indian background and his assessment of the independence struggle in India probably had much to do with centering his interest in these concepts. It is against the background of his attitudes toward the Indian Communist movement, indeed, that Roy's 1927 mission to China and his relations with the Kuomintang can best be understood.

An important basis for Roy's distrust of the bourgeoisie, for example, seems to have emerged from his perception of an important shift in British policies—and his perception, also, of how the Indian bourgeoisie had responded to this shift.

Unable, during the war, to keep Indian markets supplied with manufactured goods, Great Britain, according to Roy, had reversed its traditional policy of keeping India industrially backward, had taken the Indian bourgeoisie "into confidence," and had presented Indian capital with a free field of development.[7] In 1916 the British government even went so far as to appoint an Indian Industrial Commission, with the object of promoting industry in the country, and by the end of the war, in consequence, the Indian capitalist class had acquired such a secure economic position that it was no longer possible for the government to ignore bourgeois political demands, and these were largely met, in due course, by the Montague-Chelmsford Reforms: "The object behind this remarkable change of policy on the part of British Imperialism," Roy asserted, "was to split the revolutionary movement by making it clear to the bourgeoisie that it was no longer impossible for it to realise its ambitions under British rule." [8]

All this did not mean that the bourgeoisie would be permanently won over. On the contrary, "The more the British Government makes concessions to the Indian bourgeoisie," Roy declared, "the more ambitious the latter becomes. It knows quite well that it is necessary to make compromises with the Imperial capital, till the time comes when it will be in a position to openly contend for the right of monopoly of exploitation with the foreigner. But it also knows that the British Imperialism cannot be overthrown without the help of the masses." [9] The bourgeoisie would deceive the masses in order to win their support and achieve aggrandizement, and would entice them into the National Congress. The masses, still unconscious of their own purposes, would follow for a time, but would not remain forever a reliable force behind the political movement of the bourgeoisie.[10] "The overthrow of the British rule will be achieved by the joint action of the bourgeoisie and the masses," wrote Roy, thus revealing his position as only a few hairbreadths apart from Lenin's, "but how this joint action can be consummated still remains a question. It will be easier to solve this problem when the condition of the masses is analyzed, in order to understand what a great gulf divides these two revolutionary factors." [11] In the long run, Roy believed, the divorce of the masses from bourgeois leadership was inevitable, bourgeois nationalism would end in a compromise with Imperial supremacy, and the liberation of India would be left to the political movement of the workers and peasants—"consciously organized and fighting on the grounds of class-struggle." [12] The problem, again, was to strike just the precise balance between "revolution from above" and "revolution from below."

Between 1922 and the convening of the Sixth Congress in 1928 Roy

---

[7] Roy, *India in Transition*, pp. 28–29.
[8] *Ibid.*, pp. 33–35, 37.
[9] *Ibid.*, p. 40.
[10] *Ibid.*, p. 41.
[11] *Ibid.*, p. 41.
[12] *Ibid.*, p. 241.

differed from time to time in his assessments of bourgeois relationships with the British and with the Indian masses, but he argued almost exclusively within the same general context.

In 1922, for example, Roy told the Fourth Congress of the Communist International that the dislocation of the capitalist equilibrium in Europe was forcing the imperialists to look for new markets by which the equilibrium of world capitalism could be reëstablished. Essentially, they were attempting to accomplish this new equilibrium by promoting industrialization in countries like India and China.

Initially, Roy admitted, the various revolutionary upheavals in the eastern countries had been a spontaneous reaction to intensified economic exploitation of them by the imperialists. With increased industrialization and opportunities for profit the national bourgeoisie, which once supported the revolution, now found it more convenient to seek imperialist protection. As a consequence, "The national revolutionary movement in these countries," Roy said, ". . . is not going to be successful under the leadership of the bourgeoisie. . . . It is only under the leadership of a political party representing the workers and peasants that the national revolutionary struggle can come to final victory in these countries." [13]

The theses adopted by the Fourth Congress supported Roy's analysis. "The dominant classes in the colonies and the semicolonial countries are unable and unwilling to lead the struggle against imperialism as this struggle is converted into a revolutionary mass movement." [14] Yet the contradiction, so evident at the Second Congress, had by no means been resolved. For the Fourth Congress, while upholding Roy in the theses, was at the same time laying plans for tactical coöperation in China with the middle-class Kuomintang. How could these two courses of action be reconciled? And how was a Communist tactician to foresee the precise moment when the national bourgeoisie would expend the last of its revolutionary potentialities and "go over" to the reaction?

At the Fifth Congress in 1924, Roy asserted that in India, where national capitalism was growing rapidly, the national bourgeoisie already had been won over to support the Empire. "Because the Indian bourgeoisie knows better than anyone else that the true reason of the discontent of the masses is rooted in the economic relations and not in the national sentiment," he said, "the masses rise not against the na-

---

[13] Communist International, *Protokoll des Vierten Kongresses der K. I.,* pp. 591–597.

[14] Communist International, Executive Committee, *Kommunisticheskii Internatsional v dokumentakh,* p. 318.

tional exploitation but against the class exploitation which comes from capitalists and landlords." [15]

By 1926 Roy was writing to the effect that bourgeois nationalism had ended in a complete compromise with imperialism in India. The schism between the big bourgeoisie and the petty bourgeoisie had become wide enough to split the Swaraj, or Home Rule party, which previously had "served the purpose of a bridge" between the constitutionalism of the big bourgeoisie and the revolutionary inclinations of the petty bourgeoisie. "The split in the Swaraj Party," he declared, "means the burning of that bridge." [16] The last obstacle to a happy compromise between British imperialism and the Indian bourgeoisie had been successfully removed. Through the British policy of industrialization, Indian capitalism was permitted to grow—but within limits.

How then, in view of his distrust of the nationalist bourgeoisie, did Roy propose that the revolutionary movement should be developed in India? How was the correct balance of tactics "from above" and tactics "from below" to be achieved and maintained?

As early as 1923, when he was operating in Berlin, Roy had been writing to comrades in India about the advisability of forming a "party of Workers and Peasants," [17] and in subsequent years he expanded this idea to include the forming of a national People's party, which would draw its members from a broader class base, but would contain a "Communist party inside it." [18] Similarly, in a letter which was probably written toward the end of November, 1926, the Foreign Bureau of the Indian Communist Party, of which Roy was a member, urged the Communists to organize themselves as an illegal faction inside a legal workers' and peasants' party. In Roy's view, the Workers' and Peasants' party would be organized to include Left Wing elements of the petty bourgeoisie—always, in a Communist theory, a vacillating class—which had rejected nationalist bourgeois leadership. The object, then, was "gradually to develop the W. and P. P. into a real Communist Party by means of ideological education and political training connected with action." [19] The Workers' and Peasants' party, in due course, would enter a more broadly based national People's party.

---

[15] Communist International, *Piatyi Vsemirnyi Kongress Kommunisticheskogo Internatsionala*, p. 615; *International Press Correspondence*, Vol. 4, No. 50, July 25, 1924, p. 519.

[16] Roy "New Economic Policy of British Imperialism," *The Communist International*, No. 21, 1926, p. 70.

[17] Roy, *Political Letters*, p. 30.

[18] India, Government of, *Judgment in the Meerut Conspiracy Case*, I, 77–78.

[19] *Ibid.*, pp. 87–88.

In China Roy saw the Kuomintang serving similar broadly based functions.

At the time of the Second Congress Moscow was already in touch with scattered Marxist groups in China. In the spring of 1920 the Comintern had sent Grigorii Naumovich Voitinsky and Yang Ming-chai, an overseas Chinese, to help organize a Chinese Communist movement. In Shanghai these two men met Li Ta-chao, who introduced them to a Marxist study group organized there by Ch'en Tu-hsiu. Voitinsky established a headquarters and began organizational work. By autumn a group had been drawn together in Peking, and at about the same time Mao Tse-tung and Tung Pi-wu started similar units in Hunan and Hupeh respectively.[20]

Some months later the Comintern commissioned Hendricus Sneevliet (Maring), a Hollander, to attend the organizational meeting and First Congress of the Chinese Communist Party.[21] Under Comintern influence the Second Congress of the Chinese Communist Party, held at West Lake, Hangchow, in June and July 1922, called for closer relations with Sun Yat-sen's Kuomintang. A Party manifesto made clear, however, that the "proletariat support to the democratic revolution" should not be construed as a "proletarian surrender to the capitalists." [22]

"If we, the Communists, wish to work successfully in the southern Chinese trade unions," Maring wrote in an official Comintern publication, "we must first of all maintain the most friendly relations with southern Chinese nationalists. In China, when the proletariat is still in the first stage of development, we, while applying the theses of the Second Congress, must at the same time support in every way possible the revolutionary national elements in the South. We must try to unite [ob'edinit] these revolutionary national elements and to push [tolkat] the entire movement leftward." [23]

In the summer of 1923, having been in correspondence with Lenin and other Communist leaders in Moscow, Sun Yat-sen sent a young Nationalist military officer, Chiang Kai-shek, to the Soviet Union in order to make a brief study of the Russian Red Army. At that time, Sun Yat-sen was staying in Shanghai, having left Canton following the revolt of General Ch'en Ch'iung-ming in June 1922. Somewhat later L. M.

[20] *Chung-kuo hsien-tai ko-ming yün-tung shih,* I, 88.
[21] Hatano, "Chūgoko Kyōsan-tō-shi," *Ajia Mondai Koza,* II, 23–46. See also Chen Pan-tsu, "Reminiscences of the First Congress of the Communist Party of China," *The Communist International,* October, 1936, pp. 1361–1363.
[22] "Ti-erh-tz'u ch'üan-kuo tai-piao ta-hui hsüan-yen," in Chu Hsin-fan, *Chung-kuo ko-ming yü Chung-kuo she-hui ko chieh-chih,* I, 277
[23] Maring, "Revoliutsionno-natsionalisticheskoe dvizhenie v iuzhnom Kitae," *Kommunisticheskii Internatsional,* No. 22, 1922, pp. 5814–5815.

Karakhan, replacing A. A. Ioffe as Soviet envoy negotiating with the legal Chinese government in Peking (which the Nationalist government in Canton was seeking to overthrow), wired his greetings to Sun Yat-sen. The Nationalist leader replied in friendly terms and asked for a Comintern representative to advise him and help in the reorganization of the Kuomintang and in the training of an army for use against warlord forces of the Peking governments.[24]

The man chosen for the mission was Roy's old friend from Mexico City days, Mikhail Markovich Borodin (or Gruzenberg), who had recently been released from six months of prison in Glasgow on a charge of distributing Communist propaganda. Reaching Canton in early October, 1923, Borodin found the Kuomintang in confusion and Sun Yat-sen engaged in a military struggle with Ch'en Ch'iung-ming, a local warlord upon whom the Nationalists has been relying for support.[25]

With a staff of Russian colleagues, Borodin began reorganizing the Kuomintang and Sun Yat-sen's armies after well-tested Soviet patterns. The party structure was completely rebuilt into a hierarchy of units pyramiding upward through subdistrict, district, and provincial levels to an annual National Congress, and the whole system was tied together, like the Communist parties, by the practice of "democratic centralism."

The First Congress of the Kuomintang, held in January, 1924, reinterpreted Sun Yat-sen's Three People's Principles (nationalism, democracy, people's livelihood) along more radical lines [26] and approved a new constitution for the party written in English by Borodin.[27] Members of the Chinese Communist Party began joining the Kuomintang in considerable numbers. "Moscow," according to Conrad Brandt, "felt safe with the Kuomintang because it had fashioned it in its own image and imbued it with its own spirit." [28]

Soviet influence in Canton brought about a fundamental division in Kuomintang ranks, and the first Central Executive Committee of the party suffered disruptive upheavals almost from the day of its election in January, 1924. Conservative Kuomintang members could scarcely be expected to approve Communist-made policies.

In May, 1924, Borodin and General Galen (Vasilii Konstantinovich Blücher) supervised the establishment, under Kuomintang auspices, of the Whampoa Military Academy. Chiang Kai-shek was ap-

---

[24] Sokolsky, "The Kuomintang," *The China Year Book,* 1928, p. 1321.

[25] Mitarevsky, *World Wide Soviet Plots,* pp. 130–131.

[26] "Declaration of the First Congress of the Kuomintang," in Hsü, *Sun Yat-sen: His Political and Social Ideas,* pp. 119–141.

[27] A text of the Kuomintang Constitution is available in Holcombe, *The Chinese Revolution,* Appendix C, pp. 356–370.

[28] Brandt, *Stalin's Failure in China,* p. 71.

pointed commandant, and Chou En-lai, a founder of a French branch of the Chinese Communist Party, became head of the academy's political department. In spite of these measures, however, the Kuomintang remained critically dependent upon a number of warlords who shared very little with Sun Yat-sen other than a desire to overthrow the Peking government. Even in Kwangtung province, a main base of operations, the Kuomintang and the Communists were dependent upon a congeries of military men.

Later in the year a group of Right Wing leaders issued "A Proposal for the Impeachment of the Communist Party," [29] which charged that Communists were not acting as "individuals" within the Kuomintang, but were taking orders from the Central Committee of the Chinese Communist Party.

The deaths of two men—Lenin on January 21, 1924, and Sun Yat-sen on March 12, 1925—had a great deal to do with the confusion of conflicts which now began to appear. In Moscow, J. V. Stalin and L. D. Trotsky were vying for supremacy; in Canton a delicate balance emerged wherein Borodin, Chiang Kai-shek, and a Left Wing Nationalist named Wang Ching-wei seemed to be sharing power. The "flamboyant idol of the Left," Wang became the chief intermediary between Borodin and the Canton government.[30]

Elections for the Second Central Executive Committee of the Kuomintang at the Second Congress in January, 1926, brought defeat for the extreme Right Wingers who had urged "impeachment" of the Communist Party and a victory for those who favored coöperation between Canton and Moscow. At the close of the congress there were proposals for a northern expedition against the warlord government in Peking, with Chiang in favor and Borodin—in contrast to his position at a later juncture—strongly opposed.

During 1925, according to M. G. Rafes, the Chinese Communists, acting largely as a conspiratorial faction within the Kuomintang, had failed to create an independent local party organization of any strength in order "to avoid annoying" [ne razdrazhat] the Nationalist leaders. Under Comintern influence, the Chinese Communists corrected this tendency toward the end of the year.[31]

"Our comrades and committee members of various levels (the CC and local committees) generally work as individuals in labor unions

[29] "T'an-ho kung-ch'an-tang liang ta yao-an," *Kuo-min-tang chung-yang chien-ch'a wei-yüan-hui*, as cited in Schwartz, *Chinese Communism and the Rise of Mao*, p. 51.
[30] Brandt, *Stalin's Failure in China*, p. 71.
[31] Rafes, *Kitaiskaia revoliutsiia na perelome*, p. 150.

and the KMT, and among the student masses," admitted the Enlarged Plenum of the Chinese Central Committee, held in Peking during October, 1925, "or they limit their direction to certain specific tasks. Hence, they appear to be representatives of the various movements in the KCT rather than executors of the Party's policies and tasks while participating in such movements." [32] In order to overcome this tendency, the plenum resolved to effect a considerable reorganization in order to strengthen the Party and at the same time expand the united front and fortify co-operation with the Kuomintang. "We should simultaneously build up a clandestine organization," the plenum asserted, "and exert every effort to engage openly in the political movement." [33]

At this plenum, however, there emerged, according to Rafes, a tendency on the part of some Party members to withdraw from the Kuomintang, while others were inclined to "retreat before the advancing bourgeoisie." In the course of ensuing months these two tendencies, "both alien to the correct policy of maneuvering," took shape within the Party.[34]

In February and early March, 1926, the Sixth Enlarged Plenum of the ECCI reaffirmed the importance of the Kuomintang and its government in Canton. According to the "Theses on the Chinese Situation," passed by the plenum,

> The Kuomintang, whose basic group has entered into an alliance with the Chinese Communists, represents a revolutionary bloc of the workers, peasants, intelligentsia, and urban democracy [petty bourgeoisie] united on the basis of the common class interests of these groups in the struggle against the foreign imperialists and the whole militarist-feudal order, for the independence of the country and for a single revolutionary democratic government.[35]

The Canton government, which the Sixth Plenum designated as the "vanguard in the struggle of the Chinese people for liberation," would "serve as a model for the future revolutionary democratic order of the whole country." [36]

The Sixth Plenum warned against two equally harmful deviations threatening the Chinese Communists: *Right Wing liquidationism,* "which abandons the independent class tasks of the Chinese proletariat for a formless merging with the general democratic national movement";

---

[32] "Resolutions on the Question of Organization," as translated in Wilbur and How, *Documents on Communism,* pp. 100–103 (cited hereafter as Wilbur and How).

[33] Wilbur and How, p. 103; see also "Plans on the Organization of Party Cells," *ibid.,* pp. 104–109.

[34] Rafes, *Kitaiskaia revoliutsiia na perelome,* p. 151.

[35] Communist International, Executive Committee, *Kommunisticheskii Internatsional v dokumentakh,* p. 619.

[36] *Ibid.,* pp. 619–620.

and *extreme Left moods* "which favor skipping over the revolutionary-democratic stage of the movement straight to the proletarian dictatorship and soviet power, forgetting the most important and decisive factor of all—the peasantry." [37]

Here, then, were the two extremes: excessive "revolution from above" and excessive "revolution from below."

The fundamental problem of the Chinese national-liberation movement, according to the plenum, was the peasant situation. Indeed, the victory of the movement's revolutionary democratic tendencies depended on how many of the 400 million Chinese peasants were drawn, "together with the Chinese workers and under their leadership," into the decisive revolutionary struggle. The main task of the Chinese Communists and of the Kuomintang was to explain to the Chinese peasants that "only by allying themselves with the working class to form an independent revolutionary democratic government" could they radically improve their national and political circumstances. Beyond this, the Chinese Communists must develop a program "capable of rousing the whole peasantry to an armed struggle against the militarists and against the administrators, middlemen and gentry who support the semifeudal order in the villages." [38]

Just before the Sixth Plenum in Moscow Borodin, sometime in February, 1926, had left Canton for Shensi in order to negotiate with the so-called Christian General Fêng Yü-hsiang, a northwestern militarist who obtained arms and advisers from the Soviet Union. While the Comintern agent was gone, Chiang Kai-shek, claiming a conspiracy against him by officers of a Nationalist warship, detained the vessel, declared martial law, ordered troops to surround the house of his Russian advisers, and arrested Communist political workers attached to military units under his command. This action against the Chinese Communist Party and the Russian advisers, according to Stepanov, who was attached to Chiang Kai-shek's First Army, "came as a lightning shock." [39]

Having weakened the Communists sufficiently to ensure his own initiative, Chiang then sent a personal emissary to invite Borodin back to his post in the Kuomintang army and government,[40] and, as a further reassurance, he also ordered the arrest of several of his own erstwhile accomplices—army officers and civilian Rightists—for their part in the March *coup*. Borodin, according to reports, "was delighted." [41]

The reconciliation was effected none too soon, because Wu P'ei-fu,

[37] *Ibid.,* p. 621.
[38] *Ibid.,* pp. 621–622.
[39] "Stepanov's Report at a Meeting of the Communist Party Branch," as trans. in Wilbur and How, pp. 248–253.
[40] Fisher, *The Soviet in World Affairs,* II, 652.
[41] *Ibid.,* p. 652.

most powerful of the northern warlords, was preparing a vigorous offensive against the Kuomintang in Kwangtung. In the face of this threat, Chiang clearly needed all the Soviet arms and supplies he could muster while, for Borodin, Russian aid to the Kuomintang appeared equivalent to supporting the Chinese revolution against reactionary forces and the agents of foreign imperialism.[42]

On his return, the Comintern adviser conceded that the number of Communist members in higher committees of the Kuomintang should be limited; that organs of the Communist Party should be forbidden to instruct individual Communists within the Kuomintang without clearance; and that Communist members of the Kuomintang should be denied positions of department heads within the Nationalist Central hierarchy.[43]

Wang Ching-wei, who had "fallen ill" a few days before the *coup,* denounced Chiang as a counterrevolutionary—and disappeared. Later he reëmerged long enough to declare his retirement from public life and then, on May 9, 1926, he headed for Paris.

At least a few Comintern agents in China—probably the contingent in Shanghai—felt that Chiang's actions called for countermeasures: without formally leaving the Kuomintang, the Communists should "progress by stages" from a "bloc within" to the position of a separate party. Moscow was so advised.[44] On the surface, however, Communist-Kuomintang relations looked more cordial than ever.[45] The chief of the Comintern's Far Eastern Division, G. N. Voitinsky, tried to dismiss reports of Chiang's *coup* as imperialist propaganda,[46] and according to an article in *International Press Correspondence,* published by the Comintern, "The perspectives for the people's government in Canton" had never looked so favorable.[47] The power of the anti-Kuomintang generals was beginning to disappear under pressure from the national revolutionary movement. "The Kuomin government," the article stated, "is now proceeding to organize all district and town administrations within the province of Kwangtung according to the Soviet system." [48] A

---

[42] Brandt, *Stalin's Failure in China,* p. 77.

[43] The text of the Kuomintang resolution embodying these decisions is available in Woo, *The Kuomintang and the Future of the Chinese Revolution,* pp. 175–177.

[44] Trotsky, "Kitaiskaya Kompartiya i Gomindan," p. 6, a document in the Trotsky Archives, dated September 27, 1926, as quoted in Brandt, *Stalin's Failure in China,* pp. 77–78.

[45] T'ang Leang-li, *The Inner History of the Chinese Revolution,* p. 247.

[46] Voitinsky, "The Situation in China and the Plans of the Imperialists," *International Press Correspondence,* Vol. 6, No. 39, May 6, 1926, pp. 599–601.

[47] Tang Shin She, "The Canton Government and the Revolutionary Movement in China," *International Press Correspondence,* Vol. 6, No. 27, April 8, 1926, p. 415.

[48] *Ibid.,* p. 416.

special Politburo committee, which had been appointed to deal solely with China policy, met in Moscow on March 25 with Trotsky acting as chairman, but no mention was made of the *coup*. As pointed out by Conrad Brandt, the committee "may have known too little about the situation in Canton to appreciate its gravity." [49]

The committee, for the most part, seems to have concerned itself "with the bogy of a possible new alliance (the old one having lapsed four years previously) between Japan and Great Britain." [50] In order to avert what they perceived as a threat to the Soviet Union, the committee proposed to buy off the Japanese—at no expense to the Russians—by yielding Chinese territory. Under this arrangement, "South Manchuria [should], for the present, remain in the hands of Nippon." [51] The committee, according to Brandt, counted on the Kuomintang and the Chinese Communist Party to overcome Chinese resistance to the proposal.[52]

In his "Report to a Meeting of the Soviet Group at Canton" written in mid-April, 1926, Stepanov reported two possible conclusions to be drawn from Chiang's behavior:

One is that Chiang intends sincerely to temper the incident of March Twentieth and to cooperate with the Left for the cause of the National Revolution. If this should be the case, it will be very profitable to us.

The second conclusion is that Chiang's actions are intended to deceive his opponents in preparation for a second move.[53]

Whichever conclusion the Russians adopted, the basic policy, according to Stepanov, was to coöperate with Chiang Kai-shek "to the very end possible." The Chinese Communist Party, he added, was in complete agreement with this policy, Ch'en Tu-hsiu having reported to the effect that the Central Committee had passed a resolution supporting the utilization of Chiang by all means.

Whether Ch'en Tu-hsiu personally supported this policy is not en-

---

[49] Brandt, *Stalin's Failure in China*, pp. 73 and 203, on the basis of "Voprosy nashei politiki v otnoshenii Kitaya i Yaponii," Trotsky Archives. Those present at the meeting were Trotsky, Chicherin, Voroshilov, Dzerzhinsky—only Trotsky and Voroshilov being Politburo members.

[50] *Ibid.*, p. 73; see also *Pravda*, No. 65, March 21, 1926, p. 1. (K. Radek, on shootings in Peking and on general advance of world imperialism against the Chinese revolution); also No. 83, April 11, 1926, p. 1 (C. Voitinsky, on the significance of the change of government in Peking which overthrew "the grandiose plan of the Anglo-Japanese imperialists aimed at the advance against revolutionary nationalist China").

[51] Quoted in Brandt, *Stalin's Failure in China*, p. 73, from "Voprosy nashei politiki v otnoshenii Kitaya i Yaponii," Trotsky Archives, pp. 2–4.

[52] *Ibid.*, p. 73.

[53] "Stepanov's Report on the Present Situation," as translated in Wilbur and How, p. 255.

tirely clear.[54] Certainly there were members of the Kwangtung Regional Committee who opposed further support for Chiang, denied the existence of any reliable alternative Left leadership among Nationalist leaders and urged Communist withdrawal from the Kuomintang. In retrospect it appears, however, that Ch'en Tu-hsiu inclined strongly toward revolution "from above"—despite many claims that he was to make later.

The various restrictions on Chinese Communist action were made even more specific in resolutions passed May 15 by the Second Plenum of the Kuomintang. When telegraphic news of this session was received in Moscow, Voitinsky reported the matter to the Politburo which met in special session and decided unanimously, according to Conrad Brandt, that (1) the Chinese Communists were to try "in case of absolute necessity" to discuss with the Kuomintang the "possibility of a certain separation of functions"; (2) the "best known Communists" were to withdraw from Kuomintang institutions, but those "not yet known to Kuomintang" were not—or not yet—to withdraw; (3) the "possible separation" of the two parties might "in case of emergency" require consideration. To leave the Kuomintang at that time, however, would be thoroughly undesirable.[55]

Against the background of Chiang's *coup,* of course, these decisions appear meaningless. The "best known Communists" had already been forced out of their positions in the Kuomintang, and Nationalists demands that the Communists release their membership lists would preclude the anonymity of "those not yet known."

Early in June Voitinsky left for China "in order to correct the separatist tendency" of the Chinese Communists. Actually, what he observed on the scene soon brought about a complete reversal of his views [56]—though, as we shall see further along, he never allowed them to inhibit his own attempts, however ineffectual, to implement a conflicting policy handed down from Moscow.[57] It will become evident, too, that the

---

[54] Wilbur and How, pp. 224–227; see also Yakhontoff, *The Chinese Soviets,* pp. 123–124.

[55] Brandt, *Stalin's Failure in China,* p. 78, quoting Zinoviev, "Zayavleniye," p. 2.

[56] Brandt, *Stalin's Failure in China,* p. 91.

[57] Voitinsky, "K voprosu ob oshibkakh Kitaiskoi Kompartii v revoliutsii 1925–1927 gg," *Problemy Kitaia,* No. 4–5, 1930, pp. 84–104. This is Voitinsky's late recognition of the mistakes made by the Chinese Communist Party in 1925–1927, and in particular by Ch'en Tu-hsiu. Special stress is laid by him on the Party's failure to give sufficient attention to the importance of the agrarian revolution. Voitinsky quotes in this article the directive of the Executive Committee of the Communist International to the Chinese Communist Party's third congress in 1923, the last section (6) of which is particularly interesting: "The Communist Party must constantly push [*tolkat*] the Kuomintang in the direction of the agrarian revolution. In the localities occupied by Sun's troops, it is imperative to strive for the confiscation of land in favor of the poorest peasants and for a number of other revolutionary

Chinese Communist leadership,[58] divided geographically according to whether they headquartered in Wuhan when the Kuomintang government moved there or remained in Shanghai, were also divided on the issue of supporting Chiang Kai-shek.

Relations between the Chinese Communist Party and the Kuomintang were redefined with some precision at the Second Enlarged Plenum of the Chinese Communist Central Committee held July 12 to July 18, 1926. This meeting recognized Chiang Kai-shek's *coup d'état* of March 20, 1926, as part of a "persistent anti-Communist offensive" on the part of the Kuomintang Right Wing. Referring to the decision adopted at the Enlarged Plenum of the Central Committee of the Party, which met in the previous year, the plenum declared, that "we still recognized [then] the development of the Kuomintang and our participation in directing the Kuomintang's work as prerequisites to a victorious Chinese Revolution." And it further added:

Our policy in the National Revolution should be more precisely defined. We should make further efforts to achieve our own force among the workers and peasants in order to exert political influence over the revolutionary masses. We should organize the revolutionary [high] tide of the petty bourgeoisie and concentrate it within the Kuomintang to consolidate the Left Wing. We should bring influence of the revolutionary force of the masses of workers and peasants to bear on the Kuomintang. We thus unite with the Kuomintang Left in a strong alliance and fight the bourgeoisie for the power of directing the national movement.[59]

In its "Resolutions on the Peasant Movement," the Second Enlarged Plenum described how peasants "conscious of their own sufferings" and unable to endure them any longer, had begun, on their own initiative, to revolt against "landlords, local bullies, bad gentry, compradors, imperialists" and other oppressors and stated that the Chinese Communist Party must therefore "secure the force of the peasantry and the directing power in the peasant movement." [60] It was decided that a complete peasant political platform would have to await the Fifth Congress of the Chinese Communist Party in the spring of 1927, but minimal agrarian demands—such as rent ceilings, tax and interest reforms, popular elec-

---

measures. Only by doing so would it be possible to ensure the success for Sun's revolutionary army, gain support for it by the peasants, as well as to broaden the base of the anti-imperialist revolution."

[58] See pp. 45 ff.

[59] "Resolution on Relations Between the Chinese Communist Party and the Kuomintang," as translated in Wilbur and How, pp. 278–279; see also Rafes, *Kitaiskaia revoliutsiia na perelome* pp. 153–158 for a Russian version of the text.

[60] "Resolutions on the Peasant Movement," as translated in Wilbur and How, pp. 296–297.

tion of *hsien* (county) magistrates, and the like—were recorded. Big landlords were to be "neutralized" and overt attacks made against the "most reactionary big landlords" only.

The Northern Expedition against Chang Tso-lin, Wu P'ei-fu, and other militarist forces in the North and against the legal government in Peking was launched officially on July 9, 1926, but actually troops had been sent from Kwangsi and Kwangtung into Hunan to help T'ang Sheng-chih, a Hunanese warlord, as early as May. Chiang Kai-shek left Canton on July 26 and arrived in Changsha on August 11. The purpose of the expedition, according to Chiang Kai-shek, was to unify the Chinese nation and to secure for the country a position of equality among the other nations of the world. A more immediate objective was to join forces with T'ang Sheng-chih.[61]

Comintern reasons for supporting the Northern Expedition were presented by Rafes in these terms:

> The basic peculiarity of the Chinese revolution is found in its *anti-imperialist* nature. Every step that the Chinese revolution takes is weighed up by the Comintern first of all from the viewpoint of the blows which it deals to world imperialism, and first to British imperialism. That is why the Comintern supported the Northern Campaign of the Chinese bourgeois generals who were fighting the militarists and imperialists. Was the Comintern right in building up its tactic before anything else on this peculiarity of the Chinese revolution? Of course it was right. Since to forget about the anti-imperialist nature of the Chinese revolution is equivalent to rendering assistance to the imperialists. . . . Here [in China] the struggle for the overthrow of generals and landlords is closely bound with the struggle against imperialists. To separate one from the other is like losing one's way around three separate pine trees.[62]

What Stalin and many of his colleagues failed to perceive was that more than one "bourgeois general" was willing to use Soviet—or anyone else's—money and weapons in the struggle between warlords that was authentically Chinese, but scarcely revolutionary.

Advancing northward, Chiang Kai-shek's troops found their route cleared by an advanced army of Communist-trained propagandists and political agitators who had organized strikes and peasant revolts behind militarist lines and who, in some instances, had even infiltrated warlord armies hostile to the Kuomintang.

On August 11, 1926, Chiang Kai-shek arrived in Changsha, Hunan,

---

[61] Huston, "Sun Yat-sen, the Kuomintang and the Chinese-Russian Political Economic Alliance," an unpublished manuscript in the Huston Collection, Hoover Institution, p. 143.
[62] Rafes, *Kitaiskaia revoliutsiia na perelome,* pp. 42–43.

where he met T'ang Shang-chih. Relations between the two military men were uneasy and suspicious, but the Russians, apparently, thought that they could make good use of both. "I have been working together with Chiang Kai-shek," wrote the chief Soviet adviser with the General Political Department of the National Revolutionary Army to Borodin, "and simultaneously manipulating T'ang. I should like to inform you that Karakhan has expressed his approval of this relationship." [63]

In late October a joint conference of the Kuomintang CEC and provincial Party headquarters was held at Canton, and the Chinese Communists apparently tried to dominate the sessions. Such slogans as "Down with Personal Dictatorship" and "Democracy within the Party" were put forward, and the delegates adopted a number of resolutions which Chiang Kai-shek found distasteful. For the Communists, however, the most important gain was a resolution to recall Wang Ching-wei, who was still abroad.

Chiang, having himself proposed the resolution in a telegram to the conference, was perhaps not prepared for the enthusiasm of Communist support for the move. In retrospect it becomes evident, of course, that Wang's recall was prerequisite to Communist plans for strengthening the Left Wing of the Kuomintang against Chiang Kai-shek and other elements of the Right.[64] From this point forward, Chiang Kai-shek became increasingly aware of Communist agitation and intrigue against him [65]—even though the Communists undoubtedly were proceeding also upon the somewhat contradictory assumption that the alliance could still be maintained. Despite a feeling among some of the Chinese comrades that Moscow's concern for the freedom of China hid "imperial aspirations," [66] the Central Committee wired reassurances of good will, and relations between Chiang and the Russians were conspicuously cordial.[67]

[63] Teruni, "A Report to Borodin from Teruni [October 30, 1926]," as translated in Wilbur and How, p. 418. The reference is to Lev Mikhailovich Karakhan, assistant people's commissar of foreign affairs and ambassador to China 1923–1926, purged in 1937.

[64] Wilbur and How, p. 371.

[65] *Ibid.,* p. 374.

[66] Brandt, *Stalin's Failure in China,* p. 93.

[67] Wilbur and How, p. 375. Chinese Communist distrust of Soviet intentions was probably augmented by a dislike of Soviet aid to the Kuomintang. The Kuomintang should be dropped like a "rotten corpse," according to one Central Committee member in Shanghai. See Brandt, p. 94 and "V [Piatyi] sezd Kompartii Kitaia i Gomindan," *Kommunisticheskii Internatsional,* No. 11 (85), March 18, 1927, p. 7.

II

THE SEVENTH PLENUM

AND THE AGRARIAN QUESTION

Pressing their northern advance with spectacular *élan*, Chiang Kai-shek and his troops captured the Wuhan cities (Wuchang, Hanyang, Hankow) in early October, 1926, and somewhat later—almost contemporaneously with the Comintern's Seventh Plenum in Moscow—the Kuomintang government moved its headquarters to Hankow.[1] At that point the responsibility for law and order in Kwangtung province passed to Li Chi-shen, the commander of the Fourth Army, who was left with part of his forces to hold the base, and who promptly seized Canton in a remarkably nonrevolutionary *coup*.

Consistently, the forces of the northern warlord Wu P'ei-fu had fallen back in the face of the Nationalist drive, and many local commanders had defected. It was assumed by Borodin and others that the Kuomintang-Communist alliance could count upon T'ang Sheng-chih, the Hunanese militarist, and—after November—upon Fêng Yü-hsiang, the "Christian general," who returned in October, via Kansu, from a visit to Moscow. Yet the struggle was by no means finished. Wu P'ei-fu and Chang Tso-lin still blocked the road to Peking; Sun Ch'uan-fang held Shanghai and the eastern provinces; Chang Tsung-ch'ang guarded Shantung. There were lesser militarists on every hand who could be counted upon to support whichever side appeared to be winning.

In all quarters, meanwhile, both among the Chinese and the Russians, it became increasingly clear that the Chinese countryside was on the edge of widespread peasant revolt. Before the Northern Expedition, according to Ts'ai Ho-sen, a veteran Communist who later became party secretary for a brief time, "we had sufficiently trained workers only in

---

[1] Wilbur and How, pp. 370–371, suggest that, contrary to the usual assumption, it was Chiang Kai-shek, and not Borodin, who first proposed the transfer.

Shanghai, Kwangtung, and Hunan." [2] As Chiang's troops swept into new territory, however, the peasants were released from their old restraints by the tens and hundreds of thousands until—by the spring of 1927, according to Ts'ai Ho-sen's subsequent estimates—the number of organized peasants in Kwangtung, Hupeh, Hunan, Kiangsi, and other provinces had reached "not less than fifteen million." [3]

At what may have been a crucial moment in this rising groundswell, however, at least a part of the Communist leadership held back. In October the Kremlin sent a telegram directing the Chinese Communists to restrain the peasants in order not to antagonize Kuomintang generals —many of them obviously landholders—who were in command of the Northern Expedition.[4] Later, under attack from Trotsky, Stalin was to concede that the dispatch of this directive had been a "mistake." [5]

On the Chinese countryside, in any case, victorious Kuomintang commanders began more and more to restrict the workers' and peasants' unions, and the government in liberated areas—especially in Kiangsi province—became more and more conservative.[6] "When in Kiangsi province a number of local Communists succeeded in obtaining positions of local magistrates," wrote T. Mandalian, a young Communist from Russia who was in China at that time, "the Central Committee of the Chinese Communist Party reacted to it as follows: 'These comrades will lose contact with the masses, our Party will no longer be trusted by the masses. Therefore, these Communists must resign their posts or leave the Party.' " [7] No sooner had these orders been issued, however, than new communications from the Seventh Plenum in Moscow directed Communist Party members to *participate* in the government and thus share Kuomintang rule [*Document 1*].

On December 13, 1926, the Left Wing of the Kuomintang organized in Wuhan a Joint Council composed of members of the Kuomintang Central Executive Committee and also of representatives of the National government. Designed as a temporary organ to function until the main body of the party and government leaders had arrived from Canton, the

---

[2] Tsai Ho-sen, "Istoriia opportunizma v Kommunisticheskoi Partii Kitaia," *Problemy Kitaia*, No. 1, 1929, p. 21. (Cited hereafter as Ts'ai Ho-sen, *Problemy Kitaia*, No. 1.) The testimony of Ts'ai Ho-sen, like that of other close Chinese participants and eyewitnesses of the events dealt with in this volume, is frequently open to challenge. However, it provides additional interpretation to the already existing accounts of this period based to a great extent on the testimony of Ch'en Tu-hsiu.

[3] *Ibid.*, p. 21.

[4] Trotsky, *The Stalin School of Falsification*, pp. 165, 173.

[5] Stalin, *Marxism and the National and Colonial Question*, p. 237.

[6] Brandt, *Stalin's Failure in China*, p. 94.

[7] Mandalian, "Pochemu obankrotilos rukovodstvo kitaiskoi kompartii," *Pravda*, No. 159, July 16, 1927, p. 2.

council emerged as a nucleus for what came to be known as the "Wuhan Left Wing." [8]

As will be described later, the conflict between Chiang Kai-shek and this group in Wuhan developed almost immediately.

The same day that the Left Wing of the Kuomintang organized itself in Wuhan—December 13—the Central Committee of the Chinese Communist Party convened a special conference at Hankow. During this conference the Chinese Communists discussed at some length the increasing pitch of peasant discontent and revolutionary excitement on the countryside—and also the problem of strengthening Communist coöperation with the Kuomintang Left.

A section of the Chinese Communist movement—especially the members from Kwangtung Province, and also Mao Tse-tung—advocated radical land policies even at the price of antagonizing the Kuomintang.[9] In their view, the so-called Left Wing of the Kuomintang consisted of high-level persons who had no revolutionary sense at all, but only oppressed the workers, peasants, merchants, students, and other elements of the "true" Left. In the long run, according to this wing of the Party, only those who approved of solving the land problem could become the Left.[10] The Central Committee majority, by contrast, remained cautious in their approach to the agrarian situation. "The land is not yet a problem!" the CC declared. "The immediate problems of the peasantry are [to raise] pressing demands for the reduction of rent and interest, freedom of organization, armed self-defense, resistance against local bullies and the bad gentry, and opposition to excessive taxes and irregular levies. To lead the peasantry away from actual struggle for these demands to study the blocked land problem is to stop struggling." [11]

According to a resolution on the Central Committee's report,

The greatest danger is that the mass movement is developing towards the Left, while the political and military authorities, seeing the swift growth of the mass movement, are seized with panic, and begin to incline to the Right. Should these *extreme tendencies* continue to develop in the future the cleavage between the masses and the government will deepen and in the end the Red united front will be demolished and the whole national government will be endangered.[12]

---

[8] Wilbur and How, p. 381.

[9] Mitarevsky, *World Wide Soviet Plots,* pp. 135–136.

[10] Wilbur and How, p. 377.

[11] "Resolutions on the Problem of the KMT Left Wing . . . ," as cited in Wilbur and How, p. 376.

[12] As quoted in "The Letter from Shanghai, March 17, 1927," Trotsky, *Problems of the Chinese Revolution,* p. 398. (Cited hereafter as "The Letter from Shanghai.")

The special conference criticized those comrades who seemed to think that the Left Wing of the Kuomintang did not exist and that the real strength of the revolution lay solely with masses of the Left. "Not only is it a fact that the [Kuomintang] Left exists," the conference declared, "it is the pivot of our coöperation with the Kuomintang." The task, then, was to strengthen the Kuomintang Left.[13]

There seems to be little doubt, then, that the official position of the Chinese Central Committee tended toward support of the Left Kuomintang (tactics "from above") at the expense of the peasant movement (tactics "from below"). The question remains, however, who was responsible for this policy—the Chinese leadership, the Comintern representatives on the spot in China, or Stalin and his associates in Moscow?

Early in November, during a pause in the northward advance and while Chang Kai-shek's forces were active in eastward direction, capturing Kiukiang on November 3 and participating in the capture of Nanchang on November 9, the Communist International in Moscow had been completing its preparations for the Seventh Plenary Session of its Executive Committee. According to M. N. Roy's recollections many years later, A. S. Bubnov, F. F. Raskolnikov (Il'in), and G. N. Voitinsky were charged with writing preliminary Theses on the Chinese Situation. After a brief visit to China, Bubnov returned to Moscow with recommendations that were entirely military: the Communists should support the Northern Expedition in order to make use of the Kuomintang with its landowning officers and thus capture power across the face of China. This meant avoiding agrarian revolution at all costs. According to Roy, whose recollections, it must be noted, are not always reliable,

The preliminary theses prepared by Bubnov, Raskolnikov and Voitinsky were all but useless. So Stalin asked Bubnov, Bukharin and me to draw up another set of theses. These were divergent. On November 26, speaking of the theses that were presented, Stalin stated, "Roy has written these theses." The emphasis was on the necessity for agrarian revolution. Stalin was convinced of this necessity at the time. In those days Stalin listened carefully when someone dealt with a subject about which he knew nothing, and when he heard a fair presentation, he accepted it quickly and without equivocation.[14]

---

[13] "Resolutions on the Problem of the KMT Left Wing . . . ," as cited in Wilbur and How, p. 378.

[14] M. N. Roy in an interview with Robert C. North, Dehra Dun, India, October 15, 1951. Compare with Isaacs, *The Tragedy of the Chinese Revolution* who states that the theses were drafted by Bukharin and Stalin.

Again, in his book *Revolution and Counter-Revolution in China*, written many years later, Roy asserts,

The meeting of the Executive Committee of the Communist International in November 1926 adopted a new thesis on the Chinese question, the central point of which was that the Chinese Revolution must from that time be developed as an agrarian revolution. The leadership of the Chinese Communist Party as well as the representatives of the C. I. in China were of a different view. They still maintained that the nationalist bourgeoisie should be helped to lead the revolution and class struggle should not be accentuated for the sake of national unity. I was alone to advocate the different point of view that the Chinese Revolution had reached a critical moment in which it must strike out a new course and a fetish should not be made of the alliance with the Kuo Min Tang. The Executive of the C. I. adopted my point of view, which was opposed in the beginning by Stalin himself. But Stalin was brought around to my view and the Thesis adopted by the ECCI was drafted by me. Immediately afterwards, I left for China.[15]

In fact, it is not easy to determine the precise extent of Roy's responsibility for drafting the theses which the Seventh Plenum adopted. What does emerge from the text, however, is the inescapable conclusion that warnings against Chiang Kai-shek and the "national bourgeoisie" are obtuse, at best, and that no clear exhortation to "strike out a new course" can be found in the document. On the other hand, the theses—regardless of who was most responsible for writing them—do foresee a "regrouping" of class forces and an increasing "abandonment" of the revolution by large sections of the bourgeoisie.

Actually, there appear to have been several preliminary drafts. One copy of the theses written in Russian and allegedly seized in the Soviet military attaché's office during a raid by Chang Tso-lin's police on the Soviet Embassy in Peking on April 6, 1927, contains at the end two theses and one paragraph which are wholly absent from official publications of the Comintern.[16] No doubt a number of different Comintern "experts" contributed to the theses as they were finally approved,[17] but internal evidence also suggests that Roy's influence in shaping their content must have been considerable.

The first session of the Comintern's Seventh Plenum was opened by N. I. Bukharin November 22, 1926. Delegates and guests had packed

---

[15] M. N. Roy, *Revolution and Counter-Revolution in China*, p. 538 n.

[16] Wilbur and How, p. 33.

[17] In "The Prospects of the Revolution in China," a speech delivered before the Chinese Commission of the Seventh Plenum of the ECCI, November 30, 1926, Stalin refers specifically to theses written by Petrov and Mif, two reports by T'an P'ing-shan, and the observations by Rafes on the Chinese question. Stalin, *Works,* VIII, 373.

the hall, which was situated in the Kremlin, and stormy applause greeted Bukharin's arrival. "We address ourselves to the great Chinese people," he declared after the opening formalities, "which carries on a gigantic revolutionary liberation struggle. We promise in the name of the entire Communist International, in the name of the whole working class of the world, that we will support this world historical struggle with all means, with all forces, at any cost." [18]

Among major speakers—aside from Bukharin—who addressed following sessions of the Seventh Plenum were T'an P'ing-shan [19], M. N. Roy, and Stalin himself.

In the opinion of Bukharin, the chief error committed by the Chinese Communist Party so far—despite its generally correct policy—lay in the insufficient attention toward the peasant question. "Unnecessary fear as to the development of the peasant movement," he declared, "and insufficient insistence on the necessity of conducting agrarian reforms in the areas occupied by the Kuomintang constituted the main trend of the errors." [20]

T'an P'ing-shan, in a speech delivered November 26, referred to Bukharin's statement and tried to analyze the conditions which had led to these mistakes. The Chinese Communist Party, he said, was still weak both numerically and in terms of its organization. During the preceding year its membership had increased five times, and there had not yet been sufficient time for amalgamation and the achievement of cohesive leadership. The comrades, especially in regard to the peasant question, were largely inexperienced and deficient in theoretical training.

The peasant movement, meanwhile, had arisen spontaneously in many places—but largely without organization or experienced leadership. No clear agrarian program or uniform slogans had been developed yet, and many of the peasants themselves still suffered under the "prejudices and survivals of the feudal order." The situation of the peasantry in China was thus a complicated one. "For this reason," T'an P'ing-shan declared, "we hope that the theory and practice of the Communist In-

---

[18] Communist International, Executive Committee, *Puti mirovoi revoliutsii*, I, 1. (Cited hereafter as *Puti mirovoi revoliutsii*.)

[19] According to Roy, T'an P'ing-shan had been shipped off to Moscow because, in opposition to Borodin, he had advocated use of the Northern Expedition for the primary purpose of spreading agrarian revolution across the face of China. "But most of the big guns in Moscow supported Borodin," Roy asserted later, "and during T'an's stay there he was more or less won over. Hence, after the Fifth Congress in May, 1927, he was to join Ch'en Tu-hsiu in upholding the Kuomintang alliance. Later, of course, he was made a complete scapegoat for his Kuomintang illusions. But that sort of thing was usual." M. N. Roy interview, Dehra Dun, India, October 15, 1951.

[20] *Puti mirovoi revoliutsii*, I, 106–107.

ternational and its sections will be of great assistance to us. Only on this condition and in spite of all the difficulties shall we be able to solve the complicated Chinese problem." [21]

Yet a further difficulty emerged from Communist relations with the Kuomintang. "Since the establishment in July of last year of the nationalist government in Canton, which is nominally a government of the Left Wing," T'an stated in his written report on the situation in China, "the power has actually been in the hands of the Right Wing." [22] But the power of the party, that is, the Kuomintang, he said in somewhat contradictory fashion, lay in its Left Wing groups which, jointly with the Communists, controlled "nine-tenths" of the local Kuomintang organs. The Communist task was to strengthen the Left Wing, combat the Right Wing, and isolate the middle group (Chiang Kai-shek) and push it toward the Left.[23] All this was of pressing importance because the Chinese revolution "urgently required a national revolutionary united front, a front of all revolutionary strata of the population against the imperialists and the feudal relics." So here again the Communists confronted their basic dilemma. "We must safeguard the interests of the peasantry, but on the other hand we must maintain and solidify the united front of the national revolutionary movement. In so contradictory a situation it is far from easy to maintain a correct tactical line." [24]

On November 29, in his "Report on the Situation in China," T'an P'ing-shan revealed that, however keen his awareness of the dilemma, he was in no way able to escape from it. The Kuomintang, he said, was a "united organization of the revolutionary forces of all classes" and a Communist withdrawal from it would mean the splitting of it. The Communists, therefore, must do everything possible to "develop the Kuomintang further" and with its aid carry out the nationalist revolution. Yet at the same time the Communists must also "solve" the agrarian question. "The landowning class represents the base of Chinese militarism," he declared. "In order to put an end to the semifeudal system of the militarists we must solve the agrarian question. Only then shall we be able to shatter the militarists' base." [25]

Addressing the plenum on November 30, Roy made two major points —one concerning the imperialists and the big bourgeoisie, one pertaining to the peasants.

---

[21] T'an P'ing-shan's statement at the Seventh Plenum of the ECCI, November 26, 1926, *International Press Correspondence*, Vol. 6, No. 89, December 23, 1926, p. 1548; see also *Puti mirovoi revoliutsii*, I, 279–280.

[22] *Puti mirovoi revoliutsii*, I, 411.

[23] *Ibid.*, 407, 409.

[24] T'an P'ing-shan's oral statement to the Seventh Plenum of the ECCI, *Puti mirovoi revoliutsii*, I, 280.

[25] *Puti mirovoi revoliutsii*, I, 399.

American imperialism, he argued, was trying to recover the moral prestige it had enjoyed in China when the Chinese nationalist movement had been oriented primarily toward the United States. "America tries to get stealthily into China under the label of a liberal, humane imperialism," he said, "in the place of the old brutal and greedy imperialism. That is, America wants to kill China not with bombs and machine guns, but with kindness. We know that we have to be very careful with such a 'friend.' " [26]

In the meantime, since the revolutionary mass movement had broadened its base in China, imperialism by dialectical process must broaden its base proportionately by making alliances with some sections of the bourgeoisie which, up to now, had been marching with the revolution. These were the groups most likely to succumb to imperialist temptations.

These upper bourgeois groups, on the other hand, were a narrow segment of the population. In China the overwhelming majority of the people were peasants, and the revolutionary fight against imperialism depended upon their being drawn into the struggle under proletarian leadership. "The Chinese revolution in the immediate stages," Roy declared, "must primarily be an agrarian revolution." [27]

In order to mobilize the peasantry and bring them into the anti-imperialist united front it was indispensable that both the Chinese Communist Party and the Kuomintang develop an agrarian program. But so far, in formulating this agrarian program, no one had touched upon the basic prerequisite, which was not merely a "program of action" or "a program of daily demands" but "the agrarian revolution—clearly put." "There is the question of the nationalization of land," he reminded the plenum, "the expropriation of the big landowners' estates. This question cannot be avoided. It must be put clearly and answered in the negative or in the positive. . . . The central point of the agrarian program of the Chinese revolution must be the nationalization of land." [28]

Stalin, in his speech delivered before the plenum November 30, 1926, maintained that the national big bourgeoisie in China was weak in the extreme and hence the role of initiator and guide of the Chinese revolution and the leadership of the Chinese peasantry must inevitably fall to the Chinese proletariat and the Chinese Communist Party.

It had been said that the Japanese were beginning to show symptoms of "good will" toward the Cantonese and toward the Chinese revolution and that the Americans were not lagging behind the Japanese. "That,"

---

[26] *Ibid.*, 454; see also *International Press Correspondence*, Vol. 6, No. 91, December 30, 1926, pp. 1603–1604.

[27] *Puti mirovoi revoliutsii*, I, 455; see also *International Press Correspondence*, Vol. 6, No. 91, December 30, 1926, p. 1604.

[28] *Puti mirovoi revoliutsii*, I, 456; see also *International Press Correspondence*, Vol. 6, No. 91, December 30, p. 1604.

Stalin declared, "is self-deception." The revolutionary armies remained a most important factor in the struggle of the Chinese workers and peasants for their emancipation, and the underestimation of the importance of these armies had been an "impermissible shortcoming" of the preliminary theses. It followed from this that the Communists in China must devote special attention to work in the army and transform it into "a real and exemplary vehicle of the ideas of the Chinese revolution." [29] Beyond this, the Chinese revolutionaries, including the Communists, must undertake a thorough study of the art of war. "They must not regard it as something secondary," he said,

because nowadays it is a cardinal factor in the Chinese revolution. The Chinese revolutionaries, and hence the Communists also, must study the art of war, in order gradually to come to the fore and occupy various leading posts in the revolutionary army. That is the guarantee that the revolutionary army in China will advance along the right road, straight to its goal. Unless this is done, wavering and vacillation may become inevitable in the army.[30]

Stalin urged, also, that the most immediate demands of the peasantry ought to be met in order to draw them into the revolutionary struggle. Toward this end, he said, they could be influenced through the formation of peasant committees, through the "apparatus of the new people's revolutionary government," and especially

through the revolutionary army. I have already spoken of the great importance of the revolutionary army in the Chinese revolution. The revolutionary army of China is the force which first penetrates new provinces, which first passes through densely populated peasant areas, and by which above all the peasant forms his judgment of the new government, of its good or bad qualities. It depends primarily on the behaviour of the revolutionary army, on its attitude towards the peasantry and towards the landlords, on its readiness to aid the peasants, what the attitude of the peasantry will be towards the new government, the Kuomintang, and the Chinese revolution generally.[31]

Mif, who saw the Northern Expedition as a struggle of Canton generals against Wu P'ei-fu and Sun Ch'uan-fang, a fight for supremacy of "one group of generals against another group of generals," [32] urged the formation of peasant soviets. Stalin, on the other hand, considered it "entirely out of the question to form soviets" in the countryside and avoid industrial centers of China. As yet there were too few trained

---

[29] Stalin, "The Prospects of the Revolution in China," *Works,* VIII, 377–380.
[30] *Ibid.,* 380.
[31] *Ibid.,* 386–387.
[32] *Ibid.,* 375–376.

proletarian cadres to permeate "this ocean of peasants." Hence the Chinese Communists, while supporting the Kuomintang and the Wuhan government, must take every measure—as must "the Chinese revolutionaries generally"—"to neutralize anti-peasant elements in the army, to preserve the army's revolutionary spirit, and to ensure that the army assists the peasants and rouses them to revolution." [33]

To perceive how the Comintern tried to fuse all these concepts—preservation of the anti-imperialist and antimilitarist united front, strengthening of the Kuomintang Left Wing, development of a powerful revolutionary army, and a "solution" of the agrarian problem—we must examine the "Theses on the Chinese Situation" of the Seventh Plenum, adopted as a plan of action for China [*Document 1*].

As a result of the victorious northern sweep of the Nationalist armies, according to the theses, imperialist domination had been swept off half the country, and further victories would achieve the independence of China.

The basis for imperialist power, the theses argued, lay in the imperialist monopoly of the entire financial and industrial life of the country. This monopoly, on the other hand, was being weakened by rivalries among the imperialist states and by a developing crisis in world capitalism—and challenged by the growth of the proletarian movement in Western Europe, the rise of national revolutionary movements in the colonies, and the existence of the proletarian dictatorship in Soviet Russia.

The revolution emerging from the antagonism of these two forces, according to the Theses, was something quite distinguishable from European bourgeois revolutions of the nineteenth century. For China, as a "semicolonial" state dependent upon foreign imperialism, did not stand alone, but functioned as part of a world-wide movement toward the overthrow of capitalist society. Contained in it, moreover, were a variety of economic forces ranging from a survival of patriarchal tribal society to finance capital.

The development of the national revolution in China—and here we may possibly detect the hand of Roy—depended upon the agrarian revolution. It had to be kept in mind, however, that the situation in the rural districts was complicated with the class struggle developing against foreign imperialists, Chinese militarists, the survivals of large landownership, petty squire landowners (the so-called gentry), merchant usurers, and upper wealthy strata of the village—all more or less simultaneously.

---

[33] *Ibid.,* 384–388.

One could look forward to crucial regroupings of social forces in three stages: a first stage in which the national bourgeoisie, the intellectuals, and the students were the main driving force; a second stage in which the proletariat would emerge to form a bloc with the peasantry, the petty urban bourgeoisie, and with a section of the capitalist national bourgeoisie—a combination of forces finding its expression in corresponding groups within the Kuomintang and the Canton government; and a third stage which was "just beginning," during which the driving force would be "an even more revolutionary bloc consisting of the proletariat, the peasantry, and the urban petty bourgeoisie" to the exclusion of a large section of big capitalist bourgeoisie. This did not mean, however, that the whole bourgeoisie as a class would be excluded from the struggle for national liberation. On the contrary, "even certain strata of the big bourgeoisie may, for a certain period, continue to march with the revolution."

During this third stage the hegemony of the revolutionary movement would pass more and more into the hands of the proletariat. As the revolutionary class forces began to regroup, moreover, there would be a parallel "crystallization" of the counterrevolutionary forces. The big industrial bourgeoisie would vacillate and incline increasingly toward an agreement with foreign capitalists, who, having found warlord forces generaly ineffective, were looking for other agents to crush the revolution. Clearly, then, the Communists must take tactical advantage of antagonisms between strata of the bourgeoisie abandoning the revolution and also between imperialist groups.

Future revolutionary developments, according to the Theses, were primarily dependent upon the role of the proletariat. The feudal military cliques represented out-and-out reaction. The economically strongest section of the bourgeoisie—the financiers and compradores—had always been on the side of the imperialists. The industrial bourgeoisie would march with the national revolutionary movement as long as it preserved a purely bourgeois character, "but on the first signs of revolution they either desert the revolutionary cause or maneuver to sabotage it." As for the petty bourgeoisie—the petty bourgeois intellectuals, students, artisans, small traders, and so forth—they could not act independently, but must march either with the bourgeoisie or the proletariat. In a country like China, as contrasted to the West, the petty bourgeoisie would constitute a revolutionary force, however wavering and uncertain, because of the exploitation of them by the big bourgeoisie and because of their economic dependency upon the buying and selling of the peasant's produce. When the time came for the national bourgeoisie to "desert the revolution," therefore, the petty bourgeoisie would "come under the revolutionary influence" of the proletariat, and in view of these circumstances the "moving force" of the Chinese revolution in its present stage consisted of "a revolutionary bloc" of the proletariat, the peasantry and the petty bourgeoisie—with the proletariat functioning as the dominating factor.

Throughout this transitional stage, the agrarian question would necessarily become the "central" question. "The class which would boldly tackle this basic question and be able to give a radical answer to it," the Theses declared, "will be the leader of the revolution." The proletariat, therefore, must put forward a radical agrarian program to attract the peasantry into the revolutionary movement. "Not to approach the agrarian question boldly by supporting all the objective political and economic demands of the peasant masses," according to the Theses, "is positively dangerous for the revolution. Not to place the question of the agrarian revolution in a prominent place on the program of the national liberation movement for fear of alienating the dubious and disloyal coöperation of a section of the capitalist class is wrong. It is not the revolutionary politics of the proletariat. The Communist Party must be free of such mistakes." Specifically, then, the Chinese Communist Party must support the effort to overthrow the despotic rule of the gentry and rural officials in the village and to substitute the old semifeudal bureaucracy with organs of revolutionary authority. The peasants, in short, must participate in the establishment of the local administrations.

In territories where the Kuomintang government had authority, the Theses stipulated, the Chinese Communist Party and the Kuomintang must reduce rents to a minimum, abolish the numerous taxes in favor of a single progressive agricultural tax, and confiscate the monasterial and church lands and the lands belonging to reactionary militarists, compradores, landlords, and gentry who were waging civil war against the Kuomintang Nationalist government. In areas controlled and dominated by the reactionary militarists, on the other hand, the Chinese Communist Party must lead the peasantry against feudalism, militarism and imperialism as the surest way of demoralizing the reactionary armies [*Document 1*].

The additional articles which did not appear in the officially published version of the Theses, but which were among the documents seized by Chang Tso-lin's police in their April, 1927, raid upon the Soviet Military Attaché's office in Peking reëmphasized the role of Kuomintang troops:

The national revolutionary army is the greatest factor which brought about the victories over Sun Ch'uan-fang and the extension of the territory over which the rule of the Nationalist Government extends. The national revolutionary army has played and can play in the future its part only on condition that the revolutionary consciousness of the soldiers and their commanders will be strong. It is therefore necessary that energetic political work should be not only done in the corps of the national army, but that such work should also be organized among the politically uninstructed troops that have joined the national army, which can be done by means of travelling political workers. The Chinese Communist Party must display the greatest energy in order to intensify the political work of the army, and to strengthen the Left Wing of the Kuomintang in their military nuclei.[34]

Communist parties in the various imperialist countries, meanwhile, must support the Chinese revolution by agitating against imperialist military intervention and must at every opportunity demand the withdrawal of foreign troops from Chinese territory and of foreign naval forces from Chinese waters.[35]

Among leaders of the Chinese Communist Party reactions to the Theses were mixed when the first copies reached Shanghai and Canton early in 1927. According to Ts'ai Ho-sen, who supported the Theses,

On no account should the resolution of the Comintern be considered as an attempt forcefully to apply to China the methods of the Russian revolution. It is equally mistaken to assume that the Third International had resolved to carry out an agrarian revolution in China! The fact of the matter is that the Chinese revolutionary movement had reached on its own a stage when the peasants began to confiscate the land; the workers to aim at the establishment of their own political dictatorship; the coolies and the shop assistants to protest against the antiquated relations between them and their masters; the women to demand the overthrow of the old order. Therefore, the Comintern did not produce its resolution out of the blue sky, nor did it invent it out of its own head, but rather deduced it from the situation as it existed then in China.[36]

Later we shall see how other Chinese Communist leaders either opposed or misinterpreted the Theses and how even the Comintern representatives in China disagreed over their implementation. In any event, according to Ts'ai Ho-sen,

the most important point in the revolution on the Chinese question was the statement that the Chinese revolution might proceed along two different paths [of development]: the bourgeois path, and the non-bourgeois one. The resolution stated that it was easier for the Chinese revolution to proceed along the first path than along the second one. Therefore, the duty of the Chinese proletariat and the Chinese Communist Party lay in switching the

---

[34] "Soviet Intrigues in China," pp. 90–91, Huston Collection, Hoover Institution.
[35] Ibid.
[36] Ts'ai Ho-sen, Problemy Kitaia, No. 1, pp. 21–22.

revolution onto the non-capitalist rails. [The resolution added] that the agrarian revolution carried on by the peasants themselves, was the best means [*glavnoe sredstvo*] for achieving this end.[37]

During the first session of the Seventh Plenum, November 22, 1926, Roy as the representative of the Communist Party of India had been elected to the Presidium of the Comintern and to the Chinese Commission.[38] Then, within a few weeks after the close of the plenum, he found himself enroute to Wuhan as the head of a new delegation of the Communist International. The precise reasons for his journey have never been clear, but his own subsequent testimony suggests that a growing conflict between Chiang Kai-shek and the Chinese Communist Party lay at the heart of the matter. "When the conflict between him and the Central Committee became acute," Roy—designating himself "The Delegation of the Communist International"—declared the following April in Hankow [*Document 8*], "Chiang Kai-shek approached the Communist International with the request that it send a delegation to him in China." At any rate, according to Ts'ai Ho-sen, the leader of the Chinese Communist Party, Ch'en Tu-hsiu, "was displeased with the new representative of the Comintern and he naturally came closer to Comrade B[orodin]." [39]

---

[37] *Ibid.*, p. 16.

[38] *Puti mirovoi revoliutsii*, I, 8. Other members of the Presidium included Bukharin, Stalin, and Manuilsky for the Communist Party of the Soviet Union; T'an P'ing-shan (China); Clara Zetkin (Germany); Katayama (Japan); Kuusinen (Finland); Bernhard (France); Maggi (Italy); Jílek (Czechoslovakia); Bogucki (Poland); Birch and Bittelmann (United States of America); Furoboten and Lominadse (Young Communist International); Thälmann and Remmele (Germany); Gallacher (Great Britain); Kolarov (Bulgaria); Semaoen (Indonesia); Bosković (Yugoslavia). In the Chinese Commission, according to *International Press Correspondence*, Vol. 6, No. 83, December 1, 1926, p. 1432: Gallacher and T'an P'ing-shan were chairmen; Roy and Petrov secretaries. Other members were Bobnov and Miljuten [Miliutin] (Communist Party of the Soviet Union); Eberlein and Remmele (Communist Party of Germany); Jílek (Communist Party of Czechoslovakia); Doriot (Communist Party of France); Ercoli (Communist Party of Italy); Duncan (Worker's Party of America); Young (Communist Party of Great Britain); Turjanski (Communist Party of Poland); Sponberg (Communist Party of Sweden); Bai [Ch'u Ch'iu-pai?] (Communist Party of China); Shatskin (Young Communist International); Semaoen (Indonesia); Ferdi (Turkey); Codovilla (Argentina); Meschlscherjakoff [Meshcheriakov] (USSR); Heller (USSR); Katayama (Japan); Tjuchun [?] (Korea). Technical secretaries: Wagner and Porowoj.

[39] Ts'ai Ho-sen, *Problemy Kitaia*, No. 1, p. 28.

III

THE SPLIT BETWEEN LEFT AND RIGHT

Soon after the close of the Seventh Plenum Roy set out for China by way of Vladivostok and Canton. Traveling with him were Jacques Doriot and Tom Man, who were on their way to the Fourth All-China Trade Union Conference.[1]

Presumably, the Theses of the Seventh Plenum reached Shanghai while Roy and his companions were still enroute. During heated Central Committee discussions, according to the subsequent testimony of Ts'ai Ho-sen, it became clear that there were important differences between Moscow on the one hand and the Chinese Communist Central Committee on the other:

[Central Committeeman] P'eng Shu-chih [Pi Shu-ch'êng] concluded his report by saying that "the Comintern's instructions differed as a whole but little from the policy of the C.C." P'eng Shu-chih's report was bitterly criticized by some members of the C.C., including Comrade Ch'u Ch'iu-po [of the Central Committee] who were of the opinion that the instructions of the Comintern and the activities of the C.C. were fundamentally different [v korne razniatsia]. Other comrades expressed their strong displeasure with the opportunist methods of the C.C. and of some responsible Party workers (Li Chih-lung and others).[2]

According to Ts'ai Ho-sen,

it is sufficient to compare the C.C.'s resolution on the Shanghai uprising and the resolution of the Comintern in order to become convinced of the falsity of P'eng Shu-chih's statement regarding "small differences." The Comintern had instructed us to make a choice between the bourgeoisie and the peasantry, and to select the latter, while the C.C. and Comrade Li-Chih-lung had allied themselves with Ts'ai Yüan-p'ei [a prominent member of the Kuomintang who supported Chiang Kai-shek in April 1927 and became a member of the

---

[1] Louise Geissler in a series of interviews with Robert C. North, Zürich, June 19–22, 1958.

[2] Ts'ai Ho-sen, *Problemy Kitaia,* I, p. 16.

Nanking government], Niu Yung-chien [a Right Wing Kuomintangist appointed by Chiang Kai-shek after the April *coup* as head of the local government in Kiangsi Province], Wu Chih-hui [a veteran member of the Kuomintang, formerly an anarchist, who supported Chiang Kai-shek and after the April *coup* became a member of the CEC of the Kuomintang and of the Nanking government], Yang Hsin-fu [a prominent Left Wing Kuomintangist who later defected to Chiang Kai-shek], and others.[3]

As the discussions continued, it became increasingly evident that some of the Chinese comrades were troubled by the Theses and extremely hesitant about unleashing a large-scale agrarian revolution over the countryside of China. In months to come, as Ts'ai Ho-sen has recorded, the gap between Comintern theory and Chinese practice became wider and wider:

> The Comintern had instructed us to carry on an agrarian revolution, but we continued to support the slogan of a "united front in the countryside!" While the Comintern pointed at the possibility and the necessity of a struggle for the non-capitalist development of the revolution, at that very time, mass arrests of the members of the peasant unions, or "bandits," as the reactionaries called them, continued in Hunan. Meanwhile, the C.C. and the Shanghai Committee were helping the bourgeoisie to consolidate the latter's authority in the Southeast instead of following the directives of the Comintern.[4]

What Ts'ai Ho-sen does not make clear, of course, is that the Comintern instructions were themselves ambivalent between the policies of "revolution from below" and "revolution from above."

On reaching Canton, probably in early February, 1927, Roy was delayed by travel difficulties. During this wait he wrote a number of articles including an analysis of the role of the United States in the Chinese Revolution [*Document 2*].

Meanwhile, at a conference of army commanders and vice commanders held at Nanchang on January 1, 1927, Chiang Kai-shek was urging an attack against Chang Tsung-ch'ang and Sun Ch'uan-fang in the direction of Nanking and Shanghai to the southeast—a strategy opposed by Galen and by Teng Yen-ta and T'ang Sheng-chih, who spoke for the Wuhan Left Wing.[5] According to the Chinese Communist Central Committee, the Peking-Hankow Railway had become the center of military movement, and all Nationalist troops should be concentrated against the Mukden-Shantung forces along this line. Shanghai, on the other hand, was a place where serious encounters with imperialist forces

---

[3] *Ibid.*, pp. 16–17.

[4] *Ibid.*, p. 17.

[5] Wilbur and How, p. 382; see also Roy, *Revolution and Counter-Revolution in China*, p. 462.

could be expected, and there the Communists were relying upon a powerfully organized labor movement. "We should support the autonomous movement in Shanghai," the Central Committee declared, "in order to create a buffer zone in the clash between the Northern Expeditionary forces and the Mukden-Shanghai forces." [6]

On January 3, 1927, large crowds of Chinese began demonstrating at the edge of the British Concession in Hankow and eventually took it over. The British government voluntarily withdrew their forces the next day, and the incident was settled by the Ch'en-O'Malley notes of February 19 and March 2, 1927, which returned the Hankow concession to Chinese jurisdiction. "Nobody foresaw the events of January 3," according to three young Communists—Nassonov, Fokine, and Albrecht—reporting back to Moscow from Shanghai. "The occupation of the concessions by the Hankow workers took place spontaneously, without any leadership or instigation, either from the government, from the Kuo Min Tang or from our party. They were all confronted by an accomplished fact, by a spontaneous act of the masses, and all of them had to reckon with it." [7] The incident did much to encourage Borodin and the Left Wing to take a firm stand against Chiang, but on Voitinsky and the Chinese Communist Central Committee it seemed to have an opposite effect. "We do not entertain the slightest illusion about Borodin," Nassonov and his two colleagues wrote in their letter from Shanghai. "As a Communist, we regard Borodin as one who is greatly similar to a Left Kuo Min Tang man; and like every petty bourgeois revolutionist, he is subject to very great vacillations." [8]

Yet for the time being, at least, the Hankow incident had a considerable influence on Borodin and upon the Left Wing in the Kuomintang government. According to Nassonov and his colleagues,

against their will, they turned to the Left under the pressure and the influence of this spontaneous action of the masses; the December moods were in a certain sense destroyed and when, two weeks afterward, the conflict arose with Chiang Kai-shek over the question of the government seat, the members of the government and Borodin adopted a Left position, which would most likely have been unthinkable without the events of January 3. The Left Wing which, as many believed, hardly existed any longer, consolidated itself and this was accomplished by a certain crystallization of the Right Wing around Chiang Kai-shek in Nanking, [Nanchang?] which led to the conflict between Nanking and Hankow. [9]

_____

[6] "Political Report of the Central Committee of the Chinese Communist Party," translated in Wilbur and How, p. 428.
[7] "The Letter from Shanghai," Trotsky, p. 402.
[8] _Ibid.,_ p. 406.
[9] _Ibid.,_ pp. 402–403.

Ch'en Tu-hsiu and the CC, by contrast, were slow to react at all to the Hankow incident. "Why should we clamber over it," Ch'en was reported to have asked, "and what kind of agitation should we develop when the aggressors were not the English, but the Chinese?" [10] In the conflict that was developing between the Left and Chiang Kai-shek's "new Right," the "leading core of the Party," according to Nassonov and his colleagues, took no steps for a period of two months. Yet this line, "if it could be called a line," was not so much the course of the CC, the letter from Shanghai argued, as it was of Voitinsky.[11] The position of the representative of the ECCI, Nassonov complained, could not be "explained by any principled motives." [12]

Chiang, in pressing for a southeastern campaign, demanded also that Nanchang—rather than Wuhan—should serve as the Nationalist capital. A large contingent of the party and government staff had reached Nanchang on December 31, enroute to Wuhan, and on January 7 it was reported that these officials would remain there pending further discussion of the question at the Third Plenum of the CEC which was scheduled to be held in Nanchang. In Wuhan, however, the Left Wing stood firm in asserting that city as the capital. On January 11 Chiang visited Wuhan in an effort to gather support for his position,[13] but Borodin and the Kuomintang Left Wing gave him no encouragement.

This conflict, as pointed out by the "Letter from Shanghai,"

was not a simple dispute over the seat of the government. The question was whether the national revolutionary movement would go with the masses and the Communist party, or with the dictator Chiang Kai-shek who was already steering towards a compromise with Japan and Mukden.[14]

At a banquet in Wuhan Borodin made a number of bitter remarks about power-seeking militarists, though—almost immediately, according to critics—he "recoiled in fright," and was quoted as confessing to Fokine, "I am afraid I made a mistake. My standing up against Chiang Kai-shek was provoked by the pressure of public opinion, and I do not know if I acted correctly." [15]

Chiang soon returned to Nanchang where, on February 19, he opened a broadside against the Communists. Every true member of the Kuo-

---

[10] *Ibid.,* p. 403.

[11] *Ibid.,* p. 406.

[12] *Ibid.,* p. 408.

[13] The dispatch from Consul General Lockhart, Hankow, to Secretary of State, January 22, 1927. State Department Archives 893.00/8342, referred to in Wilbur and How, pp. 400–401.

[14] "The Letter from Shanghai," Trotsky, pp. 403–404.

[15] *Ibid.,* p. 407.

mintang, he said, must be a faithful believer "in the doctrines of Sun Yat-sen and nothing else." [16]

In its political report of January 8—just five days after the Hankow incident—the CC had described the problem of a reconciliation between Chiang Kai-shek and Wang Ching-wei as "the most important of all problems" and warned that a slogan of "Reduce the People's Burdens" would not be appropriate at the moment, particularly when military action is still in progress." [17]

The CC's reasons for caution emerged in its subsequent Political Report of January 26, 1927. The Right Wing of the Kuomintang, according to this analysis, was gaining strength and tending to join with the moderates and the foreign imperialists in a united front to oppose Soviet Russia, the Communist Party, and the labor and peasant movements. The report declared:

> The tendency toward the Right is due first to the belief of Chiang Kai-shek and Chang Ching-chiang that only one party should exist in the country, that all classes should cooperate, that class struggle should be prohibited, and that there is no need of a Communist party. Many of the bourgeois class have been influenced by this belief, since they do not realize their own sufferings.
>
> The second reason is their idea that the National Revolution will soon succeed, that there will soon be a movement for class revolution, and that the greatest enemy at present is not imperialism or militarism but the Communist Party. Hence, the tendency to oppose Russia, the KCT [Chinese Communist Party] and the peasant and labor movements.
>
> The third reason is jealousy and fear on the part of a third group, which sees that the development of the Northern Expedition and of the labor and peasant movements is controlled and directed by the KCT.

"For these reasons," according to the CC, a great anti-Communist tide "has developed within the Kuomintang," and the most dangerous aspect was the possibility that the Right Wing and the foreign imperialists might succeed in winning the moderate elements. To counter this possibility, therefore, the Communists must (1) allay the Kuomintang fear of the Chinese Communist Party; (2) convince the Kuomintang that the national revolution needed mass support to achieve an ultimate victory; (3) "criticize scornfully" the development of bourgeois ideology in the Kuomintang in order to prevent Kuomintang members from falling for Rightist inducements; (4) explain that the aim of the national revolution was not merely the transference of political power to the

---

[16] Chiang Kai-shek's address to the Kuomintang on February 19, 1927, as reproduced in Wieger, *Chine Moderne,* Vol. VIII, pp. 23–24.

[17] "Political Report of the Central Committee of the Chinese Communist Party," as translated in Wilbur and How, pp. 429–430; see also "The Letter from Shanghai," Trotsky, p. 426.

Kuomintang, but thorough reform, and that in the cities and villages the influence of imperialism and feudalism still existed; and (5) delaying anti-imperialist movements against Japan, France, and the United States, the Communists must concentrate on an anti-British movement in order to isolate Britain from the other powers.[18]

At this time Bukharin, Stalin's chief lieutenant and a major theoretician of the Russian Communist Party, spoke optimistically of the Chinese Communist future when he addressed the Twenty-fourth Conference of the Leningrad district:

> The present stage of the Chinese revolution is characterized by the fact that the forces of the revolution are already organized as a state power, with an attribute, such as the regular disciplined army which fills the imperialist with fear. The advance of this army, its brilliant victories, the systematic dislodgement of foreign imperialism by the Canton troops and by the troops of their allies are a special form of the revolutionary process.

Speaking further, Bukharin said that the revolution was far from being exhausted, nor had stability been reached in the combination of classes which made up the forces of the revolution:

> The present power of the revolutionary Canton is based on a broad bloc of various classes. Within this bloc, the commercial and industrial bourgeoisie still play a fairly important part. This bourgeoisie will, however, inevitably secede from the revolution inasmuch as the lower strata of the Chinese people—the peasantry, petty bourgeoisie, and the working class—continue to penetrate the revolutionary arena with ever growing persistency and strength. The Chinese proletariat which already plays a tremendous role in the national revolutionary movement, is striving and will continue to strive with still greater energy to take the position of a guide, a hegemon, a leader of the Chinese revolution.
>
> For this reason, in the future, a regrouping of the class forces within China is quite inevitable, as is also a shifting of the forces in the government and in the army; it is also inevitable that there should be a certain increase of contradictions within the Kuomintang, a party with a quite peculiar construction, a party which combines various classes into one political bloc. It goes without saying that this entire development cannot proceed, and indeed will not proceed quite smoothly, without friction and without certain collisions.[19]

Bukharin added, however, that "we regard the future of the Chinese revolution with optimism, hope and confidence." [20]

---

[18] "Political Report of the Central Committee of the Chinese Communist Party," as translated in Wilbur and How, pp. 431–434.

[19] *Pravda,* No. 26, February 2, 1927, p. 3: see also *International Press Correspondence,* Vol. 7, No. 14, February 17, 1927, p. 282.

[20] *Ibid.*

It was during February that Mao Tse-tung, still a relatively obscure member of the Chinese Communist leadership, submitted to the Central Committee his now famous "Report on an Investigation of the Peasant Movement in Hunan." Since he had left Shanghai no more than a fortnight after the close of the Seventh Plenum in Moscow, it is doubtful that he had yet seen the Theses of the plenum [21] which had declared, of course, that the urban proletariat was the only class capable of carrying out the radical agrarian program prerequisite to further development of the Chinese revolution [*Document 1*]. According to his report, however,

to give credits where they are due, if we allot ten points to the accomplishment of the democratic revolution, then the achievements of the urban dwellers and the military units rate only three points, while the remaining seven points should go to the peasants in their rural revolution.[22]

Mao submitted the report, first of all, to an interprovincial meeting of peasants in Wuhan, which approved it. Later, however, the Central Committee overruled this action, and at the Fifth Congress in May the conflict deepened. By that time, as will be seen later, Mao himself had come to perceive the difficulty he faced in presenting a viewpoint which seemed to contradict the prevailing trend.

On February 27, 1927, a "warning"—presumably inspired and written by Roy [23]—was issued in Canton by the Chinese Communist Party and various allied organizations [*Document 3*]. The success of the Northern Expedition had placed the national revolutionary army face to face with the two chief forces of the enemy—the armies of the northern militarists and the military and naval forces of international imperialism concentrated in Shanghai. At this crucial moment the military and political forces of the revolution must be held together at all costs. The various attempts of certain imperialist powers to enter into relations with the Nationalist government must be frustrated and any responses to such overtures must be exposed and prosecuted as treason. "Under no circumstances" the "warning" declared, "can the military or other organs of the revolutionary state be permitted to act independently." Rumors concerning a possible agreement between the "commanding staff" of the national revolutionary army and Chang Tso-

---

[21] Brandt, *Stalin's Failure in China*, pp. 107–108.

[22] An English translation of this document appears in Brandt, Schwartz and Fairbank, *A Documentary History of Chinese Communism*, pp. 80–89, especially p. 83.

[23] According to Ts'ai Ho-sen, Roy, at the time of his arrival in Kwangtung province, "stated once at a meeting of the Party active members that he did not approve [*ne odobriaet*] the movement directed at the defeat of Chiang Kai-shek which had taken root at that time." *Problemy Kitaia*, No. 1, p. 36.

lin must be flatly repudiated. Wang Ching-wei, moreover, must be re-called to his post without delay and the unity of the People's party preserved at all costs.

In a "most secret" report, unsigned but apparently written by a Russian agent in Hankow and dated March 5, 1927, the intelligence was relayed—probably by the Chinese Communist leadership—as follows:

Chiang Kai-shek has betrayed his dictatorial conspiracy in opposition to the Kuomintang Left Wing. His attitude was particularly clarified in connection with the appointment [recall] of Wang Ching-wei to the National Government. Chiang at first expressed a great desire for Wang's return, but as soon as Wang left Paris on his way back to China, Chiang cabled him and hinted that there was no need for him to return.[24]

Because of this behavior, the report asserted (erroneously, as events would reveal), Chiang had alienated "many wavering elements and a portion of the Kuomintang Right Wing" and also had "lost the greater part of his influence in the Army." [25] T'ang Sheng-chih was aligned against him. The best elements of the National Revolutionary Army, in fact, were no longer supporting Chiang. On the other hand, "it would be premature to state" that he had been completely defeated because of these realignments—or that he would no longer figure in the internal struggle.[26]

Chiang Kai-shek, on March 7, again criticized Borodin and the other Russian advisers openly—though he reiterated Kuomintang friendship for the Soviet Union.[27] "It is not [Russia's] policy to tyrannize over us," he declared, "and though her representatives have acted otherwise, insulting our every movement, I am convinced that it has naught to do with Russia, but are the individual actions of these representatives. Therefore we must not let such individual movements make any difference to our relations with that country. Their friendly attitude has not changed a whit, and ours must remain the same to the Soviet Government and the people, according to the policy of our President, which is to unite with Russia, and fight against all countries with imperialist tendencies." [28]

On March 9 Roy issued another warning from Canton [*Document 4*]. The danger of the revolution being betrayed through compromise with militarism and imperialism was real, and it was time for the Communist

---

[24] "Soviet Report on the Split Between Chiang Kai-shek and T'ang Sheng-chih," as translated in Wilbur and How, p. 435.
[25] *Ibid.*
[26] *Ibid.*, p. 436.
[27] *North China Herald*, April 2, 1927, p. 28.
[28] *Ibid.*

Party to sound an alarm. From February 19 to 24 Communist-led labor forces in Shanghai, anticipating a Nationalist military advance, had staged a strike and insurrection—only to be cut down by the forces of the militarist Sun Ch'uan-fang when Chiang failed to attack the city.[29] How was this delay to be accounted for? "The working class of the whole country had a right to know why Marshal Chiang Kai-shek allowed the imperialist henchmen to stage a bloodbath of the leaders of the Shanghai proletariat," Roy declared, "while his army stood right by the city and could have dealt a direct blow."

This warning, Roy asserted later, was refused publication by Chinese Communist officials in Canton under the pretext that it might provoke Li Chi-shen, the local Cantonese militarist, into taking repressive measures.

There were sharp divisions of opinion among Communist leaders on the issue of Chiang Kai-shek's advance. According to the "Letter from Shanghai" one group of comrades, especially the Russians and Borodin,

were of the opinion that it would not hurt for Chiang Kai-shek to break his neck on Shanghai and Chekiang, and they egged him on; Comrade Galen was of the opinion that the march on Shanghai was a hopeless military undertaking and did not participate in it.[30]

A second group representing the "Right Wing of the CC and the Shanghai Committee," failing to perceive that Chiang Kai-shek would convert Shanghai into "a fortress of the Right Wing of the Kuomintang" were in favor

of supporting, unconditionally and without circumlocution, Chiang Kai-shek's march on Shanghai, of uniting with his representative in Shanghai itself to prepare an uprising, and thereby to help the troops of the national revolutionary army to march into Shanghai. . . . Whether consciously or not, these comrades consented to hand over power to Chiang Kai-shek in Shanghai, that is, to help the bourgeoisie intrench itself there.[31]

A third group, including Nassonov, Fokine, Albrecht, "and a part of the Chinese comrades," were in favor

of supporting with all means the capture of Shanghai by the people's revolutionary army and, on the other hand, by the unleashing of a mass movement in Shanghai as a counterpoise to the Right wing, of creating a democratic people's power so that the democratic factor would predominate over the military factor and the occupation of Shanghai would simultaneously

---

[29] For a description of how Sun Ch'uan-fang's "execution squads armed with broadswords patrolled the streets, decapitating as many revolutionists as they could find," see Isaacs, *The Tragedy of the Chinese Revolution,* p. 134.

[30] "The Letter from Shanghai," Trotsky, p. 409.

[31] *Ibid.,* pp. 409–410.

result in the victory of the national revolution, of the anti-imperialist movement, and in the defeat of Chiang Kai-shek as the representative of the bourgeois Right wing of the Kuo Min Tang.[32]

Borodin and his colleagues, defying Chiang—up to a point—from Wuhan, convened the Third Plenum of the Central Executive Committee of the Kuomintang in mid-March, 1927, in Wuhan, in an effort to restore to the regular party organs the special powers which Chiang had assumed at the time of his March 20 *coup* the year before.[33] In the course of these proceedings the plenum created five new ministries— Labor, Education, Agriculture, Industries, and Health—and received from Chiang Kai-shek the following telegram:

> I, Chung-chen, elected by the Central Executive Committee to be chairman of both the Standing Committee and Military Committee, have not been able to discharge my duties because I have been busy at the war front. Now that the Central Executive Committee is in session and the Political Council is in session, it is time that new men be elected to these posts and the Military Council be reorganized. Therefore I hand in my resignation.[34]

The plenum also passed a resolution suggesting an immediate joint conference between the Kuomintang and the Chinese Communist Party to discuss methods of coöperation—particularly in connection with a united front of peasant and labor movements, with relations between the Chinese and minority peoples in the country, and with "the question of political responsibility." The plenum resolved that "nothing should be printed in the papers of the Communist Party that violates the principle of cooperation with the Kuomintang." [35]

No doubt the proceedings of this plenum did much to persuade Stalin and his colleagues of a strong leftward turn in Kuomintang policies. It cannot be assumed, however, that Moscow had no inkling of the various emerging conflicts.

That Russian Communist leaders were apprehensive of possible difficulties in China is evident from a number of letters or instructions which Moscow dispatched to the Chinese Communists and the Kuomintang during the winter and early spring of 1927. Unfortunately, in most cases no actual texts of these instructions are available. In an article of July 16, 1927, which analyzed the reasons of the failure of the Chinese

---

[32] *Ibid.*, p. 410.

[33] *People's Tribune,* March 15, 1927, pp. 1, 4.

[34] *Ibid.*, p. 1.

[35] *Ibid.*, p. 1. This revolution evidently led to the April 4 declaration of Wang Ching-wei and Ch'en Tu-hsiu. Text appears in *Pravda,* No. 78, April 7, 1927, p. 1; see also Isaacs, *The Tragedy of the Chinese Revolution,* p. 165. The text, dated April 8, 1927, is also given in Mif, *Kitaiskaia Kommunisticheskaia Partiia v kriticheskie dni,* pp. 121–122.

Communist Party, T. Mandalian, a young Communist who was in China in the early months of 1927, noted that toward the end of February, 1927, "the ECCI sent a letter to the CC of the Kuomintang in which it criticized one of Chiang Kai-shek's speeches as a treacherous and deviationist blow in the back of the revolution." [36]

On March 3 the Central Committee of the Russian Communist Party also dispatched a second letter to the Central Committee of the Chinese Communist Party warning it of its "opportunist mistakes." [37]

Another Soviet writer and specialist on China, A. Aikhenvald, has referred to this letter as "an extremely important resolution on the Chinese question," taken by the CPSU on March 3, 1927, and quotes as follows:

It is necessary to draw the attention of all functionaries devoted to the revolution to the fact that at the present moment the Chinese revolution is passing through a critical period in connection with the regrouping of the class forces and with the concentration of the imperialist armies, and that its further victory is possible only if a clear course is steered toward the development of a mass movement. If this is not done, serious danger will threaten the revolution.

It is necessary to direct our course towards arming the workers and peasants, toward transforming the peasant committees in the provinces into actual organs of power with armed self-protection. It is necessary to steer our course towards ousting the Right members of the Kuomintang, discrediting them politically and deposing them from leading positions. The Communist Party must not conceal the treacherous and reactionary policy of the Right Wing of the Kuomintang, and must mobilize the masses around the Kuomintang and around the Communist Party of China. Wherever it is and on every occasion, the Communist Party must take its stand as such.[38]

On March 31 the ECCI issued a further instruction which directed the Chinese Communist Party

to launch a campaign among the masses against the coup which is being prepared and a campaign against the Right Wing. In view of the prevailing exceedingly disadvantageous correlation of forces, not to rush into an open battle. The arms must not be surrendered, and if necessary, must be concealed.[39]

Meanwhile, an editorial in *Pravda,* which Bukharin then edited, had stated in part:

---

[36] Mandalian, "Pochemu obankrotilos rukovodstvo kitaiskoi kompartii," *Pravda,* No. 159, July 16, 1927, pp. 2–3.

[37] *Ibid.*

[38] Aikhenvald, "O takticheskoi linii Kominterna v Kitae," *Pravda,* No. 104, May 11, 1927, p. 2.

[39] Mandalian, *op. cit.*

It would be a grave political mistake and extreme wishfulness, which has nothing in common with Marxism, to believe that *the differences in the camp of the revolution* are not inevitable. Various social elements: the proletariat, the city petty bourgeoisie, the peasantry, and a section of the Chinese commercial and industrial bourgeoisie participate in the Chinese revolutionary movement. These social groupings have some *common* and some *divergent* interests. They have different aims, unequal fighting energy, unequal strength in the revolutionary consistency, and an unequal "inclination to vacillation." This motley combination of class aims and interests affects, and is bound to affect the revolutionary organizations, the government, and the Kuomintang.[40]

The editorials then referred to "contemporary liquidators" who were not aware of the fact that "their preaching of the withdrawal from the Kuomintang was equivalent to preaching liquidation of the Chinese revolution." Actually, the revolutionary movement was on the upsurge, and at peasants' conferences in Hupeh and Hunan a considerable number of Left Wing slogans had been adopted. The path of the Chinese revolution was a difficult one, the editorial concluded, but there was no room for pessimism.[41]

On March 18 Ch'en Tu-hsiu quoted a headline from a Shanghai Japanese newspaper of the previous day: "The Nanchang Party openly proclaims a pro-Japanese policy, refuses to recognize the results of the [Central Executive] Committee conference and decides to get rid of Borodin." It was up to Chiang Kai-shek, the Chinese Communist leader asserted, to repudiate these rumors and not abuse "his own associates." Beyond that, "Our duty . . . is earnestly to persuade the Nationalist revolutionary leader, General Chiang Kai-shek, to prove immediately in words and actions that what is called the reconciliation between North and South to oppose the Reds, is but the scheming of imperialistic Japan." [42]

Publicly, at least, Stalinist circles in Moscow appeared oblivious to what was happening in China. Almost as Chiang was making his statements about checking excessive Communist influence, an editorial in *Pravda,* quoted above, stated that imperialist efforts to separate Chinese military leaders from the Kuomintang were useless. "The revolutionary pressure from below is so strong that in the present stage of the [revolutionary] development, Chiang Kai-shek is compelled to maneuver, to swear allegiance to the principles of revolutionary loyalty, of Sun Yat-

[40] "Revoliutsiia v Kitae i Gomindan," *Pravda,* No. 61, March 16, 1927, p. 1.
[41] *Ibid.*
[42] *North China Herald,* April 9, 1927, p. 90, citing *Guide Weekly,* March 18, 1927.

sen's teaching of socialism, and to submit himself to the leadership of the mass party of the Kuomintang." [43]

Nationalist troops occupied Nanking on March 24. Shanghai had been captured by the Nationalist troops under Pai Ch'ung-hsi two days earlier and over the next few days Chiang Kai-shek moved on toward Shanghai at a leisurely pace. There were no "unpleasant incidents" involving Westerners, according to the foreign press, but Nationalist subversives were reported to be infiltrating the city and rumor had it that the "red general," Chiang Kai-shek, would soon attack.

Actually, the troops of the warlord Sun Ch'uan-fang, were already demoralized and deserting at every opportunity. Chang Tso-lin, however, was reported to be advancing southward and other northern troops under Chang Tsung-ch'ang were moving toward the city. Still Chiang did not attack.

Inside Shanghai Communist-dominated labor unions—having staged their February strike and insurrection in anticipation of the Nationalist advance prematurely—now pulled themselves together for a second strike to be coördinated with Chiang's attack. Actually, according to one foreign observer, the Communists were planning "to make a shambles of Shanghai" in order to prevent Chiang from "taking refuge there." However that may have been, the Chinese Communist leadership, according to the "Letter from Shanghai," denied that the "people of Shanghai" wanted to take power, and no suggestion was made to the workers, the soldiers, or the sympathetic petty bourgeoisie as to what should be done.

The Canton advance guard is twenty-five to thirty miles from Shanghai. The troops of Sun Ch'uan-fang, absolutely demoralized, begin pillaging and dispersing homewards. In the city, sections of the military forces waver, the fleet comes over to our side. Three hundred thousand workers go out on strike and pass over to armed struggle. The military commander executes dozens of workers. [44]

With early reports of Sun Ch'uan-fang's impending defeat, the atmosphere in Shanghai became "red hot," but the Central Committee of the party vacillated, reflecting on "whether the uprising should be made or not, at the very moment when the uprising is already taking place." [45]

On March 26 Chiang Kai-shek arrived unannounced aboard a gunboat and walked ashore, the city being already occupied by the forces of

---

[43] *Pravda*, No. 61, March 16, 1927, p. 1.
[44] "The Letter from Shanghai," Trotsky, p. 411.
[45] *Ibid.*, pp. 410–411.

Pai Ch'ung-hsi. The Shanghai Communists rendered no opposition.[46]

Rumors of an impending rift between Chiang Kai-shek and the Communists continued and so did the denials. "A split in the Kuomintang and hostile sentiment between the working class in Shanghai and the revolutionary soldiers is absolutely out of the question at the present moment." T'ang Sheng-chih wrote in *International Press Correspondence,* March 31: "A Revolutionary like Chiang Kai-shek will not act in cooperation with the counter-revolutionary Chang Tso-lin. . . . The only danger for the working class of Shanghai consists in the provocation by the imperialists." [47]

In Moscow, on April 5, Stalin explained to 3,000 active functionaries of the Moscow organization of the Communist Party of the Soviet Union why it was necessary to support the Kuomintang Right. Summarizing Stalin's speech a few months later, Vuyo Vuyovich, a Yugoslav Communist then in opposition to Stalin's line, quoted from notes he had taken at the time: "Why drive away the Right when we have the majority and when the Right listens to us? The peasant needs an old worn-out jade as long as she is necessary. He does not drive her away. So it is with us." Chiang Kai-shek had no sympathy for the revolution, perhaps, but he was leading the army against the imperialists—and could not do otherwise. Beyond this, the Rightists had relations with the rich merchants from whom they could raise money, and with the generals of Chang Tso-lin, whom they could induce to come over to the revolution "bag and baggage." So, according to Stalin, the Rightists had to be utilized "squeezed out like a lemon and then flung away." [48]

However, no printed text of Stalin's speech *in toto,* or that of Bukharin at the meeting of April 5, had appeared in the press. Only the resolution taken at that meeting was made available.[49]

This latter document described the Chinese revolution as democratic national liberation in nature, with the proletariat and the peasantry serving as the driving force. It also condemned as profoundly incorrect the demands by some comrades that the Chinese Party withdraw from the Kuomintang.[50] Stalin and his supporters must have been deeply in-

---

[46] According to Mandalian, the Shanghai Committee failed to heed the ECCI's order to prepare itself for a struggle (see our p. 54) and instead "tried to turn back the historical process, attempted to influence the Rightists through the personal contact, and so forth. Nor did it prepare itself for a retreat, although it was convinced, no less than anyone else, that the coup was inevitable." Mandalian, *Pravda,* No. 159, July 16, 1927, p. 2.

[47] *International Press Correspondence,* Vol. 7, No. 22, March 31, 1927, p. 446.

[48] Vuyo Vuyovich at the Eighth Plenum of the ECCI in May 1927, as reproduced in Trotsky, *Problems of the Chinese Revolution,* pp. 389–390.

[49] *Pravda,* No. 77, April 6, 1927, p. 3.

[50] *Ibid.*

fluenced by the nature of the intelligence that was coming to them through Communist channels at that time: Shanghai was in the hands of the workers, the revolutionary banners of the Kuomintang were flying in Shanghai, and the Kuomintang revolutionary army was entering the city.[51]

According to another source the Kuomintang could be relied upon to continue support for the revolutionary workers, peasants, and the democratic masses; [52] the conflict within the Kuomintang in connection with the claims for individual leadership had been solved.[53] According to the *Tass* communiqué of March 17, Chiang Kai-shek had given his complete approval of a collective settlement of differences among the members of the Kuomintang, and of the subordination by all members of the party to the decisions so taken. Chiang Kai-shek had also expressed his absolute readiness to subordinate himself to the CC of the Kuomintang.[54]

"Wang Ching-wei is my teacher and friend . . . ," *Pravda* quoted Chiang Kai-shek as asserting. "All military, political, and civil problems, the problems of finance and foreign policy must be settled under the guidance of the Chairman Wang Ching-wei." [55]

On April 6, Wang Ching-wei and Ch'en Tu-hsiu signed a joint statement denying the existence of any conflict between the Kuomintang and the Chinese Communist Party which could not be settled amicably.[56]

Consequently, it was quite appropriate for A. Martynov [57] to state on April 10:

At present the Chinese Communist Party, as can be judged by the information recently received from China, is following the right course. Thanks to its capable leadership, the proletariat begins gradually to conquer hegemony in the revolution while at the same time it maintains a united front with the peasantry, the numerous urban petty bourgeoisie, and the sections of the big bourgeoisie which have not as yet withdrawn from the movement. The latter is bound to do so because of the consolidation of the position of the proletariat.[58]

---

[51] *Ibid.*, No. 65, March 22, 1927, p. 1.

[52] "Declaration of the Executive Committee of the Kuomintang," see *Pravda*, No. 76, April 5, 1927, p. 2.

[53] "The Significance of the Plenum of the Executive Committee of the Kuomintang," *Ibid.*, p. 2.

[54] *Pravda*, No. 64, March 20, 1927, p. 2; see also *Pravra*, No. 65, March 22, 1927, p. 2.

[55] *Ibid.*, No. 77, April 6, 1927, p. 2.

[56] See pp. 60 ff.

[57] Martynov was a former Menshevik who joined the Russian Communist Party only in 1923. He bitterly criticized Trotsky and was soon made editor of the official journal of the Communist International, *Kommunisticheskii Internatsional*.

[58] *Pravda*, No. 81, April 10, 1927, p. 5.

Undoubtedly Stalin and his colleagues in Moscow were receiving a welter of conflicting information from China. Nassonov and his colleagues in China considered Voitinsky responsible for much of the misunderstanding and confusion:

He sent Moscow bastardized information, held back material, and concealed the real situation in the party from the ECCI. Without principles, as well as without political courage, he viewed everything as a functionary and did not stop at putting the CC into absurd decisions.[59]

Such a representation of the ECCI, Nassonov argued, could only ruin the work. Except for his intervention, indeed, the Chinese Communist Party might have been able to fight the Right Wing successfully with its own forces—though by now such a cause would be difficult under any circumstances. "It is not only necessary to recall Comrade V.," the "Letter from Shanghai" asserted at a time when Roy was already enroute, "but to send here a much stronger worker who is capable at the same time of representing the ECCI and of directing Borodin." [60]

Meanwhile, after a delay of more than three weeks in Canton, Roy set out for Hankow. An airplane was to have flown him to the Kuomintang capital, according to a member of the travel party, but there was engine trouble, and the group journeyed overland "five weeks in chairs carried by coolies." Roy, of course, had been in China a decade earlier, but this was his first intimate experience with the Chinese countryside. "On the way to Hankow he saw Chinese villagers hung from trees—villagers who had fought for the revolution." [61]

On April 1, 1926, Roy and his party reached Changsha, where he was welcomed by the provincial government of Hunan province and by members of peasant, merchant, student, and labor organizations. A Kuomintang newspaper described the event:

Despite the rain, 100,000 people turned out to greet the [Comintern] delegate. Today the Government entertained Mr. Roy at a dinner. He will leave at midnight by special train and will arrive in Hankow tomorrow morning. Mr. Roy is accompanied by Mr. T'an P'ing-shan, Minister of Agriculture.[62]

In Hankow Borodin received Roy warmly—though within a few weeks at most they were to find themselves in sharp disagreement.

In Shanghai, meanwhile, Chiang Kai-shek was gathering support from quarters that were scarcely revolutionary. "Bankers and merchants flocked to his standard," wrote a Western observer. "The Shanghai

---

[59] "The Letter from Shanghai," Trotsky, p. 431.
[60] *Ibid.*, p. 432.
[61] Geissler interview.
[62] *People's Tribune*, April 3, 1927, p. 1.

Chinese Bankers' Association, the representatives of the Chinese modern banks, arranged for an immediate three million dollar loan. . . . Arrangements were made with the Green and Red Societies," [63] secret organizations with which Chiang Kai-shek was rumored to have had connections of long standing.

At this point, according to Ts'ai Ho-sen,

and in spite of the energetic protests of the responsible [Party] workers, he [Roy] wished to go with Comrade B to Shanghai to meet Chiang Kai-shek there. Not two days passed when the news came of the events of April 12.[64]

Just before dawn on April 12 squads of armed men left their hiding places and began systematically rounding up and disarming Communist-organized labor pickets within the city. During the following days as Chiang pressed his attack, the Shanghai Communists and their forces of organized labor were all but decimated.

On April 13 Roy dispatched a telegram to Chiang Kai-shek urging him not to convene separate meetings of the Kuomintang Central Committee and Control Commission in Wuhan. It will be recalled that Chiang himself, according to Roy (see p. 43 above), had asked Moscow—at the time when his relations with the Communists first became acute—to send a delegation to him in China.

On the eve of our departure to [see] him [presumably from Hankow], we received the news that he had called a meeting in Nanking of several members of the Central Committee and the Central Control Commission in order to accuse the united conference in Wuhan of splitting the party. We advised him immediately by telegraph to break off the conference and to fulfill the conditions of the agreement he had concluded with Wang Ching-wei in Shanghai [*Document 8*].

Roy's telegram to Chiang read as follows:

We are informed that you requested the Executive Committee of the Communist Internationale to instruct its representatives in China to visit you in order to discuss the problems that have arisen in consequence of the meeting of the Kuomintang Central Committee in Wuhan. The delegation of the Third Internationale is now in China and has always been eager to visit you; but it could not be done because we have been visiting separately distant parts of the country.

Assembling at Wuhan a week ago we intended to proceed to Shanghai to visit you there as you desired. On the eve of our departure came news of the raids on the U.S.S.R. embassy at Peking and on the consulate at Shang-

---

[63] Sokolsky, "The Kuomintang," *The China Year Book,* 1928, pp. 1361–1362.

[64] Ts'ai Ho-sen, *Problemy Kitaia,* No. 1, pp. 36–37. At that point, Ts'ai Ho-sen asserts, Roy also supported the tactic of relying on Li Chi-shen, the militarist in control of Kwangtung Province, whose sole claim to revolutionary status was his opposition to Chiang Kai-shek.

hai, indicating that the imperialist powers are adopting the most aggressive measures. Then we were informed that you had left Shanghai. Therefore we abandoned our projected visit to Shanghai.

Now comes news that you have decided to convene several members of the Central Committee and the Central Control Committee in meeting at Nanking. This act obviously violated your agreement with Wang Ching-wei that all questions of conflict inside the party would be placed before a plenary session of the Central Committee, which should be called at Wuhan and in which you would participate. Your convening a meeting of a few members of the Central Committee at this critical moment will naturally be interpreted by the enemies of the revolution as a rupture in the ranks of the Kuomintang.

At this moment when international imperialism unites in an insolent attack upon the Chinese Nationalist Revolution the unity of the revolutionary forces is a supreme necessity. As a matter of fact it is the dissensions in the Nationalist ranks that have encouraged imperialism to assume such a high-handed attitude as to deliver identical notes of five powers. In view of the dangerous situation we advise you to abandon the projected Nanking conference which will practically split the party. And the grave responsibility of breaking the Nationalist front at this critical moment will rest on you. We advise you to stand on the agreement to place all contentions on inner party questions before a plenary session of the Central Committee. If you take this advice we shall be glad to visit Nanking in order to discuss with you personally all outstanding questions.

The Third Internationale will lend all its services to help the formation of a united nationalist front of all revolutionary forces.

Signed, for the delegation of the Third Internationale,
M. N. Roy, Hankow, April 13, 1927.[65]

Chiang did not respond to the telegram, according to Roy, but "pursued further his plan for destroying the party" [*Document 8*].

At this point, according to Ts'ai Ho-sen,

I returned to Wuhan from Moscow . . . and I became immediately aware of the problem which was disturbing everyone, namely, the problem of the second Northern Expedition. Just at that time serious misunderstandings were evident between Comrade B and Comrade R, the new representative of the Comintern. These misunderstandings ensued from the different political viewpoints [of these two men].[66]

Borodin urged that the Communists and the Left Kuomintang should launch immediately a second Northern Expedition and postpone the agrarian revolution until after Peking had been captured:

---

[65] Released by the official (Wuhan) *Nationalist News Agency,* and published in *China Press,* April 14, 1927, p. 2.
[66] Ts'ai Ho-sen, *Problemy Kitaia,* No. 1, p. 24.

Comrade R disagreed with him and believed that it was necessary to deepen [*uglubliat*] the revolution, that the agrarian revolution should not be delayed, and that its base should be strengthened. In regard to the question of "deepening" or "widening" the [Chinese] revolution, the two men disagreed also. Comrade R was of the opinion that it was necessary first to deepen the revolution, and only afterwards to widen it. Comrade B, on the other hand, wished to widen it first and then to deepen it.[67]

Roy, in these arguments with Borodin and with the Chinese Communist leadership, asserted that he was not opposed to the Northern Expedition in principle. But an immediate campaign against the north was "fraught with grave danger" [*Document 5*]. And action of this sort would certainly provide either the northern militarists or Chiang Kaishek (who probably had an "agreement" with the northern forces) an opportunity to attack the revolutionary armies from the direction of Nanking.

The plan for the Northern Expedition was built on the assumption that Fêng Yü-hsiang and Yen Hsi-shan would join the revolution, but in the person of Yen the Communists might soon find that they had "another T'ang Shen-shi" or even a Chiang Kai-shek. If the Northern Expedition were continued, Roy declared, the complications "we experienced as a result of the first stage" would be repeated, and the generals "with the help of whom we must reach Peking" would in all probability "turn into new Chiang Kai-sheks." There would be further difficulties with every advance. "We are jumping from the frying pan into the fire," he warned. "Right now we have only to cope with Chiang Kai-shek. But we are running from him into unknown territories where, in all probability, we will have to encounter many more like him."

An immediate campaign against the northern militarists, according to Roy, would be an evasion of the central realities of class conflict—"a typical petty bourgeois policy." But the petty bourgeoisie did not constitute a reliable class. In due course, the petty bourgeoisie was quite capable of turning to flight.

Agrarian revolution, in Roy's view, was the great motive force of the conflict. "The Chinese revolution will either win as an agrarian revolution," he asserted, "or it will not win at all."

According to Ts'ai Ho-sen, however,

Comrade B succeeded in introducing his plan for the second Northern Expedition to the Nationalist government and to the Kuomintang. Both accepted it and an appropriate statement was issued in which they pledged to bring the Northern campaign to a successful end or die.[68]

[67] *Ibid.*, pp. 24–25.
[68] *Ibid.*, p. 27.

Members of the Chinese Communist Central Committee were not in agreement over the issue. T'an P'ing-shan and Chang Kuo-t'ao preferred a Southern Expedition into Kwangtung where the warlord Li Chi-shen was leading a counterrevolution, while Ch'ü Ch'iu-pai argued in favor of capturing Nanking first and then marching northward along the Lunghai railway.[69] Ch'en Tu-hsiu, P'eng Shu-chih, and Chang Tai-lei, on the other hand, fully supported Borodin.

In Document 5 it is against Borodin and Ch'en Tu-hsiu that Roy is directing his arguments: Borodin has argued that the establishment of a firm revolutionary base before advancing further is a delusion. He is against developing a powerful peasant movement in Hunan lest T'ang Sheng-chih, a "100 per cent revolutionary" be antagonized. He thinks that the principal factor in the revolution is not the masses, but an ability to maneuver with the petty bourgeoisie. And Ch'en Tu-hsiu, according to Roy, is afraid to expand the red revolution of workers and peasants who will assure its future.

In opposition to Borodin and Ch'en Tu-hsiu, then, Roy proposed an organization, concentration, and consolidation of revolutionary forces by (1) pressing the agrarian revolution; (2) establishing peasant power in the villages; (3) and creating a truly revolutionary army that would not be merely a creature of landowning generals. On this basis, he argued, it would be feasible to defend Wuhan by concentrating military forces in the border between Hupeh and Honan—while developing the agrarian revolution in Hupeh and Hunan, both under control of the Wuhan government. At the same time a new political penetration of Kiangsi and Kwangtung provinces could be reinforced by suitable military action. Then, step by step, Kiangsi, Fukien, Kwangtung, and Kwangsi could be brought under the Wuhan government. Then, once this broad base had been firmly established and the revolutionary power strengthened, it would be time for launching a new northern campaign against Peking.

The northern warlords represented a constant threat to the revolution, he admitted, and the destruction of Chang Tso-lin and his Fengtien forces was essential for the consummation of the revolution. Yet an even greater danger lay close at hand—the possibility that a "counterrevolutionary feudal-bourgeois bloc aided and abetted by imperialism" might be built around Chiang Kai-shek and his new government in Nanking.

The Central Committee of the Chinese Communist Party adopted on April 16 a resolution to defer the Northern Expedition in order first to

---

[69] *Ibid.*

build a firm revolutionary base, "defeat Chiang Kai-shek and the bourgeoisie which is attempting to split the revolutionary movement," and annihilate the Fengtien [Chang Tso-lin] forces [*Document 6*]. According to Roy, however, the Central Committee reversed itself two days later, retracted the resolution, and supported the Left Wing Kuomintang's decision on the immediate dispatch of troops to the north. (See Roy's note, p. 177.)

On April 20 the Central Committee of the Chinese Communist Party issued a Declaration [*Document 7*] welcoming the Left Kuomintang's decision "to remove Chiang Kai-shek from command of the national-revolutionary armies, to expel him from the party, and to issue an order for his arrest."

The reasons behind Chiang's defection, according to this document, were not difficult to establish: ". . . as soon as it became clear that it was impossible to develop the national revolution further without [having] an agrarian revolution, and as soon as the revolutionary wing of the Kuomintang recognized the necessity [of this agrarian revolution], the feudal bourgeois elements in the Kuomintang felt that their position had become unstable." When Chiang, the leader of these elements since his March 20 *coup* of the year before, found that he could not "convert the Kuomintang as a whole into an instrument of feudal-bourgeois reaction," he declared war against it.

Now, according to the CC, the time had come to create a truly revolutionary-democratic power. "This means that the revolution must first of all be an agrarian revolution. The peasants make up 80 per cent of the Chinese population; hence, a revolutionary democratic power can be established only by means of a democratic revolution."

It remained to be seen whether or not the Chinese Communists were prepared to press an agrarian revolution at this time.

IV

THE FIFTH CONGRESS OF THE CCP

Writing in Moscow on April 21, 1927, Joseph Stalin tried to make it appear that he had foreseen events accurately and that Chiang Kai-shek's defection "confirmed the correctness" of the Communist program of action in China. The recent *coup,* indeed, marked the desertion—predicted all along, according to Stalin—of the national bourgeoisie from the revolution, the emergence of a center of counterrevolution, and the "conclusion of a deal" between the Kuomintang Rightists and the imperialists against the Chinese revolution. "Chiang Kai-shek's coup," he declared, "signifies that in South China there will now be two camps, two governments, two armies, two centres—the revolutionary centre in Wuhan and the counter-revolutionary centre in Nanking." [1]

The record shows, of course, that the Stalinist leadership had been caught almost completely off balance.

The Chinese revolution, Stalin asserted, had entered the second stage of its development—swinging away from the revolution of an all-national united front toward a revolution of the workers and peasants, an agrarian revolution which would "strengthen and broaden the struggle against imperialism, against the gentry and the feudal landlords, and against the militarists and Chiang Kai-shek's counter-revolutionary group." [2]

An article by A. Stetsky in *Pravda* of April 15 on the "Critical Point of the Chinese Revolution," stated in a similar vein:

As the revolution developed, the Chinese Communist Party and the Comintern perceived clearly the inevitability of the passing of the Chinese bourgeoisie to the camp of reaction. It is exactly because of these prospects that the efforts of the Communist Party and of the Left Kuomintang have been directed toward the consolidation of a bloc of workers and peasants,

---

[1] Stalin, "Questions of the Chinese Revolution. Theses for Propagandists," *Works,* IX, 227, 229.

[2] *Ibid.,* p. 229.

the strengthening of the organization of the working class, and the transformation of the Kuomintang into a mass party which would lean on the broadest strata of the workers and peasants. *It is exactly for these reasons that the Chinese Communist Party was preparing the workers and peasants for such a possible step on the part of the bourgeoisie and was denouncing the vacillations of the Right Wing Kuomintang. . . .*

However, the Chinese Communist Party did not wish to force the events. Its tasks, and the task of the Left Wing Kuomintang, was to utilize the bourgeoisie in the struggle against imperialism and militarism as much as it was possible. *The Party's strategic line lay in abstaining from the fight with the bourgeoisie until sufficient forces were accumulated, and the organization of the working class and the peasantry consolidated.*

Now the conflict has come. *The Chinese bourgeoisie has launched an attack against the revolution. . . .* Under such conditions, and it goes without saying, the Chinese Communist Party will help to drive away from the Kuomintang the counter-revolutionary traitors and betrayers to the cause of the national liberation. It will continue to work for the transformation of the Kuomintang into a mass organization of the working class and the peasantry.[3]

As can be seen from this quotation, the Moscow Communists continued to assert their ideological and tactical correctness—and also to reveal both an unsophisticated faith in the revolutionary character of the Left Kuomintang and a wholly naïve assessment of their own capacity for influencing its behavior.

The reaction of the Left Kuomintang to Chiang Kai-shek's *coup* coincided, moreover, with that of the Soviet leaders in Moscow. According to Liau Han-sin [Li Han-chün], who claimed to speak for the CEC of the Kuomintang,

the treachery of Chiang Kai-shek does not come unexpected. This danger has already existed a year. The Chinese revolutionaries first obtained a hint of the intentions of Chiang Kai-shek on the occasion of the coup d'état of the 20th March 1926. The present open defection has come about, first in consequence of the threats, enticements and bribes of the imperialists.

Referring to the future policy of the Kuomintang, the Chinese representative asserted:

Our people and our Party will adopt an irreconcilable attitude to this treachery. Our Party, the Kuomintang, will proceed forwards undeterred along the way which our Party leader indicated to us, and will strive for the alliance with the Soviet Union planned by him, with the Communist

---

[3] Stetsky, "Kriticheskii punkt kitaiskoi revoliutsii," *Pravda*, No. 85, April 15, 1927, p. 2; also *The China Weekly Review*, July 30, 1927, p. 190, Huston Collection, Hoover Institution.

Party, with the suppressed peoples and classes and for the policy of the workers and peasants. We will not cease for a moment to fight against the imperialists and against the feudalists.[4]

A much more thorough and serious interpretation of the Chinese crisis was supplied by Bukharin in his article which appeared in two issues of *Pravda* (April 19 and 20) and which was later published as a separate pamphlet. Writing the greater part of this article before the *coup* of April 12, and only the last section after it, Bukharin had sufficient insight to speak of the inevitable complications within the Chinese situation, and to correlate them with the complex political and social conditions of the country. His statements suggest, moreover, that he was less dogmatically certain about the future path of the Chinese revolution than were some of his colleagues. Apparently he did not overlook the possibility that "feudal" conditions might be compromised with. In his own words:

If there were only one prospect of the development of the Chinese revolution, it certainly would be very gratifying. But unfortunately the situation is much more complex. It goes without saying that if one fails to consider, as is done by Radek, the historical task of the struggle against feudal conditions, and to forget at the same time the task of the struggle against foreign imperialism, then the situation becomes quite "simple." If no feudal conditions are present, then there only remains one prospect, namely, the socialist development. But if the task of the bourgeois revolution is not completely solved, the problem [of the revolution] becomes much more complicated.

Is the prospect of the continuation of the struggle, but with the acceptance of some compromises unthinkable [ne myslima]? Is it absolutely impossible to be satisfied with the partial solution of the problem, which is not *as yet* the case, but which might become necessary? The plan to beat the northern militarists, *but* not to *erase* completely the remnants of the feudal order, and not to carry out an agrarian *revolution;* the plan to defeat the imperialists, *but* to reach a compromise with them for a joint supervision of the country's economy, and the management of this economy along the capitalist line; the plan to introduce definite social reforms, *but* on no occasion to overstep their boundaries, to go with the workers, *but* on no occasion to surrender to them the hegemony and dictatorship—we say, such a plan actually exists. *If* half of China were not as yet occupied by the northern militarists, *if* a decisive blow were already dealt to the imperialists, then the possibility of adopting such a plan would be absolutely excluded. But it cannot *as yet* be excluded, although the extension of the class struggle is bound to drive continually the supporters of such a plan of development of the revolution to the camp of the supporters of *counterrevolution.*

---

[4] *International Press Correspondence,* Vol. 7, No. 26, April 21, 1927, pp. 527–528.

The other prospect is the bringing of the revolution rapidly to the conclusion of its bourgeois stage, the steering of the revolution in the class, that is, economic direction, and following this, along the socialist path.[5]

Thus, while favoring "socialist development," Bukharin questioned whether even the "socialist" stage of the Chinese revolution had been reached. Might China not find itself isolated and unable to carry out its socialist tasks—particularly if the general international situation were not in its favor? And, what strata of the Chinese people would support the Right Wing and who would join the Left Wing?

China, Bukharin believed, was a country of "motley socialist-economic tendencies" in which one observed a multitude of shades within the classes. This, of course, in no way denoted the general economic maturity of the country. On the contrary, it was evidence of a serious technical and economic backwardness. There existed in China numerous categories of semiworkers, craftsmen, petty tradesmen. There also existed in China different nuances within the bourgeoisie itself—with different types of contact with foreign capital:

Therefore, it is quite natural for the bourgeoisie *to withdraw from the revolution in a somewhat fantastic and zigzag-like fashion.* We must not envisage the classes of China as being some firm blocs which are clearly cut and which are detaching themselves sharply and finally from the national revolutionary front.[6]

Bukharin saw this motley of class shades as revealed particularly within the urban petty bourgeoisie and as including city intelligentsia, artisans, tradesmen, petty town people, independent tradesmen, and "some individuals who, while leading themselves a miserable existence, sometimes employ the workers whom they exploit directly or indirectly." The attitude of the petty bourgeoisie toward the revolution, he believed, was far from homogeneous. On the one hand it included a very radical group and on the other hand a group which was becoming exceedingly reactionary because it found itself threatened by the so-called "vindictive demands on the part of the working class," and which, therefore, was "joining the chorus of the large scale bourgeoisie" against the so-called "workers' terror."

The withdrawal of the bourgeoisie of various shades, according to Bukharin, was an "historical *process.*" The defection of the bourgeoisie was already distinctly noticeable, expressing itself in a class struggle within the national-revolutionary front. But the bourgeois abandonment

---

[5] Bukharin, "Problemy kitaiskoi revoliutsii," *Pravda*, No. 88, April 19, 1927, p. 4; see also Bukharin, *Les problèmes de la révolution Chinoise*, p. 28.
[6] *Ibid.*

of the revolution and its passing to the camp of the counterrevolution proceeded unevenly, and in the settlement of tactical and strategic problems this unevenness and diversity of the various bourgeois groupings would have to be taken into serious consideration. Thus:

As we have stated at the Seventh Plenum of the Executive Committee of the Comintern—and the events which followed have fully confirmed the correctness of our position—the Chinese revolution is at present *in transition from the second stage of development of the revolution to the third stage.* The working class struggles with the increasing strength against the bourgeoisie, and for the hegemony in the national revolutionary movement; it emphasizes more and more its role of a leader, of a decisive force in the revolutionary movement which determines the definite *(socialist)* path in *the development of the Chinese revolution.*[7]

It was through this chain of reasoning that Bukharin brought himself to admit, at last, the possibility of socialist development in China—but not without placing heavy emphasis upon the difficulties which he perceived as inevitable. Fortunately, the revolution would find support in a variety of different forms: from the fact of the Soviet Union's existence; from the possibility of commercial transit from Europe by way of Soviet territory; from the emergence of contradictions among capitalist powers; from the possibilities of support for the Chinese revolution from the international proletariat; and from the growing colonial movement as a whole.

The time had now arrived, Bukharin warned, when the Communists must definitely decide who was their ally and who was not.

The development of the national revolutionary movement, the drawing of the workers' and peasants' masses into the huge national revolutionary stream is bound to lead to serious re-grouping within the national revolutionary front. One must not conceal this prospect. One must bring it to light. "We are at present in such a situation," we said at the Chinese Commission of the Enlarged Plenum [VII], *"when we must choose between the peasantry (as an ally in the revolution) and the big industrial bourgeoisie."* The bourgeoisie, some comrades argued, is a revolutionary force, and we must bring it to our side. This is true, *but to a certain point only, to the point when an alternative presents itself: either with the peasants or with the bourgeoisie.*

This is what was stated with sufficient clarity and worded very definitely in the resolution passed by the Enlarged Plenum of the Comintern. . . . To this we must now add that if the class struggle leads to the establishment of powerful organizations within the peasantry and the working class, it will also lead to the similar intensive self-organization on the part of the

---

[7] *Ibid.*

old enemies of the revolution, and on the part of those who had withdrawn from the revolution and passed to the camp of the counterrevolution.[8]

To Bukharin it was evident that a number of the bourgeoisie had abandoned the united national revolutionary front. These groups had a tendency to form a bloc with the feudal elements within the country and with the imperialists operating outside the country and "also within the country." The consequences were a rightward movement of the bourgeoisie and the formation of a considerable force which became increasingly hostile to the revolution. In connection with this, a great deal of further regrouping would inevitably take place within the Kuomintang, within the national government, and within the army. This regrouping, Bukharin declared, would lead to conflicts and struggle, the limits of which one could not always foresee.

Equally interesting is Bukharin's interpretation of the peculiar nature of the Kuomintang as a bloc of three parties which lacked the kind of strict party discipline that was needed:

It must be taken into account that the Kuomintang represents a *bloc of classes* who live within one definite organizational shell. One does not find in this organization the existence of a strict party discipline which usually characterizes political parties. This fact is exceedingly important. When one speaks of the Kuomintang and of its separate sections, of the Right and the Left wings, one must take into consideration the fact that here we actually have *two* parties (and the Communists are the *third* such party) who live *within the framework of one party*. These two parties do not adhere to a common party discipline. In general, the discipline of the entire Kuomintang is extremely remote from the general notion of party discipline, as it exists with us, the Communists. And further, when we speak of the national revolutionary armies we must bear in mind first of all that these are *mercenary armies* in which the principle of single command is far from being established. . . .

In the domain of *peasants and worker questions,* the policy of the national government, or rather of its *separate sectors,* its separate organs very often is far remote from the policy that would satisfy us or even would satisfy even the most modest requirements.[9]

Toward the conclusion of his article, nevertheless, Bukharin made a strong effort to prove that the revolutionary cause was not lost and that the Left Kuomintang remained a reliable force. Most of the Kuomintang Central Executive Committee belonged to the Left Wing, he argued, and the Wuhan government was under the control of that bloc. A considerable part of the army was for the government of Wuhan and

---

[8] *Pravda,* No. 89, April 20, 1927, p. 3.
[9] *Ibid.*

against the government of Chiang Kai-shek, and the army of Fêng Yü-hsiang had not as yet been brought into battle.

Freed from "the Right saboteurs in the Right Wing" and from the "conciliators and traitors," Bukharin said, the Kuomintang must now become *a true mass organization*. It would be absolutely wrong to surrender the banner of the Kuomintang to the Chiang Kai-shek clique. On the contrary, it was necessary to explain Chiang's move as treason to the Kuomintang and to the cause of the national liberation. That was why now, perhaps more than ever before, the tactic of the withdrawal from the Kuomintang was absurd.

The important thing now was to press for the strongest possible mass workers' movement, the courageous development of the agrarian revolution, the most energetic political work in the army, and the organization of the working masses. The creation of peasants' unions and committees in the villages, workers' committees, the extension of the workers' trade unions, the organization of strike committees—all these undertakings must become the tasks of the day. Thus:

> The work in the *provinces* acquires tremendous importance. It is imperative to draw in the peasant masses who represent the rear [guard] of the revolutionary movement since, in the last count, it is the strength and the living force of the peasant *masses* that will decide the outcome of the struggle. It is necessary to avoid as much as possible such *forms* of the organization which would give the occasion for the enemies of the Chinese people to shout about the "sovietization" of China.[10]

In Shanghai, Nassonov and his colleagues objected to earlier Comintern policies. To them it appeared that neither Voitinsky nor the Chinese Communist Party perceived what actions a successful exploitation of the revolution required. Basically, according to the "Letter from Shanghai," Chinese Communist leaders were afraid of the peasant masses, and this fear led to a dangerous dependence upon the bourgeoisie—big and little—and an unwillingness to carry on vital agitation in lower ranks of the army.

Until three years ago the Chinese Communist Party had been "only a small circle of intellectuals," and consequently the leadership—intellectuals and students who, with all their good qualities, had no understanding of the masses—even now found difficulty in comprehending "that it had long ago ceased to be a circle and had been transformed into a party of 30,000 members" capable of influencing the many millions of peasants and workers. In blunt fact, according to the "Letter from Shanghai," the "upper circles of the party organizations" did not want to admit the workers into leadership:

[10] *Ibid.*, p. 4.

According to the conception of the leading core of the party, the workers
and peasants are a dull, dumb mass, unconscious and inactive; this mass
must be led by the Communists along a road which they themselves outline, without consulting these masses. The party leadership declares, for
example, that the peasants do not want land. Still more, they would not
even demand the reduction of rent payments, did not the Communists incite them to it with their agitation.[11]

In place of establishing firm relations with the peasantry, the "Letter
from Shanghai" charged, Voitinsky and the Chinese Communist leadership had persisted in "fishing for Left leaders from above." The whole
tactic of the Party in Shanghai "consisted for half a year in continuous
reunions with the national bourgeoisie and its representatives"—reunions
"covered up" with assertions about the necessity of a bloc with the petty
bourgeoisie. Indeed,

the bogey of the petty bourgeoisie runs to the grotesque. No peasants'
power can be organized, for it will frighten away the petty bourgeoisie. No
demands must be raised for the workers for they will scare away the petty
bourgeoisie. No strike movement must be developed, else the petty bourgeoisie will fall away. No Communist party must be developed, for it will
frighten the petty bourgeoisie. No actions should be taken so long as the
petty bourgeoisie has not taken any.[12]

In actuality, according to Nassonov, the Chinese Communist leadership
had displayed slight interest in the *real* petty bourgeoisie, ignoring
especially the artisans, who had lost heavily in the revolution and who
"run into the millions, if not the tens of millions." On the contrary, the
Party leaders occupied themselves only with "parleys at the top with
representatives of the small and middle commercial bourgeoisie who
were closely associated with the big bourgeoisie." According to the "Letter from Shanghai,"

the responsibility for all this lies equally with the Right wing of the leader-
ship and the representative of the ECCI [Voitinsky]. *In tactical questions*
in the past he cannot be separated from the CC; on the contrary, every
time that the party hesitated and began to seek new paths, he forced it

---

[11] "The Letter from Shanghai," Trotsky, p. 415. The attitude of the Party leaders
toward workers and peasants was best formulated, according to Nassonov and
his colleagues, by the statement of a Central Committee member concerning the
selection of students to attend a special course at the University of the Toilers of
the East in Moscow. The workers, he said, could not read, could not write, and
could not "understand anything." Moreover, the workers and peasants, if allowed
to live under relatively more favorable conditions in the Soviet Union, might "have
a demoralizing effect upon them" on their return to China. It was preferable, then,
to send only intellectuals and students. *Ibid.,* p. 414.

[12] *Ibid.,* pp. 423–424.

back into the old swamp of petty combinations, tricks, of political jugglery, which have nothing in common with revolutionary tactics.[13]

These attitudes toward the bourgeoisie and the peasantry had much to do, no doubt, with the reluctance on the part of Voitinsky and the Chinese Communist leadership to carry on effective agitation among rank-and-file soldiers of the Kuomintang and allied armies:

> The CC of the party staked everything on the commanding staff, not on the commanding staff coming forward from the ranks, but on the old staff. With the aid of all sorts of combinations, oppositions, etc., our comrades hoped to maintain a balance of forces in the army, but it never occurred to them to capture it.[14]

In a military report to the Party leadership Chou En-lai, according to Nassonov and his colleagues, had urged Communists: "Go into this national revolutionary army, strengthen it, raise its fighting ability, but do not carry on independent work there." [15]

Beyond this, Voitinsky had denied the possibility of serious agitational work in the army with "particular ardor." He also "discovered a thousand difficulties" to preclude arming the peasantry and bringing them into the army.[16] Actually, in the Kuomintang and allied forces there were already

> dozens of company commanders and a few regiment commanders who are Communists and have a colossal influence, there is a Communist regiment, and through all these channels an enormous work could be conducted. But out of the fear of revolutionizing the army which pervades some party leaders, the various comrades working in the army become detached from the party, are transformed into "individual" Communist commanders, and, as one of the Russian comrades in charge of military work in the CC

---

[13] *Ibid.*, p. 430.

[14] *Ibid.*, p. 421.

[15] *Ibid.*

[16] *Ibid.*, pp. 421–422. According to Nassonov and his colleagues, "The December plenum of the CC adopted decision to build nuclei in the army (only of commanders, to be sure, with the prohibition against taking in soldiers) and in January of this year, when the other Russian comrades (not for the first time) raised the question of work in the army, Comrade V already expressed himself sharply against the organization of nuclei. In the beginning he said (to Comrade Mandalyan) [A representative of the Russian Communist Party in China; his agreement with the views expressed in this document among others by Nassonov, who represented the Russian Young Communist League in China, caused them both to be recalled to Moscow by Stalin.—Eds.] that Moscow had decided against the organization of nuclei; then he showed the impossibility of organizing them: first, because the military command, especially Chiang Kai-shek, would see in it the machinations of the Communists, which would strain the relations; second, because the Cantonese army was not susceptible to influence from below."

declared: "they probably refuse to take workers into their sections of the army, because the workers constitute a turbulent element." [17]

It remained to be seen what sort of position Roy, the new Comintern representative, would take on these issues.

In April, only a few days before the convening of the Fifth Congress of the Chinese Communist Party in Hankow, the Left Kuomintang Central Executive Committee held a two-week open conference on land confiscation. Among those present, in addition to influential leaders of the Kuomintang, were T'an P'ing-shan, Mao Tse-tung, Ch'en Tu-hsiu, two other Communists—Hsia Sü and Yi Li-chuan, who were leaders of the peasant movements in Hupeh and Hunan respectively—Borodin and Roy, who had arrived recently from Canton.

Generally, the military men attending the conference either opposed land confiscation outright or demanded that the property of "revolutionary military men" should be safeguarded. Wang Ching-wei, according to Ts'ai Ho-sen's account, was "evasive," but insisted that certain criteria should be established for large-scale landowners—with only those possessing 50 mou [18] or more of land being subject to confiscatory action. Even the Communists, according to Ts'ai Ho-sen, were by no means unanimous:

The comrades from Hunan and the Russian comrades insisted on the confiscation of all landlords' land. T'an P'ing-shan appeared to vacillate and did not speak to the point: one time he favored the taxation on land, the other time he spoke of the redemption of land, and finally, no one knows how, he came to an agreement with Comrade B and Chen Tu-hsiu and introduced his famous proposal of "political confiscation," i.e., of the confiscation of the counterrevolutionaries' property only. It was assumed that in this manner one would escape the indignation of the officers of the revolutionary army who could be considered "big landowners" if their property was duly evaluated.

Now it is clear that the so-called "political confiscation" was simply a maneuver which enabled them [i.e., T'an P'ing-shan, B and Chen Tu-hsiu] to elude the agrarian revolution.[19]

An emerging problem—which became a major issue during the Fifth Congress—concerned whether or not the Chinese Communists should support the so-called "Left militarist" T'ang Sheng-chih in a drive to the north.

---

[17] *Ibid.*, pp. 422–423.

[18] A Chinese land measure of area which varies in different provinces, but for general purposes is equivalent to 733½ square yards, that is, 6.6 *mou* is equal to one acre.

[19] Ts'ai Ho-sen, *Problemy Kitaia,* No. 1, pp. 30–31.

On April 12 the Wuhan government had decided to dispatch a military expedition to the North along the Peking-Hankow railway in order to join forces with Feng Yü-hsiang who had been advancing eastward from Shenshi along the Lunghai Railroad. The father of the plan, Roy recalled many years later, was T'ang Sheng-chih whose "ambition to be the military dictator of Nationalist China had suffered a set-back, his rival, Chiang Kai-shek, having come out of the factional struggle for power much the stronger." [20] The difficulty, according to Roy, was that the Wuhan forces were not nearly strong enough "for this gigantic task."

The Chinese Communist Central Committee on April 16 passed a resolution against the expedition [*Document 6*]: "Before advancing beyond the *Lunghai* railway," the resolution stated, "the consolidation of the base will be carried out in accordance with Comrade Roy's speech." Two days later, according to Roy's cryptic note at the end of the resolution, the Central Committee decision was reversed.

As soon as this course of action had been settled upon, according to Roy in retrospect,

the nationalist [Wuhan] Government called upon the masses to suspend all activities on the pretext that these would weaken the rear of the army fighting against northern militarism. Instead of fulfilling its previous promises, it asked the masses to make further sacrifices, so that new military victories could be won. While industrial workers were prohibited to strike for improving their economic conditions, they were obliged to labour for longer hours to keep the Army well supplied. Even the struggle against Imperialism was suspended on the pretext that the National Government should avoid international complications so long as it was engaged in the war against the northern militarists.[21]

A joint session of the Central Committee and of Communist leaders in the Hupeh federation of labor drew up an agreement for the purpose of "strengthening revolutionary discipline" among the workers in support of the expedition [*Document 9*]. It was stipulated that the Wuhan government would reach immediate agreements with principal foreign enterprises and banks and that "not a single strike" could take place against such firms without the consent of a special government commission. Trade unions were to establish "revolutionary tribunals" to penalize workers guilty of breaking this discipline.

By this time arrangements were virtually completed in Hankow for the Fifth Congress of the Chinese Communist Party at which future policies were to be argued in considerable detail. The congress opened

[20] Roy, *Revolution and Counter-Revolution in China,* p. 466.
[21] *Ibid.,* pp. 472–473.

April 27 in Hankow and lasted for two weeks. Approximately eighty delegates attended, with about the same number of visitors. The delegations of Comintern and Profintern were also present. Among those who came to greet the congress were the leaders of the Kuomintang, Hsü Chien and T'an Yen-k'ai. Wang Ching-wei attended the session at which Roy was the speaker. Hsü Chien delivered a long speech and emphasized the importance for the Communist Party, which was the vanguard of the working class, to exist side by side with the Kuomintang which, in his opinion, represented the interests of the peasantry now ready for a struggle. According to Mif, this viewpoint on the separation of the functions of the Communist Party (being concerned with the working class) and the Kuomintang (being concerned with the peasantry) was supported by some Communists. The congress rejected this viewpoint, however, and stated in its political resolution a repudiation of "the mechanical theory that the Communist Party is a party of only the proletariat, and that the Kuomintang has charge of the peasantry. . . . Being the most revolutionary class in China . . . the proletariat is the leader of the peasantry in its struggle against feudal absolutism" [*Document 15, Point 11*].[22]

On the issue of support for T'ang Sheng-chih during the continuation of the northern campaign, Borodin and Ch'en Tu-hsiu came out in favor—Roy and T'an P'ing-shan against. It was Ch'en Tu-hsiu's belief that the Chinese revolution "could not develop in Canton nor in Shanghai nor in Tientsin nor in Hankow nor in any of those regions where industry was most developed, because there imperialism and the Chinese bourgeoisie held the stronger positions." Under these circumstances the only solution was for the revolution "to retire to the northwest provinces where the influence of imperialism was weaker and where the revolution could more easily concentrate its forces for a later attack on the imperialist strongholds." [23] It was in part, at least, as a means for clearing a way in this direction that Borodin supported the plans for T'ang Sheng-chih.

The Fifth Congress, according to Mif, decisively rejected Borodin's proposal for retirement to the Northwest,[24] but T'ang Sheng-chih and his army, representing a large part of the armed forces remaining to Wuhan and to the Communists after Chiang's defection, proceeded with his offensive.

In presenting the report for the Central Committee of the Chinese Communist Party, Ch'en Tu-hsiu spoke for several hours and discussed

[22] Mif, *Kitaiskaia Kommunisticheskaia Partiia v kriticheskie dni*, pp. 31–32.
[23] *Ibid.*, pp. 45–46.
[24] *Ibid.*, p. 117; see also Ts'ai Ho-sen, *Problemy Kitaia*, No. 1, pp. 24–28.

in some detail the various developments of the Chinese revolution over the previous two years. Unfortunately, the full text of his speech is not available, and consequently we are forced to rely upon a summary which was published in *Pravda* and in the *International Press Correspondence* [25] and upon the analyses of Ch'en's speech by Ts'ai Ho-sen and by Pavel Mif, who were present at the congress.[26]

While endorsing in principle a vigorous agrarian program, Ch'en Tu-hsiu warned that the proletariat must make concessions to the petty bourgeoisie for the sake of maintaining its support. Hence, the confiscation of large and middle landed estates—inevitable in the long run—must await the further development of military action. "The only correct solution," he declared, "is to deepen the revolution after it has first been spread."

This policy was precisely the opposite of the program which Roy advocated—but did not implement.

In opening discussions on Ch'en's report, Roy placed heavy emphasis upon the peasant problem [*Document 10*]. The development of the class struggle, he declared, was the only guarantee of the future of the revolution. The petty bourgeoisie was afraid of the revolution; to rely on T'ang Sheng-chih and the other so-called Left militarists was illusory; it was not feasible to win the militarist forces over and transform them into a revolutionary force. The task of the revolution, on the contrary, was to demoralize and destroy the militarists and turn the soldiers—largely landless peasants—against their officers. Toward this end, the revolutionary energies of the peasants must be unleashed, the roots of reaction in the villages destroyed. "There is only one way," he declared, "of really winning the soldiers of the warlords' armies over to the side of the revolution, of really organizing them into a revolutionary army: it is by way of an agrarian revolution."

Under these circumstances, he warned, the Communists should not support the Kuomintang Left unreservedly, but should carry out fractional work within the Kuomintang. "The Communist Party," he said, "must create in various organs of the Kuomintang and of the government Communist factions under the political leadership of the Central Committee so that every decision of the national government will be adopted with the consent and under the influence of the poletariat and the peasantry."

In conclusion, Roy put forward the following priorities: *first,* the

---

[25] *Pravda,* No. 108, May 15, 1927, p. 2; see also *International Press Correspondence,* Vol. 7, No. 34, June 9, 1927, pp. 716–717.

[26] Ts'ai Ho-sen, *Problemy Kitaia,* No. 1, pp. 24–27; see also Mif, *Kitaiskaia Kommunisticheskaia Partiia v kriticheskie dni,* pp. 32–54.

agrarian revolution; *second,* arming the peasants; *third,* rural self-government; *fourth,* the creation of state machinery through which the "democratic dictatorship" would be realized; *fifth,* the creation of a revolutionary army—not by converting the militarists into revolutionaries—but by organization of a "firm, social basis."

The discussions which followed Roy's initial statement to the Fifth Congress brought forward a number of criticisms. Chang Tai-lei complained, for example, that the Comintern line was too far Left. Unfortunately, Chang's speech is not available, but the nub of his criticism seems to have been that a radical agrarian program would almost certainly antagonize the petty bourgeoisie and thus destroy the revolutionary bloc [*Document 11*].

In response, Roy put forward his usual argument that the petty bourgeoisie in China—as contrasted to Europe—was an exploited class and stood closer to the proletariat, objectively, than to the bourgeoisie. It was clearly Roy's belief that the petty bourgeoisie would be forced to follow the proletariat, but in any case, the Communist Party had only two courses—to support the peasant demands for the confiscation of the large landholdings, or to retard the development of the agrarian revolution for the sake of good relations with the petty bourgeoisie. "Every member of our Party considers that in the situation that has arisen," he asserted, "the Communist Party must support the peasantry in the struggle. The proletariat cannot betray the peasantry for the sake of buying an alliance with the petty bourgeoisie." The Kuomintang had already "declared war" on the Communist Party for leadership of the peasantry, Roy added, and therefore the time had come to undermine the reaction and unleash the fighting energy of the masses.

The task of the Communists, in Roy's view, was first of all to "strengthen the base of the revolution" in Hunan and Hupeh—the provinces that were most advanced in this respect. Chang Tso-lin must be crushed, but there was no use in making "vainglorious plans" until the prerequisite power was at hand.

Two days later, on May 4, Roy presented a summary report on the "Theses on the Chinese Situation" of the Seventh Plenum "for the examination of the Fifth Congress of the Chinese Communist Party," which confirmed them without making changes. "For the first time," wrote Pavel Mif, who was present at the Congress, "the Chinese Communist Party was given a truly Leninist prognosis of the events which were taking place, was given a thoroughly worked out perspective of the movement, as well as directives on a number of cardinal questions. The Chinese Communist Party received all the above from the Plenum which had provided for the first time the broad outline for the Chinese question." [27]

Among those present when Roy delivered this report was Wang Ching-wei, "who listened with much attention," and, speaking later, declared that "the Kuomintang accepted fully the Comintern's interpretation of the noncapitalist development of the revolution. No one could reproach the Kuomintang for supporting the interests of the bourgeoisie. On the contrary, the Kuomintang was following a revolutionary path." [28]

One question was not clear, however: the Kuomintang Left leader wanted the delegates to the Congress to tell him how they interpreted the position of the petty bourgeoisie. Did they think that it could follow the noncapitalist development of the revolution?

Roy answered Wang Ching-wei's presentation with a speech that was criticized by some of the delegates as a "tactless attack." At the present stage, he said, the Communist Party would work jointly with the Kuomintang—but on the condition that it shared not only the responsibility, but the power as well. The program of the three classes would lead inevitably to socialism, however, and in this development the proletariat, acting within the Kuomintang as the conscious vanguard of the revolution, would determine the stages leading in that direction.

Two possibilities lay before the Chinese revolution, according to Roy —a development along bourgeois-democratic lines; or a pattern of "noncapitalist development" created by the Kuomintang, the national-revolutionary government, and the Communist Party [Document 12].

Because the Chinese revolution still drew its support from a coalition of classes and did not have a purely proletarian character, the proletariat could not become its sole leader—though it would be the most dominant factor. In other words, the Kuomintang had already become an instrument through which the hegemony of the proletariat could be organized, the three classes participating in it—the proletariat, peasantry, and petty bourgeoisie—all being interested in a noncapitalist development. This state, taking the form of a dictatorship of the three classes,

[27] Mif, Kitaiskaia Kommunisticheskaia Partiia v kriticheskie dni, pp. 117–118. Note the discrepancies between this quotation and the version put forward by Roy in Revolution and Counter-Revolution in China, p. 538 n: "In a book published officially in Moscow in 1932, that is three years after I had ceased to be a member of the CI, P. Mif wrote: 'It was Roy who gave the young Chinese party for the first time a real Leninist prognosis of the events taking place. From Roy, the party hears for the first time a thoroughly thought-out perspective of the movement, and received directives on a series of cardinal questions. Roy gave the young Chinese party the experience of world Bolshevism.' "
[28] Ts'ai Ho-sen, Problemy Kitaia, No. 1, p. 31.

would serve as an instrument of agrarian revolution, the abolition of feudal remnants, and the nationalization of large-scale industry and public utilities.

Though no primary record is available, Roy and Borodin appear to have carried on a running debate throughout much of the congress. Roy, according to Ts'ai Ho-sen, emphatically objected to Borodin's assertion that the Communist Party should recognize the Kuomintang's hegemony in the revolution, and yet the precise differences between them were not easy to establish:

At first we were unaware of the details of disagreement between the above two comrades, but later we learned from the accounts given us [by other comrades] that the differences between Comrade R and Comrade B lay not so much in their interpretation of the actual problem as to "whether we should agree to concessions or not," but rather in their formal approach and the point of principle in this question.

Comrade B was saying, for example, that the CCP and the KMT should "make decisions together and they should carry them out together also." But the representative of the ECCI, Comrade R, pointed out that in each separate case, and as a problem arises, the CCP should approach it in its own independent and class manner.[29]

On May 5 Roy pushed further his concepts concerning noncapitalist development in the Chinese revolution and the nature of the state during this dialectical phase [*Document 14*]. The economic forces which would prepare for the transition to socialism, he said, could occur in China only with the support of capitalist methods—but not necessarily on the basis of capitalist exploitation. Drawing its support from the three exploited classes, a revolutionary state could expect to open a phase of noncapitalist development through the nationalization of heavy industry, transport, and public utilities—but without, at first, the outright abolition of all forms of private property. It would be the task of the proletariat to lead such a state toward socialism by means of class struggle. Indeed, the agrarian reforms of the state would themselves give rise to an agrarian revolution "which only the proletariat" could carry to its conclusion. "The present Wuhan government," he asserted, "will not, on its own initiative, decide to nationalize land, railroads and factories. But the objective conditions of the revolutionary struggle will force it to do so. The subjective factor here will again be the proletariat which not only supports this program objectively, but must also put it into practice."

During his interchange with Wang Ching-wei, however, Roy—wit-

---

[29] Mif, *Kitaiskaia Kommunisticheskaia Partiia v kriticheskie dni,* pp. 56–57.

tingly or unwittingly—had capitulated on an absolutely crucial point. Previously he had been placing consistently heavy emphasis on the agrarian revolution—including the confiscation of land. Just before his statement to Wang Ching-wei, indeed, he had asserted that the agrarian question could not be resolved "as long as private ownership of land is not abolished" [*Document 12*]. Yet he assured Wang that "inasmuch as the revolution, in its present stage, will be led by a coalition of classes —and the proletariat is prepared to lead the revolution in collaboration with other classes—the proletariat can not put forward a program for the immediate abolition of private property" [*Document 13*].

Here at this crucial point, the tactics of revolution "from above" and revolution "from below" had clashed head on. One or the other had to be subordinated. Subsequently there was talk in Party councils of differentiated, or "political" confiscation—the confining of confiscations to land belonging to "large" owners and the exempting of property belonging to Left Kuomintang officers. During debates within the Agrarian Commission, according to Ts'ai Ho-sen, Roy "did not object to this measure," even "severely criticized" the counterproposal of some Russian advisers.[30] This decision, as we shall perceive further along, was almost certainly Stalin's own.

The concession was fatefully expensive. From this point onward Roy's arguments about the need for independent action and support for the peasantry were, in any practical sense, wholly meaningless.

After these various debates the Fifth Congress adopted three major policy documents: "Theses on the Political Situation and the Tasks of the Chinese Communist Party" [*Document 15*]; "Resolution on the Agrarian Question" [*Document 16*]; and a "Manifesto" [*Document 17*].

The policy of supporting the Northern Expedition had been correct, according to the theses, but the Party, which underestimated the petty bourgeoisie, had overestimated the role of the big bourgeoisie. Actually, the class struggle should have been deepened in the towns and villages as the revolution expanded. Territorial expansion must be accompanied everywhere by the intensification of the revolutionary base—by radical agrarian reform and the establishment of revolutionary democratic power. The land question should be used to win over the soldiers of the various military leaders. In the meantime, according to the theses, "relations between the Communist Party and the Kuomintang at the present stage of the revolution are becoming closer than ever before."

The first task of peasant reform, as set forth by the "Resolution on the Agrarian Question," was to attack native militarism by clearing the countryside of feudal relations and patriarchal power. A radical solution

---

[30] Ts'ai Ho-sen, *Problemy Kitaia*, No. 1, p. 32.

of the agrarian problem depended, moreover, upon a fundamental redistribution of land based on the principle of equalization—an undertaking
which required nationalization. Land belonging to small owners would
not be confiscated, however, and land belonging to "officers of the revolutionary army" was also exempted.[31]

Now that Chiang Kai-shek and the big bourgeoisie had rejected the
anti-imperialist struggle, asserted the "Manifesto," they had widened
the counterrevolutionary bloc of feudal reactionary remnants, militarists
and imperialists. No longer could the anti-imperialist struggle be separated from the class struggle: the imperialists were counting on their
Chinese allies to crush the revolution. To meet this challenge the revolutionary forces, in turn, must intensify their social base, lands belonging to the large landlords must be confiscated and the *min t'uan* disarmed. The power of the gentry must be crushed and the village power
built on the basis of village democracy. A peasant militia must be
organized.

"The slogan LAND TO THE PEASANTS will give the revolution an army
so enormous that it will make the revolution invincible," declared the
"Manifesto."

While raising these aggressive slogans, however, the "Manifesto" was
careful to reassure the Kuomintang Left: by taking part in the nationalist movement and entering the Kuomintang, the Chinese Communist
Party was not acting as a rival trying to seize power, but was moving
only "to consolidate the revolutionary elements in order to assure the
development of the revolution."

In a speech welcoming the new Central Committee elected by the
Fifth Congress, Roy gave every evidence of being pleased with the
outcome of the debates [*Document 18*]. "This Congress was Bolshevist,"
he asserted. "It showed that the Chinese Communist Party is on the
way to becoming a genuine Bolshevik party."

Rejecting an exclusively radical policy which might have damaged
the revolutionary bloc, he said, the Congress had decided on a partial
confiscation of land—exempting small landowners and officers of the
revolutionary army. This decision, said Roy, "showed that the revolutionary agrarian policy and the defense of the interests of the proletariat
will not weaken our ties with the Kuomintang."

The Fifth Congress, Roy declared further on May 10, had success-

---

[31] According to Roy in retrospect, "The resolution of the Fifth Congress was
against wholesale confiscation. Only large estates were to be confiscated. There was
a controversy over the definition of a large estate! The Kuo Min Tang set the limit
at 500 [*sic*] mus, while the Communists insisted that it should be lowered down to
100 [*sic*]." *Revolution and Counter-Revolution in China*, p. 481. Undoubtedly Roy
meant 50 and 10 *mus* [*mou*] respectively.

fully fulfilled the task of evaluating the situation in China and had "dispelled all doubts regarding the future of the revolution" [*Document 19*]. Ts'ai Ho-sen, in retrospect, was far more critical. "Our slogan at the Fifth Congress should have been 'forward,' " he asserted, "and not 'backward.' We were duty bound to carry on the agrarian revolution instead of avoiding it." [32]

---

[32] Ts'ai Ho-sen, *Problemy Kitaia*, No. 1, pp. 35–36.

V

THE CHALLENGE OF THE PEASANTRY

In Moscow, meanwhile, the Stalinist leadership had begun to face growing criticism of its China policy from Trotsky and other members of
the Opposition. The chief criticism, of course, was directed against the
ill-fated attempt at allying with Chiang Kai-shek, but beyond this Trotsky
and his supporters were urging the immediate formation of soviets. In
countering this proposal—for the time being, at least—Stalin referred at
some length to the Second Congress of the Communist International in
1920 and to the significance of the role played there by Roy.

Writing to a Russian party organ, *Derevensky Kommunist* (Rural
Communist), a reader had criticized the failure to establish soviets in
China and had argued the case with a citation from the Second Congress.
Stalin replied on May 9, 1927:

> You quote in your letter a passage from the "Supplementary Theses" of
> the Second Congress of the Comintern on the National and Colonial Ques-
> tion, where it said that in the East "the proletarian parties must carry on
> intensive propaganda of communist ideas and at the first opportunity estab-
> lish *workers'* and peasants' Soviets." In so doing you make it appear as if
> these "Supplementary Theses" and the passage you quote from them are
> Lenin's. That is no so, Comrade Marchulin. You have simply made a mistake.
> The "Supplementary Theses" are Roy's.[1]

Why had Roy's theses been submitted to the Second Congress and
adopted as a supplement to Lenin's?

> In order to single out from the backward colonial countries which have
> no industrial proletariat such countries as China and India, of which it can-
> not be said that they have "practically no industrial proletariat." Read the
> "Supplementary Theses," and you will realize that they refer chiefly to
> China and India.[2]

---

[1] Stalin, "Concerning Questions of the Chinese Revolution," *Works*, IX, 237.
[2] *Ibid.*, p. 238.

How could it happen that Roy's special theses had been needed to "supplement" the theses of Lenin? The fact was that

Lenin's theses had been written and published long before the Second Congress opened, long before the representatives from the colonial countries had arrived, and prior to the discussion in the special commission of the Second Congress. And since the discussion in the congress commission revealed the necessity for singling out from the backward colonies of the East such countries as China and India, the necessity for the "Supplementary Theses" arose.[3]

Clearly, then, Lenin's speech and theses must not be confused with Roy's "Supplementary Theses," according to Stalin, nor must it be forgotten that, in the case of countries like China and India, one must envisage the formation of *workers'* and peasants' soviets, and not simply of peasants' soviets.

Would it be necessary to form *workers'* and peasants' soviets in China? Yes, asserted Stalin, it certainly would. The whole question was *when* to form them, in *what* circumstances, in *what* situation.[4] What would it mean to call for the *immediate* formation of soviets of *workers,'* peasants', and soldiers' deputies in the areas of the Wuhan government? It would mean calling for an uprising against the "power of the revolutionary Kuomintang," the skipping over of the whole Kuomintang phase of the Chinese revolution. This course of action, Stalin declared, might put the whole Chinese revolution "in a most difficult position." [5]

Once again revolution "from above" was at odds with revolution "from below."

---

[3] *Ibid.*

[4] *Ibid.*, p. 239.

[5] *Ibid.*, p. 241. The italics are Stalin's. This whole argument was further developed by Stalin in his "Talk with Students of Sun Yat-sen University," May 13, 1927, *Works*, IX, 265–266, which stated:

"In his theses at the Second Congress of the Comintern, Lenin spoke of the formation of 'peasants' Soviets,' 'toilers' Soviets,' in the backward countries of the East. He had in mind such countries as Central Asia, where 'there is no industrial proletariat, or practically none.' He had in mind countries such as Persia, Afghanistan, etc. That, indeed, explains why there is not a single word in Lenin's theses about the organisation of *workers'* Soviets in such countries.

"But it is evident from this that what Lenin's theses were concerned with was not China, of which it cannot be said that it has 'no industrial proletariat, or practically none,' but other, more backward, countries of the East.

"Consequently, what is in question is the immediate formation of Soviets of *workers'* and peasants' deputies in China. Consequently, in deciding this question it is not Lenin's theses that must be borne in mind, but Roy's, which were adopted by the same Second Congress of the Comintern, and which speak of the formation of *workers'* and peasants' Soviets in countries such as China and India. But it is said there that *workers'* and peasants' Soviets should be formed in those countries when passing from the bourgeois-democratic revolution to the proletarian revolution."

When would it be necessary, then, to establish soviets in China? Precisely at that moment, according to Stalin, when the Kuomintang, "as a *bloc of the revolutionary Narodniks of China* (the Kuomintang Left) *and the Communist Party,* begins to outlive its day, when the bourgeois-democratic revolution, which has not yet triumphed and will not triumph so soon, begins to manifest its negative features, when it becomes necessary to pass step by step from the present, Kuomintang type of state organization to a new *proletarian* type of organization of the state." [6]

It was quite proper, Stalin told the students of Sun Yat-sen University in Moscow a few days later, to put forward at this time a slogan for the immediate seizure of land by the Chinese peasantry. Actually, he said, the peasants of Hunan, Hupeh, and other provinces were already "seizing the land from below" and setting up their own courts, their own penal organs, and their own self-defense bodies. "I believe that in the very near future the entire peasantry of China will go over to the slogan of the confiscation of the land," Stalin stated. "Therein lies the strength of the Chinese revolution." [7] Beyond this,

the chief thing *now* is, while improving and revolutionising the existing army by all available means, to lay at once the foundations for new, revolutionary regiments and divisions, composed of revolutionary peasants who have passed through the school of the agrarian revolution and of revolutionary workers, to create a number of new and really reliable corps with reliable commanders, and to make them the bulwark of the revolutionary government in Wuhan.

These corps will be the nucleus of the new army which will subsequently develop into a Red Army. [8]

With the opening of the Eighth Plenum of the ECCI in Moscow on May 18, Trotsky and other members of the Opposition tried to make their criticisms of Stalin's China policy heard. The main theme of the Trotsky argument was that soviets should be established in China immediately.

Pravda, in its issue of May 15, 1927, had carried a summary of Ch'en Tu-hsiu's speech before the Fifth Congress. According to Trotsky, "Neither Stalin nor we had this speech when Stalin wrote his theses [i.e., the theses of April 21. See p. 65 above.] and we wrote a criticism of them." [9]

The ECCI, Trotsky charged, was meeting in a "strange atmosphere." In reference to the Chinese question, he asserted: "You have been given

---

[6] *Ibid.,* pp. 241–242. The italics are Stalin's.
[7] Stalin, "Talk with Students of the Sun Yat-sen University," *Works,* IX, 263–264.
[8] *Ibid.,* pp. 271–272.
[9] Trotsky, *Problems of the Chinese Revolution,* p. 73.

the theses of comrade Zinoviev which have remained unknown to the Russian [Communist] party up till now. Zinoviev was not permitted to come here, although he has the full right—politically as well as formally —to do so." [10] Trotsky's own attempts to criticize Stalin's China policy had also "remained unsuccessful." In Moscow, "every expression of opinion, oral or written, in favor of the Opposition on the basic problems of the Chinese revolution" was treated as a "crime against the party." The "completely false" theses of Stalin had been declared *de facto* inviolable. Yet the Chinese revolution could not be "stuffed into a bottle and sealed from above with a signet."

The Stalinist leadership had asserted that the development of events in China had confirmed the earlier prognosis. Surely the workers of Shanghai and Hankow would be surprised to read that the April *coup* had developed in complete harmony with the historical line of march previously outlined for the Chinese revolution.[11]

Contrary to widely held assumptions, however, Trotsky did not, at this time, press for withdrawal from the Kuomintang. As Conrad Brandt has shown, Trotsky is clearly on record as late as March 22, 1927, as opposing Communist withdrawal from the Kuomintang.[12] "Instead of continually sounding alarms about wanting to withdraw from the Kuomintang," he asserted, the Chinese Communist Party must put its own political independence "above all other considerations, even that of remaining in the Kuomintang." This could be achieved, he believed, through the formation of soviets. "The alliance between the Communist party and the real revolutionary Kuomintang," Trotsky declared, "must not only be maintained, but must be extended and deepened on the basis of mass Soviets." [13]

In replying to Trotsky's criticisms Stalin told the Tenth Sitting of the Plenum on May 24 that he would "try, as far as possible, to keep the personal element out of the controversy." At the same time, he declared, Trotsky would like to pose "as a sort of hero" and turn examinations of the Chinese revolution and other questions "into an examination of the question of Trotsky." Stalin did not think that Trotsky "deserved so much consideration." [14]

---

[10] Trotsky, "First Speech on the Chinese Question, Delivered at the Eighth Plenum of the ECCI," *Problems of the Chinese Revolution*, pp. 83–84.

[11] *Ibid.*, p. 87.

[12] Brandt, *Stalin's Failure in China*, p. 161. At the critical points, when Moscow could effectively have changed the course of events in China, Trotsky was absorbed with other problems. *Ibid.*, p. 80.

[13] Trotsky, "First Speech on the Chinese Question," *Problems of the Chinese Revolution*, p. 100.

[14] Stalin, "The Revolution in China and the Tasks of the Comintern," *Works*, IX, 288–289.

Trotsky's fundamental error, according to Stalin, was that he failed to understand that survivals of feudalism and the entire militarist-bureaucratic superstructure of *"tu-chüns,* governors, generals, Chang Tso-lins and so forth" were the predominant factors in the oppression of China and that these factors were stimulating the agrarian revolution. Stalin continued:

If in a number of provinces 70 per cent of the peasants' earnings go to the landlords and the gentry, if the landlords, armed and unarmed, are not only the economic but also the administrative and judicial power, if medieval purchase and sale of women and children is still practised in a number of provinces—then it cannot but be admitted that feudal survivals are the principal form of oppression in the Chinese provinces.[15]

It was precisely because of these "feudal survivals" that China was now passing through an agrarian revolution "of gigantic power and scope"—an upheaval that formed the "basis and content" of the whole bourgeois-democratic revolution. Yet the bourgeois-democratic revolution in China was directed not only against feudal survivals, but also against imperialism. Why?

Because imperialism, with all its financial and military might, is the force in China that supports, inspires, fosters and preserves the feudal survivals, together with their entire bureaucratic-militarist superstructure.

Because it is impossible to abolish the feudal survivals in China without at the same time waging a revolutionary struggle against imperialism in China.

Because anyone who wants to abolish the feudal survivals in China must necessarily raise his hand against imperialism and the imperialist groups in China.

Because the feudal survivals in China cannot be smashed and abolished without waging a determined struggle against imperialism.

That is precisely why the Comintern says that the bourgeois-democratic revolution in China is at the same time an anti-imperialist revolution.[16]

The Comintern's position on the revolutionary role of Wuhan, Stalin asserted, was well-known and perfectly clear.

Since China is passing through an agrarian revolution, since the victory of the agrarian revolution will mean the victory of the bourgeois-democratic revolution, the victory of a revolutionary dictatorship of the proletariat and peasantry, and since Nanking is the centre of national counterrevolution and Wuhan the centre of the revolutionary movement in China, the Wuhan Kuomintang must be supported and the Communists must participate in this Kuomintang and in its revolutionary government, provided that the

---

[15] *Ibid.,* p. 291.
[16] *Ibid.,* pp. 291–292.

leading role of the proletariat and its party is ensured both inside and outside the Kuomintang.[17]

Was the present Wuhan government the organ of a revolutionary-democratic dictatorship of the proletariat and peasantry? Stalin asked rhetorically. No, but it had "every chance" of developing into such an organ—given the further development of the revolution. On the other hand, according to Stalin:

Quite different is the way Trotsky sees the matter. He considers that Wuhan is not the centre of the revolutionary movement, but a "fiction." Asked what the Left Kuomintang is at this moment, Trotsky replies: "So far it is nothing, or practically nothing." [18]

In fact, according to Stalin, the formation of soviets of workers' and peasants' deputies in China "at the present time" would mean the establishment of dual power requiring a call for the overthrow of the Wuhan government. One must be blind to deny to the Left Kuomintang the role of an organ of revolutionary struggle and of revolt against feudal survivals and imperialism in China.[19]

Later,

when the moment of the complete victory of the bourgeois-democratic revolution approaches, and when in the course of the bourgeois revolution the paths of transition to the proletarian revolution become clear, the time will have arrived when it is necessary to set up Soviets of workers', peasants' and soldiers' deputies, as elements of a dual power, as organs of struggle for a new power, as organs of a new power, Soviet power.[20]

To an objective observer it becomes clear that Stalin must perform a Procrustean operation indeed to force the maneuvers of Wang Ching-wei and T'ang Sheng-chih into the bourgeois-democratic concept of Marxist-Leninist orthodoxy. If the Wuhan government was not quite a "fiction," it was certainly not a center of revolution in anything like the Communist sense.

Trotsky put forward the nub of his own criticism in a second speech on the Chinese Question delivered before the Eighth Plenum, May 27. Stalin, he said, wanted to "assume the responsibility for the policy of the Kuo Min Tang and the Wuhan government, as he had repeatedly assumed the responsibility for the policy of the former 'national government' of Chiang Kai-shek." The Opposition had nothing in common with this policy. "We do not want to assume even a shadow of responsi-

---

[17] *Ibid.*, pp. 299–300.
[18] *Ibid.*, p. 300.
[19] *Ibid.*, pp. 305, 308.
[20] *Ibid.*, p. 315.

bility for the policy of the Wuhan government and the leadership of the Kuomintang." [21] Only through peasants' and soldiers' soviets could the majority of Chiang Kai-shek's soldiers be won over. The Communists, then, should build up these soviets and shoot the generals, bureaucrats, and bourgeois liberals who chose to oppose them.

During the Eighth Plenum word came from China of spontaneous peasant uprisings against a militarist *coup* in Changsha (see p. 102 below). How should the Comintern respond? Had the time come to provide all-out support for the peasants? The problem was discussed at a meeting of the Chinese Subcommittee of the ECCI when Bukharin informed his two colleagues, Ercoli (Togliatti) of Italy and Treint of France that the Chinese peasants were seizing the land. "This frightens the Wuhan government," he said as quoted by Treint many years later. "If we do not curb the agrarian movement, we will lose our Left allies and it will become impossible to win a majority in the Kuomintang. On the other hand, by curbing it, we will enlarge our influence in it, and when we will have become more powerful, we will go beyond our present allies."

Treint disagreed. The problem, he said, was not whether to sacrifice all the allies of the proletariat, but to know which ones to sacrifice— the insurgent peasants or the bourgeoisie. The Comintern would be in no better position tomorrow than today to fight the Chinese revolution with constitutional decisions of the Kuomintang as weapons.

As the argument developed, Bukharin proposed that Stalin ought to be consulted. Bukharin went out to telephone while Ercoli and Treint continued the discussion.

Stalin, on joining the subcommittee meeting, supported the arguments which Bukharin had put forward. Unless the Communists opposed the peasant revolts, he asserted, the Left bourgeoisie would turn hostile, and that would mean civil war. "The armed Chinese are largely mercenaries," he said, "and we do not dispose of big enough financial resources to have them on our side."

"But the mercenaries," Treint argued, "are largely ruined peasants who will desert [to the Communists] if the agrarian program is put forth." [22]

In the course of the discussions Stalin produced telegrams from Borodin which asserted that the Kuomintang Left was determined to

---

[21] Trotsky, *Problems of the Chinese Revolution,* pp. 102–103.

[22] This conversation is drawn, with deletions, but without alterations, from "Minutes of the Chinese Subcommittee of the ECCI," *The New Militant,* February 8, 1936, p. 3. According to Isaacs, *The Tragedy of the Chinese Revolution,* p. 244 n, this account is an English reprint of "Compte Rendu Analytique de la Petite Commission Chinoise, Mai, 1927" which Treint, at Isaac's urging, had developed from notes taken in 1927.

fight against the agrarian revolution even if it meant a break with the Comintern. The Left bourgeoisie, Stalin insisted, was still too powerful. "Its armies will not disband in the twinkle of an eye, and we will then be defeated in a civil war before the insurgent agrarians are able to connect with the proletarian insurrection." The question, according to Stalin, was whether to fight or to maneuver.

"We must fight," Treint declared.

"To fight means certain defeat," Stalin countered. The Communists ought to maneuver, he said, without compromising anything. "The agrarian revolution frightens the Kuomintang only in the degree that it directly injures its members as well as the officers of the army. I propose to send instructions to Borodin to oppose the confiscation and division of land belonging to members of the Kuomintang or the officers of the Nationalist Army. . . . We possess sufficient authority over the Chinese masses to make them accept our decision." [23]

The position taken by Stalin suggests that at least one of his representatives in China may have communicated to him the reasons why it seemed preferable not to push the land revolution at this critical moment. Roy's sudden capitulation on the issue might be explained in this context.

Ercoli expressed agreement with Stalin. According to his own "Report on the Chinese Commission," [24] he considered Treint wrong in maintaining that the Stalinists had failed to estimate correctly the nature of the petty bourgeoisie—and wrong in predicting an early break with the Wuhan government. The petty bourgeoisie was not a class with homogeneity and solidarity, according to Ercoli, and not in a similar category with the big bourgeoisie. "Consqeuently, wc cannot even think of having a break with certain elements of the petty bourgeoisie." [25]

The main Communist task, Ercoli felt, was to intensify the agrarian movement, take over leadership of the emerging peasant rebellion, unchain and organize the agrarian revolution "in every possible form" including the confiscation and nationalizaton of land. At the same time, however, it was essential "to keep the peasant class within the Kuomintang," "to guarantee the inviolability of the property of the petty bourgeoisie acquired by them through their own work," and "to assist them in their struggle against usurious capital." [26]

Ercoli recognized that the agrarian revolution would "frighten away

---

[23] *Ibid.*

[24] Communist International, Executive Committee, *Die chinesische Frage auf dem 8. Plenum der Exekutive der Kommunistischen Internationale, Mai 1927*, pp. 145–151.

[25] *Ibid.*, p. 150.

[26] *Ibid.*, p. 146.

many middle-class elements" and thus encourage "partial defeats."
To guard against such defeats, the Communists must themselves organize
the agrarian movement through peasant committees and peasant unions
outside the Kuomintang—but see to it that the control was kept *inside*
Kuomintang organs. This, he thought, was entirely feasible in view of
the fact that the Kuomintang was not a party, but "some kind of
'representative' soviet-type organization." [27]

In the meantime, the Communists must press their attack against
imperialism and the militarists in the north. Toward this end it was
essential to reorganize the entire army on a revolutonary basis, clearing the army of counterrevolutionary elements and recruiting Communist and "reliable elements of the Left Kuomintang." [28]

It was the Stalinist faction, of course, which had the power to enforce
its viewpoint. "You are the majority," Treint conceded, "you can decide what you like."

"The minority must be disciplined," Bukharin said.

Treint was angered by this. "So serious a question is involved here
that no force on earth will prevent me from formulating my reservations in such a manner that they will be heard. Or are you going to
employ physical violence against me?"

"Don't get dramatic," Stalin shot back.[29]

In the light of the account given by Treint in the *New Militant* as to
what had transpired in the Chinese Section of the Eighth Plenum of the
ECCI, it is interesting to turn to the resolution on the Chinese question
passed by the same plenum. In regard to the alleged opinion of the
majority of the Commission on the need to curb the agrarian revolution,
the resolution asserted:

*Agrarian revolution, including confiscation and nationalization of land—
such is the basic, inner, and social content of the new stage of the Chinese
revolution.* The most important thing at the present time is to secure the
"plebeian" revolutionary solution of the agrarian problem from below by
the tens and hundreds of millions of the peasants themselves. And in this
the Communist Party must take the lead of the movement.

The Communist Party must conduct even *within* the government a policy
which would contribute [*sodeistvovat*] to the unleashing [*razviazyvanie*] of
the agrarian revolution by the government itself. This will transform the
government into an organizational and political center of the workers' and
peasants' revolution, an organ of revolutionary democratic dictatorship of
the proletariat and the peasantry. On the other hand, only on the basis of
such a policy enacted from below and from above will the creation of really

---

[27] *Ibid.*, p. 147.
[28] *Ibid.*, pp. 148–149.
[29] *The New Militant*, February 8, 1936, p. 3.

reliable armed detachments and the reorganization of the whole army on a sound revolutionary foundation be possible.[30]

How, then, was this task to be fulfilled? The resolution points out that "the Communist Party of China must exert all its efforts directly in alliance with the Left Kuomintang." [31] At the same time, the CCP must "preserve its own political features, distinct from the political features of even the most radical petty bourgeois revolutionaries"—presumably the Left Kuomintang:

No matter what the political situation may be the Communist Party must never merge [rastvoritsia] with any other political organization. It must represent an independent force. . . . For that reason the Communist Party must never allow restrictions to be imposed on it in advocating its views and mobilizing its right to criticize the waverings and hesitations of the revolutionary petty bourgeois democracy. On the contrary, only such criticism will stimulate [tolkat] the petty bourgeois revolutionaries to move to the Left, and will secure the hegemony of the working class in the revolutionary struggle.[32]

The resolution stated, however, that the independence of the Communist Party was not to be interpreted as the Party's isolation from nonproletarian strata of the population; it was simply to ensure the leading role of the proletariat *within* the Kuomintang:

In China the Kuomintang is the specifically Chinese form of organization in which the proletariat collaborates directly with the petty bourgeoisie and the peasantry. It is impossible, under these conditions, to claim the role of leader for the proletariat unless the Communist Party, the party of the working class, claims the role of leader *within* the Kuomintang.[33]

The task of the CCP, therefore, was to "convert the Kuomintang into a genuine mass organization embracing the toiling population in town and countryside." The CCP was to see to it that the Kuomintang developed "into a genuinely broad, genuinely elective, genuinely mass, genuinely revolutionary democratic organization." While preserving its own independence, the CCP "must exercise to an increasing degree its influence over the work of the Kuomintang." Consequently, the CCP "must take a most energetic part in the work of the Wuhan Provisional Revolutionary Government." The Communist Party must participate

---

[30] Communist International, Executive Committee, *Kommunisticheskii Internatsional v dokumentakh*, p. 722. The resolution on the Chinese Question adopted at the Eighth Plenum of the ECCI, May 18–30, 1927; see also *International Press Correspondence*, Vol. 7, No. 35, June 16, 1927, pp. 737–741.

[31] *Ibid.*, p. 722.

[32] *Ibid.*, p. 723.

[33] *Ibid.*

with much energy in the work of the organs of the government, "both centrally and locally, while criticizing the inadequate firmness revealed by its immediate allies and securing correct line of government policy," as well as bringing about a close contact, primarily through the Kuomintang, between the revolutionary government and the masses of the people:

Unless this task is fulfilled, unless the mass movement is developed, unless the agrarian revolution and the improvement in the conditions of the working class are brought about, unless the Kuomintang is converted into a genuine mass organization of the toiling masses, unless the trade unions are further consolidated and the growth of the party is ensured, unless the most intimate contact is maintained between the Wuhan government and the masses, it will be impossible to bring the revolution to its victorious conclusion.[34]

There was still another point which was taken up in the resolution of the Eighth Plenum of the ECCI dealing with China. This was the question of reorganization of the army:

The ECCI also considers that at the present time there arises with particular acuteness the question of the reorganization of the army, of establishing military units absolutely loyal to the revolution, and to establishing contact between the armies and the workers' and peasants' organizations, of securing cadres of the army, of converting the army from a mercenary into a regular army of the revolution, etc.[35]

In a similar manner Stalin had referred to the problem of the future Chinese army when he spoke to the students of Sun Yat-sen University in Moscow a few days before the opening of the Eighth Plenum session.[36]

In China, meanwhile, T'ang Sheng-chih had launched his new northern offensive in the direction of Peking. By mid-May, according to Conrad Brandt,

his campaign had progressed to a point where it seemed to Stalin that it was fairly sure to succeed and that, therefore, he could safely applaud it. So applaud it he did, giving reasons why, arguing—it seemed on the surface —exactly as Borodin had done at the party congress in Hankow. He pointed out, as had Borodin, that here was an opportunity to join hands with General Fêng Yü-hsiang, who hovered about north of Wuhan.[37]

Meeting in Wuhan, meanwhile, the Chinese Politburo argued further the proper relationship between the Kuomintang Left and the Communist Party. According to Ts'ai Ho-sen,

---

[34] *Ibid.*, pp. 724–726.
[35] *Ibid.* p. 727.
[36] Stalin, *Works*, IX, 271–272.
[37] Brandt, *Stalin's Failure in China*, pp. 121–122.

Comrade B [speaking later in the Politburo] said that "the Fifth Congress had settled the problem of the petty bourgeoisie only in principle, but failed to provide any concrete tactical formula for it and that it was our duty now to do it." At the same time he put forward the following proposals: "(1) To satisfy the trading and industrial petty bourgeoisie we should curtail the demands of the shop assistants and others; (2) In regard to the village petty bourgeoisie, we should defend the small scale landlords; and (3) We should take measures against the practices of arrest and shooting of the counter-revolutionaries directly by the populace." He also mentioned in passing, the problem of "the dictatorship of the workers' unions," but did not elaborate on it.[38]

Borodin was followed in the Politburo debate by Ch'en Tu-hsiu, who

pointed out that "it was not sufficient to discuss the above three points. It was necessary to clarify finally the problem of the popular movement as a whole, and of the leadership in it. At the present the word "hegemony" is constantly on Wang Ching-wei's lips and he loudly proclaims that the hegemony exercised by the people will lead to defeat, that the Communists are unable to guide the people," and so forth, and so forth. The basic point in all Chen Tu-hsiu's speeches has been the demand that general leadership in the movement be handed over to the Kuomintang. The basic question which called for an answer [from us] was: "to yield, or not to yield." [39]

Referring somewhat later to the above statement by Ch'en Tu-hsiu, Ts'ai Ho-sen recalled that

Comrade Chen Tu-hsiu was quite right in directing our attention to this question. At that time I, too, voted for his proposal. But Comrade R thought differently, although he gave no clear explanation of his own stand, but simply got off with some meaningless words: "Alright, we shall never again come to discuss this problem with them." It was evident that Comrade R and Comrade B had already had some heated discussions on this question, but Comrade R failed to communicate anything to us and consequently some participants in the session were displeased with him.[40]

During a second session the Politburo examined and accepted a resolution proposed by Roy for regulating relations between the Kuomintang Left and the Communist Party [Document 23]. According to this document, the Communists were to continue collaboration in order to strengthen the Left Wing and assist it in "leading the national revolution"—but without forfeiting the independence and interests of the proletariat. It was stipulated that the Wuhan Ministry of Labor should establish a court for resolving conflicts between petty entrepreneurs and

[38] Ts'ai Ho-sen, *Problemy Kitaia*, No. 1, pp. 34–35.
[39] *Ibid.*, p. 35.
[40] *Ibid.*

their employees. In this connection, the "exhorbitant demands of commercial employees" were to be restricted, and "no obstacles to the commercial activities of imperialists" were to be permitted.

Through the passage of this resolution, according to Ts'ai Ho-sen,

the basic tactical points of the Northwest theory of Comrade B were accepted: The Northern Expedition was to be undertaken which, on its part, meant the delay in the agrarian revolution. Concessions to the imperialists and the petty bourgeoisie were agreed upon. As a consequence of these concessions, two and a half months later [the congress concluded in early May], the political death of the top leadership in Wuhan and the second serious defeat of the Chinese revolution followed. The Politburo's aims, its mistakes, its activities and its ideas [in the period following the Fifth Congress] follow directly from the policy of concessions! [41]

Roy, according to Ts'ai Ho-sen, had consistently rendered ardent support to the decisions of the Comintern and of the Fifth Congress of the CCP. He firmly insisted that the fundamental political slogan was that of an "offensive," that is, the agrarian revolution and the basic hegemony of the proletariat. But,

as to the "concessions," Comrade R believed that these were the problems of a secondary and passing importance. However, it was on account of this attitude that he had unwittingly made the Politburo approve, and in that way ensured the acceptance of the Northwest theory. It is evident, therefore, that Comrade R had capitulated to this theory without even being aware of it.[42]

In March the Wuhan government had agreed to appoint two Communists, T'an P'ing-shan and Su Chao-cheng, Minister of Agriculture and Labor respectively. On assuming office May 20, T'an stated that the policy of his ministry was to carry out the agricultural policy of the Kuomintang, to stir up interest of the peasantry in the struggle against the northern militarists, to achieve closer coöperation between the peasants and the "revolutionary armies," and to strengthen the peasant organizations in Wuhan territory. He was formally welcomed in office by Wang Ching-wei who referred to him as a leader "unusually equipped to cope with the peasants' problems." [43]

On May 18, just before T'an P'ing-shan's assumption of office, one of the generals allied with the Wuhan government, the commander of the Fourteenth Division, Hsia Tao-yin, rebelled. At the head of a regiment which had been stationed on the railway line between Wuhan and

---

[41] Ibid.
[42] Ibid., p. 36.
[43] The People's Tribune, May 21, 1927, pp. 1, 5.

Changsha, he marched toward the seat of the Kuomintang Left government in order to overthrow it. According to Roy, writing many years later,

the attitude of the Nationalist Government was such as gave rise to the suspicion that it connived with the revolt against itself. Hsia Tao-yin, with a pitiable army of hardly 2000 men, reached the outskirts of Woochang without any resistance. Helplessly, the Nationalist Government awaited its fall on the pretext that it had no power to resist the rebels, all the available forces having been sent to the North. The situation revealed the motive of the hasty expedition towards Peking. Wuhan should be disarmed to facilitate the counter-revolutionary attack.[44]

The Kuomintang garrison at Hankow, according to Roy, was amply strong to resist the attack, but at least some of the officers clearly sympathized with the revolt. At that critical moment,

it became quite clear that the Kuo Min Tang, in the interest of the revolution, should break away from compromising allies, and stand alone with the support of the masses. When there was uprising against the Nationalist Government, and military forces, formally owing allegiance to it, were conspiring with the rebels, then the only way out was to arm the masses which had demonstrated their loyalty to the revolution.[45]

For tactical reasons, according to a footnote which Roy added to the Party's "Declaration" which an extraordinary session of the Politburo charged him to write concerning the revolt [Document 21], it seemed necessary to "intensify the conflict" between the Left Wing petty bourgeoisie and the generals. "Certain concessions should have been made to the petty bourgeoisie in order to alienate it from the openly reactionary officers." Instead, an "orientation toward T'ang Sheng-chih" prevailed in the Central Committee—an orientation which, according to Roy, was encouraged by Borodin.[46]

Ts'ai Ho-sen's account provides a somewhat different perspective:

We [Ts'ai and Li Li-san] recommended intensified training of armed forces in order to be able to meet the enemies' insurrections with insurrections of our own. But Comrade R and Ch'ü Ch'iu-po were of the opinion that the central issue that concerned us was the question of our relations with the Left Wing Kuomintang, and not the military problem. Only after these relations were rectified were we to center our attention on the problem of establishing a military base and devote our energy to that end.[47]

---

[44] Roy, *Revolution and Counter-Revolution in China*, p. 513.
[45] *Ibid.*, p. 514.
[46] *Ibid.*, pp. 518–519.
[47] Ts'ai Ho-sen, *Problemy Kitaia*, No. 1, p. 37.

Roy's "Declaration," according to Ts'ai Ho-sen, made two serious errors:

1. The excesses were admitted in the peasant movement, and it was stated that these excesses were committed by the peasants themselves, and that the CCP had no participation in them. In other words, the CCP washed its hands of all responsibility for the intensification of the peasant movement.

2. It was admitted that the CCP was defending not only the interests of the workers and peasants, but also the interests of the middle strata of in-dustrialists and merchants. It was hoped that by making the latter statement it would be possible to prevent the industrialists and the merchants from joining Hsia Tou-yin. However, the above argument made it evident that Comrade R had completely lost his head and had surrendered the basic principles [of the revolution].[48]

It was under these circumstances, at any rate, that the "Declaration" was issued in order, according to Roy, to "win the confidence of the petty bourgeoisie [and] to incite it against the reactionary officers." An "Appeal" was also issued to rebel soldiers urging them to desert their commander [Document 22]. Communists working in the "highest organs of the Kuomintang," however, failed to press the Wuhan government into formally condemning Hsia Tao-yin—an action which, according to Roy's footnote, would have proved a turning point in the revolution.

Workers in the nearby Hanyang Arsenal "laboured day and night" to keep the [Wuhan] Nationalist armies supplied. "If they were given only a part of the weapons they manufactured," Roy asserted years later, "the workers could easily disarm the counter-revolutionary garri-son. An open declaration by the Kuo Min Tang that the military offi-cers were rebelling against the Nationalist Government, because the latter wanted to give land to the peasants, would have won over the soldiers, who were all landless peasants." In later years, however, Roy perceived clearly what in mid-May, 1927, he seems to have perceived dimly, if at all: "The Kuo Min Tang neither wanted to arm the workers, nor give land to the peasants. Consequently, it could not defend the revolution, and joined the conspiracy against it." [49] The further "trag-edy," according to Roy in retrospect, was that many Communist leaders shared the predispositions of the Wuhan government.

It was the Communist general Yeh T'ing, who crushed the Hsia revolt.

According to Ts'ai Ho-sen,

Li Li-san and I proposed that the troops of Yeh T'ing, jointly with the cadets of the Military Political School, would occupy the Canton-Hankow

[48] *Ibid.*, p. 39.
[49] Roy, *Revolution and Counter-Revolution in China,* p. 514.

railway line and put down Hsia Tou-yin's mutiny. In the case of T'ang Sheng-chih's treason, our forces were to make Hunan their base and advance on Hupeh and Kwangtung. While proceeding in that manner, they were to assist the development of the workers' and peasants' detachments so that the latter could render us considerable assistance at the positions which we held.[50]

Writing several years later, Roy recalled that

the city [of Wuchang] was defended by a couple of hundred soldiers; but the garrison commander happened to be a Communist. The rebels appearing on the outskirts of the city, the Communist commander could no longer wait for the instruction of the Nationalist Government, the headquarters of which were situated just on the other side of the river. As there was no chance of any reinforcement coming from Hankow, the garrison commander Yeh-tin [Yeh T'ing] acted on his own initiative. He got together an irregular army of about 1500 men, including several hundred students from the local military school. They were mostly petit-bourgeois intellectuals, all members of the Kuo Min Tang. After a week's hard fight the rebels were driven back.[51]

Ts'ai Ho-sen charges that Roy, failing to arouse the Politburo to deal with the counterrevolution, centered attention on the problem of establishing proper relations with the Kuomintang Left. The proposals put forward by Ts'ai and Li Li-san, moreover, were only partly accepted:

Yeh T'ing and the cadets of the Military Political School were sent to fight Hsia Tou-yin. The workers' pickets demanded from the Nationalist government 2,000 rifles from Hanyang Arsenal and several thousand dollars per month, to which demand Wang Ching-wei and others gave only a verbal consent. [Meantime], the Left Wing Kuomintang continued to remain the central problem of the party, while Hsia Tou-yin's mutiny was interpreted as a temporary occurrence.[52]

Borodin and T'an P'ing-shan were now making their voices heard everywhere, according to Ts'ai Ho-sen. Did this not mean a break with the Nationalist government? Surely the Communists were not yet strong enough to do it, Borodin argued, and if the Arsenal workers went on strike the consequences would be suicidal. What could be done? All Nationalist leaders were turning against the Communists. "What is being planned now," they said, "is simply nonsense! Naïveté! Madness!" [53]

The masses, according to Ts'ai Ho-sen, began to sense the situation

---

[50] Ts'ai Ho-sen, *Problemy Kitaia*, No. 1, p. 37.
[51] Roy, *Revolution and Counter-Revolution in China*, pp. 514–515.
[52] Ts'ai Ho-sen, *Problemy Kitaia*, No. 1, p. 38.
[53] *Ibid.*, p. 46.

and to wonder why the Communists were so indifferent and passive in their attitude toward "the horrors that were being perpetrated, and why they did not fight" against the exploiters and the Nationalist government. The chief Communist leaders, for their part, still failed to understand the character and motivations of men like T'ang Sheng-chih, Wang Ching-wei, Fêng Yü-hsiang, and the others.[54]

On May 21 the Left Kuomintang Central Executive Committee issued a manifesto on the "All-Class Nature of the Revolution." Stating that the peasants and workers needed "proper guidance," the Manifesto criticized them for making "excessive demands" on their employers. "The revolutionary allies, the manufacturers and merchants," the manifesto asserted, needed "adequate protection" also. "It is our policy to unite them all on the same battle front and enable them all to benefit equally from the Revolution." [55]

The following day Borodin told a meeting at the Central Kuomintang headquarters:

The imperialists will not adopt military force to deal with China. They can further their economic aggression through three methods: first, utilize all Chinese reactionaries who have feudal notions; second, use Chinese capitalists as their tools of expansion; third, frighten the small capitalists in China and break the unity of the Chinese revolutionary masses.

Therefore, true Kuomintang members must cooperate with the small capitalists in completing the Revolution.[56]

Roy, on May 24, presented to the Chinese Politburo a resolution on "Relations with the Kuomintang and the Independence of the Communist Party" [*Document 23*] which, according to his own subsequent notation, was "neither adopted nor rejected." The resolution restated the necessity for Communist support of the Kuomintang Left, but warned against any blindness to the essential hostility of many elements in Wuhan toward the Communist Party. The essential fact was that the Kuomintang Left rank and file were legitimately petty bourgeois in nature, while the leadership consisted of "agents of the feudal-bourgeois reaction." Wang Ching-wei, indeed, was the only major leader trying to maintain friendly relations with the Communist Party. According to Roy,

our tactic under these circumstances must be determined not by the desire to maintain good relations with the leaders, but by the necessity of using the party as a whole as an instrument for developing the revolution.

I do not propose effecting an internal coup in the Kuomintang. The task lying before the Communist Party is one of freeing the Kuomintang

[54] *Ibid.*
[55] *The People's Tribune*, May 21, 1927, pp. 1–2.
[56] *Ibid.*, May 22, 1927, p. 1.

from its present leadership; however, it is impossible to achieve this immediately. [*Document 23*]

The task, in short, was to "rebuild the Kuomintang from below," to mobilize the revolutionary Kuomintang masses against their reactionary leadership, to mobilize the peasantry and establish in the villages and districts an armed "democratic power" [*Document 23*].

No sooner had Hsia Tou-yin's revolt been put down than General Hsü K'e-hsiang and other Nationalist officers in command of troops stationed in Changsha, staged a *coup d'état* on the night of May 21, overthrew the Hunan provincial government and imprisoned its members, dissolved local committees of the Kuomintang Left and initiated repressive measures against local Communist organizations. "The insurgents," Roy recorded many years later, "were direct subordinates of the Commander-in-Chief of the [Wuhan] Nationalist Army, Tang Sheng-chih. From the front, he remained in telegraphic communication with them." [57] In the meantime, the retreating peasants were brutally massacred. [58]

Still, according to Ts'ai Ho-sen, the Communists remained primarily concerned with relations between themselves and the Wuhan government:

The entire energy of the Politburo was directed upon the regulation of the relations with the "Left Wing." Herein lies the reason for our defeat in Hupeh and Hunan. If, and from the beginning, the Politburo had concentrated its attention upon the suppression of the counterrevolution, and by its own efforts had strengthened the bases in Hunan and Hupeh, we would not have suffered the terrible and shameful defeat. If, at a required moment, we would have given our attention to the task of liquidating Hsü K'e-hsiang and Hsia Tao-yin, and of suppressing the counterrevolution of T'ang Sheng-chih and T'an Yen-k'ai, the "Left Wingers" would have ended their vacillations which, on its part, would have led to the improvement of our relations with them. [59]

In these circumstances it was Ts'ai Ho-sen's conviction that Roy bore considerable responsibility. "At that time I and Li Li-san had not had as clear a picture of the situation as one has it now. But if Comrade R had made use of our proposal and had directed the attention of the Politburo to the task of suppressing the counterrevolution and other conspiracies with our own forces, then there would have been no defeats in Hunan and Hupeh." [60]

In Changsha the Communists, together with members of the local

[57] Roy, *Revolution and Counter-Revolution in China*, p. 517.
[58] *Ibid.*, p. 552.
[59] Ts'ai Ho-sen, *Problemy Kitaia*, No. 1, p. 38.
[60] *Ibid.*, pp. 38–39.

Kuomintang Left organizations, began organizing an armed attack against the rebels. Their plan was to retake the city and thus "save the revolution." According to Roy, writing in retrospect:

> More than twenty thousand peasants marched upon Changsha from all sides. Nearly at the gates of the city, they were ordered to go back and dissolve their military formations. The instruction came from the Communist headquarters at Wuhan. In the meantime, the Commander-in-Chief of the Wuhan Army, T'ang Sheng-chih, had declared that he was personally going to Changsha in order to establish order there. The counter-revolutionary insurgents there were his subordinates. The Communist leaders allowed themselves to be deceived by the unmistakably dishonest manoeuvre; they decided to call off the armed uprising, since T'ang Sheng-chih had taken the matter in his own hand. A sudden, unwarranted retreat is extremely demoralizing even for a regular army; it is more so for an improvised force. The mobilised peasants retreated in a chaotic manner. The counter-revolutionary insurgents availed themselves of the opportunity. They attacked the retreating peasants and massacred them ruthlessly.[61]

Almost all the Communist leaders in Hankow, according to Roy, believed the stories that were reaching Wuhan about the "excesses" of the peasants, and there was a wide concensus that the most effective method of combatting counterrevolution would be to check them.[62]

The chairman of the National Peasant Federation was none other than Mao Tse-tung who had only recently presented his report on the peasantry in Hunan, and now it became his duty, under party discipline, to discourage the very kind of action on the countryside that he had just finished advocating. Under these circumstances it is not difficult to understand how Roy, writing some years later, should recollect Mao as belonging to the extreme Right Wing of the Party.[63]

In seeking to contain the peasantry the Chinese Communists tried every channel at their disposal. "The Communist Minister of Agriculture, Tan Ping-san [T'an P'ing-shan], was ready to go to Hunan with that object," Roy recorded. "But on the spot, things appeared differently." [64] There the peasants and local Communist leaders were in danger of extermination.

Wang Ching-wei, according to a Kuomintang Left account, de-

---

[61] Roy, *Revolution and Counter-Revolution in China*, pp. 551–552.

[62] *Ibid.*, pp. 550–551; see also "Deklaratsiia priniataia no avgustovskoi konferentsii KKP," as translated from Chinese in Mif, *Kitaiskaia Kommunisticheskaia Partiia v kriticheskie dni*, pp. 215–221; also Brandt, Fairbank and Schwartz, *A Documentary History of Chinese Communism*, pp. 109–114.

[63] Roy, *Revolution and Counter-Revolution in China*, p. 615.

[64] *Ibid.*, p. 551. One month after assuming office T'an requested leave of absence in view of his failure to put the peasants "on the right track." *The People's Tribune*, June 30, 1927, p. 1.

manded to know of Borodin on what authority he justified the policy of land seizure in Wuhan:

> Borodin denied that he was responsible for the movement, but mentioned his colleague M. N. Roy, an Indian Communist, as the instigator of all the troubles, stating that Roy had the complete confidence of Stalin, even more so than himself.[65]

It was possible, Roy thought, to raise an irregular force several thousand strong for temporary operations against Changsha—pending the formation of the revolutionary army with peasant volunteers. To secure the services of the improvised force, however, it was necessary to pay the troops a month's wages in advance, and Borodin controlled the purse strings. In the beginning, according to Roy, Borodin promised to supply the required money, but when all arrangements were made— "in spite of the criminal non-cooperation of the leaders of the CP"— and when the peasants' unions had been able to besiege Changsha, he failed to keep his promise.

According to Ts'ai Ho-sen,

> Comrade B became very much disturbed and desired to proceed to Hunan immediately with the Commission which was organized by T'an P'ing-shan and the CC of the Kuomintang (it consisted of Comrade B, T'an P'ing-shan, Ch'en Kung-po and two representatives of T'ang Sheng-chih) to investigate the reasons of Hsia Tou-yin's treachery and the excesses in the peasant movement. Such was the decision made by Comrade B. Comrade R disapproved of it.[66]

On May 26 the All-China Trade Union Federation and the All-China Peasant Association wired the provincial peasant and labor unions that the Wuhan government had "appointed a committee of five which left here this morning for the settlement of the Changsha incident" and instructed all peasant and labor comrades of the province "to be patient and wait for the government officials in order to avoid further friction."[67]

At that point, according to Roy's later account,

> I vigorously objected to the Communists undertaking the task of checking the revolutionary action of the peasants, in order to placate the reactionary army officers. I pointed out that the suicidal policy of restraining the development of the agrarian revolution on the plea of not disturbing the rear, when the army was fighting on the front, had already enabled the forces of reaction to go over to the offensive. Further restraint would demoralise the peasants'

---

[65] T'ang Leang-li, *The Inner History of the Chinese Revolution,* p. 273. (Cited hereafter as T'ang, *The Inner History.*)

[66] Ts'ai Ho-sen, *Problemy Kitaia,* No. 1, p. 39.

[67] *The People's Tribune,* May 28, 1927, p. 5.

movement, and encourage counter-revolution to raise its bloody head in the villages. But my objection was disregarded.[68]

Roy then suggested that T'an P'ing-shan might proceed to Changsha with the instruction that "his mission should not be to check the 'excesses' of the peasants' movement, but to set up village self-government, investing the peasants' unions with the necessary political power." That, Roy believed, would be setting up soviets in fact, if not in name. The peasants' unions, he thought, were the rallying ground of the rural oppressed and exploited masses. T'an P'ing-shan, in his capacity as minister of agriculture, was in charge of local self-government and police. The action proposed, therefore, was within his official competence, Roy maintained, and the peasants' unions, "properly and courageously guided," could easily "become basic units of the revolutionary State, disarm the rowdies and ruffians in the pay of the landlords, and create a militia as the nucleus of a real revolutionary army." [69]

In this respect Ts'ai Ho-sen's views were not much different from those of Roy:

Several mistakes were made at that time by Comrade B. First, the investigation of "excesses" in the peasant movement was by itself wrong in principle. Second, the idea of a struggle against the counterrevolutionaries by legal means, and not by force, was simply and highly amusing. Third, the failure to carry out the intended investigation led to the loss of confidence in the Nationalist government and Comrade B, and it encouraged the growth of counter-revolution.[70]

T'an P'ing-shan and his "Commission of Five" proceeded to the Hunan border. There, according to one version, they were turned back by the troops of Ho Chien, a militarist who had supported Hsü K'e-hsiang with reinforcements.[71] According to Ts'ai Ho-sen, on the other hand, "when Comrade B and the commission arrived in Yochow, Hsia Tou-yin issued an order for their immediate arrest and execution." Whereupon all members of the commission hastened back to Wuhan.[72]

It was now clear that whoever would reach Changsha must have an army at his back.

Roy, according to Ts'ai Ho-sen, had been against the venture from the outset, "and he was right in his opinion, but his fault lay in failing to take measures against it." [73]

At one of the Politburo sessions both Borodin and Roy took the

---

[68] Roy, *Revolution and Counter-Revolution in China*, p. 551.
[69] *Ibid.*
[70] Ts'ai Ho-sen, *Problemy Kitaia*, No. 1, p. 39.
[71] Brandt, *Stalin's Failure in China*, p. 131.
[72] Ts'ai Ho-sen, *Problemy Kitaia*, No. 1, p. 39.
[73] *Ibid.*

floor in an argument over the next move. Borodin, according to Ts'ai Ho-sen, made five major points:

1. The present position of the Left Kuomintang is entirely acceptable [to the CCP]. They do not display any deviationist tendencies or shortcomings. The mistakes in the past were due to the extreme nature of the workers' and peasants' movement. Actually, the leadership in this movement was not that of the peasants, but of the Society of Elder Brothers (Ko-lao-hui) and bandits. [The Society of Elder Brothers was a secret peasant organization, particularly strong in the northern provinces, which directed the peasants' struggle against demands of the militarists and government authorities.]

2. We must yield to the Kuomintang in order to be able to continue collaboration with it; if we break with the Kuomintang, the Chinese revolution will suffer defeat.

3. Collaboration with the Kuomintang means collaboration with its CC, since the present composition of the CC is quite acceptable to us. The withdrawal from it, or its overthrow, would be equivalent to a break or a political coup. A tendency in favor of a break is evident among some of our party members (for example, the representative of Comrade R).

4. Reduction of rent, elimination of usury and the introduction of local self-government in the countryside—these measures represent the agrarian revolution.

5. The CC of the CCP must issue jointly with the workers' and peasants' organizations an appeal to the masses urging them to follow the orders of the CC of the Kuomintang and of the Nationalist government which require the discontinuation of the excesses in the workers' and peasants' movement, as well as the recently issued orders.[74]

Roy argued, on the other hand, that

1. The CC of the Kuomintang and the Nationalist government no longer represent the Left Wing; rather, they support the interests of T'u-hao, the gentry, landlords, and imperialists. We must direct the people to overthrow them.

2. The overthrow of the present CC of the Kuomintang does not mean as yet a political coup.

3. At present we must aim at the democratic dictatorship of the workers and peasants (Comrade R did not elaborate any further on this point).

4. The CC of the CCP must issue immediately an appeal to the people, and explain in it the reactionary nature of all orders which had been issued recently by the CC of the Kuomintang and its government. These orders aim at the suppression of the workers' and peasants' movement and the defense of the feudal system.[75]

At this juncture a Chinese Communist "manifesto" commemorating the incident of May 30, 1925—when British police fired on a student

---

[74] *Ibid.*, p. 40.
[75] *Ibid.*

demonstration in Shanghai—emphasized the inevitability of national bourgeois "betrayals" and the responsibility of the proletariat for providing the motive force of the revolution [*Document 24*]. Again, the central proletarian task was to enlist the broad masses of the peasantry—including the rank-and-file soldiery—and the urban petty bourgeoisie against militarism, feudalism, and imperialism. No mention was made of the Changsha killings.

In Hunan, moreover, the five-member Provincial Committee of the Communist Party decided to promote an insurrection of three hundred thousand armed peasants and march against Changsha on May 30. But, according to Ts'ai Ho-sen,

once Li Wei-han [a Politburo member] heard of this decision he lost his temper and announced that the undertaking was a mere child's play. His interpretation of this move was as follows: "If Changsha is captured [by us], T'ang Sheng-chih will march on Wuhan and will overthrow the Nationalist government. In that way, by capturing Changsha we shall loose Wuhan. As long as the Wuhan government exists we must ask it to end [Hsü's] insurrection by lawful means." [76]

Meanwhile, according to Roy's subsequent account,

in despair I tried to act over the head of the impossible Political Bureau of the Communist Party. I demanded a plenary meeting of the Central Committee to be attended by local leaders. The demand was opposed on the plea that important members of the party could not leave their respective posts in those critical days. The top leaders were against the plenary session, because local workers were impatient for decisive action and would have surely endorsed my plan. [77]

The leading figures of the Communist Party, Roy felt, simply did not see the chances for revolutionary action. "They mostly came from the petit-bourgeois intellectuals," he observed, "and were closely connected with the Kuo Min Tang politicians." [78]

Roy then appealed directly to Moscow and, on June 1, received this telegram from Stalin:

Without an agrarian revolution victory is impossible. Without it the Central Committee of the Kuomintang will be converted into a wretched plaything by unreliable generals. Excesses must be combatted, not, however, with the help of troops, but through the Peasant Unions. We are decidedly in favor of the land actually being seized by the masses from below. The fears regarding Tang Pin-shan's visit are not devoid of foundation. You must not

[76] *Ibid.*, p. 42.
[77] Roy, *Revolution and Counter-Revolution in China*, p. 552.
[78] *Ibid.*, p. 550.

sever yourselves from the worker and peasant movement, but must assist it in every way. Otherwise you will ruin the cause.

Certain of the old leaders of the Central Committee of the Kuomintang are afraid of what is taking place. They are vacillating and compromising. A large number of new peasant and working class leaders from the ranks must be drawn into the Central Committee of the Kuomintang. Their bold voice will stiffen the backs of the old leaders or throw them into the discard. The present structure of the Kuomintang must be changed. The leadership of the Kuomintang must be freshened and reinforced by new leaders who have come to the fore in the agrarian revolution, while local organizations must be enlarged by bringing into them the millions belonging to the working class and the peasant unions. Otherwise the Kuomintang runs the risk of becoming divorced from realities and losing every atom of authority.

It is necessary to liquidate the dependence upon unreliable generals.* Mobilize about 20,000 Communists and about 50,000 revolutionary workers and peasants from Hunan and Hupeh, form several new army corps, utilize the students of the school for commanders, and organize your own reliable army before it is too late. Otherwise, there can be no guarantee against failures. It is a difficult matter, but there is no other course.

Organize a revolutionary tribunal headed by prominent non-Communist Kuomintangists. Punish officers who maintain contact with Chiang Kai-shek or who set soldiers on the people, the workers and peasants. Persuasion is not enough. It is time to act. The scoundrels must be punished. If the Kuomintangists do not learn to be revolutionary Jacobins, they will be lost both to the people and to the revolution.[79]

Even this directive was not sufficient, apparently, to change Chinese Communist policy. Borodin considered the instructions "ludicrous." The only solution was to "shelve them." [80] A diplomatic reply was dispatched to Moscow: "Orders received. Shall obey as soon as we can do so." [81] Roy, as a last resort, solicited the coöperation of "individual comrades" —Chinese as well as Russian:

Galen [V. K. Blücher] (the Chief Military Adviser to the Nationalist Government) was fully in agreement with me. Many other Russian com-

---

* The English translation of this sentence reads in the published volume: "This dependence upon reliable generals must be put an end to." On the other hand, Ch'en Tu-hsiu's version of this sentence which he records, but does not quote, reads: "It is necessary to liquidate the unreliable generals." (Ch'en Tu-hsiu, *Kao ch'üan-tang t'ung-chih shu* [Letter to All Comrades of the Party], p. 6B; also the Russian text of this letter in *Biulleten Oppozitsii*, No. 15–16, p. 22.)

[79] Stalin, *Marksizm i natsionalno-kolonialny i vopros*, pp. 186–187; also *Marxism and the National and Colonial Question*, p. 249. This document does not appear in Stalin's *Works* either in the Russian or English editions.

[80] Brandt, *Stalin's Failure in China*, p. 135.

[81] Huston, "Sun Yat-sen, the Kuomintang, and the Chinese-Russian Political Economic Alliance," p. 187.

rades had also come around to my view by that time. But all power was
centered in the hands of Borodin. Moscow had backed me up politically
as against his opportunism. Nevertheless, in other respects, he was still left
in the controlling position, and consequently functioned as the dictator of
the Communist Party. Being mostly his disciples, and ideologically akin to
his way, the top leaders of the CP of China followed him, disregarding
repeatedly the instructions of the International, and in defiance of its representative on the spot.[82]

Still struggling to preserve the Communist-Kuomintang Left alliance,
Roy, on June 1, wrote an article entitled "Revolution and Counter-
Revolution in China" [Document 25] which held "foreign imperialists"
basically responsible for the revolt of Hsia Tao-yin and for the Changsha coup. The fundamental mission of the reactionary elements, therefore, was not merely "the extermination of communism and of future
Communists"—as they had asserted—but to destroy the whole national
anti-imperialist revolution. To whom, indeed, did the reactionaries refer
when they spoke of "future Communists?" To the nonproletarian revolutionary classes—the peasantry and petty bourgeoisie.

The Wuhan government under which these revolutionary classes were
united with the proletariat stood, therefore, as a symbol of the anti-
imperialist struggle against the Chinese people. Those elements who,
under imperialist orders, organized insurrections to exterminate "communism" and "future Communists" were therefore enemies of the
national revolution, traitors to the Kuomintang, and insurgents against
the national government.

In an effort to arouse the Kuomintang Left into more radical action,
Roy

as the representative of the Communist International suggested that the
[Chinese] Communist Party should address an Open Letter [Document 26]
to the left wing leaders of the Kuo Min Tang, setting forth the Platform of
the National Revolution.[83]

This document urged the dissolution of the insurrectionary committee in Changsha and the appointment of a legal provisional government,
the mounting of a punitive expedition against the revolt, and the arming of the peasant masses. The document left an impression that Roy
himself must have been deceived by T'ang Shen-chih who, according to
the Open Letter, should be authorized "to dispatch to Wuhan the necessary troops for crushing the revolution.[84] The Chinese Communist

---

[82] Roy, Revolution and Counter-Revolution in China, pp. 552–553.
[83] Ibid., p. 481 n.
[84] Compare the text of this version of the Open Letter with "The Parting of the

Politburo, in any case, decided that T'ang Sheng-chih, as a "Leftist general," was the man to solve the problem in Changsha.[85]

Unfortunately, according to Roy, writing many years later, the submission of the Open Letter to leaders of the Kuomintang Left

did not find favour with the leaders of the Communist Party and others guiding its policy. The Platform with a preamble setting forth the facts recorded in the preceding paragraph was, however, drafted by the author and was published without the official sanction of the Executive of the [Chinese] Communist Party.[86]

By now Roy had cast off any lingering illusions he might have had about T'ang Sheng-chih and about the Central Committee of the Kuomintang Left. On June 9 he put forward a proposal—"The Counterrevolution and Communist Tactics: Defense or Offense" [*Document 28*] —which was a clear, if hopelessly belated call for action. In seeking to preserve friendly relations with the Kuomintang, he charged, the Communist Party was agreeing to the liquidation of the whole mass movement. "What do these demonstrations represent which the Kuomintang brands as 'excesses' of the workers' and peasants' movement and which Comrade Ch'en Tu-hsiu condemns as an infantile disorder? They are, in fact, revolutionary actions of the working class and the peasant masses."

A break with Wuhan was becoming more inevitable each day, he asserted. Could the Communist Party betray the working masses for the sake of preserving the ties? On the contrary, the Communists must create a really revolutionary army; develop peasant insurrections to destroy the power of the gentry; begin reorganizing the Kuomintang "from below"; begin planning the immediate conquest of Kwangtung to recover that province for the revolution. There was no time to lose.

In actuality, it was entirely too late. "If Comrade R had acted with more decisiveness and persistence," Ts'ai Ho-sen asserted later, "the Politburo would have given in and would have accepted his plan. Unfortunately, Comrade R was unable to defend sufficiently vigorously his proposal—and finally capitulated." [87]

Ways in China," an editorial in *The Communist International*, No. 11, July 30, 1927, p. 212.

[85] Ts'ai Ho-sen, *Problemy Kitaia*, No. 1, p. 48. Around that time T'ang Sheng-chih in Honan sent an order to the Hunan provincial government forbidding "the troops to act on their own initiative." He also ordered that peace be maintained and that all arms be returned to "the peasants and workers picket corps." *The People's Tribune*, May 29, 1927, pp. 1, 4.

[86] Roy, *Revolution and Counter-Revolution in China*, p. 481 n.

[87] Ts'ai Ho-sen, *Problemy Kitaia*, No. 1, p. 47.

VI

We have perceived how, in the course of developing their alliance with the Kuomintang, both Russian and Chinese Communists had found it necessary to rely not only upon the newly organized armies of Chiang Kai-shek, but also upon the forces of more traditional militarists such as Li Chi-shen, Hsia To-yin, T'ang Sheng-chih, and Fêng Yü-hsiang. Of these four, Fêng was undoubtedly the most colorful.

Rising to power in the Northwest through a series of carefully calculated political maneuvers, Fêng had first come to the attention of Westerners as the "Christian general" who insisted that his soldiers learn hymns and his officers keep themselves in Cromwellian simplicity. With Borodin's arrival in China, however, he had begun to perceive the utility of Russian arms, money, and military advisers. After a visit to Moscow, he announced himself as the son of a laborer and proclaimed a new crusade to awaken the masses, drive out Western imperialism, and secure the freedom and independence of China.

By June, 1927—with the defections of Chiang Kai-shek, Li Chi-shen, and Hsia Tou-yin—the Communists found themselves dependent upon the forces of T'ang Sheng-chih, whose "devotion" to Comintern purposes was becoming increasingly doubtful, and upon Fêng Yü-hsiang and his Russian-trained and Russian-equipped Kuominchün, or People's Army.

In the meantime, a Pandora's box of difficulties were proliferating from the receipt of Stalin's telegram, from the deterioration of relations with the Kuomintang Left, from the emergence of revolution in the countryside, and from the tendency of various military men to show their true colors. During this last period, according to Ts'ai Ho-sen, the Politburo was to reveal its utter incapacity to direct Party affairs.[1]

Roy, by now, had come to perceive Wang Ching-wei as a man in a "quandary," a "tragic figure standing hopelessly on board the sinking

---

[1] Ts'ai Ho-sen, *Problemy Kitaia*, No. 1, p. 50.

ship of the National Democratic Revolution." In Roy's view the "foolish tactics" of the Communists—Borodin's policy of a military combination under T'ang Sheng-chih's leadership—were driving Wang "into the embrace of the reactionary clique." [2] Roy had reason to believe, or thought he had reason to believe, that Wang stood ready to be rescued. In the words of Ts'ai Ho-sen,

both Comrade R and Comrade B wished to draw Wang Ching-wei to their side, but while the first wished to rule over him and be his chief, the second [i.e., Comrade B] wished to trail behind him. Consequently, R failed "to command and to subordinate," while Comrade B "knew very well how to adjust himself and to guess the wishes of other people." [3]

The whole Politburo, indeed, was "resurrecting once again" its illusions about Wang Ching-wei as the leader of a revolutionary Kuomintang Left. The Politburo also imagined that T'ang Sheng-chih was still anxious to achieve an effective alliance with Wang. "In that way," according to Ts'ai Ho-sen, "Wang Ching-wei became the center of our entire policy." [4]

On his return to China from Europe, Wang had passed through Moscow. There, according to Roy's account, the Communist International and the Soviet government had promised him full support. In wiring Moscow for support of his own plan, Roy had seen his proposals—those for confiscating land, destroying the power of "unreliable generals," establishing a revolutionary court, and arming the workers and peasants —as constituting a "reassurance" for Wang. "He [Wang] agreed with the plan," Roy recorded later, "provided that the necessary help would be forthcoming." [5]

It was almost too late when the needed reassurances came. Meanwhile, believing that the Communists had betrayed him Wang Chin-wei [sic] had entered into negotiations with the right wing which was clamouring for the blood of the Communists to propitiate Chiang Kai-shek. I thought at that juncture a final effort must be made to regain the confidence of Wang Chin-wei. I communicated to him the message from Moscow. . . . Besides, the plan was already known to him. He had expressed his agreement with it. He was willing to stand by his agreement if I could produce definite proof that the necessary help would be forthcoming.[6]

Wang Ching-wei, according to T'ang Leang-li writing from the Wuhan point of view, was "very astonished" when he discovered the

[2] Roy, *Revolution and Counter-Revolution in China*, pp. 518–519.
[3] Ts'ai Ho-sen, *Problemy Kitaia*, No. 1, p. 55.
[4] *Ibid.*, p. 50.
[5] Roy, *Revolution and Counter-Revolution in China*, p. 520 n.
[6] *Ibid.*

nature of Stalin's "new attitude" toward the Kuomintang as revealed in the telegram received on June 1, and he told Roy that Wuhan could not accept the conditions of the telegram on any account. The two men argued about it for a time, but without result. On leaving, Wang inquired whether Roy would let him have a copy of the translation.

Roy hesitated for a moment and then said, "Yes. I will send you a copy of it tomorrow, as there are one or two verbal alterations to be made." Wang received the promised copy next day, and at once showed it to Madame Sun and Eugen [sic] Ch'en. Eugen Ch'en's face became pale on learning its contents, "That means war between the Kuo-Min Tang and the Communist Party." [7]

Roy saw Wang again the following day. "I am glad that I have shown you the telegram," he said, according to T'ang's account, "which you can take as an ultimatum. If you accept the tenor of the telegram and grant facilities for its execution, the Communist International will continue to cooperate with you. If not, it will have nothing to do with the Kuomintang." [8]

Wang replied that the conditions for coöperation between the Kuomintang and the Third International laid down by Ioffe and Borodin in 1923 were "entirely different from those presented in your ultimatum. It is not for us to refuse your conditions, for it is you who have violated the agreement." [9]

According to T'ang, Roy then made a statement to the effect that he did not agree with Borodin's conditions and policy. Wang replied that he was not interested in the new conditions. "We only care for the conditions we have agreed on before." [10]

According to Roy's subsequent account, Wang had shown the telegram to his associates—"known reactionaries like Sun Fo, Eugene Chen, Tan Yan-kei [T'an Yen-kai], trusted by Borodin and the leaders of the CP as left-wingers"—"who were already in communication with Nanking" and who "had come to a secret understanding with Chiang Kai-shek." [11]

Roy, according to T'ang, was "severely taken to task by Borodin," who at once cabled Stalin and "requested him to withdraw Roy." [12] Ts'ai Ho-sen's account is similar:

To pass on the content of the telegram to Wang Ching-wei was a very serious lack of tact on the part of R, and all members of the Politburo

---

[7] T'ang, *The Inner History,* p. 281.
[8] *Ibid.*
[9] *Ibid.*
[10] *Ibid.*
[11] Roy, *Revolution and Counter-Revolution in China,* p. 520 n.
[12] T'ang, *The Inner History,* p. 282.

expressed their profound displeasure with it, while B telegraphed to the ECCI and R was [in due course] recalled.[13]

In the opinion of T'ang Leang-li,

Roy's idea was that the Left Kuo-Min Tang could only survive when in alliance with the Communists, as otherwise they would be crushed by the Rightists. They should, therefore, be informed of Stalin's cable. Borodin, however, realized that the Left Kuo-Min Tang was much stronger than Roy thought it was, and knew that if they saw the resolution, they would at once sever their relations with the Communists. He had, therefore, suppressed the resolution, and was naturally annoyed when he learnt about Roy's reckless-ness in making it known to Wang. A majority of the Chinese Communists sided with Borodin, being also of the opinion that the time for overt action had not come yet, and they drove Roy back to Russia.[14]

As things stood at this point Borodin wanted the Chinese Communists to restrain the agrarian revolution and to rely on Wang Ching-wei and the military forces of T'ang Sheng-chih. This amounted to a pure tactic "from above." Roy, on the other hand, still hoped to push Wang into a more revolutionary frame of mind and to unleash the agrarian revolution. Having lost faith in T'ang Sheng-chih, Roy differed from Borodin also in proposing to rely on the military forces of Fêng Yü-hsiang rather than on those of T'ang—though there was increasing evi-dence that Fêng might not be reliable, either. Thus Roy wanted "revolu-tion from below" but saw no way of triggering it except through Wang and the Wuhan forces.

Borodin, in one sense, enjoyed a distinct advantage in this controversy. For, as Ts'ai Ho-sen saw it,

Comrade R supported, on one hand, an alliance with Wang Ching-wei and, on the other hand, "was proposing" a program which was unacceptable to the latter. The disparity between R's ideas and practices explains very well why gain was always on Comrade B's side. Comrade R's proposals were always contradictory, while Comrade B's suggestions had a plan, because he had always taken into account Wang Ching-wei's psychology, as well as that of others.[15]

Roy's weakness has been a familiar one in twentieth-century revolu-tionary history. "Now, when the events are already behind us," Ts'ai Ho-sen stated a few months later, "I can see that Comrade R was

---

[13] Ts'ai Ho-sen, *Problemy Kitaia,* No. 1, p. 59. According to Geissler, either Borodin or one of his staff reported back to Moscow unfavorably on Roy. Only Galen stood by Roy. As for Stalin, he was predisposed toward a military puppet government in any case. Geissler Interview, June 19–22, 1958.

[14] T'ang, *The Inner History,* p. 282.

[15] Ts'ai Ho-sen, *Problemy Kitaia,* No. 1, p. 55.

essentially an intellectual. He always supported principles on paper, but in practice he did not settle a single problem." [16]

In Moscow, meantime, as in Hangkow, the Communists were vociferously reassuring themselves that Fêng Yü-hsiang could be relied upon. Trotsky, of course, had been leveling unpleasant accusations against Fêng, and there were "imperialist rumors" to the effect that the "Christian general" was about to reach an understanding with Chiang Kai-shek. According to an official Comintern publication, however,

this statement is absolutely false. . . . None of the [Wuhan] leaders is maintaining any connection with Chiang Kai-shek. Fêng Yü-hsian and his army have not trusted Chiang Kai-shek since the latter's action in Canton in March 1926.[17]

After his confrontation with Roy over Stalin's telegram, Wang Ching-wei proceeded forthwith to Chengchow with other members of the Wuhan government—T'an Yen-k'ai, Sun Fo, Ku Meng-yü, and Hsü Ch'ien—in order to inform T'ang Sheng-chih and other army commanders "about the contemplated coup d'état of the Communist Party." [18] It was proposed that the military leaders should disarm the Communists in their armies and return to Wuhan:

But was there any work actually being carried out at that time among the Left-minded masses? The work for the unification of all Leftist forces in the provinces of Hunan and Hupeh, Kiangsi, Kiangsu, Chekiang, and Fukien, and the launching of propaganda against Wang Ching-wei, T'an Yen-k'ai, Fêng Yü-hsiang, and Chu P'ei-te was just initiated. T'an Yen-k'ai and others came to know of it (since Comrade Mao Tse-tung and others carried on propaganda quite openly), and they immediately came out with a harangue of abuses against the CCP, saying that the Communists were plotting to overthrow the Kuomintang. Ch'en Tu-hsiu, likewise, was vexed and considered such policies incorrect. Actually, the propaganda against the CC of the Kuomintang was undertaken in accordance with instructions of the Secretariat of the CC of the CCP.[19]

The Wuhan government, having decided at that time to move northward against Chang Tso-lin rather than eastward against Chiang Kai-shek, was dependent upon Fêng Yü-hsiang, whose troops had been massed behind Tungkwan Pass at the northwest gateway to Honan. Now, as the best troops of the Kuomintang Left moved from Hupeh into Honan, Fêng came down the Lunghai railway to occupy Loyang and Kaifeng. With this move, the "Christian general" put himself in

---

[16] *Ibid.*

[17] Tang Shin She, "The Advance on Peking," *International Press Correspondence,* Vol. 7, No. 34, June 9, 1927, p. 711.

[18] T'ang, *The Inner History,* p. 282.

[19] Ts'ai Ho-sen, *Problemy Kitaia,* No. 1, p. 51.

control of the road to Peking. Announcing his victories by telegram to both Chiang Kai-shek and Wang Ching-wei, he called upon the Wuhan leaders to meet with him on June 12 in Chengchow.

Meanwhile, according to Ts'ai Ho-sen, the Chinese Politburo held three important meetings:

> At its first session, and following the capture of Chengchow, the question of the Northern Expedition was discussed. Now the anti-Communist position of Fêng Yü-hsiang became evident, while Ch'en Tu-hsiu realized his own past mistakes in the question of the Northern Expedition. Ch'en Tu-hsiu feared that Fêng Yü-hsiang would now propose to collaborate with the Communists in the expedition, since it was now evident to the latter that once victory was won in the Northern Expedition the unification of all militarists against the CCP would immediately follow. Therefore, Ch'en Tu-hsiu and also Comrade B were of the opinion that the only way to improve the difficult situation was to undertake an Eastern Expedition. Li Li-san and Ch'ü Chiu-po were in favor of it; Comrade R and T'ang P'ing-shan proposed to march southward instead and to capture Kwangtung. I, on my part, insisted on the solution of the Hunan-Hupeh problem. I said: "In my opinion, which may appear at first somewhat strange, the Northern Expedition is the business of Fêng Yü-hsiang; the Eastern one is that of T'ang Sheng-chih. But none of these expeditions concern us. Let us stop then to serve the interests of others; let us busy ourselves with our own affairs, and find our own territory and our own forces. In other words, let us attend to the task which confronts us directly, i.e., the settlement of the problems in Hunan and Hupeh." [20]

On June 9 Roy submitted a new warning to the Chinese Communist leadership [*Document 28*]. Despite the broad reassurances of Ch'en Tu-hsiu, it was now evident that T'ang Sheng-chih wanted to "play the role of a Leftist" only in order to become master of the situation. It was now perfectly clear, asserted Roy, that he had been in constant touch with Hsia Tou-yin all along. To believe in the Leftist protestations of T'ang was tantamount to betraying the masses. Forces of reaction were becoming more active not only in the army, but also in the Central Executive of the Kuomintang Left which, in fact, was "preparing for an open struggle against the Communists." A break between the two parties was becoming more inevitable every day. Yet the Communists, in seeking to preserve friendly relations, were actually liquidating the mass movement. There was no time to be lost in creating a truly revolutionary army, developing the peasant insurrection by destroying the power of the gentry and taking over leadership, and in reorganizing the Kuomintang "from below."

The Politburo continued to reassure itself, however, that T'ang Sheng-

---

[20] *Ibid.*, pp. 42–43.

chih—and also Fêng Yü-hsiang—wanted at all costs to work with the Kuomintang Left and with the Communists. Ts'ai Ho-sen recalled later, for example, that "Comrade B used to say: 'There is still food in our box; he [*i.e.,* T'ang Sheng-chih] is hungry, and therefore he will not run away.' " [21]

On learning how the "Christian general" had made good his advance down the Lunghai railroad, Roy, on June 10, addressed an open letter to Fêng [*Document 30*]. "By the instructions of the Communist International I send you warm congratulations on your brilliant victories," he wrote, "and express confidence that these victories will be followed by new ones." The letter was signed: "with revolutionary greetings." Fêng's great task, according to Roy, was to join with other "national armies" in coördinating the capture of Peking with the liquidation of Chiang Kai-shek's "center of counter-revolution in Nanking." Against the background of this document, Roy's later account of what happened at the Chengchow conference reveals as much about Roy as it does about Fêng, T'ang Sheng-chih, and the Kuomintang Leftists:

Fêng had a surprise for the Wuhan leaders. He did not appear at the conference as an officer reporting to his Government. Only two months ago, the Central Executive Committee of the Kuo Min Tang had appointed him the Commander of a section of the Nationalist Army. But he came to the conference obviously to dictate his terms. Leaving his train of luxurious saloon cars, in which his Staff was lodged, some miles outside, the "Christian General" rode into Chengchow on an open truck together with the ill-clad ordinary soldiers. He appeared in the gathering of the pompous politicians and gorgeous Generals in an ordinary soldier's uniform, munching a chunk of dry bread.

There was no prolonged negotiation. He laid down the following terms: The newly acquired province of Honan should be under his control; the Wuhan Government must pay him a large subsidy in return for formal inclusion of his troops in the Nationalist Army; the command of the expedition to Peking should be given to him; and the Wuhan group must forthwith enter into negotiations with the Nanking clique for unification.

The road to Peking was blocked for Tang Shen-chi [T'ang Sheng-chih]. Should he dare pursue his ambition, his troops would be caught between those of Fêng from the West and of Chiang from the East. Not willing to draw the chestnuts out of the fire for Fêng, he decided to return to his base.[22]

So much for Fêng Yü-hsiang, whose "brilliant victories" Roy had hailed with "revolutionary greetings." Meanwhile, the Communists and the Kuomintang Left continued their exchange of views.

---

[21] *Ibid.,* p. 50.
[22] Roy, *Revolution and Counter-Revolution in China,* pp. 474–475.

In response to the Communist Party's "open letter" [*Document 26*] the Kuomintang Central Executive Committee in Wuhan admitted in a formal reply of June 15 that some of the Nationalist "comrades" had been careless in their relations with the peasants and workers, that such carelessness should be corrected, and that "improper actions" on the part of the military must be curbed. The Kuomintang, however, had sent "responsible comrades" to Hunan to investigate the difficulty there and to settle it [*Document 33*].

The chief "responsible comrade" was none other than T'ang Sheng-chih.

At a Chinese Politburo meeting of June 15 Roy presented the "Draft Platform of the National Revolution" [*Document 31*] which included proposals for (1) the immediate reconquest of Kwangtung; (2) support of Fêng Yü-hsiang in his campaign against Peking; (3) liquidation of counterrevolutionary forces; (4) strengthening of the authority of the Kuomintang "as the leader of the national revolution"; (5) subordination of the army and provincial administrations to central Wuhan government control; (6) establishment of local self-government in the villages; (7) confiscation of land according to previous resolutions; (8) complete freedom for the peasant movement; and (9) creation of a peasant militia under the control of the Ministry of Internal Affairs.

Borodin's immediate response to this program was, according to Ts'ai Ho-sen, that "there was no need to advocate the agrarian revolution . . . since now one treachery followed another." Communist relations with the Kuomintang Left were hanging "on a thin thread" and therefore to discuss with Wuhan the problem of an agrarian revolution would be "sheer nonsense." Only an Eastern campaign against Chiang Kai-shek could lead the Communists out of their dangerous situation. After a Left Wing capture of Nanking it might once more be feasible to discuss a radical program.[23]

Addressing the Politburo in support of his draft platform, Roy declared that the time had come "to separate the goats from the sheep"; to determine who was against the revolution and who was for it [*Document 32*]. The Communist relationship with the Kuomintang could not be considered an end in itself. If the Nationalist party was no longer an instrument of national revolution, the Communist position and tactics toward it should be radically changed. "If the Kuomintang will not collaborate," he declared, "we must regard it as an enemy rather than an ally."

Both Borodin and Ch'en Tu-hsiu considered that the Communist

---

[23] Ts'ai Ho-sen, *Problemy Kitaia,* No. 1, p. 52.

task was to ascertain what the Kuomintang wanted and to reach an agreement with it, Roy asserted. This was a serious error. The task was to accelerate the process of class differentiation within the Kuomintang with the object of replacing the current leadership with leaders of a more revolutionary character.

Specifically, according to Ts'ai Ho-sen, Borodin proposed (1) that the agrarian question be withdrawn from the general program; (2) that there be no more insistence on the arming of the workers' and peasants' pickets; (3) that "something" ought to be said in defense of the interests of the merchants and industrialists—particularly in view of the demands of the Eastern campaign; and (4) that earlier decisions to restrain the shop assistants' movement, the workers' and peasants' organizations, and "the mass movement in general" should be reasserted.[24]

After prolonged discussion, the Politburo adopted the draft platform —but not without the changes indicated by Roy's footnotes to the text. No decision was made whether or not the document should be "insisted on before the Kuomintang." Actually, events soon revealed not only that "no offensive had been launched," but that "even Comrade B's minimum program" had not been followed.[25] As Ts'ai Ho-sen recalled later:

After the repudiation of the "offensive" policy, the Politburo's mood was thoroughly pessimistic. The comrades wandered aimlessly, looked depressed, and did not expect that the situation could improve. They vacillated and were unable to make definite decisions on the problems that were confronting them, or to agree upon a definite and firm stand on anything.[26]

The Politburo did approve a telegram, dispatched by Ch'en Tu-hsiu to the Comintern [*Document 29*], which stated that it was not simply the confiscation of land which antagonized the military officers, but rather the "excesses" of the peasantry. For this reason it would be necessary to "regularize the excesses" as well as to "moderate the practices in the confiscation of land." Thereafter the Communists might reasonably

---

[24] *Ibid.*

[25] *Ibid.*

[26] *Ibid.*, pp. 56–57. According to Ts'ai Ho-sen, the Central Committee had previously sent instructions to Party functionaries in Hupeh and Hunan to carry on propaganda against the Kuomintang and to prepare peasant uprisings. "A large group of army comrades was sent to Hunan to assist in developing the peasant insurrection and to defeat Hsü K'e-hsiang. Before their departure the comrades were told by the Presidium of the CC that we were preparing ourselves for a struggle against the coming reactionary attempts on the part of T'ang Sheng-chih. A special commission was organized by the CC and the delegates from the ECCI to attend to the problems of Hunan, and it took exclusive charge of the Hunan uprisings. This commission held several sessions at which the plan for insurrections was examined and corrected by competent comrades. However, the funds which were needed were not forthcoming." *Ibid.*, p. 44.

expect to attract the more Leftist leaders around a common platform and gradually create reliable military forces.

On June 11 the Hunanese members of the Kuomintang asked the Central Kuomintang in Wuhan that "an order should be at once issued to punish Hsü K'e-hsiang," and that "General T'ang Sheng-chih should be asked to return to Hunan in order to restore the Hunan provisional government." [27]

Once it had been decided that T'ang Sheng-chih should be sent to investigate the Changsha revolt and to "restore peace," the Communists could only assure themselves that the general was a loyal revolutionary and would "further the interests of three classes." Consequently, in their Propaganda Theses on the Events in Hunan and Kiangsi Provinces, dated June 14, 1927, they stated that "the *coup* in Changsha was carried out by T'ang Sheng-chih's adversaries, since it has been known that T'ang sympathized with the people's movement in Hunan and has expressed good will toward the oppressed peasantry.[28]

A few days later more than two hundred delegates from the various organizations in Hunan petitioned T'ang for a prompt action against Changsha militarists. "Laborers and peasants will never be suppressed," he assured them, "although some immature actions in labor and peasant movements should be corrected by the Central Kuomintang." And he added:

We should support the three policies of our Tsungli, so that the national revolution will be accomplished. Hsü K'e-hsiang did not receive any orders from his superiors to kill the revolutionary masses. The Central Kuomintang has worked out concrete plans to settle the case and all that I can do now is to obey [it]. Long live the revolutionary masses of Hunan! [29]

In due course T'ang Sheng-chih established that the revolting officers had been acting under grave provocation, and advised the immediate explusion of the Communists from the Left Kuomintang. Being informed of the secret decision of the top Left Kuomintangists to expel the Communists, he at once dismissed all the officers under his immediate command who were known to have Communist affiliations. There were not many of them, as his policy had always been to reserve all important posts in his army to the pure Kuomintang members.[30]

---

[27] *The People's Tribune,* June 12, 1927, p. 5.
[28] Quoted in the Chinese Communist Party's Declaration to All Members of the Party, August 7, 1927, as reproduced in Mif, *Kitaiskaia Kommunisticheskaia Partiia v kriticheskie dni,* p. 235; see also *Kung-ch'an Kuo-chi tui Chung-kuo ko-ming chüeh-i-an,* p. 174.
[29] *The People's Tribune,* June 21, 1927, p. 3.
[30] T'ang, *The Inner History,* pp. 284–285.

The result of T'ang Sheng-chih's investigations, according to T'ang Leang-li, "confirmed the existence of the Communist conspiracy against the Kuo-Min Tang."

On June 26 T'ang Sheng-chih telegraphed Wuhan:

Since I received the Central Government's order to take charge of the Changsha Affairs, I came to the Hunan capital on the same day, and have gone thoroughly into the matter. I have examined the different official complaints sent in from the country, and have found that the workers' and farmers' movements, under the misguidance of their leaders, have broken loose from control and precipitated a reign of terror to the people. In defiance of the explicit orders of the Central Government for the protection of the revolutionary soldiers' families, they have everywhere extorted taxes and fines, abused people and even murdered people. While they talk everyday about the union of farmers, workers, scholars and soldiers, their daily activities are such as to make such a union impossible and to encourage a bitter class-struggle. Added to this, there are certain opportunist elements who take advantage of this chaotic state of things to seek private vengeance. As a result of this, there is great deal of hardship among the workers and farmers themselves.

Seeing this state of things, and while personally under the oppression of these leaders, the soldiers who were stationed in Hunan rose for their self-defense, and thus the incident of June 21st arose. A few disgruntled politicians and idle soldiers took advantage of this situation and formed "Party Salvation" societies for the purpose of securing personal power for themselves.

Having regard to all these facts, I have, therefore, decided on the following methods of settlement of the question. Since the local Kuomintang and people's organizations have not been keeping within the limits of law and order, on account of the misguidance of their leaders, they should be suspended in accordance with the previous order of the Central Government, while awaiting future reorganization. Chou Ao, a politician who tried to secure personal benefits under the pretext of "saving the party," should be dismissed from the party and never again admitted into our service. Chang Ching-i, who, under his queer opinion, is harbouring a secret purpose, should also be expelled from the Kuomintang and deprived of all his military titles. Although Hsu Keh-hsiang's actions were animated by a passion for justice, he has overstepped the limits of law and discipline. He should receive a light punishment in the form of a demerit, but should be retained in the army service. Others who have no important connection with the affair need not be dealt with, in my opinion.

The above is the proposed method for dealing with the affair which I submit hereby for your approval.

I have also received reports saying there are few party members who are in the habit of defying the Central Government's orders. It is reported they are not only unwilling to stop their activities, but are planning on the contrary to defy the Government to the end. I should be glad to receive and carry out your instructions as to whether these people should or should not be dealt with under the charge of being anti-revolutionary, in order that the supremacy of the party may be upheld.

Signed: T'ang Sheng-chih [31]

June 26th

Just as T'ang's report was being published in Hankow, an official organ of the Comintern declared:

The panic-makers of the [Trotsky] Opposition have raised clamour about the defeat of the Chinese revolution. This clamour, prompted by malicious joy, will not convince anyone. Our Party is following with undiminished attention the events in China . . . with firm faith in the power of the Chinese revolution. The revolt of the officers in Changsha which met with decided resistance of the workers and peasants, has already been suppressed.[32]

At the Chengchow conference on June 12, meanwhile, Honan province had been "assigned" to Fêng "who was also informed of the Communist activities in Hunan and Hupeh." According to T'ang Leang-li, "Fêng, on his part, also reported on the measures he had taken in the matter of restricting Communist activities in Shensi." [33]

While the Chengchow discussions were still in progress word came that Chiang Kai-shek was preparing an attack on Wuhan. Under these circumstances, according to T'ang Leang-li,

the question of the separation with the Communists was a complicated one, owing to the differences of opinion existing among the Kuo-Min Tang members of the Central Executive Committee. Madame Sun and Eugen [sic] Ch'en, while opposed to the Communist dominance of the Kuo-Min Tang and favouring the ultimate termination of the Communist alliance, held that the moment of actual separation had not arrived yet, owing to the danger of attack from Nanking. They were of opinion that Chiang Kai-shek should first be dealt with and eliminated, and that the expulsion of the Communists should take place afterwards. Otherwise, the Wuhan forces would be divided against themselves, and be powerless against Chiang.[34]

From Chengchow Fêng proceeded to Hsüchow, the junction of the Lunghai and Pukow-Tientsin railways, where he conferred with Chiang Kai-shek—having apparently decided "to join hands with Chiang." [35]

---

[31] *The People's Tribune,* June 29, 1927, pp. 1, 6.
[32] Zeitlin, "The New Stage of the Chinese Revolution," *International Press Correspondence,* Vol. 7, No. 37, June 30, 1927, p. 783.
[33] T'ang, *The Inner History,* p. 282.
[34] *Ibid.,* p. 283.
[35] Roy, *Revolution and Counter-Revolution in China,* p. 476.

Chiang was reported to have said that there was no real conflict between Nanking and Wuhan, but that Borodin should be sent back to the Soviet Union and the Communists expelled from the Wuhan government and from the Kuomintang.[36] In a telegram to Wuhan, the "Christian general" promptly urged the unification of all nationalist forces against the northern militarists. The wire, according to Roy, demanded that the Wuhan leaders should immediately dismiss their Russian advisers and suppress the Chinese Communist Party. "The demand was backed up by the thinly-veiled threat that Fêng would attack Wuhan from the north in case his advice was not accepted."[37] In reply, the Wuhan government assured Fêng that these measures "had already been decided upon at Chengchow" and that active preparations were being made for carrying them into effect.[38]

During the Fourth Congress of the All-China Federation of Labor, meanwhile, Roy presented on June 20 an analysis of the situation at that juncture [*Document 34*]. After a period of rapid development, he said, the Chinese national movement now found itself in an extremely dangerous crisis. Hampered in its progress by imperialist rule and feudal control over the economic and political life of the country, the petty bourgeoisie had proved itself incapable of carrying the revolution further. Taking advantage of this vacillation, the big bourgeoisie had begun trying to win the petty bourgeoisie over to the side of counterrevolution. As a consequence, according to Roy, the full responsibility for the future development of the revolution had fallen upon the proletariat. "The development of the agrarian revolution," he declared, "i.e., the development of the peasants' struggle against the landlords, the gentry and all the reactionary strata is the only guarantee of a successful outcome of the national revolution." It was the task of the proletariat to lead the peasants in this undertaking.

At this juncture the Secretariat of the Chinese Communist Party, in a letter to the Shanghai Committee drafted June 23, put forward a new proposal. On the one hand, it was essential to oppose Chiang Kai-shek, but on the other hand, if the Communists continued to insist on the confiscation of land and the arming of the workers and peasants, the result would be an immediate break with the Kuomintang. In this circumstance the preferable course, according to the Secretariat, was to provoke the imperialists into seizing Shanghai, Fuchow, Nanking, and other cities. Then the Communists could raise a new anti-imperialist war, arm the peasants and workers, and confiscate the land [*Document 35*].

---

[36] T'ang, *The Inner History*, p. 289.
[37] Roy, *Revolution and Counter-Revolution in China*, p. 479.
[38] T'ang, *The Inner History*, p. 289.

After a long and heated discussion, the Politburo decided against the dispatch of this letter and proposed to substitute for it a resolution on the anti-imperialist struggle. The Secretariat then declared that the letter had already been sent to Shanghai.

During the debate, Roy characterized the Secretariat letter as "extremely dangerous" and its proposed plan of action as "adventure" [*Document 36*]. The authors of the document were proposing, in effect, that the class struggle be replaced by an anti-imperialist struggle which must form the basis of the Chinese revolution. "You refuse to lead the proletariat into a revolutionary struggle against reaction in an area where there are considerable chances of success," he declared. "You refuse to head a revolt of the Hunan peasantry against the decaying feudal reaction. Yet you make plans for sending the Shanghai proletariat, debilitated by three revolts, tortured by the white terror, to certain defeat at the hands of the imperialists, who are considerably stronger than are our enemies here!"

The development of an anti-imperialist movement on a national scale was essential, but it must be advanced at the same time as—and coördinated with—the class struggle. "I make a motion," he declared, "to reject the letter, and I propose that another plan be drawn up for an anti-imperialist campaign."

In Moscow, on June 30, Bukharin issued a new warning to the Chinese Communist leadership. Fêng Yü-hsiang had gone over to the counterrevolutionary camp, and merciless war must be declared against him. "Trust in your own forces alone," Bukharin advised. "Do not trust the generals and officers! Organize your armed troops!" [39] Only Wang Ching-wei, according to Bukharin, was "firmer than the others" who were betraying the revolution.

It soon became clear, however, that Wang was no "firmer" than his colleagues. Bukharin now perceived "an abrupt turn in the Chinese revolution." At last even Moscow had to admit that the "revolutionary role of Wuhan" had come to an end.[40] On July 14 the ECCI issued a new resolution: Support for the Northern Expedition and for the Wuhan government had been perfectly correct as long as revolutionary purposes were served, but these same tactics had become fundamentally wrong with the change of events.

In spite of Comintern advice, the Kuomintang leaders had "not only failed to support the agrarian revolution" but had "unfettered the hands

---

[39] Bukharin, "Tekushchii moment kitaiskoi revoliutsii," *Pravda*, No. 145, June 30, 1927, p. 2; see also Bukharin, "The Position of the Chinese Revolution," *International Press Correspondence*, Vol. 7, No. 39, July 7, 1927, p. 875.

[40] Bukharin, "Na krutom perevale kitaiskoi revoliutsii," *Pravda*, No. 154, July 10, 1927, p. 2; see also Bukharin, "An Abrupt Turn in the Chinese Revolution," *International Press Correspondence*, Vol. 7, No. 41, July 14, 1927, p. 898.

of its enemies." They had sanctioned the disarmament of the workers, the dispatch of punitive expeditions against the peasants, and the bloody reprisals of T'ang Sheng-chih. As a revolutionary duty the ECCI now called upon the members of the Communist Party of China openly to fight against the opportunism of its Central Committee. However,

the Communists should remain in the Kuomintang, in spite of the campaign carried on by its leaders for the expulsion of the Communists. [They should seek] closer contact with the mass of the members of the Kuomintang, who should be induced to accept resolutions decidedly protesting against the actions of the CC of the Kuomintang, demanding the removal of the present leaders of the Kuomintang, and to make preparations on these lines for the Party Conference of the Kuomintang.[41]

The Chinese Communist Central Committee then issued on July 13 a manifesto "to all Workers, Peasants and all Revolutionary Masses of the Country." "Our Party," the document asserted, "clearly sees that the policy of the majority of the top leadership in the CC of the Kuomintang and in the Nationalist government is disastrous for the revolution. It leads to the transformation of Wuhan, similar to Nanking, into a new militarist grouping." [42] Therefore,

the Communist Party will oppose such a policy since it [the Party] places the interests of the people above everything else. Thousands of Communists have fallen in the struggle [against the militarists] which is the best proof of the Communist Party's willingness to remain always with the working class and the peasantry in spite of all the sacrifices [that it may be called upon to bear]—and even when the leadership of the KMT and the Nationalist government betray the toiling masses of China. *Therefore, the CC of the CCP has resolved to recall its representatives from the Nationalist government.*[43]

The Communist Party, the manifesto asserted, would continue to struggle uncompromisingly against imperialism, for the dissolution of all unequal treaties, concessions, extraterritoriality, for Chinese customs autonomy, for the national liberation of the country and for the alliance with the USSR and "all the workers of the world and all oppressed peoples." Toward this end, according to the manifesto,

the Communist Party will carry on all its work jointly with the truly revolutionary elements of the Kuomintang and together with the Kuomintang masses. Therefore, the CP sees no reason for withdrawing from the KMT,

---

[41] "Resolution of the ECCI on the Present Situation of the Chinese Revolution," *International Press Correspondence,* Vol. 7, No. 44, July 28, 1927, p. 984.

[42] Mif, *Kitaiskaia Kommunisticheskaia Partiia v kriticheskie dni,* p. 171.

[43] *Ibid.,* p. 172. The italics are from the text of Mif.

and still less for withdrawing its cooperation with the KMT. Inasmuch as the KMT leadership and the Nationalist government will carry on the policy enumerated above, and will truly struggle against imperialism, militarism, feudal order, and against the reactionary conspiracies, the CCP will fully support the revolutionary policy of the Nationalist government. But the CCP will always place the interests of the masses, the interests of the revolution above everything else, and ten times above the individual wishes to retain this or that political bloc.

The Communist Party will not permit the generals who have betrayed the revolution or the vacillating politicians to hide behind the name of the KMT and of Sun Wen. The Communist Party will collaborate with all revolutionary elements who are ready sincerely and decisively to work in the spirit of three principles: National liberation (nationalism), democratization of the political authority (democracy), and the improvement of the living conditions of the people (socialism), as well as for the three instructions bequested by Sun Wen: Alliance with the U.S.S.R.; Alliance with the peasantry; Support of the workers' and peasants' interests. At the same time, the CCP will mercilessly denounce all quasi-Kuomintangists who are misusing the great name of Sun Wen in order to betray the revolution.[44]

On July 16, according to T'ang Leang-li, Wuhan officials found documents, dated three days earlier, which revealed these decisions and which instructed Party members to establish secret nuclei within the Kuomintang and to utilize every opportunity "to incite disorders to discredit and destroy the [Kuomintang] Party." [45] Under these circumstances, "the intention of the Central Executive Committee to grant full protection to the Communists as citizens . . . proved impracticable." [46] The Kuomintang's Central Executive Committee directed Communists within the Kuomintang government and the Nationalist army to renounce their Communist membership or "be dismissed from their offices immediately." If the member of the Kuomintang joined another party, presumably the Communist Party, he was to be "charged with having revolted against the Kuomintang." [47] Meantime, execution squads were put to work, and the Chinese Communists who were not apprehended in the first raids lost no time in fleeing the city.

Ch'en Tu-hsiu resigned from the Central Committee of the Chinese Communist Party—though he was not formally deposed from Party office until the August 7 Conference which established a new leadership. According to Harold Isaacs, "the remaining Communist leaders, Ch'ü Ch'iu-po, Chang Kuo-t'ao, Li Li-san, Mao Tse-tung, and others fled.

[44] *Ibid.*, pp. 172–174.
[45] T'ang, *The Inner History*, p. 287.
[46] *Ibid.*
[47] *The People's Tribune*, July 26, 1927, p. 6; see also *Pravda*, No. 172, July 31, 1927, p. 1.

On July 27, with executions going on in the streets of Hankow, the leaders of the Left Kuomintang gathered at the railway station to bid farewell to their 'honored guest' Borodin. He left nominally 'to confer with Fêng Yü-hsiang,' but everybody understood that he was starting on the long trek across the northwestern provinces to the distant Soviet frontier, Moscow's retreat from Hankow." [48]

According to T'ang Leang-li's account,

Borodin had wanted to resign earlier, as his position had been made impossible by the open attacks by the Communists on the Kuo-Min Tang. But at that time his wife was being detained by Chang Chung-ch'ang's men. And as his departure under those circumstances might induce Chang Chung-ch'ang to play with her life, he had been asked to remain at his post for the time being.[49]

Madame Borodin had been released on July 12, however, and the Wuhan government therefore "allowed" her husband to depart.

Borodin left Hankow with full honours. He first went to Lusan in Kiangsi to take some rest, although afterwards it was found that when at Lusan he had secret conferences with the Communists there, who were preparing for an insurrection. Borodin then returned to Wuhan and on July 27 took the Hankow-Peking Railway to Loyang, where he stayed for three days as Fêng Yü-hsiang's guest, and then through Mongolia proceeded to Russia.[50]

Roy left Hankow in late July or early August. The Comintern provided three large touring cars equipped with heavy-duty springs and gasoline cans lashed to the running boards. The drivers were agents of the GPU. From Hankow the caravan headed for the Northwest, crossed the Mongolian deserts, and proceeded to the Soviet Union by way of Urga.[51]

After a brief sojourn in Moscow, Roy continued on to his Berlin headquarters, where he began work on his report to the Comintern, on a book which appeared in German under the title *Revolution und Konterrevolution in China* [52] and on a pamphlet concerned with agrarian revolution. About three months after his arrival in Berlin his Comintern salary was suddenly cut off—the first forewarning of the serious trouble that began with the Ninth Plenum in February, 1928.

In the foreword to his Comintern report [*Document 37*], Roy argued

---

[48] Isaacs, *The Tragedy of the Chinese Revolution*, pp. 269–270.

[49] T'ang, *The Inner History*, p. 286.

[50] *Ibid.*, p. 287.

[51] Geissler interview, June 19–22, 1958.

[52] This work was published in Germany in 1931 but was withdrawn from circulation after Hitler's advent to power. The English edition was not published until 1945 (in Calcutta).

that the Communist International had correctly anticipated the development of the Chinese revolution and had carried out a correct policy. The Chinese Communist Party, on the other hand, had failed to understand the full meaning of the resolutions of the Communist International and was therefore unable to act in accordance with them. At the crucial moment, moreover, its leaders had refused to accept Comintern instructions.

In Roy's opinion these Chinese Communist failures were understandable, however, because the Party was too young for the task that lay before it and because the Party leadership "could not keep in step with its own sudden organizational growth."

Was the Comintern's policy of supporting the Kuomintang correct? Roy clearly thought that it was: The task of the Communist International in China, as in other colonial and semicolonial countries, was to mobilize all available forces that could be led into the struggle against imperialism. It was perfectly evident, Roy felt, that the classes making up these anti-imperialist forces could not all be mobilized on a Communist platform, and consequently a much broader basis had to be found for this purpose. In China, Roy asserted, such a basis could be created by the Kuomintang.

In Roy's view, the purpose of Communist collaboration with the Kuomintang during the Wuhan period—after the Right Wing under Chiang Kai-shek had "gone over to the imperialists" by predictable dialetic process—was to free the Left Wing "once and for all" from feudalbourgeois influence and convert it into an organ of the democratic dictatorship under the hegemony of the proletariat. Unfortunately, according to Roy, the Chinese Communist Party could not understand this. "For collaboration they substituted capitulation"—an error that inhibited mass revolutionary action and stifled the agrarian revolution "which could crush the forces of reaction."

For the detached observer—with the advantage of historical perspective—the documents suggest somewhat different conclusions. Roy was undoubtedly correct in emphasizing the misunderstandings and confusions that prevailed at that time within Chinese Communist ranks. It is equally clear, however, that Stalin—and also Roy—persistently miscalculated the intentions of the Wuhan "petty bourgeois" leadership and overestimated Communist influence upon and control over Wang Chingwei, his Left Kuomintang colleagues, and the so-called "Left Militarists." Undeniably, too, the open disagreements between the two Comintern representatives, Roy and Borodin, compounded the confusion that already prevailed within the Chinese Communist movement. Finally, the Comintern policies of supporting the Kuomintang and supporting, at

the same time, the agrarian revolution were mutually exclusive, recipro-
cally antagonistic, and inevitably conducive to operational disruption.
"Revolution from above" could not be combined with "revolution from
below" without dangerous confusion and risk of disaster.

For his own participation in the China debacle Roy paid dearly.

Attending the Ninth Plenum in February, 1928, Roy expected his
report to be accepted by the Comintern and his role in China to win
Stalin's personal approval. But Stalin—for whom Roy had a "senti-
mental attachment" [53]—refused to see him after the failure in China.
As the plenum proceeded, Roy came to realize that his Comintern career
was virtually over, that his life as well as his career might well be in
jeopardy. Indeed, when he left Moscow some weeks later, he found it
necessary to travel by night—clandestinely—and until he crossed the
Soviet frontier it was not certain whether he would make good his escape.

---

[53] Geissler interview, June 19–22, 1958.

THE DOCUMENTS

1

THESES ON THE SITUATION IN CHINA

BY THE SEVENTH EXTRAORDINARY PLENUM

OF THE EXECUTIVE COMMITTEE

OF THE COMMUNIST INTERNATIONAL,

NOVEMBER 22-DECEMBER 16, 1926

THE SITUATION IN CHINA

1. Imperialism and the Chinese Revolution.

The Chinese revolution is one of the most important and powerful factors that disturb capitalist stabilization. During the last two years, imperialism had suffered a heavy defeat in China, the effects of which will contribute considerably to the aggravation of the crisis of world capitalism. As a result of the victorious advance of the Nationalist army toward the North of China, imperialist domination has actually been undermined in half of the country.

The further victories of the revolutionary armies of Canton, supported by the broad masses of the Chinese people, will lead to the victory over the imperialists, to the achievement of the independence of China, and to its revolutionary unification, which will consequently increase in numerous ways its power of resistance to imperialist influence.

The failure of Sun Ch'uan-fang to stop the advance of the Canton troops has convinced the imperialist powers that the traditional method of using the native militarists as instruments to crush the national-revo-

---

This document has been translated from *Kommunisticheskii Internatsional v dokumentakh,* 1919–1932, pp. 668–680; it appears also in Communist International Executive Committee, *Puti mirovoi revoliutsii,* II, 435–449, and in *The Communist* (London), Vol. I, No. 2, March, 1927, pp. 59–72.—Eds.

lutionary movement no longer meets the situation. At the same time mutual rivalry does not permit the imperialist powers to unite for open military intervention. Imperialism seeks new methods to meet the new situation. The new policy tends toward recognition of the Canton government. The initiative comes from American imperialism. Even England and Japan consider the recognition of the Canton government as a permissible political measure. However, these are but diplomatic maneuvers which cover hostile imperialist designs against the revolution.

The basic strength of imperialism in China is in its monopoly of the entire financial and industrial life of the country (monopoly of the salt tax, mortgage of customs revenue, railways, waterways, mines, heavy industries—all are mostly owned by foreign capital). If imperialism retains for itself this solid base, it will find a substantial support in China in its task of stabilizing the capitalist system. Because of its colossal population, China is a market of unlimited potentialities. It may prove to be the most profitable field for the investment of capital if the necessary political guarantees are ensured. China's enormous sources of raw material have hardly been tapped. Consequently, imperialism will make desperate efforts to defeat the Chinese revolution which threatens to overthrow it. Failing to defeat it by the traditional method of provoking a civil war or by eventual armed intervention, imperialism will try to disrupt the movement for national liberation which is developing along revolutionary lines.

In spite of mutual antagonism among the imperialist powers the possibility of armed intervention still remains. Foreign intervention takes a peculiar form in China. Under present conditions imperialism prefers to intervene by means of organizing civil war by financing counterrevolutionary forces against the revolution. Exactly at this moment, attempts are made to unite the forces of Chang Tso-lin, Wu P'ei-fu, and Sun Ch'uan-fang to hold back the advancing Nationalist army. It is obvious that this united counterrevolutionary front will be formed under the direction and with the help of imperialism. The victory of the revolution in China will mean such a severe blow to world capitalism that the imperialist powers will try by every means to crush it.

From the point of view of its external situation the Chinese revolution—by the mere fact of its anti-imperialist character—is an inseparable part of the international revolution. Other factors favoring the development and deepening of the Chinese revolution are:

a) Mutual rivalries of the imperialist powers in China, which weaken the positions of world imperialism;

b) The crisis of world capitalism;

c) The growth of the proletarian movement in Western Europe (an open armed intervention in China is bound to be resisted by the working class in the imperialist countries);

d) The development of national-revolutionary movements in the colonies, which undoubtedly must grow as the Chinese revolution grows;

e) The existence of the proletarian dictatorship in the Union of Soviet Socialist Republics; the proximity of the U.S.S.R. to China; and the remoteness of China from the principal centers of the economic, military, and political power of the imperialist states.

II. Social Forces of the Chinese Revolution and Their Regrouping.

Side by side with the rapid development of the national-revolutionary movement the social forces which participate in it are drawn into an equally rapid process of regrouping. The national revolution in China is developing amid peculiar conditions which radically distinguish it from the classical bourgeois revolution of the West European countries in the last century, as well as from the 1905 revolution in Russia.

The principal difference is China's semicolonial status, its dependence upon foreign imperialism. Moreover, the Chinese revolution differs from the bourgeois-democratic revolutions of the last century because it is taking place in a period of world revolution and is an integral part of the world-wide movement for the overthrow of the capitalist order. This factor will determine the history of the Chinese revolution and the alignment of the social forces participating in it.

The class forces of the Chinese revolution develop on the background of extreme economic backwardness, which is the result of the low state of development of industrial capitalism, the primitive technique employed in agriculture, the incredibly low standard of living of the overwhelming masses of the Chinese population, and the numerous survivals of a semi-feudal character which are being destroyed by the pressure of the revolutionary armies and the toiling masses of town and the countryside, as they are being drawn into the struggle.

The principal failure of the present economic situation in China is its variety of economic forms, ranging from finance capital to the economic survivals of patriarchal and tribal society—the predominant form, however, being merchant capital, and petty trades and home industry in town and countryside.

This to some extent results in a low class differentiation of the Chinese population, and explains the inadequate state of organization among the principal social-political forces of the national revolution.

Other factors are the collapse of the central machinery of the government, which has been going on since the interrupted revolution of 1911 and with greater acceleration in the last year, and the widespread domination of the political organizations of Chinese militarism.

Chinese militarism represents a sociopolitical force which, at the present time, dominates over a large sector of the Chinese territory. The peculiar feature of Chinese militarism is that, while it represents a military organization, it is also one of the principal channels of primitive capitalist accumulation in China, resting upon a whole system of state organs of semifeudal character. The existence of the state organization of Chinese militarism is determined by the semicolonial position of the country, the dismemberment of the territory of China, the backwardness of Chinese economy, and the state of tremendous agrarian overpopulation in the rural districts of the country.

The development of the national-revolutionary movement in China at the present time rests upon the agrarian revolution. The economy of the Chinese village presents a picture of numerous survivals of a semifeudal character closely interwoven with elements of developing capitalism.

The extreme backwardness of Chinese economy generally, the parceling of landed property into minute allotments, the fact that an enormous proportion of the agrarian population are tenant-farmers or semitenant-farmers, the primitive state of technique in both small and large-scale agricultural enterprises, the extreme agrarian overpopulation, and simultaneously with this, the development of commercial agriculture and the process of class differentiation which is going on in the villages—render the general situation in the rural districts of China extremely complicated and considerably hinder the development of the agrarian revolution.

As a consequence of objective circumstances, the class struggle in the rural districts of China acquires a tendency to develop in the following directions: against foreign imperialism, against Chinese militarism, against the survivals of large land ownership, against gentry, against merchant-usurer capitalists, and partly against the upper kulak strata of the peasant population.

The successive stages of development of the revolutionary movement in China are marked by important realignments of social forces. In the first stage one of the driving forces of the movement was the national bourgeoisie and bourgeois intelligentsia which sought support in the ranks of the proletariat and the petty bourgeoisie.

In the second stage the character of the movement changed—its social basis was shifted to a different class combination. New and more revolutionary forms of struggle developed. The working class appeared in the arena as a political factor of prime importance.

Economic strikes are merging into political struggles against imperialism and are acquiring an exceptionally important world-historic significance. The proletariat is forming a bloc with the peasantry, which is actively taking up the struggle for its interests, with the petty urban bourgeoisie and a section of the capitalist bourgeoisie. The combination of forces has found its political expression in corresponding groups in the Kuomintang and in the Canton government. Now the movement is on the threshold of the third stage, on the eve of a new realignment of classes. In this stage the driving force of the movement will be a bloc of an even more revolutionary nature—of the proletariat, the peasantry, and the urban petty bourgeoisie, to the exclusion of the majority of the capitalist bourgeoisie. This does not mean that the whole bourgeoisie as a class will be excluded from the struggle for national liberation, for, besides the petty and middle bourgeoisie, even certain strata of the big-scale bourgeoisie may, for a certain period, continue to march with the revolution.

At this stage, the leadership of the movement passes more and more into the hands of the proletariat.

In this period of transition of the national movement of liberation to a new revolutionary stage, the big bourgeoisie sees that under the leadership of the proletariat, the anti-imperialist struggle is getting beyond its control, and that it objectively menaces their class interests. They endeavor, therefore, to regain their leadership for the purpose of defeating the revolution. They try to influence the movement with the ideology of bourgeois nationalism and against the ideology of the class struggle.

Parallel to this regrouping of the class forces of the revolution, there proceeds a crystallization of the counterrevolutionary forces. This process, in its turn, is closely related to and influenced by imperialist politics, just as the development of the revolutionary forces is related to and influenced by the world revolution (the Union of Soviet Socialist Republics and Western proletariat).

Chang Tso-lin, Wu P'ei-fu, and Sun Ch'uan-fang attempt to unify their forces to oppose the victorious revolutionary movement. This counterrevolutionary bloc is formed under the influence and with the aid of imperialism. The big industrial bourgeoisie reveal increasing signs of vacillation and become inclined toward an agreement with foreign capitalists leaving to the latter the role of a dominating agent.

Finding that the militarists are not fully effective instruments for crushing the revolutionary movement, imperialism seeks new allies within the national movement by means of the policy of reconciliation. It attempts to induce the national bourgeoisie to break away from the revolutionary bloc. To strengthen the position of the imperialists' agents within the national movement, some sections of the big bourgeoisie and even militarists, who up till now have avoided or even condemned the national-revolutionary struggle, have begun to pass to the side of the Canton government. The object of this move is to wrest the leadership of the national-revolutionary movement from the revolutionary bloc of the proletariat, peasantry, and urban petty bourgeoisie, and thereby to stem the tide of the revolution. World imperialism stands behind all these maneuvers of the counterrevolutionary forces.

In this transitional period, when the gradual abandonment of the revolution by the big bourgeoisie is historically inevitable, the proletariat must, of course, make good use of such bourgeoisie as remains actively engaged in the revolutionary struggle against imperialism and militarism.

On the other hand, the proletariat and the Party must utilize by tactical moves the antagonisms both among the bourgeoisie who are abandoning the revolution, and among the various imperialist groups, all without losing sight of the principal aims, to which it must subordinate all its strategic maneuvers and tactical moves.

III. The General Perspectives of the Chinese Revolution.

Considered from the point of view of class alignments in both camps, the general prospects of the Chinese revolution become very clear. Although historically the Chinese revolution in its present stage of development is a bourgeois-democratic revolution, it is bound to asume a character of a broad social movement. The outcome of the Chinese revolution should not necessarily be the creation of such sociopolitical conditions which will lead the capitalist development of the country. Taking place in the period of capitalist decline, the Chinese revolution is a section of a general struggle for the overthrow of capitalism and the establishment of socialism. The structure of the revolutionary state is determined by its class basis. Therefore, the Chinese revolutionary state will not be a purely bourgeois-democratic state, but a democratic dictatorship of the proletariat, peasantry, and other exploited classes. It will be a revolutionary anti-imperialist government of the period which represents a transition to noncapitalist (socialist) development.

The Communist Party of China must exert all its efforts to concretize the revolutionary possibility for a noncapitalist development. Otherwise, that is, in the event of a bourgeois victory over the proletariat and the assumption of leadership by the bourgeoisie, actual domination over the country will pass into the hands of the foreign imperialists, although this domination may take new forms.

The future development and the prospects of the Chinese revolution depend primarily on the role of the proletariat. The events of the last few years have proved that a revolutionary fighting national front can be organized only under the leadership of the proletariat. The struggle against the hegemony of foreign capital can be successfully carried on only under the hegemony of the proletariat. This is the basic principle determining the tactics of the Chinese revolution.

The feudal military cliques that exercise political power over a considerable section of the country, represent reactionary forces and are imperialists' agents. The native bourgeoisie is comparatively undeveloped and weak as a class. The economically stronger section of the bourgeoisie (bourgeois financiers and compradores) is so closely connected with foreign capitalism through commercial and financial bonds that they have never participated in the anti-imperialist struggle. The industrial bourgeoisie would march with the national-revolutionary movement as long as it preserved a purely bourgeois democratic character; but on the first signs of the revolution it either deserts the revolution or maneuvers to sabotage it. The petty bourgeoisie (petty bourgeois intellectuals, students, artisans, small traders, and so forth) constitutes a revolutionary force in a country like China. Petty bourgeoisie has played an important role in the past and will do so in the future. But they are not able to act independently; they must either march with the bourgeoisie or with the proletariat. When the bourgeoisie desert the revolution or conspire against it, the exploited middle classes come under the revolutionary influence of the proletariat. Under these conditions the moving force of the Chinese revolution in its present state is the revolutionary bloc of the proletariat, peasantry, and the petty bourgeoisie. The proletariat is the dominating factor of this bloc.

IV. National Revolution and the Peasantry.

In the present transitional stage of the development of revolution the agrarian question becomes the central question. The class which examines most thoroughly this problem and succeeds in giving a radical answer to it, will be the leader of the revolution. In the present stiuation in China the proletariat is the only class that is in a position to carry on their radical agrarian policy which is a condition for the successful outcome of the anti-imperialist struggle and further development of the revolution.

The power of Chinese militarism lies in its support by foreign imperialism on one hand, and native landowners, on the other hand. The domination of the militarists is based on the enslaving semifeudal system of oppression and exploitation of hundreds of millions of peasants by the military bureaucratic machinery of authority—the landlords, the gentry, and merchant-usurer capitalists. It is a system which is based on the total lack and shortage of land among the peasants who are consequently compelled to place themselves in a bondage to the landlords and usurers or fill the ranks of the millions of coolies in the towns and in the armies. Overthrowing the imperialists, abolishing all survivals of the old feudal relations, national liberation, the revolutionary reforms of internal and social relations—these tasks are organically connected with each other and represent the one task of the Chinese revolution.

The overthrow of the militarists completely, the economic and political struggle of the peasantry, which constitutes the overwhelming majority of the population, must be developed as a part of the anti-imperialist struggle. The fear that the aggravation of the class struggle in the countryside will weaken the united anti-imperialist front is baseless. The rout of the Second People's Army not by forces of counterrevolution but by the revolt of the discontented peasantry indicates the danger of the situation. Not to approach the agrarian question boldly by supporting all the economic demands of the peasant masses, is positively dangerous for the revolution. To refuse to assign to the agrarian revolution a prominent place in the national-liberation movement, for fear of alienating the dubious and disloyal coöperation of a section of the capitalist class is wrong. This is not the revolutionary policy of the proletariat. The Communist Party must be free of such mistakes.

The present situation is characterized by its transitional nature when the proletariat must choose between allying itself with a considerable section of the bourgeoisie or further consolidating its own alliance with the peasantry. If the proletariat does not put forward a radical agrarian program, it will fail to attract the peasantry into the revolutionary struggle and will lose its hegemony in the national-liberation movement. Under the direct or indirect imperialist influence, the bourgeoisie will regain the leadership of the movement once more. This, on its part and under the present conditions, will eventually lead to the consolidation of the positions of foreign capital in China, that is, to the stabilization of imperialism.

The national government in Canton will not be able to retain power in the course of the revolution and will not gain complete victory over foreign imperialism and over the native reaction, unless national liberation is identified with agrarian revolution. The developing process of class differentiation in the rural districts intensifies the struggle between the peasants and the exploiting classes. This class differentiation and the struggle resultant from it, require the closest attention on the part of the Communist Party. The latter must assume the leadership in the peasant movement and develop it by adopting corresponding economic and political slogans.

Although the Communist Party should make nationalization of land the fundamental plank of the agrarian program, it is necessary to differentiate in the agrarian tactics the peculiar economic and political conditions in the different districts of China.

On the question of power which has already been raised by the peasant movement, the Communist Party of China must support the [peasants'] striving to overthrow the despotic rule of the gentry and the rural officials in the villages, and substitute this old semifeudal bureaucracy with the organs of revolutionary authority chosen from the lower strata [of the peasantry]. These organs will then carry out the decrees of the revolutionary government and will protect the interests of the main peasant masses. The peasants must participate in the hub of the local administrations.

The program of the agrarian revolution must be rendered concrete in the territories under the authority of the Kuomintang national government. The Communist Party of China and the Kuomintang must immediately carry out the following measures in order to bring over the peasantry to the side of the revolution:

a) Reduce rents to a minimum;

b) Abolish the numerous forms of taxes imposed upon the peasantry and substitute them with a single progressive agricultural tax;

c) Regulate and reduce as far as possible the burden of taxation now being borne by the principal masses of the peasantry;

d) Confiscate the monasterial and church lands and the lands belonging to the reactionary militarists, compradores, landlords, and gentry who are waging civil war against the Kuomintang national government;

e) Guarantee the tenant farmers perpetual leases of the land they cultivate and the fixing of maximum rent jointly by the peasant unions and representatives of the revolutionary authority;

f) The Canton government must render the utmost support to the interests of the peasantry, and particularly protect the peasants from the oppression and encroachments of the landlords, gentry, and usurers;

g) Disarm min-t'uan [people's militia] and other armed forces of the landlords;

h) Arm the poor and middle peasants and subordinate all armed forces in the rural districts to the revolutionary authorities;

i) The government must give maximum support to the peasant organizations, including the peasant unions;

j) Grant loans to peasants at low interest, suppress usury, and support the various peasant mutual-aid organizations;

k) Grant state aid to the coöperatives and mutual-aid organizations.

The Communist Party must see to it that the Canton government enforces these measures as a transition to a more developed state of agrarian revolution. This very important task will be accomplished by creating the peasant committees under Communist leadership. As the revolution develops the peasant committees not only will assume the authority and power to enforce the above demands, but also will intensify the struggle by putting forward more radical demands. The peasants' committees will be the basis of the people's government and the people's army in rural districts.

In areas still controlled and dominated by reactionary militarists, the task of the Communist Party is to lead the peasantry against feudalism, militarism, and imperialism. In these areas revolutionary work among the peasantry is of particularly great importance because this will be the surest way of demoralizing the reactionary armies. The Communists must utilize such spontaneously created peasant organizations as the "Red Spears" and strengthen their influence among them.

The attitude of the peasantry toward the revolution is influenced to a great extent by the behavior of the Nationalist armies. It is by the good or bad behavior of the revolutionary armies that the peasantry judge the nature of the new government. Upon the conduct of the revolutionary army, upon its attitude toward the peasantry and landlords, upon its readiness to assist the peasantry depends the attitude of the peasantry toward the new government. It is true that the peasants greet the revolutionary army with enthusiasm, but it is equally true that this enthusiasm evaporates in time. Exigencies of a prolonged and difficult military campaign impose additional burdens on the peasantry. The warm support that the peasants have given to the revolutionary armies will be more stable if the Communists and other revolutionary elements who control the movement, take steps to compensate the peasants for their hardships by a bold and correct agrarian policy. The revolutionary armies will strike root in the peasant masses as the standard bearer of agrarian revolution.

V. The Communist Party and the Kuomintang.

The supreme necessity of winning influence over the peasantry determines likewise the relation of the Communist Party to the Kuomintang and to the Canton government. The machinery of the national-revolutionary government provides a very effective way to reach the peasantry. The Communist Party must use this machinery.

In the newly liberated provinces [local] governments of the type of the Canton government will be set up. The Communists and their revolutionary allies must penetrate the new government, so as to give practical expression to their agrarian program by using the government machinery to confiscate land, reduce taxes, and invest real power in the peasant committees, thus carrying on progressive reforms on the basis of a revolutionary program.

For this reason and many other equally important reasons, the point of view that the Communist Party must leave the Kuomintang is incorrect. The whole process of development of the Chinese revolution, its character and its prospects, demand that the Communists must stay in the Kuomintang and intensify their work in it. In order to intensify their activities in the Kuomintang with the object of assisting further development of the revolutionary movement, the Communists should enter the Canton government. Since foundation the real power of the Canton government has been in the hands of the Right Wing Kuomintang (five out of the six commissars belong to the Right Wing). Even though the Canton government could not exist without the support of the working class, the workers' and peasants' movement has had to overcome numerous obstacles. Recent events have shown that the Communists must enter the Canton government in order to support the revolutionary Left Wing in its struggle against the weak and vacillating policy of the Right. The extension of the Canton government's authority to new areas makes the question of the participation of the Communists in it still more imperative.

The Communist Party of China must strive to develop the Kuomintang into a real people's party—a solid revolutionary bloc of the proletariat, peasantry, the urban petty bourgeoisie, and the other oppressed and exploited strata of the population who wage a decisive struggle against imperialism and its agents. For this the Communist Party must work along the following lines:

a) Systematic and determined struggle against Tai Chi-t'ao's ideology and the Right Wing attempts to convert the Kuomintang into a bourgeois party;

b) Definite formation of a Left Wing in the Kuomintang and establishment of close coöperation with it, except in the matter of trying to replace its leaders by members of the Communist Party;

c) Consistent criticism of the Center which is vacillating between the Right and Left wings, between the further development of the revolution and compromise with imperialism.

*VI. The Tasks of the Chinese Revolution and the Character
of the Revolutionary Government.*

Lenin wrote: "While formerly, before the epoch of world revolution, movements for national liberation were part of the general democratic movement, now, after the victory of the Soviet revolution in Russia and the opening of the period of world revolution, movements for national liberation are part of the proletarian world revolution."

The program of the Chinese revolution and the structure of the revolutionary state created by it should be determined from this point of view. The process of class differentiation that follows as the revolutionary movement develops, bears out this [Lenin's] conception. The Canton government, in spite of its bourgeois-democratic character, essentially and objectively contains the germs of a revolutionary petty bourgeois state—a democratic dictatorship of the revolutionary bloc of the proletariat, peasantry, and the urban petty bourgeoisie. The petty-bourgeois democratic movement becomes revolutionary in China because it is an anti-imperialist movement. The Canton government is revolutionary primarily because it is anti-imperialist. Being primarily anti-imperialist, the Chinese revolution and the government created by it must strike at the root of imperialist power in China. Repudiation of unequal treaties and abolition of territorial concessions will not be sufficient to weaken the position of imperialism. The blow must be dealt at the economic basis of imperialist power; the revolutionary government must gradually confiscate the railways, concessions, factories, mines, banks, and other business enterprises owned by foreign capital. By so doing it will immediately outstrip the narrow boundary of bourgeois democracy and enter into the stage of transition to revolutionary dictatorship. Thus, it is a mistake to limit the immediate tasks of the Chinese revolution to (1) overthrow of imperialism and (2) liquidation of the remnants of feudalism, on the ground that in its first stage this revolution bears a petty bourgeois nature. The Chinese revolution cannot defeat imperialism without passing over the boundaries of bourgeois democracy. Under the present conditions the proletariat will lead the peasantry to the revolutionary struggle. The movement for the liquidation of feudalism, now led by the proletariat, is bound to develop into an agrarian revolution. Therefore, the tasks of the Chinese revolution become:

a) Nationalization of railways and waterways;

b) Confiscation of large-scale enterprises, mines, and banks having the character of foreign concessions;

c) Nationalization of land, to be realized by successive radical reform measures enforced by the revolutionary state.

VII. The Communist Party and the Proletariat.

To play the dominant role in the revolution the Chinese proletariat must solidify its class organization—political and economic. To organize and train the proletariat for this heroic role is the primary task of the Communist Party. The numerical weakness and youthfulness of the Chinese proletariat must be counterbalanced by strength of organization and clarity of ideas.

The general federation of trade unions, embracing now hundreds of thousands of industrial workers, as well as the national railwaymen's and seamen's unions are the basis of the Communist Party. To strengthen these organizations by drawing in broader masses of workers is the immediate task of the Communist Party. In the national revolutionary struggle of the last two years the working class has displayed tremendous power. In actual struggle it has won the hegemony in the revolutionary movement. On the basis of these traditions and achievements the working-class organizations must be further strengthened and developed on the following lines:

a) Creation of mass industrial unions, unification of all unions on an industrial basis, strengthening of the Chinese Federation of Trade Unions;

b) Intensification of work among the masses, consolidation of the contact of the leading trade-union organs with the wide masses of Chinese workers, unionizing of workers in small enterprises and cultural-educational workers;

c) Greater attention to the economic struggle of the workers which should grow into a political struggle, elaboration of tactics for the strike movement, organization of mutual aid and strike funds, formation and support of coöperatives, etc.;

d) Intensified educational work among the masses of the workers by means of denunciation of the practice of reformist methods;

e) Strengthening of contact between the Chinese trade-union movement of the Far Eastern countries.

In order to attract the bulk of the working class into the movement and strengthen its position in the national revolution, the Chinese Communist Party should agitate for:

a) Complete freedom of activity of the revolutionary peasants' and workers' organizations, legalization of the trade unions, enactment of advanced trade-union laws, and right to strike;

b) Labor legislation: eight-hour working day, weekly day of rest, minimum wage;

c) Social legislation: sanitary inspection of working conditions; housing; insurance against illness, injury, disablement, and unemployment; regulation of labor of women and children, prohibition of night work for women, prohibition of factory labor for children below fourteen years of age;

d) Institution of factory inspection;

e) Abolition of the system of fines and corporal punishment;

f) Withdrawal of all kinds of military units and police detachments from the factory premises;

g) Measures to deal with unemployment; extension of trade-union influence over the unemployed; organization of labor exchanges by trade unions.

At the present state of the revolution an almost untapped source of revolutionary energy which has not yet been fully utilized is the masses of artisans and handicraft workers who have been ruined by imperialism and are definitely hostile toward foreign capitalists. The Communist vanguard of the Chinese proletariat has the task of organizing these masses and drawing them into the common stream of the national-revolutionary movement. Particularly, the Communist Party must seek for these workers:

1. The alleviation of tax burdens;

2. The organization of handicraft and artisan workers' unions;

3. The organization of workers' associations.

VIII. The Organizational Tasks of the Communist Party of China.

The Communist Party of China is an organized force. It has its leaders; it is establishing its cadres and is leading the masses. Its work has acquired a fairly considerable sweep and a stable form of organization. During the last half year, the party had made a considerable progress in filling up its ranks, mainly from among the workers.

The peasants' section of the Communist Party is not large numerically, but the party is constantly increasing its activities among the peasantry.

One of the Chinese Communist Party's most important tasks is to widen, intensify, improve, and consolidate the work of the party training.

The party has done considerable work in organizing the Young Communist League. The Young Communist League of China recently has grown numerically and is active in the numerous fields of work. The youth is a tremendous revolutionary force in China. The revolutionary students, the young workers, and the peasant youth, all these represent a force which could speed up considerably the revolution, if they were brought under the intellectual and political influence of the Communist Party. No one realizes the imperialist oppression so profoundly and sensitively, no one realizes the necessity to struggle against this oppression so acutely as does the youth. This circumstance must be taken into account by the Communist Party of China, and it must prompt it to intensify its work among the youth.

One of the fundamental tasks of the Party is to fight for the right to exist openly.

Systematic recruiting of new members must be conducted principally in the industrial districts. The new members must be trained by short-term courses, by special discussions of the Party's program and tactics, by drawing them into everyday work in their respective cells, and through these cells, into general Party work.

It is necessary to develop collective leadership in the Party organizations, from the Central Committee to the factory street cells.

Persistent and more energetic efforts must be made to draw the best Party workers into the Party leadership and to strengthen and build up the Party's cadres. Special attention must be paid to training of cell secretaries, leaders of factions and of mass organizations, and the leading personnel of district and regional Party committees. The Central Committee and regional committees must choose permanent traveling instructors from among the best local Party workers.

Cadres of traveling organizers must be established for work in the rural districts.

Increased activity and initiative must be encouraged among the lower Party organizations in the cells, at general meetings of Party members, etc.

The [Communist] factions, particularly in the trade unions in the leading organs of the peasant unions, and in local organizations of the Kuomintang must be strengthened.

Systematic, firm Party guidance of the work of the factions must be maintained.

2

We are living in an epoch of the downfall of capitalism. At first glance, it might seem that capitalism has overcome the post-war crisis by a series of measures lowering the standard of living of the working class. In certain countries, there are obvious signs of the flourishing of capitalism. This is particularly conspicuous in Germany. However, with the exception of the United States of America and, in part, Japan, the stabilization of capitalism is but a temporary phenomenon. Even in the United States, the flowering of capitalism has already reached its peak, and the first signs of decline are noticeable.

The fact that the Chinese revolution is occurring in an epoch of the decline of capitalism is itself a fundamental determinant of the character and import [of this revolution].

Any social system that happens to be in contradiction with progress is doomed to destruction. Capitalism has long ago ceased to be an instrument of progress and has become a definitely reactionary force, an impediment to civilization, a curse on humanity. Capitalism, in its most highly developed form, that is, imperialism, has led to colonial plunder, to the enslavement of millions of human beings, to the most brutal form of economic exploitation and political slavery. It has obstructed social progress in a series of countries that make up a large part of the earth. It has led to wars of conquest, to plunder and coercion. And the end result was a world conflagration which erupted in 1914. Capitalism has become a destructive force. In its place must come a new social order to permit the continuation of human progress. All over the world the forces of a great revolution are beginning to develop, a revolution that will liberate the human society from the oppressive clutches of capitalism and build a new world on the ruins of the old.

An article by M. N. Roy, Canton, February 22, 1927.—Eds.

One of these forces is the revolt of colonial peoples. The Chinese revolution is the most advanced and the most intense expression of this force. That is why the fundamental significance of the national-liberation movement in China is that it is an integral part of the world revolution which will abolish the exploitation of man by man and put an end to national oppression and class supremacy.

The Chinese revolution poses a potent challenge to the stabilization of capitalism. It has already dealt cruel blows to British foreign trade. Its successes are ruining the plans of the imperialist powers whose aim is to ensure the stabilization of the capitalist system.

Capitalism is now undergoing an unparalleled crisis. It is a crisis at once of overproduction and underproduction. In recent years, the industrial productive capacity of all major capitalist countries has grown tremendously. This occurred as a result of attempts to lower the prime cost of production by improving the techniques of production. But at the same time, actual production is far below the production capacity. The world market has narrowed down considerably. The destruction wrought by the imperialist war lowered the level of consumption in a number of countries. In many countries, the credit system was destroyed by post-war inflation. Depressed wages and heavy taxes, brought about by the necessity of liquidating war debts and defraying the enormous expenses of post-war militarism, lowered to a considerable extent the buying power of the people in the majority of industrial countries. As a result, the goods that are produced can not be sold at a sufficiently high profit, whereas the goods that the people need most of all are not accessible to them in spite of the enormous growth of the general industrial capacity of the world industry. This situation typifies most vividly the vicious circle in which capitalist production finds itself.

Capitalism sees only two ways out of this vicious circle: to lower the standard of living of the proletariat in its parent country and to increase the exploitation of the cheap labor force of the colonial masses. Imperialism is feverishly seeking its salvation in these two paths. But every step it takes in one direction or another worsens its position and amounts to merely one more revolution of the vicious circle. Lowered wages destroy the domestic market and serve to intensify the industrial crisis, to increase unemployment, and to push the proletariat further into the path of revolution. Utilization of the cheap-labor force in the colonies can be increased only if the colonies are industrialized. If industrialization could be accomplished by the capital exported from imperialist countries, it would mark a big step forward in the direction of stabilizing world capitalism. But this, too, cannot be accomplished. The accumulation of capital in all imperialist countries, with the exception of the United States of America, has undergone a sharp decline mainly because of the militarization of the basic branches of industry during the war and to the long fall-off in trade following the war. Furthermore, colonial industrialization displaces from colonial markets the goods produced by the parent country. The intensification of contradictions between industrial and finance capital leads to violent clashes which undermine the foundation of parliamentary governments.

The imperialist policy in China is determined by this intertwining of contradictory economic interests that lie at the basis of international politics. Trade with China is an important factor in the stabilization of world capitalism. For those countries which have export capital, China will prove to be an extremely profitable market for investments. The ostensibly liberal policy of the government of the United States can be ascribed to two circumstances: (1) American manufacturers are soliciting trade with China, and (2) American financiers are interested in investing their capital there. As long as peace is not restored in China, none of these aspirations of American imperialism can be realized. It is for this reason that American imperialism is pursuing a policy of peaceful penetration. It is to the interest of American imperialism that a bourgeois-democratic government becomes consolidated in China. In fact, it would merely serve to strengthen its position in the country. This is why this American policy of "enlightened and reasonable imperialism" is supported by a significant section of the bourgeoisie in other imperialist countries. Even Great Britain, which is attempting to terrorize the national-revolutionary movement by a show of armed force, follows this policy. Brandishing a mailed fist, British imperialism takes every opportunity to proclaim its desire to conclude an agreement with "the real and legal" national government. In other words, British imperialism is saying: "Let the healthy national movement create favorable conditions for capitalist development in China, and I will lay down my arms." The hostile schemes of the liberal American government and the maneuvers of British imperialism are obvious. Their aim is to split the national ranks, to achieve a rapprochement with the bourgeois elements in the national movement, and to prevail upon them to betray and destroy the revolution.

Any bourgeois-democratic government in China will receive the approval and the recognition of the imperialist powers, but only on the condition that it agrees to recognize the domination of foreign capital. Times change—and, inevitably, the forms of imperialist domination in China must also change. Unequal agreements, extraterritoriality, concessions, were all necessary under certain conditions, under certain forms of exploitation. At the present time, however, when conditions are different, capitalist domination in China can be maintained without these coercive privileges. Even the British government has repeatedly stated that these methods are outmoded and can give way to newer, more subtle forms of domination.

The Chinese bourgeoisie is young and weak. It is economically backward and politically immature. If the national liberation movement were to lead the country to capitalist development, it would find itself inevitably under the heel of imperialism. For if national independence is to be realized by a government of the native bourgeoisie pursuing a policy of home capitalism, then this will be an independence in word only. Imperialism will remain the ruling force. Unequal agreements may be abrogated, extraterritoriality abolished, even concessions may be liquidated, yet the so-called national government will still be but a toy in the hands of international capital.

However, such a misfortune will not befall the revolutionary-liberation movement. It will not follow this course. The international conditions in which this movement is taking place secures it against such a course.

Most of the imperialist powers bending every effort to preserve their positions in China are in a state of an insoluble economic crisis. In all these countries, the accumulation of surplus capital available for export—the instrument of colonial exploitation—is declining at an increasingly rapid rate. Only the United States of America can afford to continue the policy of liberal imperialism and thus undermine the Chinese revolution. The United States has export capital. But the imperialist powers which have hitherto occupied positions of dominance in China will not permit themselves to be squeezed out by America. The competition between the various groupings of imperialist powers is all to the favor of the Chinese revolution. The grouping headed by England is prepared to adopt as a last resort a policy of violence and aggression in order to suppress the national-revolutionary movement by force and to preserve the old regime of reactionaries and militarists. However, such a policy would only serve to accelerate the development of the revolution, just as it did last year.

Consequently, the Chinese national-liberation movement will either continue to develop and emerge victorious as a workers' and peasants' revolution, or it will not win at all. Capitalism has become a reactionary force throughout the world. The bourgeoisie can not lead the revolutionary struggle. The revolutionary democratic movement of China represents a great social revolution.

3

The successes of the Northern Expedition placed the national-revolutionary army face to face with the chief forces of our enemy. These are: (1) the military and naval forces of international imperialism concentrated in Shanghai, and (2) the armies of the Northern militarists. The defeat of Sun Ch'uan-fang was a cruel blow to foreign imperialism and native militarism; at the same time, it cleared the field for a decisive engagement between the forces of revolution and reaction. The unsuccessful attempt of Sun Ch'uan-fang to delay the national forces' advance on Shanghai forced the imperialists to resort to the last means—to open armed intervention. Hence, in the fight for the possession of Shanghai, a direct clash between the armed forces of international imperialism and the national-revolutionary army is inevitable. On the other hand, Chang Tso-lin is mobilizing all his forces to counteract and drive back the national-revolutionary armies. In this plan, in this vile crime against the Chinese people, he is relying on extensive support from international imperialism.

The first stage of the Northern Expedition has reached its maximum

---

This is an appeal issued just at the time that Chiang Kai-shek was preparing to betray the national revolution. Within the Kuomintang, the struggle followed the lines of personal enmities. The Central Committee of the Communist Party which was still situated in Shanghai had taken no definite stand on this conflict. The first estimate of the political significance of the crisis in the Kuomintang was given in this appeal. This was the first attack against the feudal-bourgeois Right Wing of the Kuomintang. The appeal pointed out the imminent danger and advanced a political platform to counteract it. However, this was the first step, and it had to be made with great circumspection. Its formulation had to be very carefully done. However, the fact was that the majority of the working class in Canton had arisen under the Communist guidance to a struggle against the feudal-bourgeois reaction. Before it was published, the appeal was submitted through proper Communist factions for examination by all the organizations that were to sign it; it was discussed by them and accepted. The Canton Committee of the Communist Party did not wish to take the initiative in the struggle and held up the appeal for one week after the decision to publish it had been taken. [M.N.R.]

tension. Final victory will be achieved only in the brutal struggle to come. At this critical moment, all the democratic and progressive forces of the people must staunchly support the national-revolutionary army in order to enable it to carry the Northern Expedition to a victorious conclusion and to clear the whole Yangtze Valley of the combined forces of international imperialism and domestic [*otechestvennyi*] militarism.

Until now, the national armies have been accomplishing with honor the heavy tasks imposed upon them by the people. Let us congratulate them for the glorious victories they have won for the revolution, fighting under the leadership of the people's party and the people's government. To assure the success of the coming brutal and decisive struggle, the people's party must exercise stronger political leadership of the military forces of the revolution than at any time in the past. Strict coördination of all the forces is the only guarantee of the final victory of the revolution. In the absence of modern means of transportation and communication in the country, the national armies are scattered over an enormous range of territory. The front has become extended over hundreds of miles. Under these conditions, only a central political power possessing supreme authority can assure real coördination of action in the aim of realizing the principles of the national revolution. This power belongs to the people's party (the Kuomintang). Therefore, a relaxation in the supreme authority of the party, under whatever pretext it may be, is extremely dangerous for the revolution. This can not, and must not, be allowed to happen. We appeal to all popular organizations to rally around the Kuomintang with even greater solidarity and greater faith than ever before in order that the party's authority could become really supreme with respect to the organs of the revolution, that is, the national government and the national army.

Leadership of the revolution at its highly developed stage of the present requires the unification of all the forces of the party in order to lead the national armies to victory and to build a revolutionary-democratic state machinery for the purpose of consolidating the people's power in the provinces just occupied. Every possible opportunity for consolidating the party leadership must be turned to account. At a time such as this, the party cannot do without Wang Ching-wei. We hope that his health is restored sufficiently to enable him to return to his post without delay. We are appealing to all popular organizations and all the organs of the revolution to join us in asking Wang Ching-wei to return to his native land at once.

The unity of the people's party must be preserved at all costs. Attempts at undermining or infringing upon the unity and the supreme authority of the party can not be tolerated. Such attempts, direct or indirect, are extremely dangerous to the revolution, and it is essential to combat them resolutely. We regard the Peking Conference as an attempt of this type. It was a breach of the party's authority and an attempt to usurp the party's power. There still remain persons in the party who are seeking to undermine its unity. All popular organizations must demand of the Central Committee of the Kuomintang that it categorically condemn the conduct of these enemies of the party and reply with disciplinary action to the unpardonable infringement on the unity and authority of the party.

In the realm of war, it is highly desirable to maintain close coöperation with the people's armies under the command of General Fêng Yü-hsiang. Coördinated actions between the national armies on the Yangtze and the people's armies in the western provinces will place the forces of northern reaction in a strategically dangerous position. This coördination and coöperation of all the available forces of the revolution must be swiftly accomplished through the medium of the central organ of political power—the central national government which is firmly consolidated in Wuhan. Armed forces are a weapon in the hands of the revolutionary state which is an expression of the power of the people.

The Chinese people have arisen against imperialist exploitation and native reaction—this instrument of imperialism. The fact that the vanguard of the intervention contains only one or several of the imperialist powers should not mislead us regarding the intentions of the rest of the imperialist powers. International imperialism as a whole is an enemy of the Chinese people. Our struggle is aimed first of all against this enemy. We concentrate our forces against one or more of those imperialist powers which are the most aggressive toward us. But, at the same time, we must not forget for a minute that the freedom of the Chinese people depends ultimately on the annihilation of imperialism as a world force.

The French government's announcement of "neutrality" is an outrageous lie. In addition to supplying the reactionary government of Yunnan with arms and ammunition, the French government is tacitly supporting the policy of intervention pursued by British imperialism. American liberalism is hypocritical bigotry. America is pursuing an insidious policy of peaceful penetration into the Chinese national-liberation movement in order to demoralize it by encouraging and strengthening the conciliatory elements. The hypocrisy of American imperialism was exposed in its proposal for the neutralization of Shanghai. In effect, it is a proposal for the annexation of Shanghai by international imperialism in order that foreign military and naval forces could "legally" prevent the revolutionary army from advancing on Shanghai. The policy of Japan is hardly a secret to anyone. The Chinese people will never forget the insolence of the twenty-one demands, the attempt to restore the monarchy with the help of the counterrevolutionary Yüan Shih-k'ai, and the continued support of Chang Tso-lin in the entire course of the many years of struggle against the democratic and progressive movement.

The various attempts on the part of certain imperialist powers to enter into relations with our national government have only one object, that of demoralizing our forces. Therefore, any response to such attempts is a betrayal of the revolution, and must be exposed and prosecuted as treason.

The tactic of splitting the forces of imperialism by exploiting the rivalry between imperialist powers is admissible and may prove useful in demoralizing the forces of our enemies and in consolidating our power. But before such a tactic is applied in practice, it must be thoroughly examined in every individual case and affirmed by the central organs of the revolution—the Kuomintang and the national government. If negotiations with foreign governments are necessary, they must always be conducted by the national government with the consent, and under the direction, of the Kuomintang. Under no circumstances can the military or any other organs of the revolutionary state be permitted to act independently.

We direct the attention of the people to rumors of a possible agreement between the commanding staff of the national-revolutionary army and Chang Tso-lin. These rumours must be flatly repudiated as being completely groundless. The pretensions of Chang Tso-lin and his agents that they are fighting for the same goals as those of the armies of the national government are absurd. We can not admit for a moment that the revolutionary armies can or will some day entertain the idea of some sort of an agreement with the standard bearer of reaction, Chang Tso-lin. He may, of course, suggest all kinds of negotiations because his army is threatened with destruction at the hands of the national-revolutionary forces. It stands to reason that he is ready to conclude any kind of an agreement in order to save himself. A contemptuous refusal is the only reply that can and must be given to his proposals. China's emancipation from the curse of reactionary militarism is one of the basic principles of the national revolution. It is inconceivable that the revolutionary armies should oppose this principle of the revolution out of strategical considerations, regardless of how serious these considerations may be.

The popular organizations firmly support the national party and the national government. By this support they want to make certain that the military forces of the revolution are led straight on the road to victory. They will not tolerate the slightest compromise with either Japanese imperialism or northern militarism. Such a compromise would in no way create—as it may be asserted—an alliance against the most vicious enemies of the Chinese people. It would mean becoming a victim of the intrigues of international imperialism. It would mean the capitulation of the revolution. Now, when the revolution stands on the threshold of victory, the popular organizations will assist the national party and the national government in protecting the revolution against any possibility of such a capitulation.

In order to make the national government the chief executive organ of the revolution, the Kuomintang must rally the laboring masses around the government. This must be done by carrying out the workers' and peasants' program of the national revolution through the proper organs of the revolutionary state. The progressive agrarian policy of the government will remove the danger of the disintegration of the revolutionary forces. The sympathy of the population in the rear will assure 50 per cent of the victory on the front. The peasant masses will give enthusiastic support to the revolutionary army if it brings to them the tidings of liberation from the more unbearable burdens—the exhorbitant taxes, the fluctuating rentals, illegal requisitions, banditry, and so on. The peasant masses will welcome the national armies if they defend them against the pillaging of the *min-t'uan* and the gentry and democratize the political power of the village by creating local self-government.

The army is the most powerful weapon of the revolution. As the army becomes imbued from top to bottom, from the commanding staff to the rank and file, with the consciousness of its liberational mission, this weapon will become ever more terrifying to the enemies of the revolution. In order to achieve this, one must consolidate and reinforce the political section of the army under the direct leadership and control of the Kuomintang. Greatest attention must be paid to the improvement of the material conditions in the armies. Regular wage payments to soldiers must become the chief concern of the military budget.

The organized forces and the will of the people can and will defend the revolution against the danger of compromise and capitulation. We appeal to all popular organizations to consolidate, through this force and this will, the national party and its revolutionary government.

DOWN WITH IMPERIALISM!
DOWN WITH MILITARISM!
DOWN WITH THE POLICY OF COMPROMISES AND CAPITULATION!
ALL POWER TO THE PEOPLE'S PARTY!

The Chinese Communist Party
The All-China Federation of Labor, Canton
The Conference of Cantonese Workers' Delegates
The Peasants' Union
The Union of Railroad workers
The Seamen's Union
The Combined Union of Peasants, Workers, Merchants
    and Teachers [*rabotniki prosveshcheniia*]
The Hong Kong–Canton Strike Committee
The Hong Kong General [*Vseobshchaia*] Federation of Labor

Canton, February 27, 1927

4

WATCH THE LEADERS

The danger of the revolution being betrayed as a result of a policy of compromise with militarism and imperialism is not a product of our imagination, as the enemies of the Communist Party may assert. This danger is real, and it is becoming even more serious. As the staunch vanguard of the struggle for national liberation, the Communist Party must sound the alarm in order to channel the people's will and energies into the cause of saving the revolution.

Can one remain calm in view of the persistent rumors about secret negotiations with Liang Ch'i [?], the president of the political commission of Ankuochun? Behind the scenes looms the hand of Japanese imperialism. General Yang Yü-t'ing from Fengtien, who plays the principal role in these negotiations for an agreement between the North and the South, maintains close contact with the Japanese mission. It is reported that agents of Marshal Chiang Kai-shek are also taking part in these negotiations. The popular masses who are fighting and making heroic sacrifices for the revolution have the right to demand an explanation from the persons involved in this attempt to reach a compromise.

The imperialist press reports that negotiations are proceeding between Northerners and Southerners for the joint control of Shanghai. It is further reported that the "political heads" of the Southerners are making efforts to "seize" Shanghai by any means other than military force. The working class wants to know who these "political heads" are; it is certain that they do not represent the interests of the people, but the interests of a minority, the interests of a small group of compradores closely connected with imperialist capital. Any fool can un-

---

This article was written for the organ of the Canton Committee of the Communist Party. The Committee refused to publish it under the pretext that it might provoke the Cantonese dictator, Li Chi-shen, into taking repressive steps against the Communist Party. [M.N.R.]

derstand that one cannot drive the imperialist robbers out of Shanghai by means of persuasion. If this were possible, the military and naval forces of international imperialism would not have made a rush for Shanghai as soon as the revolutionary armies approached it. The "seizure" of Shanghai in alliance with Chang Tso-lin and Chang Tsung-ch'ang would mean selling out the right of the national government to establish its power in the economic capital of China. Such a "seizure" of Shanghai would mean the capitulation of the revolution.

Were not these the "political heads" at whose counterrevolutionary advice the direct advance of the national armies on Shanghai was delayed at the very moment when the Shanghai proletariat declared a general strike in order to help the nationalists to occupy the town? The working class of the whole country has the right to know why Marshal Chiang Kai-shek allowed the imperialist henchmen to stage a bloodbath of the leaders of the Shanghai proletariat while his army stood right by the city and could have dealt a direct blow and while Sun Ch'uan-fang's forces defending Shanghai were seriously debilitated, disorganized, and demoralized. The Shanghai proletarians threw themselves into the front lines of the battle, they braved the imperialist cannon fire heroically in order to assure victory to the revolutionary armies. The proletariat took the stand at the most dangerous point of the battle and extended its mighty hand to the national army for a revolutionary alliance and brotherhood. But the national army, being evidently under some evil influence, did not accept this hand; it refused to take the road to victory and betrayed its valiant ally to the terror of the counterrevolution.

There is talk that the Northern militarists are ready to reach an agreement with the national forces on the three following conditions: (1) expulsion of Russian advisers, in other words, a rupture of the revolutionary alliance with the Union of Soviet Republics, (2) concession to the national army of territories lying south of the Yangtze, with the exception of Shanghai, and (3) suppression of the Communist Party and the workers' movement. Agreement on joint control of Shanghai with Northern military leaders and the refusal to take decisive action during the strike of the Shanghai proletariat evidently correspond to two of these three conditions. The national army refused to come forward when the proletariat raised a rebellion. As a result, it has forfeited the right to occupy Shanghai and has breached the alliance with the proletariat.

In the face of these formidable facts, our warning is not a false alarm. It is justified by the gravity of the situation. A definite tendency toward compromise with domestic [otechestvennyi] militarism and foreign imperialism, toward a betrayal of the revolution, exists in the national movement. This tendency is represented in the Kuomintang by a well-organized faction. To it belong those "political heads" who advocate an agreement with the Northern militarists, who work for a rapprochement with Japanese imperialism to counterbalance the revolutionary alliance with the USSR, and who recommend a policy of inaction at a time when the Shanghai proletariat is boldly defying imperialist intervention. Among these "political heads" who by their counterrevolutionary aspirations have earned the admiration of the imperialists are such ardent reactionaries as Wang Fu, the former premier of the Wu P'ei-fu cabinet in Peking. This situation demonstrates that there are very *weighty reasons* compelling the Communist Party to sound the alarm and to advise the people: "Watch your leaders and check their actions!"

The policy of the Japanese imperialists in China is no secret. Without the support of Japan, Manchurian militarism would have long been a thing of the past. Chang Tsung-ch'ang, the Shantung warlord, is a protegee of Japanese imperialism. Japanese forces have been dispatched together with other imperialist forces to defend Shanghai against the national-revolutionary armies. Yet, in spite of this, *secret negotiations are being conducted with the Japanese government.* Moreover, Tai Chi-t'ao is leaving for Japan with instructions "to establish friendly relations." Tai Chi-t'ao's mission to Japan would have been understandable if its purpose were to create among the popular masses of Japan a mood against military intervention, against the policy of Japanese imperialism in China which supports Chang Tso-lin and Chang Tsung-ch'ang. But he has evidently set out to kowtow to the Japanese bourgeoisie and its imperialist government. He is meeting with cabinet ministers. The Chinese people on whose behalf Tai Chi-t'ao is acting have the right to know the real purpose of his mission and to recall him if his actions are calculated to compromise the revolution. In a conversation with the foreign minister, he took the trouble to explain that the demands of the Chinese nationalists are by no means excessive, that the Chinese nationalists are opposed to communism (by which he evidently implied the revolutionary movement of the working class). In conclusion, he declared that China hopes to act in contact with Japan and is seeking her aid in the cause of the national revolution.*

As an unofficial representative of the Kuomintang and the national government, Tai Chi-t'ao declared that on the condition of support

---

* A highly significant resemblance exists between this statement of Tai Chi-t'ao and those conditions on the basis of which—according to available information—the Northern militarists are ready to reach an agreement with the Southerners. [M.N.R.]

from Japanese imperialism, the Right Wing of the national movement would be prepared to restrict the program of the national movement, to break the alliance with the USSR, and to suppress the workers' and peasants' movement. Thus, the apostle of "pure Sun Yat-senism" brazenly violated all the principles established by Sun Yat-sen on the eve of his death.

The danger of a compromise and betrayal of the revolution is not a product of the imagination. Strenuous efforts are applied to achieve these goals. The working class, in alliance with other revolutionary elements, must save the revolution.

Canton, March 9, 1927.

5

THE BASE AND THE
SOCIAL FORCES OF THE REVOLUTION

The arguments for continuing the Northern Expedition, in regard to which a decision has already been adopted by the national government, are as follows: Wuhan has the necessary military forces at its disposal to carry out the expedition. With the help of the forces of Fêng Yü-hsiang and of Yen Hsi-shan, Chang Tso-lin will be forced back into Manchuria. Peking and Tientsin will be occupied by the national government. It is reported that Yen Hsi-shan has issued a declaration in which it is stated that he supports the Kuomintang and will submit to its leadership. This is viewed as a new factor in favor of the Northern Expedition. It is reported that this plan has been approved by military experts. It has also been pointed out that the Northern Expedition cannot be stopped, because if the national army does not advance to the north, then Chang Tso-lin can advance to the south. Further, the idea is suggested that Fêng Yü-hsiang is on the move. He can no longer remain in Shensi since this province is very poor. But if Fêng Yü-hsiang is advancing, he must be helped and in order to do so, it is necessary to move the national armies to the north.

The new objections raised against my proposal can be summed up as follows: We can not consolidate our base in the South, because a revolutionary democracy can be established solely by means of ruthless terror and the dictatorship of the proletariat. Therefore, it is impossible to remain in Hankow. The fundamental meaning of my proposal is that it is necessary for us to establish a firm base before advancing any further. Borodin says that this is a delusion, that this can not be accomplished in China, that only a dictatorship of the proletariat can lead to this goal, but a dictatorship of the proletariat is impossible to establish.

Presumably a speech given by M. N. Roy before the Party leadership.—Eds.

In my opinion the tasks of the revolution in the present crisis are as follows:

1. Expansion of the working-class and peasant movement.

2. Democratization, centralization, and consolidation of the state machinery.

3. Reform and the centralization of the army.

Arguments Against an Immediate Campaign Against the North

For the sake of avoiding any misunderstanding, I emphasize the word "immediate." I am not against a Northern Expedition in general, but I am against an immediate campaign. I take exception to the decision of the Kuomintang that in ten days the troops must move along the Peking-Hankow railroad to occupy Peking and Tientsin. Comrade T'an P'ing-shan is in favor of the Northern Expedition provided that some necessary preparations are made.

I, too, am in favor of the Northern Expedition. But it must be preceded by a certain amount of preparation.

The arguments of those Kuomintangists who stand for an immediate campaign against the North follow first of all from considerations of a military nature. They say that a rapid advance to the North would give us an opportunity to shatter the Fengtien forces and not only to occupy Peking and Tientsin, but at the same time to drive the Mukden forces back beyond the Great Wall. This is a very tempting proposal. According to Comrade Borodin, all the military experts support it unanimously. I will not harbor an appraisal of military strength, but will merely mention certain facts to demonstrate that one cannot always rely on the opinion of military experts.

Two weeks ago they were saying that in two or three months they would be able to occupy Shanghai without any difficulty. Yesterday, however, Comrade Borodin admitted that he has always been opposed to an eastward advance because it would have wiped out our troops. Thus, he himself testified that two weeks ago the military experts were wrong. But one cannot rely so readily on the opinion of experts who were absolutely wrong two weeks ago.

The policy is now being defined by the opinion of military experts in spite of the fact that two weeks ago, in proposing that [we] advance and occupy Nanking, these specialists lost sight of a completely elementary factor, namely, that the distance between Hankow and Nanking is four times as great as that between Shanghai and Nanking. Railroad transportation exists between Nanking and Shanghai, and Chiang Kai-shek could have turned up in Nanking four times sooner than the Wuhan forces. They forgot about this. These military experts are not familiar

with the a-b-c's of strategy, yet this does not prevent them from determining our policy. It should be said that Comrade Galen was opposed
to the plan of occupying Nanking. All the Chinese specialists, especially
Ch'ên Ch'êng, were for it. The plan for the Peking expedition was also
drawn up by generals. *An immediate campaign against the North is
fraught with grave danger.*

If we really want to smash the Northern forces, we must set about
this seriously. We will have to concentrate all our forces on the Peking-
Hankow railroad. This would mean that Wuhan will be left without
defenses. If we move toward the north, we will provide either Chiang
Kai-shek or the Northern forces with an opportunity to attack us from
the direction of Nanking. This danger becomes even more heightened as
a result of yesterday's events, that is, the second occupation of Pukow
by the Northerners and their threat to Nanking. This victory by the
Northern forces indicates, first, that the Northerners did not suffer as
serious a defeat as we had assumed and, second, that there probably
exists an agreement between Chiang Kai-shek and the Northern forces.

Thus, on the right flank we are threatened by quite a substantial combination of armed forces. Our rear is not defended, we have no base,
and yet we want to advance into a new region. Under such conditions,
the Northern Expedition represents nothing but a military adventure.

The plan for the Northern Expedition is built on the assumption that
Fêng Yü-hsiang and Yen Hsi-shan will join us. But even if they were to
join us, the danger will not be removed. When we reach Peking, the
alignment of forces will be unequal. Our forces will be in the minority,
whereas in the person of Yen Hsi-shan we will have another T'ang
Shêng-chih or even a Chiang Kai-shek. It is equally unknown what stand
Fêng Yü-hsiang will take. The same [situation] we were in in Nanchang
awaits us in Peking. The bourgeois and feudal elements in the national
army will clash with the revolutionary elements, and another split will
occur. The reactionary forces, headed by Yen [Hsi-shan], and, possibly,
by Fêng [Yü-hsiang] will occupy Peking, and we will be forced either
to surrender or retreat. We will have to abandon Peking; by that time,
Wuhan will probably be already under the control of the reaction and,
in the end, we will have nowhere to go.

An immediate campaign against the North means that we are leaving
a territory where we have at our disposal the powerful organizations of
the Kuomintang, the Communist Party and the workers' and peasants'
organizations, for an unknown land where we have no organized forces
apart from the armies of Fêng [Yü-hsiang] and Yen [Hsi-shan]. There
are no guarantees that these forces will always remain friendly toward
us. On the contrary, there are sufficient grounds to suppose that after a

certain amount of time has elapsed, a crisis will arise and these forces will take action against us, but we will have no sound base for a struggle against them.

The fundamental objection to an immediate campaign against the North (this argument was advanced yesterday by T'an P'ing-shan) is that this campaign would reinforce the position of the militarist elements and have harmful consequences for the basic forces of the revolution, that is, the workers and peasants. The balance of the forces of the revolution will be destroyed. Its base will not be the might of the organized masses, but the unreliable military forces in the hands of reactionary-feudal generals. Comrade Borodin admits that a direct result of the Northern Expedition will be the creation of a military combination out of heterogeneous elements; this, of course, is exactly what will happen, and the reactionary elements will have the dominant role.

The present crisis has caused the fundamental problems of the revolution to take precedence. An immediate campaign against the North means an evasion of these problems. This is a typically petty bourgeois policy. But the proletariat can not save itself by flight just because the problems of the revolution are difficult to solve. If we do not solve problems posed by the development of the movement, the future of the revolution will be in the greatest jeopardy.

As the revolution developed, the process of class differentiation unfolded. At a certain stage, the bourgeoisie turned against the revolution. The social base of the revolution came to consist of the proletariat, the peasantry, and the urban petty bourgeoisie. At the present stage, the revolutionary bloc of these classes must establish a democratic dictatorship.

Recent events have substantiated the correctness of this view. The hour has struck when the future of the Chinese revolution must be assured by the establishment of a democratic dictatorship of these classes. But instead of doing this, it is proposed that the Northern Expedition be continued; this means an escape from the fundamental problems of the revolution.

We are retreating, but where to? We are jumping from the frying pan into the fire. Right now we have to cope only with Chiang Kai-shek. But we are running from him to unknown territories where, in all probability, we will have to encounter many more like him.

An immediate drive against the North not only fails to resolve the problem of class destratification, but it denotes collaboration with the reactionary elements that are betraying the revolution on every step. If history teaches us anything at all, we may be certain that another Nanchang awaits us in Peking. Instead of aiming for many Nanchangs, we ought to create safeguards against future repetitions of Nanchang. Why did we have the Nanchang crisis? Because the democratic revolutionary forces were not sufficiently consolidated in the preceding Northern Expedition. When the clash with the bourgeoisie occurred, we could not suppress it. Before proceeding any further, it is necessary to have a guarantee that we will not find ourselves again so unprepared. We must mobilize the democratic revolutionary forces. Before proceeding any further, it is necessary to strengthen the base.

An immediate campaign against the North means that the petty bourgeoisie, under the pressure of certain military leaders, will turn to flight and abandon the masses. It is tantamount to a betrayal of the peasantry; of the proletariat in Shanghai, Canton, and Wuhan; [and] of these masses who had suffered, gained victories and sacrificed themselves, and who will lead the revolution to a victorious conclusion. Can the Communist Party, the political party of these masses, follow the petty bourgeoisie in this shameful desertion? It is not as serious a matter for the petty bourgeoisie. With the Don Quixotism peculiar to it, it will oscillate from one venture into another, and if a catastrophe occurs, it will go over to the side of the bourgeoisie. It has nothing to lose. The working class can not behave like this.

I will now turn to the second point I wanted to make, namely, my criticism of Borodin's plan and the perspectives of the Chinese revolution as outlined by Borodin.

I could elaborate on this in detail, and a detailed criticism, in my opinion, would be of great benefit to our young Chinese party. But I will bypass this now and merely touch on those points in Comrade Borodin's speech which dealt with our immediate tasks.

The only deduction which can be drawn from Borodin's speech adds up to the fact that he and those whose views he expresses consider that the Chinese revolution has broken down—that the leadership of the national movement has definitely been seized by the bourgeoisie. The revolutionary forces must therefore retreat somewhere to the hills, or to the Mongolian desert. If this is so, that is to say, if the comrades who have been responsible for leadership acknowledge that the revolution has been defeated under their leadership, it means that their policy was wrong and they have forfeited the right to lead the revolution.

Comrade Borodin and those whose opinions he expresses propose that the revolution withdraw from the provinces where there exists an organized proletariat with political experience, that it withdraw from the territories where the revolution has been partly achieved and go [to regions] where the reaction is stronger.

They propose that we leave the provinces where the revolution has a social base, where there are an organized proletariat, a revolutionary peasant movement, and powerful party organizations, and go into the backward provinces where the social base is very weak, where the counterrevolution is stronger and better organized.

I will note one contradiction in the theory and the plan of Comrade Borodin. There are, in fact, many such contradictions, but I shall touch upon only one of them. He says that if the Northern Expedition proves successful and the Mukdenites are smashed, then a widespread peasant movement will develop in Honan under the auspices of Fêng Yü-hsiang. Then, why doesn't he stay home and do this under the auspices of T'ang Shêng-chih? In declaring himself against the tactic of developing a powerful peasant movement in Hunan, he said: "If we attempt to carry out an agrarian revolution in Hunan, we will be forced immediately into a conflict with very imposing forces." But if such is the case in Hunan, then what grounds are there to believe that it would be any different in Honan or in Shangtung? If T'ang Shêng-chih—and, in the opinion of Borodin, he is a "100 per cent revolutionary"—is against an agrarian revolution, then how can one expect that Fêng—another one like to him—will be for it? This is a contradiction and an illusion.

The petty-bourgeois Left, onto whose wagon Comrade Borodin wants to harness the Communist Party, has neither the daring, nor, simply, the desire to start an agrarian revolution. This is a fact which must be recognized. The Northern Expedition will merely provide these elements [the petty bourgeoisie] with a pretext to postpone the solution of the agrarian question.

The Chinese revolution will either win as an agrarian revolution or it will not win at all. The bourgeoisie is against the revolution; the petty bourgeoisie does not have the daring for it; it must be accomplished by the proletariat. If the proletariat does not accomplish it, the national revolution will not succeed. The petty bourgeoisie is betraying the national revolution. If the Communist Party supports the plan for an immediate campaign against the North, it will aid the petty bourgeoisie in betraying the revolution. The Communist Party is faced with the following question: should the proletariat drag behind [plestis' v khvoste] the essentially counterrevolutionary policy of the petty bourgeoisie or should it take over the hegemony in the national revolution?

I will now turn to Comrade Borodin's objection to the consolidation of the revolutionary-democratic forces in the Southeast. This objection is dictated by an underestimation of the proletariat and a disdainful attitude toward the strength of the masses. Comrade Borodin thinks that the principal factor in the revolution is not the masses, but our ability to maneuver with the petty bourgeoisie, and not only with the petty bourgeoisie but also with various military elements. Yesterday he told us that a result of a military advance would be "a bouquet of military forces. China will become a land without a master, and we will have the opportunity to maneuver between these forces." To Comrade Borodin the Canton proletariat is "dust," whereas the Shanghai proletariat is "a cotton-fibred [*khlopchato-bumazhnyi*] proletariat." *

The revolution must not be "tied down to them." Borodin does not mention the Wuhan proletariat whose revolutionary action brought the Left Wing elements to power. He does not want the Wuhan peasantry to go too far, because this might not please T'ang Shêng-chih. If one is so disdainful of the social forces, the revolution will lose its ground and cease to exist.

Comrade Borodin's theory holds that the consolidation of democratic power in the southeastern provinces can be achieved only on the basis of a dictatorship of the proletariat and ruthless terror. Unfortunately, he furnished no evidence for this theory, he offered no arguments to back it up. According to this theory, there is no intermediate stage between the feudal-bourgeois reaction and the dictatorship of the proletariat. This contradicts the perspective given in the theses of the Communist International. I do not wish to say that the Chinese revolution, or any revolution in general, can be made to fit theses that are written on paper, albeit these theses are good and even wise. I consider that if what Borodin says is correct, then the Comintern has an erroneous conception of the Chinese revolution and, consequently, an erroneous conception of the world revolution.

The fundamental task of the Chinese revolution at the present moment is the consolidation of the social and territorial base of the revolution. The bourgeoisie has turned against the revolution. The Left Wing bourgeoisie is disoriented and has no definite perspective. What is most essential now is the organization, concentration, and consolidation of the revolutionary democratic forces. Without this, there is no guarantee for the success of the revolution. And yet, this can be done. The democratic forces can be united under the leadership of the proletariat. It is a very auspicious moment for this. The petty-bourgeois Left Wing power can not exist another day without the support of the working class. That is why the present moment is extremely auspicious for the proletariat actually to realize its hegemony in the struggle. The hegemony of the proletariat can become a reality. Under the hegemony of the proletariat, the revolution can develop further. What constitutes the hegemony of the proletariat in the struggle? What is the difference be-

---

* Probably a reference to the numerous prolitarians employed in the cotton industry in Shanghai.—Eds.

tween leadership of the revolution and achievement of hegemony in the struggle? The time has not yet come when the proletariat can assume the supreme leadership of the revolution; but because of its dominant position, it can determine the future development of the revolution. Instead of this, the comrades are proposing that the working class and the Communist Party simply capitulate before the panic-stricken petty bourgeoisie. An immediate campaign against the North is incompatible with the interests of workers, peasants and the urban petty bourgeoisie —it is hostile to their interests, even if the petty bourgeoisie itself does not realize it. That is why the Communist Party, as the vanguard of the most revolutionary class, must stand up against the Northern Expedition. If the Communist Party stands up against it, the Left Wing elements will not dare to insist on this policy because the Left Wing power cannot exist without the working class. We must establish a democratic dictatorship, but in order to do so, we must first expand the forces of democracy. The revolution is confronted with three tasks. These can be accomplished by consolidating our power in the central and southeastern provinces, but not by an immediate campaign against the North.

These tasks are:

1. Mobilization of the democratic forces through an agrarian revolution, and realization of the minimum demands of the proletariat;

2. Seizure of political power in the village by the peasantry;

3. Reorganization and centralization of the revolutionary army, in other words, the creation of a revolutionary army.

The opportunity for this exists. Two of the most important ministries are in the hands of Communists and can be used for realizing these tasks. If we use our power in these two ministries properly and with sufficient energy, in a few months our position will not only become secure, but we will become almost invincible. Then we will be ready to go ahead— to develop the revolution territorially.

Here, in rough outline, is a plan for consolidating our forces:

1. The necessity of defending Wuhan. Concentration of forces on the northern border of Hupeh. The troops of Fêng Yü-hsiang and Yen Hsi-shan can gradually advance to the Peking-Hankow railroad to threaten the flank of the Northern troops in the event that the latter attempt to drive on Wuhan.

2. An agrarian revolution in Hupeh and Hunan which are completely under the authority of the Wuhan government. The results of an agrarian revolution in Hunan and Hupeh will affect the northern provinces and the way to them will be open.

3. Political penetration into Kiangsi and Kwangtung, reinforced by necessary military actions. The results of the agrarian revolution in Hunan

and Hupeh will have an immediate effect on the neighboring provinces.

4. Subjection of Kiangsi, Fukien, Kwangtung, and Kwangsi to the Wuhan government. Extension of Wuhan's influence to the southwestern provinces.

5. Highly energetic work on organizing, propaganda and agitation in Shanghai and in the entire Chekiang province.

6. Maximum use of the power of the Ministries of Labor, Agriculture, and Internal Affairs. The arming of peasants and workers.

7. Improvement of relations with Fêng Yü-hsiang and Yen Hsi-shan.

As soon as these conditions are fulfilled, the campaign against the North must be launched in order to seize Peking and lay seige to Shanghai by creating an economic blockade and cutting it off from the hinterland.

I am not against the Northern Expedition, but I consider that it must pass through definite stages. During the first stage of the revolution, Kwangtung served as the base. Now we find ourselves at the second stage. Before passing on to the third, it is necessary to develop, strengthen, and concentrate the revolutionary forces on a much larger scale.

The Northern warlords represent a constant threat to the revolution. The destruction of Chang Tso-lin is essential for the consummation of the revolution. But there is yet another enemy, one that is much closer and no less dangerous. An immediate campaign against the North under the pretext of fighting Chang Tso-lin would disarm the revolution in the face of this danger. One should not lose sight of the possibility of the creation of a counterrevolutionary feudal-bourgeois bloc aided and abetted by imperialism. The nucleus of this bloc is the Nanking government and in its person the revolution will have a much stronger and more dangerous enemy than Chang Tso-lin. It is perfectly obvious that the present policy of imperialism consists of promoting the establishment of a feudal-bourgeois bloc which would create a so-called "anti-Red front" under the guise of nationalism. This is precisely what constitutes the greatest and the most immediate danger to the revolution.

The threat of danger is from this direction, and not from any military grouping in the south, north or west. The danger is political and not geographical in nature, and it may arise anywhere in the country. Attempts are being made to create an alliance of all reactionary forces, including the bourgeoisie, and this danger is a threat to our base. By our base I mean not only Wuhan, but all the territories under the control of the Kuomintang, all the territories in which the revolution has been partially achieved. And this danger exists in the entire territory. An attack on our base is not a thing of the future. It is already underway. It has already commenced in Chekiang, Fukien, and Kiangsi. These provinces are already outside the control of the national government. Li Chi-shen is transforming Canton into a center of the counterrevolution. We have just received reports that Chiang Kai-shek has sent his agents to Szechuan. The attack has begun. The reaction is surrounding us. And when our house is being attacked, when the forces of reaction are threatening our base, instead of defending our base we are going to the North to find a new base for the revolution.

What are we looking for in the North? Again the military support of Fêng Yü-hsiang and Yen Hsi-shan? The reliability of these allies is not particularly great. This is common knowledge. We must make a choice. On the one hand, we have the worker-peasant masses as a social base, and on the other hand a few thousand bayonets which may at any moment be turned against us, against the revolution.

It has been repeatedly pointed out that the military factor plays a highly important role in the Chinese revolution. I do not underestimate the military factor, but I am afraid that the Chinese revolution is in danger of becoming militarized. Not only in the Kuomintang, but in the Communist Party as well, priority is given to the policy of maneuvering between military forces and not to mobilizing the masses which represent the genuine revolutionary-democratic force. The Communist Party must be oriented toward the working class, and only when it finds itself on this sound base will it be able to make use of and maneuver between the military forces. But instead of this, the prevailing tendency is to attribute the highest importance to maneuvering with generals.

Comrade Ch'ên Tu-hsiu said that the revolution can not die in Wuhan. But no one is demanding that the revolution commit suicide. When I say that the base must be defended, I have in mind not only Wuhan or Hupeh, but all the southeastern provinces. This precisely is what I consider to be the base. And if in the course of the next six months or a year we consolidate our positions creating a real Left power, developing the democratic forces, building a state machinery and a real revolutionary army—then not only will the revolution not die, but it will have a most intensive life and will be in a much better position than it would have been as a result of an immediate Northern Expedition.

Even if we assume that the campaign against the North will be successful, that it will be possible to drive Chang Tso-lin's forces back into Manchuria and to occupy Peking, Tientsin, and so on, even then, the situation will not be definitely favorable to us. A number of difficulties will arise before us. The complications we experienced as a result of the first stage of the Northern Expedition will repeat themselves. The generals with the help of whom we must reach Peking will in all probability turn into new Chiang Kai-sheks. For Chiang Kai-shek is not an individual person. He is a representative of definite reactionary, social forces which supported the revolution up to a certain point and then turned against it. The revolution must organize its basic forces in order to safeguard itself against these unreliable allies. During the first Northern Expedition, the democratic social forces were neither sufficiently powerful nor sufficiently well organized to make their influence prevail. The bourgeois elements in the national movement were attempting to seize supreme power. It is true that they did not completely succeed in their aim, but still they did split the Kuomintang. If the revolutionary-democratic forces were sufficiently well organized, Chiang Kai-shek's *coup* could have been crushed. But before the first Northern Expedition, it was impossible to create a better and stronger organization of revolutionary forces. This work only started from Kwangtung and the forces developed rapidly in the very process of the Northern Expedition. Now the revolution has a much broader base on which the democratic forces can be organized to create a guarantee against reactionary groupings against the revolution.

If we go to Peking immediately, the democratic forces will prove to be even less organized and weaker than during the Nanchang crisis. In Peking, Fêng and Yen will wrest the power from our hands and we will be left with no support. If we find ourselves in such a crisis in the north, there is absolutely no guarantee that the base of the revolution would still remain in our hands. To think that we will be able simultaneously to move *to the north and to consolidate our base in the south* is sheer illusion. To consolidate the base means to fight against the forces of reaction, against the counterrevolution which is being organized in the rear of the revolution. In order to carry this out, it is necessary to concentrate on resolving the basic problems of our forces. We need military strength for the defense and consolidation of the base. An immediate campaign against the North will result in our being cut off from our base and our encountering new enemies.

Today, however, Comrade Borodin drew an entirely different picture for us which changes the situation considerably. Today he no longer wants to move on Peking, Kalgan, the Chinese Wall. Today he says that the plan consists merely of occupying the Lunghai railway. I am prepared to agree to such a plan. An advance no further than Lunghai is a purely defensive measure. It enters into the plan for defending our base. This is already not so much of a Don Quixotic adventure as the plan for expanding the revolution to Tibet and for transferring its base to Mongolia. If the Northern Expedition consists of this, then I agree to it. This is simply a defensive measure, and not an offensive. I am not compromising at this point, for in my speech yesterday I proposed that troops should be sent for the time being to the border of Honan, and that an agreement should also be reached with Fêng to enable his gradual advance toward the Lunghai railway. When I objected yesterday to Comrade Borodin's plan, I said that it was necessary for us to advance to the Lunghai railway in the interest of defense. I am opposed to an immediate campaign against the North, but I do not deny the necessity of defending ourselves against the North.

I will now turn to the basic question. Whether to advance to Peking or to Lunghai is only the practical aspect of the basic problem of the revolution. This morning Comrade Ch'ên Tu-hsiu said that the immediate task of the revolution consists not of intensifying it but of expanding it. This constitutes the real difference in our views: whether to intensify or to expand the revolution. The theory is advanced that in those provinces where the revolution has occurred in part it is impossible to consolidate the power of the Left: we will not be able to exist if the revolution is not expanded.

The bourgeoisie has turned against us. The petty bourgeoisie is vacillating; it is looking for ways to evade the basic questions posed by the development of the revolution. *We must develop the forces of workers and peasants—this is the only measure that will assure the future of the revolution.* To attack the North immediately means to run from this necessity. The petty-bourgeois government is being confronted with the necessity of pursuing a really revolutionary policy, of achieving an agrarian revolution. It is evading this task under the pretext of the necessity of launching an immediate campaign against the North. By declaring themselves in favor of an immediate Northern Expedition, Comrades Borodin, Ch'ên Tu-hsiu, and others register their approval of the actions of the petty bourgeoisie who are evading the necessity of pursuing a revolutionary policy. This is not the way a revolution is developed. Not only is this opportunism, but it can also be interpreted as a betrayal of the working class and the peasantry. Thanks to this theory, we have already suffered defeat in Shanghai. Thanks to this theory, we have refused to intensify the revolution. It is true that a campaign against the North would give rise to a peasant movement there, that the first stage of a mass movement would begin there. But, after all, the peasant movement in Kwangtung, Hunan, and Hupeh has already passed through the first stage—the stage of expansion, and is now ready to enter the second stage, the stage of intensification. It cannot be held back mechanically on the first stage. It must either develop in the process of intensification, or it will begin to rot and deteriorate. The objective situation favors the peasantry assuming the offensive against the reaction in order to annihilate it. If the peasants do not assume the offensive, they themselves will be subjected to attack, as was the case in Kwangtung and Kiangsi, and as will be the case in Hunan if T'ang Shêng-chih becomes the master of the situation there; the same will happen if the national-revolutionary troops are sent to the North.

If we carry the banner of peasant revolt to Chihli or Shantung, we will lose the positions won in the southern provinces. In addition, the objective situation in the northern provinces—in Chihli and Shantung—is no less favorable to the rapid development of the peasant movement than it is in the South. There are more well-to-do peasants in the North, whereas in the South it is the poor peasants that make up the majority. The well-to-do peasants will not join the revolution as quickly and unreservedly as will the poor [peasants]. In southern provinces the social base is better for the revolution than in the northern provinces.

Today Comrade Borodin elucidated his theory [which holds] that only by means of the dictatorship of the proletariat and ruthless terror can a genuine Left [Wing] democratic power be established in the southern provinces.

The peasant movement in Hunan, Hupeh, and Kwangtung is ready to enter the second stage. The development of the movement posed the question of a radical solution to the agrarian question. Comrade Borodin points out that in order to consolidate the base of the revolution in the South it is necessary to support the peasantry in its demand for radical agrarian reform; from this it follows that the Communists must turn against the national government, and this will inevitably lead to an armed uprising which will prove very dangerous. Follow his argument in reverse order: an armed uprising is dangerous; but opposition to the government leads to an armed uprising, and the Communists must stand in opposition to the government. Shouldn't one, therefore, refuse to support the peasant movement? What conclusion can we draw? The conclusion is that the Communists must not support the peasantry in its demand for a revolutionary solution to the land question. This is the advice that Comrades Borodin and Ch'ên Tu-hsiu give us.

Such advice is very dangerous in the present situation and the Communist Party must reject it if it wants to play a historic role, if it wants to lead the Chinese revolution.

The struggle against imperialism and militarism will not expand as a result of our evading the necessity of intensifying the revolution. On the contrary, this struggle can be developed only if we are prepared to meet this necessity, if we assume the offensive on the basis of reaction in our own house before giving battle to the external foe. It would be stupid to overextend ourselves when our base is insecure and open to enemy attack (this attack has already begun). The only guarantee of the future of the revolution is to provide it with a revolutionary democratic base, and in China the core of the revolutionary democracy is the peasantry.

Not to want an agrarian revolution, to consider it premature in China denotes a lack of understanding of the Chinese revolution . . . an absence of a correct perspective. Those who favor an immediate campaign against the North do not want to carry out the program of agrarian revolution. Therefore, I pointed out this morning that Comrade Ch'ên Tu-hsiu's viewpoint contradicts the theses of the Communist International, and I reiterate this.

Mobilization of the revolutionary-democratic forces—the proletariat, the peasantry, and the urban petty bourgeoisie—and the establishment of a democratic dictatorship are the only guarantee of the victory of the Chinese revolution. The time has come when the Communist Party is able to undertake these steps. The Left [Wing] power in Wuhan will not last a single day without the support of the Communist Party, that is, without the inspired and conscious support of the laboring masses. The time has come when the Communist Party must participate in revolutionary power and not lag behind [*plestis' v khvoste*] the Kuomintang. The Communist Party must understand this. *An immediate advance to the North will prove detrimental to the development of the revolution.* If the Communist Party announces its opposition to an immediate campaign against the North, and if it clearly explains its point of view, the petty-bourgeois Left will not dare to attempt this adventure. The Communist Party will not let it deviate from the fulfillment of the most urgent tasks of the revolution.

In this way, the proletariat will achieve hegemony in the national struggle. Although the leadership of the revolution is still in the hands of a coalition of classes, the proletariat, as the most revolutionary and best organized class, will determine the policy of the revolution.

I shall summarize my objections to an immediate campaign against the North. They add up to the following:

1. In the military respect, the expedition might end in victory as well as in defeat, and there is no guarantee that it will emerge victorious.

2. Even if it is successful in the military respect, a series of problems will arise as a result of a military victory; there is every ground to believe that it would strengthen the military forces and weaken the democratic masses.

3. An advance to the north, which requires the concentration of all

the military forces available to the national government, would expose the southern base of the revolution to attacks by the reaction. The reactionary forces will consolidate and overthrow the democratic forces which have only partial power there.

4. At a time when the bourgeoisie has definitely turned against the revolution, the only guarantee [that remains] is the development and consolidation of democratic forces—the proletariat, the peasantry, and the urban petty bourgeoisie. This task cannot be realized simultaneously with a serious campaign against the North. An immediate expedition will serve as a pretext for preventing the development of the democratic forces; hence, it will be damaging to the revolution.

Concretely, I propose the following:

1. To distribute the military forces in the north, east, and west in such manner as to ensure the defense of the second line of the revolution— the Yangtze Valley. The elaboration of this plan should be assigned to military experts. To recapitulate: dispatch of forces to the Honan front; collaboration with Fêng who will gradually advance to the Lunghai railway; the advance of the Second and Sixth armies to the western section of Anhwei.

2. To restore the power of the national government in the provinces of Kiangsi, Kwangtung, and Kwangsi.

3. The return to power in Kwangtung does not require a southern expedition. This can be achieved by local forces; by a revolt of troops which have remained loyal to the national government, and by the action of workers and peasants.

4. When Kwangtung is conquered, it will not be difficult to conquer Kiangsi.

Here I would like to say a few words about financial difficulties. Some may have formed the impression that I am an utopian who draws up glorious plans, but loses sight of the practical problems of the movement.

A radical solution of the agrarian problem would not worsen the financial crisis—on the contrary, it would aid considerably in resolving it. The large, confiscated estates and temple lands can serve as security in the issuance of bank notes. The example of the German *rent* [*rentnyi*] bank will help us in resolving the financial difficulties of the revolutionary government of China. In Germany the rate of exchange of the mark was restored on the basis of guaranteeing the new emission by large estates. There the landowners gave assistance to the state on the condition that it submit to their influence. In China, the revolutionary state can find a way out of its financial difficulties by doing away with feudal reaction. In taking a stand for the agrarian revolution, we are not declaring war on the petty bourgeoisie, we are not intensifying the conflict with it, we are not establishing a dictatorship of the proletariat. On the contrary, we are consolidating the power of the Left, we are creating a base for a genuine revolutionary power.

April 13–15, 1927

NOTE: For concrete proposals, see Appendix II. [M.N.R. Page 186 in this book. —Eds.]

6

RESOLUTION ON THE CONTINUATION

OF THE NORTHERN CAMPAIGN

Adopted by the Central Committee of the
Chinese Communist Party in Hankow, April 16, 1927

In order to expand and intensify the Chinese revolution, it is necessary to deliver a decisive blow to the Fengtien forces. This must be achieved, since the complete annihilation of the Fengtien forces will signify a mortal blow to imperialism.

At the same time, all the forces of the revolution must be mobilized for defeating Chiang Kai-shek and the bourgeoisie which is attempting to split the revolutionary movement. In order to be able to conduct a successful struggle against imperialism, against native militarism which is a tool of imperialism, and against the counterrevolutionary bourgeoisie, the national government must possess a solid base.

Under existing conditions, an immediate military advance to the north with the aim of capturing Peking, Tientsin, and so forth is not only undesirable, but will be harmful to the revolution. Military operations aimed at territorial expansion to the north must be preceded by a consolidation of the base of the revolution in those regions which are already under the control of the Kuomintang or in which the revolution has already been partially accomplished. Nonetheless, it is necessary properly to defend the seat of the national government. Without such defense, the cause of consolidating the base of the revolution can not be continued successfully. The following measures must be carried out for defense purposes: (1) the immediate occupation by national forces of the territory extending right up to the southern border of Honan; (2) the establishment of close and efficient collaboration with Fêng so that his troops could gradually make their way forward to the Lunghai railway; and (3) the Second and Sixth armies which have withdrawn from Pukow must advance to the north occupying the western sector of Anhwei. These defensive military actions will ultimately lead to the occupation of the Lunghai railway which will become the first line of defense of the revolution. The second line will be the Yangtze behind which the main forces of the revolution will be developed to consolidate the base of the revolution.

Before advancing beyond the Lunghai railway, the consolidation of the base will be carried out in accordance with the suggestions made in Comrade Roy's speech. The theory according to which the revolution's forces in the southern and southwestern provinces can obtain no further development pending the immediate capture of new territories by the national government is incorrect.

It is assumed that the opinion of the Communist Party will be taken into consideration before the Kuomintang and the national government decide in favor of an advance to the north.

NOTE: Two days later, the Central Committee of the Communist Party retracted this resolution and supported the Kuomintang's decision on the immediate dispatch of troops to the north. [M.N.R.]

7

DECLARATION OF THE
CHINESE COMMUNIST PARTY

The Chinese Communist Party wholeheartedly welcomes the decision of the Central Executive Committee of the Kuomintang to remove Chiang Kai-shek from command of national-revolutionary armies, to expel him from the party, and to issue an order for his arrest.

Chiang Kai-shek has become an open enemy of the national revolution and an ally of reaction. He has become an instrument of imperialism. Hence, he can not be tolerated in the ranks of the people's revolutionary party, and he can not be entrusted with the command of the national-revolutionary army. As a traitor to the revolution, he deserves the highest punishment at the hands of the national government against which he revolted and which he is now attempting to overthrow. *The working class will give every possible help to the Kuomintang and the national government in weeding out all the reactionary elements and crushing the enemies of the national revolution.*

The conflict within the Kuomintang which led to this harsh but absolutely necessary action against Chiang Kai-shek has a deep social meaning. The revolt against the party's authority and against the revolution was not accomplished by an individual person. Chiang Kai-shek and his clique are representatives of a social stratum that exists both within and without the Kuomintang. From the moment the Kuomintang was reorganized, it became the revolutionary party of the oppressed and exploited masses. Nevertheless, bourgois elements and even elements of feudal reaction continued to remain within the party. They continually tried to divert the Kuomintang from the path of revolutionary democracy. An internal struggle was going on around the decision of the vital question: *should the Kuomintang become a class party or a people's party, and should its program and policy be defined by the interests of the upper classes (the large-scale bourgeoisie and the feudal lords) or by the interests of the oppressed and exploited majority of the people.*

This struggle is the social background against which the crisis in the Kuomintang intensified in connection with the rapid development of the revolution resulting from the Northern Expedition.

The bourgeoisie and the feudal elements within the Kuomintang overthrew the revolutionary-democratic power in Canton by the *coup* of March 20. For this purpose, they even resorted to such vile methods as individual murders (the murder of Liao Chung-k'ai). They seized power with the intention of directing the revolution according to the interests of their class. In order to ensure their own power, they began to destroy the mass organizations which supported the revolutionary wing of the Kuomintang (the attack on the workers' and peasants' movement, the dissolution of the Canton town committee, and so on).

While the masses supported the Northern Expedition as a way of developing the revolution and made big sacrifices for its sake, the bourgeois and feudal elements in the Kuomintang saw the expedition as a way of expanding their own power. But the enormous forces of the revolution raised by the victorious march of the national armies caused alarm in the reactionary-bourgeois and feudal wing of the Kuomintang. The masses defied the feudal-bourgeois leadership and supported the revolutionary wing of the Kuomintang, overthrown on March 20. The power struggle between the feudal-bourgeois Right Wing and the revolutionary-democratic wing of the Kuomintang became greatly heightened.

The Northern Expedition served to expand the power of the national government to a considerable extent. When the national forces reached the Yangtze Valley, they threatened the main citadels of imperialism. It was perfectly clear that imperialism would not yield a single position of importance without an open armed struggle. While negotiating with the national government on the question of concessions, imperialism was preparing simultaneously for intervention. In order to repel the combined forces of imperialism and its instrument, native militarism, the national government must rely on full and class-conscious support from the masses whose power of self-sacrifice is the only defense of the revolution. In other words, *national China must create a revolutionary-democratic power.* This means that the national revolution must first of all be an agrarian revolution. The peasants make up 80 percent of the Chinese population; hence, a revolutionary-democratic power can be established only by means of an agrarian revolution. The French peasantry supported Napoleon for twenty years because of the agrarian reforms of the great revolution. In those provinces of China through which the national army had marched, the peasant movement spread like forest fire. If the arrival of the national army and the national government means the removal of those servile and destitute conditions under which the peasantry has existed and labored for centuries, the victory of the national revolution will be assured, and the national army will be invincible. The French peasantry helped Napoleon to conquer feudal Europe. The Chinese peasantry will support the national government and the national army for the cause of liberating China from imperialism and militarism.

But an agrarian revolution, inseparable from the national revolution, runs counter to the interests of feudal elements and, under the present conditions of China, even to those of the bourgeoisie. Agriculture is the main branch of production while the peasantry is the chief producing class and is, therefore, the object of all forms of exploitation—feudal, imperialist, and capitalist. Thus, as soon as it became clear that it was impossible to develop the national revolution further without [having] an agrarian revolution, and as soon as the revolutionary wing of the Kuomintang recognized the necessity [of this agrarian revolution], the feudal-bourgeois elements in the Kuomintang felt that their position had become unstable. They attempted to steer the revolution in another direction which would have led inevitably to a compromise with reaction and a surrender to imperialism. They were ready sooner to prostitute party principles, to defame the memory of Dr. Sun Yat-sen, to sell out the whole nation, than to harm their class interests. Chiang Kai-shek came to represent these reactionary aspirations of the feudal-bourgeois elements in the Kuomintang. Ever since March 20 he has been the standard bearer of these elements. When he failed to convert the Kuomintang as a whole into an instrument of feudal-bourgeois reaction, he declared war against it. If the national movement does not pursue a policy desirable to the bourgeoisie which is bound up with imperialism, then the bourgeoisie does not hesitate to split the movement, to turn against it and to join forces with militarism and imperialism in order to destroy it. And Chiang Kai-shek, as a representative of the feudal-bourgeois elements within the Kuomintang and outside of it, resolved to do all this.

The Kuomintang's decision to remove Chiang Kai-shek from his post, to expel him from the party, and to issue an order for his arrest means a declaration by the Kuomintang that the feudal-bourgeois elements have turned against the revolution and must therefore be regarded as enemies whose defeat is necessary for the final and complete victory of the national revolution. This decision ushers in a new stage in class differentiation which develops as the revolution progresses. The Communist Party endorses this decision, because not only must the proletariat consolidate the revolutionary-democratic power, but it must also serve as its leverage.

When Chiang Kai-shek declared war on the Kuomintang in the name of the practical interests of the bourgeoisie, his actions were directed first of all against the working class. The violent hatred of the counter-revolutionary bourgeoisie descended on the workers and peasants of Kiangsi, Chekiang, and Shanghai. The Communist Party became the target of its hatred. Chiang Kai-shek understands that one can not discard the Left Wing power and establish a bourgeois monopoly of the national movement if the organized forces of the working class are not destroyed. On its part, the proletariat understands that Chiang Kai-shek is merely a henchman executing the will of the counterrevolutionary feudal bourgeoisie. To destroy Ching Kai-shekism, it is necessary to crush the feudal-bourgeois elements within and without the Kuomintang. As long as the counterrevolutionary social forces are not destroyed, the overthrow of Chiang Kai-shek alone, who is a representative of these forces, will merely vacate the place for other, similarly traitorous, cruel, and bloodthirsty Chiang Kai-sheks.

The feudal-bourgeois elements who just recently gave grudging support to the national revolution have now deserted to the camp of the counterrevolution. The neomilitarism of Chiang Kai-shek became an auxiliary weapon in imperialism's attack on the Chinese people. The feudal-bourgeois elements failed to seize the leadership of the national movement; hence, they are trying to split the Kuomintang and to form a party and a government which, under the false banner of nationalism, would betray the people, would unite with reactionary militarism, and compromise with imperialism. Chiang Kai-shek's expulsion from the Kuomintang does not remove the danger. He will attempt, as before, to create a parallel "national government." In spite of the decision of the Kuomintang, a considerable number of military forces remain under his control. He wants to deceive the national-democratic elements by a propaganda of lies about Wuhan, namely, that the Kuomintang has become an instrument of the Communist Party. By this cunning lie, he is attempting to cover up for the fact that he and the class he represents have become instruments of imperialism.

Even after his expulsion from the party, the roots of Chiang Kai-shekism can be found everywhere in national territory. It is a question of the reactionary social strata, the landlords, the gentry, and so on. Chiang Kai-shekism weakens as the national revolution destroys these forces by a radical agrarian reform. For tactical considerations, the class struggle had to develop gradually as long as the feudal-bourgeois elements supported the national revolution. But now, when they have openly declared a class war, no tactical considerations can delay any more an attack on the reactionary classes. This will be the most effective and, moreover, the only method of overthrowing the neomilitarism of Chiang Kai-shek; it will nullify his attempts to form a parallel "national government" and will create a solid revolutionary-democratic front for the repulsion of and victory over the combined forces of imperialism, militarism and the feudal bourgeoisie, and for their destruction.

DOWN WITH CHIANG KAI-SHEK, REPRESENTATIVE OF THE FEUDAL BOURGEOIS REACTION AND INSTRUMENT OF IMPERIALISM!
DOWN WITH MILITARY DICTATORSHIP!
LONG LIVE THE ALLIANCE OF THE REVOLUTIONARY DEMOCRACY!
LONG LIVE THE DEMOCRATIC DICTATORSHIP OF THE PROLETARIAT, THE PEASANTRY AND THE MIDDLE CLASSES!

The Central Committee of the Chinese Communist Party
Hankow, April 20, 1927

8

CHIANG KAI-SHEK—TRAITOR TO THE PEOPLE

AND INSTRUMENT OF IMPERIALISM

*Declaration of the Delegation
of the Communist International*

The fast tempo of the development of the Chinese revolution has intensified the struggle against imperialism. [The attempt] to arrest the victorious march of the revolution by indirect pressure through native militarism did not succeed, *and international imperialism decided upon open military intervention.* Not only is Shanghai virtually occupied by imperialist powers; other important points inside the country and, especially, Wuhan—the seat of the national government—are under the threat of an imposing line of warships. This is a grand-scale "demonstration."

Arguing with weapons, the imperialist bandits present the Chinese people with a demand for surrender. Identical notes from England, America, France, Italy, and Japan lay down impossible conditions to the national government. If these conditions are fulfilled, the national government would have to declare foreign imperialism, and not the Chinese people, to be the master of China. Nevertheless, the national government gave a very reasonable—perhaps overly conceding—reply to the brazen ultimatum of the powers. But this does not temper the wrath of imperialism which prefers to demonstrate the use of brute force rather than turn to the League of Nations, as the national government suggests. The League of Nations is a smoke screen for the predatory policy of imperialism. But in China the rapacity of imperialism is so frank that there is no need for such a smoke screen.

The Chinese people must meet this imperialist attack with a united revolutionary front. Never in the history of the national movement has it been so essential to have unity of purpose and leadership of revolutionary forces as at the present time. Nevertheless, it was at this very time that the feudal-bourgeois elements in the Kuomintang, headed by Chiang Kai-shek, destroyed the unity of national forces. Thus Chiang Kai-shek and all those whose interests he represents have become a counterrevolutionary instrument of imperialism. It was precisely Chiang Kai-shek's revolt against the central national power and his efforts to split the Kuomintang that allowed imperialism to adopt such an aggressive position.

The counterrevolutionary activities of Chiang Kai-shek culminated in the creation of a parallel "national government" in Nanking. This action of his is even more unpardonable than his numerous acts of violence that preceded it, namely: the *coup* of March 20, the actions against the revolutionary wing of the Kuomintang, the suppression of the workers' and peasants' movement in Kiangsi and Chekiang, the attempt to establish his own dictatorship and, finally, the executions of Shanghai workers. We followed with great anxiety all these violent actions by Chiang Kai-shek and his agents, and we hoped that he would not bring himself to become an open traitor of the national movement. In this critical period of the national revolution, the maintenance of a united front is so essential that the crimes of those who fight against imperialism can be left temporarily unpunished. But the egoistical interests of the feudal-bourgeois class are hostile not only to the interests of workers and peasants, but also to the entire people. The crimes of Chiang Kai-shek, therefore, were not confined to murders of workers in Kiangsi and Shanghai. They culminated in a revolt against the people's party and the people's government. Chiang Kai-shek is trying to deceive the people when he proclaims his loyalty to the Kuomintang and places the responsibility for the split on the Central Committee of the Party. We testify that this is an outrageous lie. When the conflict between him and the Central Committee became acute, Chiang Kai-shek approached the Communist International with the request that it send a delegation to him in China. On the eve of our departure to him we received the news that he had called a meeting in Nanking of several members of the Central Committee and the [Central] Control Commission to accuse the united conference in Wuhan of splitting the party. We advised him immediately by telegraph to break off the conference and to fulfill the conditions of the agreement he had concluded with Comrade Wang Ching-wei in Shanghai on referring all questions at issue to the plenum of the Central Committee, with his participation. In the same telegram we informed him that if he accepts our advice we will meet with him to discuss ways and means of preserving the unity of revolutionary forces in the face of an attack by the imperialists. He did not respond to our telegram and pursued further his plan for destroying the party.

In declaring Chiang Kai-shek to be an instrument of imperialism, a murderer of workers and peasants, and a traitor to the people, we assert at the same time, before the broad public, that the defection of Chiang Kai-shek is not merely a revolt of one or more individual persons: an entire class has deserted and has turned against the national revolution. It is necessary to overthrow not only Chiang Kai-shek and the Kwangsi generals—the murderers who surround him and who have usurped the power. *The feudal-bourgeois elements must be annihilated* in the whole country. The roots of Chiang Kai-shekism must be destroyed. One must not only move on Nanking and Shanghai in order to fight Chiang Kai-shek. One can fight his power in any village, in any town, by destroying the power of feudalism and the reactionary bourgeoisie. Destruction of the roots of Chiang Kai-shekism—this is what will be the principal feature of the next stage of the national revolution.

The consolidation of the alliance of the revolutionary-democratic forces in territories under the control of the Kuomintang will compensate for the losses inflicted on the national-revolutionary movement by the betrayal and the revolt of the bourgeois-feudal elements. Encouraged by the betrayal of the feudal-bourgeois class and by the counterrevolutionary activity of the neomilitarism of Chiang Kai-shek, the imperialists are trying to threaten the national government. *But supported by the combined forces of the town and village democracy, that is, the proletariat, the peasantry and the petty bourgeoisie, the national government will be in a position to rebuff the attack by imperialism and to develop the national revolution in a direction which will lead to the consolidation of its base in the popular masses.* Then the national revolution will be rid of the dangers of betrayal by reactionary elements, and its victory will be assured.

DOWN WITH CHIANG KAI-SHEKISM!
DOWN WITH THE COUNTERREVOLUTIONARY FEUDAL BOURGEOISIE!
DOWN WITH IMPERIALISM!
LONG LIVE THE NATIONAL GOVERNMENT!
LONG LIVE THE KUOMINTANG!

Delegation of the Communist International in China
Hankow, April 22, 1927

9

MEASURES WHOSE IMMEDIATE IMPLEMENTATION IS NECESSARY FOR STRENGTHENING THE BASE AND THE REAR OF THE NORTHERN EXPEDITION

Adopted at the Joint Session of the Central Committee of the Communist Party and the Communist leaders of the Hupeh Federation of Labor

1. The immediate establishment of labor exchanges for the unemployed and free food for the unemployed.

2. The immediate creation by the government and the labor unions of a commission for strengthening revolutionary discipline among workers, especially among workers in foreign firms. The creation by trade unions of a revolutionary tribunal for investigating actions and for penalizing all workers guilty of a breach of revolutionary discipline.

NOTE: The trade unions must propose special rules which would establish the definition of an offense; these rules must be adopted by the Ministry of Labor.

The need of this document might be traced to the disrupted economic condition in the Wuhan party caused by excessive demands of the workers and by strikes. Business became stagnant, shipping ceased, large numbers were unemployed; foreign factories, banks, and shipping companies had nearly ceased, and business, tax revenues had fallen off seriously. This created serious difficulties at the very base of the second northern expedition, created mounting opposition among Chinese business classes, and strengthened the hand of the Right Wing of the Kuomintang. Borodin, as well as Wang Ching-wei and other Kuomintang leaders in Wuhan, came to believe that the labor movement, led by Communist and Kuomintang radicals, simply had to be brought under control so that economic life could be revived.—Eds.

3. The government must immediately reach an agreement with the principal foreign enterprises and banks to enable them to conduct business in Hupeh, Hunan, Kiangsi, Southern Anhwei, Southern Honan, and in the West right up to Wanhsien.

A commission must be created composed of representatives from the government and the trade unions in the aims of implementing the agreement concluded with foreign enterprises and banks.

Pickets and armed forces must be placed at the disposal of this commission.

4. The government must in the shortest possible time establish fixed prices on all articles of prime necessity.

The government, with the consent of bankers, must regulate the prices of rice by creating reserves and by throwing them on the market to lower prices.

The Economic Commission must draw up other measures of a similar nature.

5. Not a single strike can take place in foreign enterprises or firms without the consent of the commission referred to under paragraph 3.

6. An energetic campaign should be conducted among the broadest masses of the population to explain that the solution of the vital economic problems now confronting the revolution is dependent upon the success of the Northern Expedition and the destruction of the counter-revolution, headed by Chiang Kai-shek, as well as upon the abrogation of unequal agreements and the conclusion of new agreements based on equality.

The basic requirement of the present moment is revolutionary discipline, self-sacrifice and the unity of revolutionary forces.

Hankow, April 25, 1927

10

THE PROBLEMS OF THE CHINESE REVOLUTION

AND THE ROLE OF THE PROLETARIAT

Comrades, the delegation of the Communist International would find it highly desirable if the discussion on the report of the Central Committee were opened by the Chinese comrades themselves. But since the Presidium insists on the discussion being opened by the representatives of the Comintern—we agree to speak first.

The eleven basic points set forth in the report of the Central Committee concern the most important problems of the Chinese revolution. These problems have been discussed in detail in the Communist International. Hence, although the delegation of the Comintern was not given the opportunity to hear the opinion of the Chinese comrades, it will nevertheless be able to state its view on these questions.

I will not speak on each of these eleven points separately. I will group them around three themes and will comment separately on each of these.

The first theme concerns *the perspectives of the revolution.* Under it I have subsumed questions pertaining to the development of the revolution; the past, present, and future role of the bourgeoisie; the interrelations of the proletariat and the petty bourgeoisie; the agrarian revolution; and the hegemony of the proletariat.

For a correct determination of the perspectives of the revolution, the situation should be examined from three different aspects: (1) from the standpoint of the development of the revolution, (2) from the standpoint of the interrelationship of classes within the movement itself, and (3) from the standpoint of the international situation.

On May 30, 1925, the national-revolutionary movement in China and the anti-imperialist struggle entered a new stage. This was the

M. N. Roy's speech at the Fifth Congress of the Chinese Communist Party.—Eds.

stage of revolutionary mass struggle, the struggle of the proletariat for hegemony. The preceding period was characterized essentially by: (1) the Shanghai events, (2) the events in Peking and in the North, (3) the events in the South—particularly the Hong Kong strike.

The proletariat had hegemony in the struggle in Shanghai, but only for a short time. As soon as the revolution began to spread, the bourgeoisie left the movement, the petty bourgeoisie followed the bourgeoisie, and thus it turned out that the proletariat became isolated. The proletariat captured the hegemony for a short period of time, but it could not retain it.

In the North, the question of the hegemony of the proletariat was not even raised, because there the movement was not based on the proletariat. It was primarily a movement of the petty bourgeoisie which was supported by the liberal bourgeoisie and which also found response in certain circles of militarists opposed to the more reactionary elements.

In the South—in Canton—the development of forces went further. There the proletariat not only seized the hegemony, but retained it for a considerable period of time. For one whole year the policy of the Canton national government was largely determined by the influence of the Hong Kong strike. It has even been said that the strike committee actually performed the function of a second government. This means that the policy of the national government was largely determined by the strike committee—the political organ of the combatant proletariat. In other words, for almost one year, the proletariat led the anti-imperialist struggle in the South. This emergence of the working class in the role of a leader [gegemon] in the national-revolutionary struggle affected the positions of the bourgcoisie and the so-called Left militarist circles. The attempt of the proletariat to seize the leadership resulted in the crystallization of the bourgeois forces; to a certain extent, this crystallization also affected the feudal-militarist elements.

This process of the political crystallization of the bourgeoisie—which came as a response to the proletariat's aspiration for hegemony— passed through several stages of development. The culminating point of this process was March 20. The process began with differentiation in the milieu of the militarists; there arose a sort of a Left militarism. The revolt of Fêng Yü-hsiang, the change in the orientation of T'ang Shêng-chih and the revolt of Hsia Tou-yin were the concrete manifestations of this [proccss]. Such was the first stage.

The appearance of the notorious brochure by Tai Chi-t'ao, the Western Hills Conference, and the Shanghai Conference can be considered as being the basic features of the second stage.

Both of these stages are but different manifestations of one and the same process; at the same time, each is somewhat different from the other.

The split that occurred in the ranks of the militarists during the first stage was objectively revolutionary in character, because it tended to weaken militarism. The second stage contained already the objective germs of the counterrevolution. In this period, the consciously aggressive policy of the bourgeoisie which sought to deter the revolutionary development of the national-liberation movement began to make its influence felt. When the proletariat definitely took the course of fighting for hegemony, it became clear that the development of the movement under the leadership of the proletariat would lead to a nonbourgeois revolution. The bourgeoisie mobilized its forces to counteract this prospect of development put forth by the proletariat; it sought to prevent the revolution from developing a proletarian character and to steer its course into the narrow channel of its own class interests. There exists an organic tie between these two stages of the single process of crystallization. These were stages in the crystallization of forces which sought to prevent the Chinese revolution from taking a nonbourgeois path of development.

The third stage of this process was the Canton *coup* of March 20. The significance of the *coup* was not local, but marked an event of nationwide importance. The crystallization of all the forces that were united against the proletariat was expressed in this event. The transformation of the bourgeoisie, led by Chiang Kai-shek, into an objectively counterrevolutionary force was the result of a lengthy process which started considerably earlier than March 20. It was not after he entered Shanghai and shot the workers there that Chiang Kai-shek became a revolutionary. The forces which he represented and which showed themselves to be so aggressively counterrevolutionary in Shanghai, had been undergoing a process of crystallization for a certain period of time.

During this period, our Party made several mistakes which stemmed from an overestimation of the bourgeoisie. This was not a subjective mistake. The Party had no desire to negotiate with the bourgeoisie. The mistake was a result of an insufficiently clear understanding of the process of the crystallization of the counterrevolution. During the period of reaction—starting from March 20 until the beginning of the Northern Expedition—our Party pursued the policy of a united front and ignored its basic task, that of developing the class struggle. A united front is, of course, very necessary. But while the Communist Party was creating it, it should not have overlooked the necessity of developing the energies of the working class as an independent force. It was obvious that the bourgeoisie was mobilizing its forces against the proletariat;

yet the Communist Party was participating in the united front without simultaneously preparing the working-class organizations for becoming an independent political force.

This, precisely, is what constituted the basic error. The consequences of this error made themselves felt at the sharpest point of the crisis. When Chiang Kai-shek occupied Shanghai and declared war on the proletariat, the Party was faced with the necessity of making a cruel choice between overthrowing him or surrendering. Due to our earlier policy, no sufficient premises were established for a middle road, [that is], not entering into battle for the immediate overthrow of Chiang Kai-shek, and not surrendering to him. This perspective already existed before the Shanghai crisis, beginning from the very events of March 20. The argument of whether or not to collaborate with the Right Wing should not have been understood as a question of either a final break, or a surrender. It is only on the basis of a class struggle that we can enter a united front [and] collaborate with the bourgeoisie. In collaborating with the bourgeoisie, we must at the same time prepare ourselves for the forthcoming, inevitable class struggle.

Overestimation of the necessity of a united front with the bourgeoisie and the Left militarists had led the Party to underestimate the role of the petty bourgeoisie. When it formed a united front with the bourgeoisie and the Left militarist elements, the Party was unable at the same time to win the petty bourgeoisie over to its side by explaining the actual meaning of the crystallization of the bourgeoisie and the feudal-bourgeois elements. As a result, at first the petty bourgeoisie began to waver, then it became frightened and, finally, it joined the side of the bourgeoisie when the latter openly declared war. The proletariat found itself isolated. The principal reason for the failure of the Shanghai uprising is rooted in our inability to appreciate the importance of the petty bourgeoisie, in our inability to subject it to the influence of the proletariat. This was our mistake not only in the Shanghai events, but during the entire period beginning with March 20. This underestimation of the importance of the petty bourgeoisie was not an isolated mistake committed in Shanghai, but has been the historic mistake of the Party.

Next, the fourth stage in the crystallization of the bourgeois forces, which went over to a counterattack against the proletariat's attempts to consolidate its hegemony, was the first Northern Expedition. Objectively, the Northern Expedition served as an instrument for expanding the forces of the revolution, for developing the energies of the masses. But subjectively, it represented an attempt by the bourgeoisie to extend the power it had seized on March 20. I will speak about the Northern Expedition in greater detail in another part of my speech. Here I will only say that the Northern Expedition resulted in an extremely rapid development of the revolution. The bourgeoisie saw that its plan to use the expedition as a means of expanding its own power was not developing in the right direction. The bourgeoisie turned against the revolution, because the revolution did not follow the course it desired.

Such, in brief, was the process of the development of the revolution in the course of the past three years. Class conflict was the cardinal feature of this process. The development of the revolution has reached a stage where the question arises of whether the next period will be a period of decline * or one of further development. It is perfectly obvious that the next period of the revolution will be a period of development and not one of decline. There is no place in the Communist Party for the theory that the coming period will be a period of decline. Just why this is so, I will now explain.

We must examine the future perspectives from two points of view. The first bears in mind the internal class forces. At present, the large-scale bourgeoisie and the feudal-bourgeois elements have deserted the ranks of the national revolution. Consequently, class contradictions in the nationalist ranks have been reduced to a considerable extent. The social forces which now form the base of the revolution are not as contradictory to one another as were the social forces from which the revolution drew its support in the preceding stage. The proletariat, the peasantry, and the petty bourgeoisie—this is the base of the revolution at the present stage. Foreign imperialism and native [*tuzemnyi*] militarism are exploiting and oppressing all three of these classes. A united front of these three classes will therefore be more homogeneous than the united front of the preceding period. It stands to reason that the elimination of internal contradictions increases the potential power of the revolution. At the present stage, the possibilities of developing the energies of the masses are increasing. In the class coalition which now forms the base of the revolution, the peasantry constitutes the overwhelming majority. Therefore, the basic question at the moment is one of unleashing the revolutionary energies of the peasantry. The very course of the development of the revolution has demonstrated the necessity of radical agrarian reform, the necessity of an agrarian revolution. This question is placed before the revolution not subjectively, but in the order of its objective development. On the other hand, the revolutionary movement is now able to solve this problem. In the preceding stage, the feasibility of a radical agrarian program involved extreme difficulties with respect to tactics because the landowning classes participated in the

* In his report, Ch'ên Tu-hsiu said that the next period of the revolution would be a period of decline. [M.N.R.]

national ranks. Now the situation has changed. The classes against which, for tactical considerations, it was impossible to declare war have deserted the revolution and have turned against it. We did not force them out—they left on their own. Therefore, there are no longer tactical or other considerations which could interfere with the development of the class struggle in the village. Indeed, the development of the class struggle is the only guarantee of the future of the revolution. The only possibility that can arise of a decline of the movement, a decline of the revolution, is in the event that the Communist Party and its revolutionary allies are not audacious enough in solving the agrarian problem that was posed to the revolution by the very course of its objective development. Objectively, the revolution is on the upgrade—there are no grounds for a decline. But there also exists a subjective factor. If the Communist Party and the other revolutionary elements subjectively promote the development of objective forces, the revolution can only follow the ascending line of the social base of the revolution. There are no reasons for misgivings that the intensification of the class struggle in the village might lead to a split in the united front. The united front which we were afraid of breaking up is already broken. The feudal-bourgeois elements have already split the united front; they have already joined the side of the counterrevolution. We must act on the basis of accomplished facts. We must accept the challenge of the counterrevolutionary bourgeoisie.

Our task can not be formulated in terms of our having either to intensify the revolution, or to expand it. The right approach to the question is that we must destroy the roots of reaction in the village. There is no other way. Such is the objective necessity dictated by the present stage. If we are able to destroy the counterrevolution by intensifying the revolution, then we must intensify it; if we are able to achieve the same by means of expansion, then we must expand the revolution. If both the one and the other have to be done, then we will do it. The petty bourgeoisie has become frightened by this critical period of the revolution. It does not want to carry out agrarian reforms. Never has the petty bourgeoisie led an agrarian revolution. If the Chinese proletariat, if the Chinese Communist Party want to lead the agrarian revolution with the sanction and approval of the petty bourgeoisie, then the agrarian revolution will never happen unless the peasants take it up themselves. Actually, they have already taken up this cause.

The revolution is entering a period of intensive development, and not decline. Yet the ranks of the petty bourgeoisie are overpowerd by a spirit of defeatism. Some of the Kuomintang leaders are already talking about a Chinese 1905. By this they want to say that the Chinese revolution has suffered defeat. It must begin to retreat. This reference to the year 1905 conceals dangerous intentions. Frightened of the revolution, the petty bourgeoisie wants to run to Mongolia, to Tibet, to Turkestan. Let us be frank. In the ranks of the Communist Party, in the ranks of the proletariat, there can be no place for such defeatist and panic-stricken moods. The time has come when the proletariat must have the courage to demonstrate that it is willing and able to lead the revolution if the petty bourgeoisie proves incapable of doing so. On May 30, the proletariat began the struggle for hegemony. The stage has now been reached when the proletariat must capture this hegemony and carry it out in practice.

Was it necessary to start the struggle for hegemony? If it was necessary, then we cannot evade the consequences that ensued. We find ourselves in a situation where we must take the hegemony into our own hands. If we fail to do so, we will ruin the results of the brilliant and heroic fight of the Chinese proletariat. The Communist Party can not allow this to happen. Having started on May 30 the struggle for hegemony, the proletariat seized the hegemony either temporarily or at different times in different places. Now the time has come when the proletariat must establish [its] hegemony on a national scale in the entire national revolution. If the proletariat accepts the role that history has bestowed on it, the petty bourgeoisie will have only two possibilities: either to return to the camp of the counterrevolutionary bourgeoisie, or to follow the path of revolution together with the proletariat. Without a revolutionary policy, the national government will not hold out here, it will not preserve its power. If it does not accept such a policy, it will be overthrown by the internal forces of counterrevolution and reaction.

The petty-bourgeois Left can not return to Chiang Kai-shek: this would be political suicide. Politically, perhaps, the petty bourgeoisie may not be particularly shrewd, but it understands this. If we assume the initiative, if the Communist Party will lead the proletariat to hegemony, the petty bourgeoisie will be on our side. It will follow the path of revolution.

The rise or decline of the revolution at the present time does not depend upon objective conditions. All the objective conditions speak for the revolution being on the upswing. Only the subjective factors inspire doubt. And this subjective factor is first of all the proletariat and the Communist Party. If the actions of the proletariat and its party will correspond to the objective conditions, the only future perspective of the revolution is not one of decline, but that of continued development.

Permit me, in connection with the question of the hegemony of the proletariat, to say a few words about the Shanghai events. In Shanghai, the Communist Party had the opportunity of leading the proletariat in a struggle for hegemony. An analysis of events will permit us to assess whether the Communist Party was able to exert hegemony in the struggle, whether it knew how to lead the proletariat to the struggle for hegemony. I must first of all note that only during the third uprising did the question of the hegemony of the proletariat become acute. The first uprising can be disregarded, because it was an insignificant putsch-like adventure devoid of any great political significance. There is no need to dwell upon it. But the second uprising, the February uprising, was already a serious affair. A study of the events makes clear the following: the uprising was premature, the movement was not under the leadership of the Party—it developed spontaneously; as soon as the movement began, the Party understood its prematureness. Nevertheless, the Party did nothing to gain control of the masses; the Party dragged behind instead of acting in the capacity of a conscious leader of the masses. After the masses had come forward prematurely and without political guidance, the Party got the idea of pushing them into even more premature actions. I have in mind the project for creating a town committee which would actually have been a disguised soviet.

In this struggle for power, the Party did nothing to induce the petty bourgeoisie to follow the proletariat, or to coördinate the Shanghai movement with the nation-wide movement. Shanghai was regarded as a small China within a larger China. In this small China, irrespective of the position of all the rest of the movement, an attempt was made to create a workers' state. This was not the leadership of the proletariat in a struggle for hegemony. This was a premature struggle for power which, naturally, ended in defeat.

When I emphasize the shortcomings and make critical comments, I do not for a minute lose sight of the tremendous achievements in this period.

Illusions about Chiang Kai-shek continued to exist in the period between the second and third uprisings. The Party led the proletariat to a premature attempt at seizing power, but was unable to explain to it that the bourgeoisie had turned against the revolution. Even then, the Party still did not properly understand, nor did it explain to the democratic masses, that Chiang Kai-shek had already deserted to the side of the counterrevolution. The Party did not explain to the proletariat or to the petty-bourgeois masses that Chiang Kai-shek wants to seize Shanghai in order to convert it into a base not of the revolution, but of the counter-revolution, in the interests of the feudal-bourgeois elements who are fighting against the revolution. If the illusions about Chiang Kai-shek persisted even among the working class—the vanguard of the national-revolutionary struggle—then there is nothing surprising in the presence of much greater illusions among the petty-bourgeois masses. The revolutionary democracy of Shanghai was not prepared for the inevitability of the struggle against Chiang Kai-shek. As a result, the Shanghai proletariat found itself isolated during the third uprising when it started its heroic fight, full of revolutionary self-sacrifices, when it declared war on the counterrevolution. This occurred because the Party failed to help the petty bourgeoisie to understand the counterrevolutionary essence of Chiang Kai-shek. When the latter occupied Shanghai and pursued an openly counterrevolutionary policy, the petty bourgeoisie began to falter, it became frightened and, in the end, it rejected a united front with the proletariat. In view of this, the local government which, according to the initial plan, was supposed to have become a disguised Soviet of Workers' Deputies, found itself dependent upon the large-scale bourgeoisie. Otherwise, it could not have functioned. If the proletariat is unable to realize its hegemony in a united front with the petty bourgeoisie, then it will be even less able to realize it with the large-scale bourgeoisie. But, anyway, such were the practical results of the third uprising. The way out at that moment should under no circumstances have been one of either the seizure or the surrender of power, of the proletariat either having to lead or to surrender. After all, there is a distance of enormous measure between these two perspectives. It is at this point that the question of the hegemony of the proletariat arises. In order to carry out its hegemony with success, the proletariat must win the sympathy of the urban petty bourgeoisie and the peasantry. The proletariat did not carry this out in Shanghai, because it did not know how to win the petty bourgeoisie over to its side.

Let us turn to a determination of the perspectives of the revolution from the third standpoint, from the standpoint of the international situation. This question can be discussed in detail in my report on the theses of the Communist International. I will say only a few words now. There is nothing in the international situation predetermining a decline of the Chinese revolution during the forthcoming stage. On the contrary, the situation favors an upswing of the revolution. If this were not the case, if the international situation were not favorable to the development of the revolution, the theses of the Communist International would be at variance with the facts. In that event, the Communist International would be compelled to alter its viewpoint on the Chinese revolution.

The second theme concerns *mutual relations with the military forces,* their relation to the revolution and the disproportion between the military and the social forces of the revolution.

We can not accept the schematic plan of Dr. Sun Yat-sen according to which the revolution must pass through three stages: (1) military,

(2) educational and organizational, and (3) democratic. It is possible that this schematic plan is the fruit of brilliant petty-bourgeois thought, but the proletariat can not act on the basis of such a scheme.

Militarism is a peculiar feature of the Chinese society. Its connection, to a certain degree, with the Chinese revolutionary movement is inevitable. But it is necessary to establish the extent to which these forces can be used for the revolution. For this, one must examine the social base of militarism. Militarism * in China is not an accidental phenomenon. Why is it that we find this particular type of militarism here and not in other countries? We can establish the possibility of using this force only when we find out the causes of this phenomenon. We will treat this question in detail in the discussion of the agrarian problem. Here I will only touch upon the general aspects of this question.

The base of militarism lies in the rural overpopulation of the country. What are the causes of rural overpopulation? The rule of imperialism interfered with the normal economic development of China. Imperialism interfered with the establishment of a normal ratio of productive forces. Thanks to imperialism, the overwhelming masses of the population remain tied to the land. In its present state of backwardness, agriculture can not support all the population that is dependent upon land. Thus, these militarist forces are used directly for perpetuating the feudal character of the village economy and the patriarchal features of rural government.

Indirectly, militarism is an instrument of imperialist domination. In short, militarism is the expression of all reactionary forces in the country. This bloc of counterrevolutionary forces contains contradictions and conflicts. The revolutionary classes can exploit these conflicts for the development of the revolution. But it would be a mistake to think that these forces of militarism can become a base of the revolution. Objectively, the revolution will destroy the roots of militarism. One cannot count on these forces to further the process of their own destruction.

Theory which holds that we can win the militarist forces over to our side and transform them into a revolutionary force is very dangerous. That this is impossible has been demonstrated in practice; and it can be demonstrated in theory. The danger of any one theory or another can sometimes be judged by its source of origin. Two months ago, during a discussion with General Li Chi-shên, I raised the question of a compromise with militarism. He said: "And why not? Only yesterday some of the units of our revolutionary army were still in the militarists' armies;

---

* The partition of the country by individual military leaders who wage a continuous civil war among each other disrupts the economic life and destroys the political unity of the country. [M.N.R.]

today they have joined the revolution. It is a question of gradualness. There is no reason to believe that the rest of the militarists, too, will not join us in the future. Is it not possible to win over to our side all the forces of Chang Tso-lin?"

1. Fêng Yü-hsiang. His conduct in Peking. When the attempt was made to seize power in Peking, calculated on the assistance of Fêng Yü-hsiang, at the last moment he refused to come forward. The nationalists thought of taking power by relying solely on the military forces of Fêng Yü-hsiang. No use was made of other social forces which could have influenced the situation. Consequently, when Fêng Yü-hsiang backed out, the movement collapsed.

2. Hsia Tou-yin. We know that his revolt was crushed as a result of betrayal by his own officers who were bought out by Japan. A force of this type can not serve as a reliable base for the revolution.

3. Generals: supporters of Chiang Kai-shek. These generals participated in the national-revolutionary movement as long as it was led by Chiang Kai-shek. As soon as Chiang Kai-shek turned against the movement, they followed him.

4. The most important fact: the experience with T'ang Shêng-chih. We must elucidate this fact, because it is very relevant. What was the position of T'ang Shêng-chih? Since he joined the revolution, his military forces have increased by 100 percent. This army is subordinated not to the national government, but to T'ang Shêng-chih. He will use these military forces, created by him in the process of the revolution, not for developing the revolution, but for consolidating his power in Hunan and Hupeh. During the past three weeks, a number of resolutions have been adopted on the further advance into the North. In the Political Council of the Kuomintang, T'ang Shêng-chih had always declared himself in favor of the advance. But when the question was raised as to what troops were to be sent, he proposed the Fourth and Eleventh armies. In the end he agreed to send three of his divisions. But when the order had to be given, he imposed the condition that his troops were not to go beyond the boundaries of the Hupeh province. The Fourth and Eleventh armies were to be dispatched to Honan, while T'ang Shêng-chih's troops were to remain in Hupeh.* There are a number of other highly interesting facts that I could tell you about, but this by itself is enough.

In short, the militarists—even those of them who incline most to the Left—in no way constitute a reliable base for the revolution. If the revolution does not develop the social forces that are capable of re-

---

* This "Left" military ally of ours will simply use the banner of the national revolution to increase his own forces. [M.N.R.]

sisting militarism, then militarism will destroy the national revolution.

5. *One more example important for the future.* It is essential to understand it thoroughly, since it serves as grounds for numerous speculations. It concerns Yen Hsi-shan from the province of Shansi. During the Northern Expedition, while the expedition army had not yet reached Nanking and Shanghai, Yen Hsi-shan maintained close association with Chiang Kai-shek and agreed to start an offensive against Peking provided that the national-revolutionary forces would also advance to the north along the Tientsin-Pukow railroad. But now, thanks to the split in the national front, a serious offensive against Peking has become virtually impossible. Yen Hsi-shan's position has changed accordingly. If large enough forces are sent from Hunan to the Hankow-Peking railroad, if the Fêngtien forces are repelled, if the Lunghai railroad is captured, only then will Yen Hsi-shan perhaps come forward and occupy Peking. But Yen Hsi-shan would occupy Peking for himself and not for the national government. However, should the Fêngtien forces rout the national-revolutionary army and should Fêng Yü-hsiang come to its aid, it is equally possible that Yen Hsi-shan will attack Fêng Yü-hsiang from the flank. He has very large forces on the left flank of Fêng Yü-hsiang.

These are a few facts which demonstrate the unreliability of the so-called Left militarists. This has already been repeatedly demonstrated in the past. It follows objectively from the alignment of class forces in the country.

The national revolution can not migrate from the east to the north and from the north to the west depending on [the whims of] these unprincipled, unreliable, and disloyal Left militarists. The national revolution must have a social base; it must have social roots; it must find a territory where this social base is most developed.

Our attitude toward militarism should be determined by (1) considerations of substance, and (2) tactical tasks. For tactical considerations we must make use of the contradictions between militarists in our own interest. But our policy must not be based on pulling them over to our side. It would be an illusion to think that the militarists could some day become revolutionaries. The task of the revolution is to demoralize and destroy them. This is the aim of our work. According to the theses of the Comintern—this is the aim of the work of Communists in the militarists' armies. One must destroy them and not preach to them the gospel of the national revolution. Differentiation in the forces of the militarists is possible and is, in fact, occurring. The interests of officers and soldiers in the militarists' armies are not the same. Who are they, these soldiers? These are landless peasants who are forced to go into the militarists' armies because they have no other means of livelihood. To this extent, they are revolutionary material. But there are a number of practical difficulties which militate against winning them over to the side of the revolution. Besides, whenever any unit of the militarists' forces joins our side, the national army is admitting both revolutionary and reactionary elements into its ranks; and this applies to soldiers as well as officers. The reactionary corps of officers remains in the army. It retains its influence over the soldiers. The military units retain their former composition. There is only one way of really winning the soldiers of militarists' armies over to the side of the revolution, of really organizing them into a revolutionary army: it is by way of an agrarian revolution. If the national government and the national-revolutionary movement will fight—not only through propaganda, but in practice as well— for the extirpation of the very causes of their poverty, the soldiers will join their side and fight for them—but only then, and not before.

This means that the schematic plan of Dr. Sun Yat-sen, with all due respect to his memory, must be rejected. Communists cannot accept a theory according to which the revolution, in its first stage, must rely entirely on military forces; [a theory which says] they'll gather a motley army, reëducate it in the revolutionary spirit, and only then will they take measures for democratizing the revolution. The national revolution must organize its own army, created in the process of the revolution, and not an army which comes and goes from the revolution. If the national government gives land to the peasants, if it emancipates the peasants from feudal oppression and arms them, it will be able to create in a short time an army which will fight consciously for the revolution, which will fight for what the revolution has given to it.

Propaganda is a good thing, of course. Political work is essential. But it must have an economic basis. Until now, it was not possible to impart a practical character to our propaganda. Now we can do this. The national government can create a revolutionary army. There is no more need to speculate on these so-called Left militarists. We can have our own revolutionary army. We return once again to the basic problem: to the question of creating and developing a genuine national-revolutionary army; and this depends on our ability to carry out a program of agrarian revolution.

The Question of the Base of the Revolution

First of all, I would like to repudiate the romantic orientation toward the Northwest. This, also, is a tradition inherited from Dr. Sun Yat-sen. It, too, we must reject. The plan according to which it is necessary to withdraw to somewhere in the Northwest, further removed from places where the revolution might be attacked by imperialism, and to build a movement on a combination of various militarists' forces, can only be advanced by those who have no faith in the masses. It is clear that the Communist Party can have no place for a plan such as this. As concerns the danger of an imperialist attack, experience has shown that we will not be entirely safe, even in Mongolia. An example of this was the defeat suffered by Fêng Yü-hsiang's forces even on the other side of the Nankow Pass.

There are differences of opinion regarding the importance of Shanghai as a revolutionary base. For us there can be no doubt as to the greatest importance of Shanghai to the national revolution. In Shanghai, we have a proletariat which is organized, which possesses tremendous revolutionary experience, which has received its political training in combat. The Shanghai proletariat is the bulwark of the Chinese revolution. It alone is worth all the "Left" militarists put together. But there are also inconvenient aspects to Shanghai. It is the center of the most revolutionary forces, but it is at the same time the base of imperialism. Therefore, Shanghai should not be selected as a point from which to launch an immediate attack against imperialism. This is a question of tactics. Tactically, it would be disadvantageous to convert Shanghai into a base for direct attack against imperialism. The significance of Shanghai must be defined in terms of the revolutionary movement in the entire country. As experience has shown, the Shanghai proletariat, because it is isolated from the country, is incapable of overthrowing imperialism. However, also incorrect is the theory that whoever goes to Shanghai is going to compromise with imperialism.* This holds true for the bourgeoisie. But the Shanghai proletariat will do away with imperialism. This theory merely bespeaks of the absence of faith in the masses, the inability to understand the role of the proletariat. There are some who say that if Chiang Kai-shek compromised with imperialism immediately upon his arrival in Shanghai, it follows that the proletariat, too, will be forced to make an agreement with imperialism; but to say this is to reveal your lack of understanding of the class character of society. Chiang Kai-shek made a compromise not because he found himself in Shanghai. He went to Shanghai with just this very aim to conclude an agreement with imperialism. But the Shanghai proletariat has always fought against imperialism.

In connection with the question of the base, it is necessary to discuss the question of the Northern Expedition. One cannot formulate the question in terms of our having to go somewhere—either to the north,

---

* In his report to the Congress, Ch'ên Tu-hsiu said: "Whoever goes to Shanghai is going to a compromise with imperialism." [M.N.R.]

or to the east, or to the south. What is the basic purpose of this expedition? To develop the revolutionary movement. The essential problem is one of finding a base for the revolution. Everything else must be examined from this point of view. If the expedition promotes the consolidation of the revolution—we are for it. If its objective is to transfer the base of the revolution to somewhere in Mongolia—we are against such an expedition.

There was a big discussion in our Party before the beginning of the first expedition. Events have proved the wrongness of the comrades who opposed it. But events have also proved that the Communist Party was unable to take advantage of the situation created by the Northern Expedition for developing the revolution. As I have already pointed out earlier, the subjective motivation [*dvigatel'*] of the expedition was the aim of the bourgeoisie to increase its own power. But objectively, the expedition provided the possibility of developing the revolutionary forces. It was precisely in view of this objective possibility that the Communist Party led the proletariat to support the Northern Expedition. The Party supported the Northern Expedition. But did its activity correspond to objective necessity? No. The Communist Party supported the Northern Expedition, but it did not devote sufficient attention to the interests of the working class. Carried away with the expansion of the Northern Expedition, the Communists neglected the task of organizing, crystallizing, [and] consolidating the social forces of the revolution that were raised by the Northern Expedition. And it is this unreserved support of the expedition that is to a large extent responsible for Chiang Kai-shek's success in breaking off such a considerable number of military and social forces from the national front.

If the Communist Party, while supporting the Northern Expedition, had at the same time been clearly aware of the crystallization of the forces of the bourgeoisie and its basic aims, if the Party had at the same time promoted the crystallization of the forces of the revolution, then Chiang Kai-shek would have found himself isolated at the time of the split. One more comment, and an extremely serious one at that: One result of the unreserved support of the Northern Expedition was the loss of Kwangtung. We lost Kwangtung, because we supported the Northern Expedition without any reservations. For the sake of preserving a united front with the bourgeoisie, for the sake of the support of the Left-militarist combination, the Communist Party did not intensify the class struggle, it did not destroy the roots of reaction. After the departure of the revolutionary armies, Kwangtung—this traditional base of the revolution—was left exposed to the forces of reaction. One should guard against committing similar mistakes in connection with the second expedition. It is not a question of the North or the East, but one of consolidating the base. Only by proceeding from this point of view should we support a northern, an eastern, or a southern expedition.

This question has been repeatedly discussed in the Central Committee, even before the Congress. There is no need to repeat all these discussions here. Still, it is necessary to touch briefly upon these themes. The peculiar feature about the second expedition is its fictitious nature. It would therefore be simply absurd for the Communist Party to worry about whether or not it should support this nonexistent second expedition. Since the Northern Expedition does not exist, since the national government and the Kuomintang supporting the Northern Expedition have rejected this plan, there is no need to criticize it. And perhaps, comrades, it would be appropriate to point out that the Kuomintang has accepted the plan of the delegation of the Communist International, submitted to the Central Committee of the Party as a counterplan to the plan [calling] for the conquest of Mukden, Peking, Mongolia, and Tibet. But then, the Central Committee rejected this plan. What has been depicted as the Northern Expedition simply amounts to the dispatch of troops to the north to assist Fêng Yü-hsiang in occupying the Lunghai railroad and, if possible, to assist Yen Hsi-shan in occupying Peking. The Central Committee rejected this plan when it was proposed by the delegation of the Comintern, but now, after it has been accepted by the Kuomintang *, it supports it enthusiastically in the form of a plan for the Northern Expedition.

The present plan consists of advancing to the Lunghai railroad and making it possible for Fêng Yü-hsiang's forces to leave Shensi and seize Honan; then Fêng, with the probable support of Yen Hsi-shan, would move on Peking. The principal objective of this plan is to rescue the Wuhan government from the military dictatorship of T'ang Shêng-chih. As soon as Fêng Yü-hsiang's troops occupy the Lunghai railroad, the national army will return immediately to consolidate the base of the national government by capturing Kiangsi, Kwangtung, and Fukien. Such, then, is the substance of the so-called Northern Expedition. But this is the very plan which the delegation of the Comintern advanced as an alternative to the plan that was based on the assumption that only by means of capturing Peking can the nationalist power be defended in

---

* The initial plan for occupying Peking and Tientsin and forcing Chang Tso-lin back into Manchuria was rejected by the Political Council of the Kuomintang and by the national government, since T'ang Shêng-chih did not want his troops to be too far removed from his base in the Hunan and Hupeh provinces. Nevertheless, agitation under the slogan of "seizure of Peking" continued. The Kuomintang did not want to draw the attention of the masses to questions of future military achievements of the revolution. [M.N.R.]

the Yangtze Valley, that only after the territorial expansion of the revolution can the base of the revolution be intensified, that not until the
Mukdenites are finally driven back beyond the Great Wall can the
agrarian question be solved. The Central Committee of the Communist
Party rejected the plan proposed by the delegation of the Comintern in
order to support the underhanded [*mosheinnicheskii*] plan for the capture
of Peking advanced by the petty bourgeoisie with the aim of deceiving
the masses.*

A few words about why we did not support an immediate expedition
to the north in its original version. We pointed out that it was unfeasible
from the military standpoint. At that time, supporters of the Northern
Expedition were saying that it was quite impossible to drive the Mukden
forces back belond the Great Wall. For this operation, the national government could have sent only two of its army corps to the north—the
Fourth and the Eleventh. The second expedition could lead to the capture of Peking only if the national-revolutionary forces dissolve in the
forces of Fêng Yü-hsiang and Yen Hsi-shan; if, in other words, the revolution relies primarily on the "Left" militarists.

I have pointed out earlier how dangerous this is. That is why we were
against this project. To force Fêng Yü-hsiang and Yen Hsi-shan to move
on Peking and to try to wipe out the Fêngtien forces is highly expedient,
tactically speaking. However, we must not think that this would contribute to the expansion of the revolution. We can not sacrifice the
genuine base of the revolution for the sake of accomplishing this task.
Only after having created and consolidated the base of the revolution
in southern and central provinces which are now under the national
power can we agree to such a tactic.

The Northern Expedition does not exist. The government has rejected it. Why, then, do responsible members of government speak
about a fictitious nonexistent Northern Expedition? They do so, because
they want to avoid an agrarian reform, because they are against the
development of revolutionary forces. They want to speculate by counting on Left militarists. At present we already have occasion to hear the
argument that while we are in a period of revolutionary war, we must
not begin a class struggle in the village.† No agrarian reforms. We must
wait for the occupation of Peking. Then we will carry out an agrarian
reform.‡ But the Northern Expedition, after all, does not exist, and

---

* See the resolution on the continuation of the Northern Expedition (Appendix
I). [M.N.R. Page 176 in this book.—Eds.]

† Ch'ên Tu-hsiu in his speech during the discussion of the Northern Expedition.
[M.N.R.]

‡ Wang Ching-wei made a statement to this effect at several public meetings.
[M.N.R.]

Peking will never be captured. The point here is not the Northern Expedition, but the intensification of the social base of the revolution; it
is just this which should determine the Communist Party's plan of action. We support the Kuomintang and the revolutionary government on
everything that promotes the intensification of the revolution. We will
oppose any policy that evades this.

I am appealing to you, and through you to the whole Communist Party,
not to chase after illusions. Before you lies an enormous task: you must
intensify the base of the revolution in order to assure its future, in order
to spread the revolution over all of China.

Now we come to the extremely important question of our relations
with the Kuomintang. We have entered the stage when our relations
with the Kuomintang signify that we are assuming a share of the responsibility for its policy. But we cannot share the responsibility without sharing the power. The Communist Party must not support unreservedly the petty-bourgeois policy of the Kuomintang. Our support,
our bloc with the Left-Wing Kuomintang should not mean that the
Kuomintang decides everything while we agree with it on everything.
If we intend to support the government and the Kuomintang—and we
must support them—then we have to demand that all decisions on the
present and the future of the national revolution be taken with the conscious participation of the proletariat acting through the Communist
Party. It is necessary to recognize that in the past our relations with
the Kuomintang were not what they should have been. The Communist
Party usually acted as an appendage, and not as an independent force.
In the Chiang Kai-shek affair, the Kuomintang created a fracas. Its
entire policy was determined by interests of petty-bourgeois prestige
and not by a political line. And the Communists fully supported this
absence of a political line on the part of the Kuomintang. It happens that
Leftists forget who they are and go along with the Rightists—and the
Communists follow them. And when the Leftists decide on a split, the
Communist Party does the same. This is not an independent policy. This
is not a Communist policy.

We must take stock of this past mistake in order to be able to work
out the correct policy for the future. Mistakes of the past interest us
only in terms of the lessons we can derive from them in order to pursue
the correct policy in the future. Henceforth, our policy will be such
that we will neither support nor oppose the decisions of the Kuomintang
post factum. We must have our own say in the matter of the development of the revolution. In other words, the Communist Party must carry
out the hegemony of the proletariat in the revolution. This should be
achieved through factional work within the Kuomintang. The Communist

Party must create in various organs of the Kuomintang and the government Communist factions under the political leadership of the Central Committee so that every decision of the national government would be adopted with the consent and under the influence of the proletariat and the peasantry. Various mixed committees have been formed. Factional work becomes particularly important in such circumstances. When Communists participate in these committees, they must have a policy of their own that has been worked out beforehand and defined by the interests of the proletariat and the peasantry. Through the many different organs to which the Communists belong they must propose this policy to the national government.

The Communists have accepted two ministerial posts in the national government. At the present stage of the revolution, these ministries carry very great significance. But the point is that the Kuomintang, in offering to the Communists that they assume responsibility, does not at the same time give them any power. Officially, our comrades have been appointed ministers several months ago, but they are still virtually unable to organize their ministries. One receives the impression that the Communists were appointed ministers for reasons of propaganda. Under no circumstances must they be engaged in real work. The other ministries receive all that is necessary: a budget, premises, personnel; but the Communist ministers have nothing. They do not even have the premises. If we do not take resolute steps to change this situation, our Party will be discredited and will become the scapegoat for the petty-bourgeois policy. In the event of unrest among workers and peasants, the Kuomintang will say: "But what can we do? We have placed two Communists at the head of ministries that are in charge of matters pertaining to the position of workers and peasants. If they have done nothing, this is not our fault, but the fault of the Communist ministers." The Communist Party must demand that they be given power not only formally, but in practice. The Communist ministers must have a real possibility of effectively carrying out the agrarian and the labor policy of the national revolution.

The financial problem is also connected with our relations with the Kuomintang. Here, too, the petty bourgeoisie is raising a panic, shouting about the big financial difficulties. The meaning of this panic is obvious. The proletariat and the peasantry must make sacrifices to aid the national government in overcoming financial difficulties. The meaning behind this is that the masses must be prepared for sacrifices and that under no circumstances must they press for the immediate satisfaction of their demands. The Communist Party must introduce revolutionary methods for overcoming financial difficulties. It is not enough to demand so-called self-discipline of the working class. This does not solve the basic problem. While agreeing to self-discipline and to slow-ing down the struggle against imperialism, the proletariat should say bluntly that the financial question can and must be solved by taxing the rich bourgeoisie and by carrying out an agrarian revolution [that is to say] confiscation of land. This would increase the revenues of the state, raise the living standards of the peasantry, and expand trade which, in turn, would ease the difficult economic position of the petty bour-geoisie. This would indeed be a radical solution of the financial diffi-culties.

It is necessary to sound the alarm. Under the pretext of financial dif-ficulties—it may be that this is being done unconsciously—the workers are being pushed too far back. Some of the resolutions and circulars issued by various working-class organizations in the aim of introducing so-called self-discipline in the working class, are simply disgraceful. Workers are being dragged to the revolutionary tribunal and sentenced to imprisonment for demanding higher wages. The Federation of Labor in the Hupeh province is ordering a halt to the struggle against capital-ism. The proletariat is being ordered to refrain from any resistance to imperialist coercion so as "not to weaken the bases at a moment when our armies are going to conquer Peking." These are nothing but fables.

The petty bourgeoisie fears the revolution. Therefore, it is creating a panic and is sounding an alarm about an immediate imperialist inter-vention with the object of inducing the working class to agree to a policy of retreat. This means foisting petty-bourgeois defeatism on the working class. The Communist Party must save the working class from this danger. The next stage of the revolution will establish a revolutionary-democratic power. This power can be established only on the basis of the defense of the interests of workers and peasants. In other words, a revolutionary-democratic power can be created only by intensifying the base of the revolution. The question is not one of whether or not we should sharpen the class struggle. The class struggle is sharpening of itself. A class war has been declared on the workers and peasants. Only two roads are open: either to give battle and win, or be defeated. In concrete terms, we will strive for the establishment of a revolutionary-democratic power, a democratic dictatorship of the proletariat, the peasantry, and the urban petty bourgeoisie on the following basis:

First of all, and at the basis of all—the agrarian revolution.

Second, the arming of peasants for defending the gains of the revolu-tion.

Third, the organization of rural self-government for destroying the power of feudal lords in the village.

Fourth, the creation of a state machinery through which the demo-cratic dictatorship will be realized.

Fifth, the creation of a revolutionary army, not by converting militarists into revolutionaries, but by organizing a revolutionary army on a firm, social basis.

The revolution is confronted with these tasks as a result of its own development. And it is the proletariat who must fulfill these tasks. By following this path, we will not weaken our revolutionary alliance with the petty bourgeoisie. On the contrary, we will strengthen this alliance. Only on these conditions will the petty bourgeoisie participate effectively in the revolutionary struggle. If we do not spur it on, it will begin to waver, it will liquidate the revolution and desert to the side of the reaction.

At the present stage, the hegemony of the proletariat is no longer abstract theory. It has become a living fact. And the future of the Chinese revolution depends not upon the objective forces, which are totally on its side, but upon the subjective ability of the proletariat to lead the revolution.

April 30, 1927

11

THE PROLETARIAT AND THE

PETTY BOURGEOISIE

The discussion revealed that certain theses of my report were incorrectly understood; it is also possible that I did not expound them clearly enough. Permit me, therefore, once again to touch upon one of the most important questions in the report of the Central Committee.

First of all, I want to eliminate the confusion that Comrade Chang T'ai-lei has created by his criticism of some of the points in my first speech. I am not about to indulge in personal attacks on Comrade Chang T'ai-lei, but it is absolutely necessary to speak against the point of view he represents. The confusion he has created must be eliminated.

What did he say? He said: "Because the Communist International accuses us of having Rightist tendencies [is no reason why] we must plunge immediately to the other extreme." He considers that the line proposed by the delegation of the Communist International does not correspond to the objective situation; that it is much too Left; that it is dangerous for the Party to plunge into such extremes. Specifically, he advances the argument that we are lending a completely mechanical formulation to the question when we say that the petty bourgeoisie must either join the revolution or turn back to Chiang Kai-shek. Let us see whether or not Comrade Chang T'ai-lei's criticism is correct.

In the revolutionary-democratic bloc of the proletariat, the peasantry, and the petty bourgeoisie, it is the proletariat that constitutes the dominant force. The proletariat must exercise hegemony in the revolutionary struggle in order for this bloc to become an organ of democratic dictatorship. Therefore, the policy must be determined by the proletariat. The proletariat is in a position to determine the policy of this bloc. In what way is the petty-bourgeois opposition to the proletarian policy to

M. N. Roy's second speech at the Fifth Congress of the Chinese Communist Party.—Eds.

be counteracted? Now, when the bourgeoisie has turned against the revolution, the petty bourgeoisie is left with two courses: either to join the revolution, or to reject it; either to save itself under the leadership of the proletariat, or to follow the bourgeoisie into the camp of the counterrevolution. There is nothing mechanical about this point of view. Chang T'ai-lei thinks that our policy is so far to the Left that we are closing to the petty bourgeoisie the possibility of joining us. It is a well-known fact that the petty bourgeoisie never represents an independent political force. It joins either the bourgeoisie or the proletariat. In the present period of the revolution, the petty bourgeoisie will join the proletariat not on the strength of a conscious choice; it will join the proletariat and will participate in the revolutionary-democratic bloc, because under existing conditions the petty bourgeoisie in China is an oppressed class. For this reason, it must join the bloc of oppressed classes. Under certain circumstances, the bourgeoisie may offer the petty bourgeoisie certain privileges, certain economic rights, and then the petty bourgeoisie joins the bourgeoisie. But in China the bourgeoisie is so weak itself that it is not in a position to toss a hand-out [*brosit' podachku*] to the petty bourgeoisie in order to draw it over to its side.

Imperialism is exploiting and oppressing the petty bourgeoisie. Therefore, the petty bourgeoisie objectively stands closer to the proletariat than to the bourgeoisie. Thanks to this objective class alignment, a revolutionary-democratic bloc can be created on the condition that the proletariat determines its policy and the petty bourgeoisie joins the proletariat on the revolutionary path.

In European countries, the petty bourgeoisie does not represent an independent force; this is even less possible in China. It is unable to provide an independent political existence for itself. Once it rejects the revolutionary-democratic bloc, it will have to return to the counterrevolutionary bourgeoisie. This is what I said. And I would like to know what is mechanical about it.

In criticizing my point of view and in labeling it mechanical, Comrade Chang T'ai-lei has something else in mind. He thinks that the policy we proposed will destroy the revolutionary-democratic bloc. If this is the point, then a very serious question arises here which it is necessary to examine.

What is there in our proposal that can be considered as being too far Left? We are proposing a program dictated to the movement by the objective development of social forces. The fundamental question at issue between the Communist Party and the Kuomintang, that is, the petty bourgeoisie, concerns the solution of the agrarian problem at the present stage of the revolution. The principal argument of Chang

T'ai-lei is that our proposed agrarian program of the national revolution is much too Left. The petty bourgeoisie will not accept it and, as a result, the revolutionary bloc will fall apart. The basic demand of our agrarian platform is a partial confiscation of land—the confiscation of large landholdings. This suggestion is not ours. It is what the peasants are, in fact, carrying out. The national revolution has developed into an agrarian revolution. Two courses lie before the Communist Party: either to support the peasant demands on land, or to retard the development of the agrarian revolution for the sake of good relations with the petty bourgeoisie. I do not believe that anyone in our Party would hesitate in the choice of his decision. Every member of our Party considers that in the situation that has arisen the Communist Party must support the peasantry in its struggle. The proletariat cannot betray the peasantry for the sake of buying an alliance with the petty bourgeoisie. Moreover, the agrarian revolution corresponds to the interests not only of the peasantry, but of the petty bourgeoisie as well. The proletariat will win the support of the petty bourgeoisie in the revolutionary-democratic struggle by explaining to it its real interests, by freeing it from feudal-bourgeois influence. But this can be done only in the process of a genuine revolutionary struggle. And it must be achieved through action. The petty bourgeoisie must become convinced that there is no middle road between revolution and counterrevolution.

When the proletariat tries to convince the petty bourgeoisie that the agrarian problem is an objective necessity of the given period of the revolution, it is not foisting anything on it, but is merely trying to evoke in it an awareness of its own class interests. This in itself means exercising hegemony in the revolutionary-democratic bloc. Being the motive power of this bloc, the proletariat must intensify the revolutionary struggle by such demands which correspond objectively to the interests of its allies—the peasantry and the petty bourgeoisie—but which are not advanced by them independently in view of their political backwardness. Such a tactic not only will not threaten the integrity of the revolutionary bloc, but will merely serve to strengthen it.

I do not intend to explain in detail here the advantageousness of a radical agrarian reform to both the petty bourgeoisie and the peasantry. I will restrict myself to a few comments. What will be the immediate result of a radical agrarian reform? Innumerable forms of the feudal-military bureaucracy, hampering the development of the economic life of the country, will be abolished. Owing to the fact that a considerable part of the land rental is paid in kind, agricultural products are being concentrated in the hands of feudal-bureaucratic elements. Taking advantage of this monopoly and inflating the prices, the landowners exploit the producing peasantry, on the one hand, and the proletariat and the urban petty bourgeoisie, on the other. If, in the order of agrarian reforms, measures are adopted for abolishing this monopoly on agricultural products, prices will decline. This will benefit the urban population; the existing system of feudal-capitalistic exploitation deprives the peasantry of all surplus; moreover, the peasants are often unable to satisfy even the most elementary vital needs. The peasantry finds itself constantly on the verge of starvation. If, as a result of agrarian reforms, the economic position of the peasants improves, it will bring about the flourishing of internal trade. The peasantry will be in a position to sell more and buy more, thereby increasing the volume of trade. The town tradesmen will derive their benefits from this.

Such are the direct advantages accruing to the petty bourgeoisie from a radical agrarian reform. But due to its shortsightedness and to its economic and political backwardness, brought about by feudal conditions, the petty bourgeoisie is unable to understand that the agrarian reform is advantageous to it. We are faced with the question of whether the proletariat should really become the leader and awaken in the petty bourgeoisie an awareness of its class interests, thus strengthening the revolutionary-democratic bloc, or whether it should, out of faulty considerations, reject this hegemony. This is the whole question. To doubt the correctness of the policy suggested by the Communist International, to consider that this policy contains the danger of "radicalism" [*levizna*], means to doubt that at the present stage of the Chinese revolution the proletariat is capable of exercising its hegemony in the struggle.

I want to touch upon still another question. It was said here (also by Comrade Chang T'ai-lei) that there are elements of passiveness in the policy proposed by the delegation of the Comintern. The criticism was directed particularly against my point of view concerning the so-called Left militarists. The delegation of the Communist International considers that at the present stage of the development the revolution cannot rely primarily on the support of the so-called Left militarists. Those who see elements of passiveness in this viewpoint believe that the most effective activity of the revolution consists of maneuvering with the so-called Left militarists. In their opinion, the Left militarists comprise the basic force of the revolution. In my first speech, I pointed out the danger of overestimating the importance of the "Left" militarists and stated why the revolution must be freed from the domination of the corrupt [*prodazhnyi*] hired militarist forces.

The delegation of the Comintern is by no means defending the policy of passiveness. On the contrary, we proposed to the Congress a program of intensive action. We rejected the viewpoint which appraised the next period of the revolution as a period of decline, and established that the revolution stands before the prospect of intensive activity. We came out against the theory of retreat and defense. We condemned this theory as defeatist. We do not think that political action consists entirely of maneuvering with the "Left" militarists.

A program that can be carried out only through the revolutionary action of proletarian and peasant masses is not a program of passiveness. We propose that the Communist Party act jointly with the masses, relying on an organized bond with the workers' and peasants' unions which unite over ten million members. One must look for passiveness and defeatism in comrades who criticize our program as being too Left. These comrades are suggesting retreat at a time when the objective conditions require a bold advance. To satisfy the petty bourgeoisie, they are creating a theory of so-called self-discipline of the masses. They are demoralizing the movement by an inadmissible spirit of defeatism. The danger of radicalism [levizna] does not threaten the Chinese Communist Party. But a danger from the Right does exist within it, and we must fight with this.

Permit me to cite an example of how the theory of self-discipline expresses itself. A few days ago, the so-called revolutionary tribunal,* at the request of the national government, sentenced a workers' picket to three months' imprisonment for demanding a wage increase. The Federation of Labor in Hupeh issued an appeal to workers, calling upon the workers to terminate all struggle against capitalism for the duration of the Northern Expedition. In the same appeal, workers in foreign enterprises are urged not to strike, but to direct their complaints to the Ministry of Foreign Affairs. This capitalist tactic is being pursued in the name of avoiding further aggravation of relations between the national government and imperialism. A member of the Communist Party, the chief editor of the central organ of the Kuomintang, writes in the editorial of May 1 that workers must be prepared for sacrifices; they must work not only 16, but 20 hours.

Here is another example of defeatism and capitulationism, and it is very serious. In my speech at the opening of the congress, I said that in the present period the base of the revolution will be the democratic bloc of the proletariat, the peasantry, and the petty bourgeoisie, and that the proletariat will become the leading force of this bloc. Speaking at that same meeting, a representative of the Kuomintang declared that the Communist Party is the party of the proletariat, whereas the peasantry

---

* By order of the Kuomintang, the trade unions have established so-called revolutionary tribunals for the propagation of "revolutionary self-discipline" among workers (see Appendix II). [M.N.R. Page 186 in this book.—Eds.]

must be led by the Kuomintang. It is obvious that this was said in reply to my words. This was a challenge to the Communist Party. The Kuomintang has declared war on the Communist Party. The Kuomintang has anounced its intention to fight the Communists for the leadership of the peasantry. It has warned the Communist Party not to go to the peasantry with a program of an agrarian revolution.

And so, speaking at the congress two days later, Comrade T'an P'ing-shan, ostensibly with the aim of restoring peace with the Kuomintang, said at the congress: "We are the party of the proletariat, while the Kuomintang can conduct work among the peasantry." What does this signify? In practice, the supporters of passiveness are those very comrades who are so afraid of in any way offending our petty-bourgeois allies. To concede the peasantry to the Kuomintang which is openly opposed to any agrarian reform, and to conduct negotiations with reactionary generals—such are the actions proposed by the critics of the line of the Comintern delegation.

One more comment. In discussing the question of the base of the revolution, many comrades have said that Hupeh and Hunan are not sufficient. This is perfectly right. But we, in our proposals, have never said that we must remain in Hunan and Hupeh. We propose to strengthen the base of the revolution in those provinces where the national revolution has been partially accomplished. We do not propose to lock ourselves in in Hupeh and Hunan. It is natural that the consolidation of the revolutionary base must begin in these provinces, because it is here that the peasant movement is most developed and it is here that we have the opportunity of continuing our work. But this does not mean that we must work in these two provinces alone. If we neglect work in places where we do have the opportunity, if we refuse to intensify the revolution in any region in expectation of the time when the whole country will be under the power of the national government—then we will lose both Hupeh and Hunan, just as we have lost Kwangtung.

We do not for a minute belittle the necessity of fighting against militarism and the bourgeois reaction. The Mukden forces must be destroyed, and Chang Tso-lin must be crushed. But to say this is one thing, and to crush him is another. What is the use of forming vainglorious plans for driving back the Mukden forces beyond the Great Wall when we do not have the requisite power.

The revolution must develop in the social as well as in the territorial sense. It must be intensified and expanded. Chang Tso-lin must be overthrown. Chiang Kai-shek and his neomilitarism must be destroyed. These are the tasks of the revolution. We must prepare the forces necessary for accomplishing these tasks. The bourgeoisie has deserted to the side of counterrevolution. The petty bourgeoisie is wavering. Therefore, the correct tactic at the given stage of the revolution is one which undermines the strength of the reaction and unleashes the fighting energy of the masses.

In conclusion, I will say a few words about the achievements of the Chinese Communist Party.

The discussion has centered chiefly on the mistakes and the shortcomings of the Party. Nevertheless, this discussion has been of great value, and the Party stands to gain extremely by it. The criticism of the Right-Wing deviations, the condemnation of defeatist theories and the warning about capitulationist tendencies—all this merely serves to strengthen the Party which, after this congress, will become prepared for the great struggle to come. Taking stock of the achievements of the Party gives us a clear perspective and convinces us that the revolution is not on the decline, but on the rise. In two years, the Party has grown from 900 members to 50,000. This phenomenal growth has occurred under conditions of revolutionary struggle. It tells that 50,000 Party members represent a strong revolutionary army which has proven its ability to lead the proletariat in the revolutionary struggle. The gigantic growth of the Party is one more proof of the fact that the perspective of the development of the revolution is correct. The history of the Party proves that in the last two years the proletariat has, in the process of struggle, become the motive power of the national revolution.

The Chinese Communist Party is a young party. Not possessing sufficient experience, it has naturally made mistakes and displayed weakness. Nevertheless, the Communist Party has demonstrated that it is the only political force in the country which stands staunchly for the revolution. It will discard all Menshevik and conciliatory tendencies which have become manifest in its ranks. There is no place for Menshevism and opportunism in a party that has matured in revolutionary struggle. The Chinese Section of the Communist International is a mass party in the real sense of this word, and it will become a genuine Bolshevik party. If the Chinese laboring masses—the workers and the peasants—will be led in the revolution by the Bolshevik mass party, the success of the revolution is assured. From discussions that have taken place at this congress, the Party will emerge stronger, more experienced, more developed; it will demonstrate its ability to lead the revolutionary bloc of the proletariat, the peasantry and the petty bourgeoisie in the struggle against imperialism and the counterrevolutionary bourgeoisie.

May 3, 1927

12

THE PERSPECTIVES AND THE
CHARACTER OF THE CHINESE REVOLUTION

The delegation of the Communist International intends to deliver a summary report on the theses of the Seventh Plenum of the Executive Committee of the Communist International on the question of the Chinese revolution and on the question of the international situation.

The Communist International had the opportunity of determining a clear perspective of the Chinese revolution and of setting before the Chinese Communist Party concrete tasks with respect to the subsequent development of the revolution, because it gave an analysis of its past and of the paths of its development without separating these questions from questions of the world revolutionary movement.

The theses which the delegation of the Communist International is submitting for the examination of the Fifth Congress of the Chinese Communist Party are the result of the most careful analysis of not only the Chinese, but also the international, situation.

The Seventh Enlarged Plenum of the Executive Committee of the Comintern had very great significance. It discussed and adopted resolutions on a series of questions of world-wide importance: on the domestic and international situation of the U.S.S.R., on the general strike in England and the lockout of miners, and on the Chinese revolution. In its significance, this plenum can be equaled to a world congress.

At the plenum, a number of questions were discussed relating to the development of the world revolution. Among them, the question of the development, the character, and the perspectives of the Chinese revolution was one of the most important. The discussion of these problems was determined by a correct appraisal of the basic problem of the stabilization of the capitalist world. Can the world economy become

M. N. Roy's report to the Fifth Congress of the Chinese Communist Party on the Theses of the Seventh Plenum of the ECCI.—Eds.

stabilized on a capitalist basis? This question was subjected to thorough examination. The question of the stabilization of capitalism is, in the given epoch, the most decisive one for all world-political problems. A correct appraisal of the position of the capitalist world is necessary not only for determining the tactics of the Communist parties in capitalist countries, but is also necessary for working out a distinct perspective of the development of the Chinese revolution and for understanding its character.

During the past few years, there was a certain amount of uncertainty, even confusion, on the question of the stabilization of capitalism. Following the world war there began a period of intensive revolutionary activity. The world was enveloped by a gigantic wave of revolutions. In a series of European countries, especially in the defeated countries, the revolution became an accomplished fact. On the other hand, in colonial countries there developed a powerful movement for national liberation. This period was interpreted as being a period of world revolution. And the tactics of the Communist International were aimed at leading the proletariat into an attack on capitalism in order to overthrow it and to establish socialism.

But this period ended in a series of defeats for the revolution. Its concluding event was the utter defeat of the German revolution in October of 1923. A result of the temporary defeat of the revolutionary movement in a number of major countries was that capitalism began to strive for stabilization. The abatement of the revolutionary wave gave birth to the theory that capitalism has not yet played its role out to the end, that the world can still develop within the framework of a capitalist system. The social-democratic leaders came forward as the heralds of this theory of defeatism and fatalism. Social democracy even advanced the theory that the economic development of the world is still in need of capitalism, that subsequent development can occur only under conditions of a capitalist organization of production.

During the period of reaction which followed the defeat of the German revolution, this theory demoralized certain elements even in the ranks of Communist parties. When capitalism becomes a definitely reactionary force obstructing the economic and cultural development of society, then the struggle for the immediate establishment of socialism is necessary and inevitable. But if it is true that capitalism can still become stabilized, that the application of capitalist methods and principles of production are necessary for the subsequent economic development of the world, then a struggle that assumes the offensive does not enter into the task of the proletariat. In that case, the correct tactic for the revolutionary proletariat would be not a direct offensive, but the development of its forces, the winning of allies, and the preparation for a decisive struggle that would begin at a favorable moment. The essence of the social-democratic theory of the stabilization of capitalism adds up to the following: capitalism continues to play a progressive role—capitalism is still necessary to world development. In other words, the world is still going through a period of bourgeois revolution. It still has not entered the period of the proletarian revolution whose aim is the establishment of socialism.

In view of such confusion in the conceptions of the world situation, the Comintern found it necessary to subject the question to penetrating analysis in order to provide a correct appraisal of the position of capitalism. After a thorough scientific analysis of the world economic situation, the Seventh Plenum of the Executive Committee of the Comintern ascertained the presence of a temporary capitalist stabilization and established at the same time that the theory according to which capitalism can still contribute to the development of the world economy cannot withstand criticism. Facts demonstrate, however, that the bourgeoisie has succeeded in repelling the forces of the revolution and has thus created conditions [which allow] for attempts to stabilize capitalism. Capitalism can strengthen its position only by means of lowering the living standards of the working class in its parent country and suppressing the liberation movement in the colonies. In other words, attempts to stabilize capitalism inevitably lead to the destruction of domestic markets and to colonial wars which, in turn, reduce the foreign market. The precariousness of such stabilization thus becomes obvious. Stabilization is the result of but a temporary victory of the bourgeoisie.

The following facts tell of the stabilization of capitalism:

1. Adjustment of currency circulation: A series of leading capitalist countries have passed through a period of inflation. Money had virtually lost its value. The entire credit system was destroyed. This situation has now changed. In a number of countries, the currency has been stabilized. The value of paper money has been restored.

2. Growth of production: Immediately after the war, industry was gripped by a depression which entailed the rise of unemployment. At present this situation, too, has changed. The growth of production is occurring in a series of capitalist countries.

3. Expansion of trade: The growth of industry also served accordingly to develop trade. In the past year, the volume of foreign trade showed a marked increase.

All these factors demonstrate that the position of capitalism has improved.

On the other hand, there are facts which bespeak of the transient nature of the stabilization; namely:

1. The uneven and unstable nature of the growth of industry and commerce.

2. The large disparity between the production apparatus and the actual volume of production. The growth of industry does not correspond to the enormous development of the production apparatus during and after the war.

3. The decline of the British Empire.

4. The decline of capitalism in France. During the depression and the post-war crisis, France was in a relatively better position. At a time when almost all the capitalist countries were suffering from chronic unemployment associated with the depression in trade, France knew no unemployment. As a result of the Versailles treaty which crippled Germany, France turned into a first-class capitalist power. At the present time, France, too, has entered a period of crisis, the signs of which are the constantly growing unemployment and monetary inflation.

5. America is the only country with capitalist prosperity. But even there, signs of depression and crisis can be observed.

6. The gigantic economic development of the U.S.S.R.

7. The national-revolutionary movement in China which menaces the very existence of imperialism.

In spite of the period of temporary stabilization, the crisis of capitalism continues. The temporary stabilization is but a short spike [*interruption*] on a general downward curve. The nature of the present crisis is most peculiar. It is a crisis of at once overproduction and underproduction. Production must be increased with the aim of expanding trade. Otherwise, attempts a stabilization will prove unsuccessful. But there is no way that the actual volumes of production can be made to reach the level of the productive capacity of the industrial apparatus. Therefore, in spite of the relative growth of production, the crisis of underproduction remains basically unresolved. On the other hand, even with this limited growth of production there still remains the crisis of overproduction.

As a result of the war and the "rationalization" [system of "streamlining"] of industry, the buying power of the internal market has diminished considerably. The capitalist "rationalization" reduces wages and creates unemployment. The stabilization of capitalism is being achieved at the price of destroying markets. One of the methods of stabilization is the capital's attack on the wages of the working class. This method entails the diminution of the buying power of the internal market. As a result, the necessity of new markets arises. We are returning to the situation which led to the World War of 1914. The race for markets is a characteristic feature of the contemporary international situation. As a result of the growing competition, the world is confronted with the threat of a new war, one even more burdensome and more destructive than the last war.

The revolt of the colonial peoples has, on the other hand, decreased the possibility of creating overseas markets. In fact, the markets in a number of colonial countries have already shrunk to a considerable extent. In some countries, the shrinkage of markets was caused by chronic colonial wars. In other countries, it is the result of the growth of local industry. In yet others—a typical example of which is China—a serious threat is developing to the domination of imperialism itself.

In the current situation, the following conditions are necessary for the stabilization of world capitalism:

1. Further lowering of the living standard of the proletariat in the parent country, that is, the further destruction of the internal market.

2. The preservation of colonial markets and their further development. This requires the successful suppression of colonial uprisings. But in some of the colonial and semicolonial countries, the national-liberation movement has taken such deep roots that it can be liquidated only by means of protracted military action. This applies especially to China. However, predatory wars for the purpose of maintaining imperialist domination in the colonies destroy colonial trade and thereby weaken the base of imperialism.

The conditions necessary for the stabilization of capitalism may, consequently, be created only by further destroying the markets which are so necessary for capitalist stabilization. From this follows the conclusion that firm stabilization of capitalism is impossible. The perspectives for the development of revolution in capitalist as well as in colonial countries become clear in the light of such an appraisal of the world situation. This appraisal has permitted the Communist International to outline distinct perspectives for the development of the Chinese revolution.

Under the objective, international conditions of the present, the Chinese revolution will develop into a gigantic force for the destruction of capitalism. It is one of the most powerful factors militating against the stabilization of capitalism.

The Theses on the Chinese Situation of the Seventh Plenum of the Comintern do not derive from a casual analysis of the world situation. The Communist International began to study the colonial question and to develop its conception of the colonial revolution back in the time of the Second Congress in 1920. The perspective of the noncapitalist development of the Chinese revolution was advanced by Comrade Lenin in the Second Congress when he indicated the possibility of the non-capitalist development of colonies. The revolutionary movement in the colonies occurring in the period of the decline of capitalism is, essentially, an anticapitalist force. It is an instrument for the overthrow of capitalism.

At first, the leadership of the colonial revolution belongs to the native [*tuzemnaia*] bourgeoisie. The colonial revolution has as its aim not only the overthrow of imperialism. Before it lies yet another task—that of the abolition of native feudalism. The colonial revolution is generated by a contradiction between imperialism and the native bourgeoisie and, at the same time, it assumes objectively the role of an antifeudal force. As a result, it acquires the character of a bourgeois revolution.

In the theses of the Second Congress of the Communist International, the colonial revolution was portrayed as a bourgeois revolution. But, at the same time, in his speech at the Congress, Comrade Lenin pointed to the possibility of noncapitalist development. Neither in the theses nor in Lenin's speech was it said that the liberation movement in the colonies must develop inevitably as a purely bourgeois revolution thus creating conditions for the capitalist development of the colonies. The experience of colonial revolutions from the time of this congress and the Chinese revolution, in particular, have demonstrated that in the process of the development of the revolutionary movement the national bourgeoisie deserts the revolution and even turns against it; that the revolution does not remain under bourgeois leadership to the end. In countries where the bourgeoisie remains as the leader, the revolution perishes, the anti-imperialist struggle weakens, and the bourgeoisie compromises with imperialism. The development of the revolution in colonies inevitably outgrows the bourgeois leadership, and the leadership of the revolution passes to nonbourgeois elements. When the bourgeoisie leads a revolution directed against feudalism, it does so in the name of establishing capitalism inasmuch as feudalism interferes with capitalist development. But when the task of abolishing feudalism is accomplished by a colonial revolution that is led by a more revolutionary class and not by bourgeois elements, then the liquidation of feudalism is no longer accomplished for the purpose of establishing capitalism. The revolution then goes beyond these narrow frames. So far as the revolution destroys feudalism, it still retains the objective character of a bourgeois revolution. But its results go beyond the establishment of capitalism. It ushers in a period of non-capitalist economic development that leads directly to socialism.

Such are the basic considerations which enabled the Communist International to advance before the Chinese revolution the perspective of noncapitalist development. In the process of the development of the

Chinese revolution, facts have demonstrated the correctness of the analysis of the Communist International. How was it possible to arrive at such a correct analysis of the future? This was easy to do thanks to the clear and correct understanding of the world situation as a whole.

One of the conditions for the stabilization of capitalism is the suppression of colonial revolutions. In carrying out this task, imperialism can no longer count on its former allies in the colonies. In the past, the imperialist power in the colonies drew its support, on the one hand, from reactionary, feudal elements (their expression in China is militarism); on the other hand, its existence was favored by the passivity of the broad national masses. The first gave active support to imperialism. Since their own existence was dependent upon the continuation of imperialist rule, they became active allies of imperialism. The second [the broad national masses] were a passive factor inasmuch as they did not revolt against imperialist exploitation. The development of the national-liberation movement involved these masses in a widespread revolutionary struggle. As long as imperialism was not threatened with mass uprisings, the support of the feudal elements sufficed. However, in recent years, it became increasingly difficult for imperialism to maintain its rule in China with a base composed exclusively of feudal-militarist elements. The ease with which the national-revolutionary army routed the northern militarists in the Yangtze Valley serves as proof of this. Hence, imperialism is seeking to expand its social base in the colonies. This opens up the possibility of a compromise between imperialism and the upper strata of the bourgeoisie.

The gigantic development of the revolution went beyond the narrow confines of bourgeois leadership. The bourgeoisie sensed the threat of danger. It feared that the movement would not confine itself to establishing conditions for capitalist development, that the revolution might go further. On the other hand, the willingness of imperialism to make certain concessions to the native bourgeoisie in order to assure itself of continued colonial exploitation showed to the colonial bourgeoisie that provided it collaborates with imperialism, its economic growth was still possible. Its development can also transpire under imperialist rule. Hence, the national bourgeoisie is trying to narrow down the aims of the revolution and to lead it to make a deal with imperialism. By acting in such manner, the bourgeoisie is betraying the national revolution; it is running to the side of the counterrevolution, entering a united front with imperialism, and turning into an instrument for the destruction of the revolution. At this stage, the leadership of the revolution is passing into the hands of those classes which are being exploited by imperialism, which have no grounds for making a compromise and, consequently, the interests of which require the complete overthrow of imperialism and a radical democratization of the country.

The removal of the bourgeoisie from the leadership of the revolution and the transfer of leadership to the more revolutionary classes—the bloc of the petty bourgeoisie, the peasantry, and the proletariat—make the Chinese revolution an inseparable part of the world revolution. Under the leadership of the bourgeoisie, the national revolution would end with a deal with imperialism. China would become a base for the development of capitalism thus contributing to its stabilization. However, the Chinese revolution is now moving in the direction of establishing a political power which not only would not contribute to the development of capitalism in China, but would lead to the establishment of socialism.

Thus, the Chinese revolution is becoming an inseparable part of the world revolution. In the present epoch, it is, strictly speaking, the most important, leading participant in the world revolutionary struggle. Already the assistance that it is giving to the world proletariat in its struggle for socialism is not merely indirect. It has become the direct instrument of the struggle for socialism in the whole world. Since this is so, the danger of an imperialist intervention in China is becoming real. The development of the Chinese revolution under the leadership of the revolutionary-democratic bloc will be a severe blow to attempts at stabilizing world capitalism. For this reason, imperialism is concentrating all its forces on crushing the Chinese revolution. However, it follows from our evaluation of the international situation that these efforts on the part of imperialism will prove unsuccessful. The danger of an imperialist intervention does exist. Measures must be taken to parry it. But it must also be known that an imperialist intervention can not crush the Chinese revolution. Mutual competition and the fight for colonial markets constitute the basic feature of the contemporary international situation. Most of all, capitalism now stands in need of markets. Intervention in China prevents the realization of this immediate necessity. An attempt by imperialism to crush the Chinese revolution by military intervention will be extremely detrimental to the position of capitalism in its parent countries. Attempts at smashing the Chinese revolution will merely precipitate the destruction of capitalism in its parent countries. Imperialism is unable even to effect a prolonged economic blockade of China, since this would prove to be a two-edged sword. An economic blockade would be no less detrimental to the interests of imperialism than it would to China itself. It has already once been shown (during the Russian revolution) how the revolution is capable of resisting a blockade. In the present period, however, when the very existence of capitalism hinges on its ability to find new markets—and China is a market of tremendous importance—a prolonged blockade would deprive imperialism of the opportunity of using the Chinese market. This would cause enormous damage to imperialism.

Furthermore, an armed intervention or a prolonged economic blockade would intensify the competition and the internal contradictions between the various imperialist powers. While one or several of the imperialist powers which have already invested considerable capital in China may want to maintain unconditional political dominance in the country for the sake of preserving their interests, the other powers might be interested in creating a situation that would open opportunities for further development of trade. Contradictions exist even within each of the imperialist powers. One segment of the bourgeoisie, namely, the financiers and bankers, is in favor of war in China for the sake of defending the capital investments; the industrial bourgeoisie, however, is opposed to war: it wants peace in order to trade with China. Under such circumstances, the danger of imperialist intervention is not immediate. Imperialism knows that it cannot afford either the luxury of a war with China or the creation of a prolonged economic blockade. Hence, it is pursuing a policy of intimidation. It knows that if in a short time it succeeds in terrorizing the national government and in forcing it into submission, it will find itself the master of the situation. But imperialism will have to alter its policy if the national-revolutionary government is able to hold out for some time. The danger lies in an imperialist intervention of another order. It is the imperialist policy of demoralizing the national government that is dangerous.

The fundamental principle of the policy of imperialism is that of promoting the seizure of the leadership of the revolution by such classes which would lead the revolution to compromise with imperialism and thereby create conditions for the development of capitalism in China. As it turned out, it was impossible to subject the national-revolutionary movement as a whole to the leadership of the bourgeoisie. Then it was split with the aim of creating a second center under the leadership of the bourgeoisie, supported and inspired by imperialism. In this lies the real danger of imperialist intervention. This is the basic threat to the future development of the revolution. The only guarantee against this danger is the development and the intensification of the revolution under the hegemony of the proletariat. The revolution, led by the revolutionary-democratic alliance of the proletariat, the peasantry, and the urban petty bourgeoisie, must assume a decisive offensive against the social base of the feudal-bourgeois classes.

Let us now turn to the question of the perspectives of the Chinese revolution from the point of view of the internal alignment of class forces. Although the revolution is to a large extent determined by the international situation, basically its development will correspond to the existing class relations in the native society. One should look at whether the bourgeoisie is able to lead a struggle against imperialism and feudalism given the present alignment of class forces. It is necessary to clarify whether the perspective of the noncapitalist development of the Chinese revolution is a mechanical concept or one which follows from the objective conditions that exist in the country.

The structure of the Chinese society is for the most part feudal. The overwhelming majority of the population lives in the village. The urban population constitutes the minority. The national economy is still widely subjected to the dominance of feudal or semifeudal relations. This backwardness of the Chinese society is to a large degree the result of the pernicious effect of imperialism. Imperialism has kept the Chinese society in a state of backwardness. The Chinese people are interested in the struggle against imperialism, because a radical change in existing socioeconomic relations will only be possible after the destruction of their basic cause—imperialism. The social task of the Chinese revolution in the present epoch consists of destroying feudalism and of creating conditions for the free development of economic forces. This task, in a number of Western countries, has been accomplished by the bourgeoisie. The bourgeois revolution created conditions for capitalist development. Are there any grounds to assume that it will be any different in China? That the revolution will not be a bourgeois revolution and will not lead to the establishment of conditions for the development of capitalism?

In order to answer this question, it is necessary to give an analysis of the position of the Chinese bourgeoisie. The Chinese bourgeoisie is weak and undeveloped. That segment of the bourgeoisie which is comparatively better developed in the economic respect, that is, the *compradores* and the bankers' group, is extremely closely associated with imperialism. This segment will never join the anti-imperialist struggle. An independent industrial bourgeoisie is almost nonexistent. It is very weak. It is not in a position to lead the peasantry in a struggle against feudalism.

In contrast to Europe, the Chinese bourgeoisie did not grow out of the handicraft industry. The handicraft base of the Chinese bourgeoisie was destroyed by the interference of imperialism. The Chinese bourgeoisie sprung primarily from the landowning classes and is even now very closely connected with the feudal strata. Even the petty-bourgeois intelligentsia is closely connected with the feudal system of land ownership. Therefore, not only the bourgeoisie, but also a certain segment of the petty-bourgeois intelligentsia, are objectively incapable of, and are subjectively even hostile to, the cause of realizing the social aim of the Chinese revolution—the destruction of feudalism.

At the present stage of its development, the anti-imperialist struggle coincides with the struggle against feudalism. Therefore, the bourgeoisie is no longer capable of continuing the struggle against imperialism.

The social aim of the revolution—the overthrow of feudalism—is closely connected with its anti-imperialist character. The Chinese people must fight against imperialism. But, as a result of imperialist rule, the entire national economy is still under the yoke of feudal relations. The bourgeoisie and a segment of the petty-bourgeois intelligentsia are so intertwined with the feudal economy, while comprising an integral part of the feudal structure of the Chinese society, that they cannot lead a revolutionary struggle against imperialism, for a decisive struggle against it develops inevitably into a struggle against feudalism and its political expression.

Only by weakening the feudal support [opora] of the bourgeoisie will imperialism be really destroyed and definitely overthrown. The bourgeoisie cannot lead a revolution that leads to its own downfall. Events have proved the correctness of this theoretical principle. The bourgeoisie deserted the revolutionary front [and] turned against it, because the path of the revolution's attack against imperialism runs through the destruction of feudalism. This is why in the theses of the Communist International it is clearly stated that in the present epoch the Chinese revolution is first of all an agrarian revolution. And since, owing to their origin, their social bonds and economic interests, the bourgeoisie and a certain segment of the petty-bourgeois intelligentsia are opposed to an agrarian revolution, they cannot lead the revolution and must, therefore, go against it. These elements have withdrawn from the revolution and have turned objectively into an instrument of imperialism. The attempts of imperialism to alter the character of the Chinese revolution, to deflect it from its objective perspective of noncapitalist development, are calculated on these traitorous classes. There exists the possibility of a third party arising, a bourgeois-national party which would screen itself behind a false banner of nationalism. This means that there is the prospect of a struggle for hegemony between the bourgeoisie and the proletariat.

Two perspectives lie before the Chinese revolution.

One points to a development along bourgeois-democratic lines. This perspective means the onset of a period of capitalist development under the hegemony of imperialist finance capital; this perspective means China's conversion into an instrument for the stabilization of capitalism.

This perspective means the defeat of the Chinese revolution. The objective conditions, national as well as international, belie such a perspective. But subjectively, imperialism and the reactionary classes, including the national bourgeoisie, support the perspective of an imperialist intervention and the defeat of the Chinese revolution.

The second perspective is the path of noncapitalist development.

The international situation as well as the internal class forces incline in the direction of this perspective. The Kuomintang, the national-revolutionary government and the Communist Party are the subjective forces created by this perspective.

The national government is the political and military organ of the revolutionary-democratic classes, whereas the Communist Party is the political spokesman for the interests of workers and peasants.

The development of a revolution, such as in China, is new in the history of mankind. Nowhere has the revolution developed in a way such as in China. Being a new type of a revolution, it will bring to life a new type of a revolutionary state. Since the revolution will be under the leadership of a bloc consisting of the petty bourgeoisie, the peasantry and the proletariat, the revolutionary state of the given period cannot become a class state. It will be a petty-bourgeois state, but, in addition, a revolutionary petty-bourgeois state. Never yet in the history of mankind has a petty-bourgeois state been revolutionary; in China, however, it will be revolutionary thanks to its anti-imperialist character. The Communist Party is entering the national-revolutionary government, because it is the government of a revolutionary state. This is not a reformist coalition. The Communist Party is entering the government, because this is a revolutionary government. At the present stage of the revolution, hegemony in the struggle belongs to the proletariat, and it is participating in the national-revolutionary government in order to use the state machinery as an instrument for achieving hegemony.

Since the revolution still draws its support from a coalition of classes and does not possess a purely proletarian character, the proletariat cannot become the sole leader of this revolution. But the proletariat is the most important, dominant factor in this coalition and will be the one which determines the policy of this bloc. The Communist Party is the party of the proletariat and fights for socialism. But there are also other classes which participate in the struggle that is leading directly to socialism; not being proletarian, they cannot join the party of the proletariat. The immediate struggle in which these classes participate and which leads directly to the struggle for socialism is likewise a struggle of the proletariat. Therefore, the proletariat participates in and guides the development of this struggle in the direction of socialism.

Such are the considerations which determine the relations between the Communist Party and the Kuomintang at the present stage of the revolution. The development of the revolution has turned the Kuomintang from a tenuous coalition of classes in which the dominant factor was the bourgeoisie and even the feudal elements into an organ of democratic dictatorship. In other words, the Kuomintang, in its present social composition, can become and has already become an instrument through which the hegemony of the proletariat can be exercised. The three classes participating in the Kuomintang are interested in having the Chinese revolution develop in a noncapitalist direction, because capitalism exploits and oppresses all three of these classes. The difference lies in the fact that the proletariat is consciously fighting for socialism whereas the other two classes—the peasantry and the petty bourgeoisie—although they seek objectively the same goal, are moving toward it unconsciously.

Under the leadership of the bourgeoisie, the very same classes, that is, the petty bourgeoisie and the peasantry, could become an instrument for the development of capitalism. Finding themselves under the hegemony of the proletariat as a consequence of the development of the revolution, they have become a factor in the struggle for socialism. The state, created by the revolution and based on these three classes, is therefore an instrument of the dictatorship not of one class, but an organ of the dictatorship of three classes, an organ of a democratic dictatorship. This state represents a dictatorship, because it is not a bourgeois-democratic state. It will be a dictatorship, because it will be an instrument for the suppression of counterrevolutionary classes. It will be a dictatorship, because it will be an instrument of the agrarian revolution and of the abolition of feudal classes. It will be a dictatorship, because in the near future it will become an instrument for the abolition of the large-scale bourgeoisie through nationalization of large-scale industry and public utilities.

The base of the capitalist development of the country will remain untouched if the land, the large-scale industry, the railroads, and waterways are not nationalized. The revolutionary state becomes a dictatorship, because through it must be destroyed the base of capitalism in China.

If this democratic dictatorship does not fulfill this task, it will betray the interests of the three classes from which it draws its support.

If this revolutionary bloc is unable to carry out the dictatorship which fell into its hands in the course of the development of the revolution, the leadership will return to the bourgeoisie, and imperialism will become consolidated. If this state does not carry out a dictatorship and tries to become a bourgeois-democratic state, the revolution will be destroyed. The establishment of this dictatorship is necessary as a guarantee of the noncapitalist development of the revolution. The proletariat is fighting consciously for socialism. Therefore, the proletariat is the class that is most of all interested in such a development of the revolution. The main support of this dictatorship is the proletariat, even though this is not a proletarian, but a democratic dictatorship. The proletariat is aware of the objective sense of this dictatorship. It consists of the hegemony of this proletariat. Although at the present stage the proletariat is leading the revolution jointly with the petty bourgeoisie and the peasantry, it guarantees at the same time that the dictatorship will not forfeit its character. The proletariat is the support, the center of this bloc, while the petty bourgeoisie and the peasantry are its two wings. The proletariat is a class exploited thoroughly and to the hilt. That is why it fights consciously and objectively for socialism. But the other two classes still contain the germs of private property, that is, the germs of future capitalism. These two classes in their entirety will join the proletariat's struggle for socialism only when the germs of private property are destroyed. The task of the dictatorship is to destroy these germs within the bloc. Those germs of capitalist development in China which lie outside of the bloc must be destroyed by force and dictatorship. Within the bloc, however, this process must be clothed in another form.

In the course of the later development of the revolution, the proletariat will undertake the task of persuading its allies that the road to socialism is the only way out of the poverty in which the petty bourgeoisie and the peasantry find themselves. The proletariat will not use violence in its fight against prejudices of private property, against the sense of private property rights which still exists among its allies. But it will prove in practice that the agrarian question cannot be resolved as long as private ownership of land is not abolished. On the other hand, the proletariat will prove that without the abolition of private ownership in all means of production and distribution, one cannot avoid the development of capitalism, that is, the enslavement of the petty bourgeoisie, the proletariat, and the peasantry. Thus, in exercising its hegemony, the proletariat will transform this revolutionary-democratic state into a democratic dictatorship without transforming it immediately into a dictatorship of the proletariat. The theses of the Communist International did not touch upon the question of whether this democratic dictatorship will be capable of leading [the country] directly to socialism, or whether an intermediate period of a dictatorship of the proletariat will be necessary; I assume that the discussion of this question can be postponed to a future time.

But even today, it is clear to us that objectively there exists only one perspective for the Chinese revolution: the perspective of noncapitalist development. This perspective will be lost only if the subjective forces of the revolution fail to fulfill their roles. The development of the Chinese revolution along noncapitalist lines hinges on the ability of the Communist Party to become clearly aware of this perspective and to translate it resolutely into reality.

No less clear is the fact that the development of the revolution has created a state which objectively bears the character of a democratic dictatorship. The proletariat and its party are likewise responsible for the machinery of this revolutionary state being properly used for intensifying the struggle for noncapitalist development and for the realization of socialism.

Thus, the Fifth Congress of the Chinese Communist Party must set this perspective before the Chinese revolution; it must be capable of developing the struggle in this direction. The basic task of the Communist Party at the present stage of the revolution is to organize the revolutionary bloc with the participation of the peasantry and the urban petty bourgeoisie; to establish a democratic dictatorship; to lead the Chinese revolution on a noncapitalist path; and to transform the national revolution into a struggle for socialism.

May 4, 1927

13

THE NATIONAL REVOLUTION AND SOCIALISM

Having heard the speech of Comrade Wang Ching-wei,* the delegation of the Comintern considers it necessary to express itself more clearly.

At the present stage, the Communist Party will work jointly with the Kuomintang, but on the condition that it shares with it not only the responsibility, but the power as well. Therefore, it is absolutely necessary that each side clearly defines its conception of the revolution. The Communist International does not set before the Chinese Communist Party the task of struggling for the immediate realization of socialism. The perspective of the Chinese revolution is one of a development toward socialism, not through a period of capitalism, but through a period of economic development founded on a noncapitalist basis. In this period of noncapitalist development, complete abolition of private property will not be included in the immediate program of action. Only one class—the proletariat—stands for the abolition of private property. Since the revolution, in its present stage, will be led by a coalition of classes—and the proletariat is prepared to lead the revolution in collaboration with other classes—the proletariat cannot put forward a program for the immediate abolition of private property. The proletariat neither expects nor demands of the peasantry and the petty bourgeoisie that they enter this revolutionary bloc on conditions laid down by the proletariat

M. N. Roy's reply to Wang Ching-wei's statement at the Fifth Congress of the Chinese Communist Party.—Eds.

* Wang Ching-wei was not among the delegates of the Kuomintang present at the opening of the congress. He expressed the desire to be present for the Comintern representative's report on the theses of the plenum of the Comintern. After listening attentively to the report, he pronounced a characteristic speech. The congress welcomed him enthusiastically, and my reply to his speech was censured by the leading comrades as being "a tactless attack on the Left [Wing] Kuomintang." [M.N.R.]

alone. The block will fall apart if the proletariat attempts to foist on it a program for the immediate abolition of all forms of private property. The Communist Party does not propose to lead the proletariat along this path. Let us be clear on this point, and then the mutual relations between the Communist Party and the Kuomintang will become well-defined. Essentially, the relations between the Kuomintang and the Communist Party at the present stage of the revolution are very clear: the proletariat and its party—the Communist Party—form an integral part of the Kuomintang, that is, of the revolutionary-democratic bloc; therefore, the problem is not one of adjusting the relations between the parties, but one of adopting a platform of the national revolution that corresponds to the interests of the three classes comprising this revolutionary bloc. Historically, all three of these classes are foes of capitalism; and since all objective conditions favor a noncapitalist development, this program, too, will by its very essence lead inevitably to the struggle for socialism. The interests of the proletariat are not hostile to the interests of the Kuomintang. The proletariat is in the Kuomintang and it cannot fulfill its historical role without being in the Kuomintang. If the proletariat and its party do not understand the interests, attitudes, and desires of their revolutionary allies, they will be unable to remain in the Kuomintang and pursue the right policy. The Kuomintang in its present social composition was created by the revolution, and its later development will be determined by the proletariat acting within the Kuomintang as the conscious vanguard of the revolution. The proletariat will participate in the determination of the program of the national revolution in its later stage, guiding itself by the interests of the three classes which make up the revolutionary bloc and by the peculiarities of the situation in China. In pursuing our struggle toward socialism, it is necessary to take proper account of the difficulties and peculiarities of the struggle. On behalf of the delegation of the Comintern I assure Comrade Wang Ching-wei and, in his person, the whole Kuomintang, that we will not forget this for a minute. The Communist International furnished a general perspective and outlined a program of the Chinese revolution. The task of the Chinese Communist Party is to apply this program to local conditions in such a way that the revolution would move toward socialism through a period of noncapitalist development. The Chinese Communist Party which has entered the revolutionary-democratic bloc, that is, the Kuomintang, will be able to carry out this program of the revolution in accordance with the demands of objective conditions and will strive for the consolidation of the revolutionary bloc in the process of the struggle. There are no contradictions here; the very possibility of contradictions does not exist. The Kuomintang is a revolutionary organization and shall remain a revolutionary organization, because it is fighting against imperialism. And for this very reason, the proletariat will collaborate with the Kuomintang until final victory.

May 4, 1927.

14

NONCAPITALIST DEVELOPMENT AND SOCIALISM.
DEMOCRATIC DICTATORSHIP AND THE
DICTATORSHIP OF THE PROLETARIAT

The theses of the plenum of the Comintern contain two basic principles: concerning the noncapitalist development of the Chinese revolution and concerning the nature of the state in this period of noncapitalist development.

I will not reply separately to the opinions expressed by various comrades on these two questions, and will confine myself only to general comments.

I will start with the question of noncapitalist development. There are two determinant factors in the perspective of the noncapitalist development of the Chinese revolution: (1) the international situation—I have dwelt on this sufficiently in my first speech—and (2) the class character of the Chinese revolution.

The basic feature of the world situation at the present time is the decline of capitalism. Capitalism has become a definitely reactionary force in every part of the world. In our epoch, any revolutionary movement is aimed essentially against capitalism. All these movements represent a means of overthrowing capitalism. This is why the Chinese revolution acquires the character of a struggle against capitalism; that is why there lies before it the perspective of noncapitalist development.

The class basis of the revolution is the second factor determining the noncapitalist character of the Chinese revolution. Events of the past year have proved that the base of the Chinese revolution is becoming narrower. This was very clearly brought out in the discussions that took place here. At its present stage of development, the base of the Chi-

M. N. Roy's final speech at the Fifth Congress of the Chinese Communist Party.—Eds.

nese revolution is comprised of an alliance of classes which are not interested in capitalist development. These classes are suffering, to one degree or another, from the yoke of capitalism. Therefore, they are interested in its destruction. As a result, the question arises as to what course noncapitalist development will take.

The theory that there must be a period of capitalism in between feudalism and socialism is common knowledge. In what way, then, will China arrive from feudalism to socialism if this intermediate period —capitalism—is eliminated?

The essence of this period is not the capitalist system as such, but the development of new productive forces and forms of production. Before the struggle for the realization of socialism can begin, society must reach a certain level of economic development. In all countries heretofore, this development occurred under conditions of a capitalist system. This gave rise to the theory that between feudalism and socialism there must be an intermediate period of capitalism. However, the capitalist principles of production (for profit) by themselves are not inevitably necessary for creating conditions that are ripe for the struggle for socialism; the determinant conditions for the realization of socialism are the methods and forms of production which arise under capitalism.

According to the theses of the Comintern, the immediate perspective of the Chinese revolution is not socialism, but one of noncapitalist development. It is clear that before reaching socialism, the economic development of the country must rise to a certain level.

Thanks to the presence of certain forces, it is not necessary in China to apply capitalist principles of production in order to reach this level of economic development.

What does this mean? This means that the economic development which prepares for the transition to socialism can occur in China with the help of capitalist methods, but not necessarily on the basis of the capitalist system of exploitation. What is the capitalist system? The fundamental feature of the capitalist system is production for the sake of profit, production based on surplus value. In the process of social evolution, as new productive forces emerge, the feudal system becomes destroyed and higher forms of production are established. In this historical period, the dominant factor in the whole economic and political life of a society becomes a certain social class—the bourgeoisie— which owns these means of production.

The new method of production arising in this period—machine production instead of handicraft—becomes identified with the capitalist system which is based on the exploitation of human labor.

However, these are two essentially different things. The system of capitalist exploitation and the method of capitalist production (arising in the period of capitalism) are not one and the same thing. They are by no means inseparable. From the example of the U.S.S.R., we see that industry can develop without a capitalist system of production.

Such precisely will be the nature of the economic development which China, as a result of the revolution, will experience in the period of noncapitalist development. Every method of capitalist production will be used to raise the national economy to the necessary level for the establishment of socialism.

A question was raised here about the difference between the perspective of China's noncapitalist development and the program of the Russian *Narodniks* [Populists].

The perspective of the Chinese revolution does not deny the necessity of an economic development which would be more or less comparable to the development of other countries under the capitalist system. In China a certain stage of economic development must be reached at which all methods of production inherent to the capitalist system will be applied.

The program of the *Narodniks* was reactionary. When they asserted that Russia had no need of a capitalist system, that Russia differed from other countries, they thereby denied the necessity of the economic development that was occurring in other countries under the capitalist system. They thought that Russia would remain forever under the conditions of an economy of small-scale production. This program, this point of view objectively expressed the desire to perpetuate forever in Russia the rule of feudalism. The human society has outgrown feudalism, it has freed itself from its fetters in order to develop higher methods of production. If the need for this is denied, then there is no necessity of overthrowing feudalism.

Plekhanov and Lenin have branded this theory as reactionary and have pointed out that capitalism must develop in Russia as a preparatory stage to the struggle for socialism. In proving the necessity of a period of capitalist development, Plekhanov and Lenin did not thereby establish that the economic development of a society can occur only on the basis of the capitalist principle of commodity production (for profit). They wanted to say that the economic development of Russia must follow the path of so-called capitalist countries, that feudalism must be overthrown, and that the road to socialism will be opened along this path.

But here one might raise the question: Why, then, did not Lenin and Plekhanov, at the beginning of the twentieth century, set before the Russian revolution the perspective of noncapitalist development? If this is possible for the Chinese revolution, then why was it not possible for the Russian? It was not possible, because the two factors which today determine the noncapitalist development of the Chinese revolution did not exist at that time. At that time, capitalism was still making progress all over the world. The decline of capitalism had not as yet begun. In the second place, there was still a lack of those internal forces which could undertake the task of economic development on a noncapitalist basis.

The difference between the program of the *Narodniks* and the perspective of the noncapitalist development of the Chinese revolution is enormous. The former is reactionary in character, the latter—revolutionary.

I shall turn to the next question: what will be the practical forms of achieving noncapitalist development? In the theses of the Comintern it is pointed out that this period will start with the nationalization of transport, heavy industry, and public utilities. But the nationalization of heavy industry alone still does not represent a sufficient guarantee of noncapitalist development. In several highly developed countries, railroads and other public utilities have already been nationalized. Just the same, the economic development in those countries is based on capitalism. Even bourgeois economists have been known to propose a program of nationalizing the basic branches of industry. During the war, heavy industry in almost all the powers at war was placed under government control. But this still did not create conditions for noncapitalist development or for the development of socialism. Therefore, nationalization must occur under different circumstances in order to become a condition for noncapitalist development. The nature of the state in which nationalization of large-scale industry occurs—that is the decisive factor. If nationalization is carried out in a bourgeois state, not only does it not serve as a prerequisite for socialism, but it produces higher forms of capitalist exploitation.

In China, the nationalization of heavy industry, transport, and public utilities will mark the beginning of a period of noncapitalist development, because it will be carried out by a revolutionary, and not a bourgeois, state. Created by the national revolution, the state will draw its support from the three exploited classes. All three classes are oppressed and exploited. The proletariat is the most important and determinant of these three classes, since it has absolutely no ties with the institution of private property. Next, the basic and most important function of this state will be the struggle against imperialism, and this will endow it with an essentially revolutionary character. If this state does not fight against imperialism, if it agrees to a deal with imperialism, it will contribute to the stabilization of capitalism which, in turn, will lead to the temporary defeat of the Chinese revolution. The very existence of this state depends on its unrelenting struggle against imperialism and capitalism. Consequently, if it starts with the confiscation of the basic branches of industry, transport, and public utilities, this would provide a sufficient guarantee of the development of the country on a noncapitalist basis.

During the discussions here, comparisons were drawn between the New Economic Policy in the U.S.S.R. and the perspective of the noncapitalist development of China. I think that such a comparison is only misleading and erroneous. The NEP came after the period of War Communism, it was introduced by the proletarian state and was carried out under the dictatorship of the proletariat. NEP is not an intermediate stage between feudalism and socialism, but a component part of the developing process of socialist construction. In the Soviet Union, NEP was preceded by the abolition of private property. In China, the period of noncapitalist development represents an intermediate stage of economic development from feudalism to socialism. This stage of noncapitalist development does not coincide with the complete abolition of private property. Private property will be gradually abolished in this process of noncapitalist development. It is wrong, therefore, to compare noncapitalist development in China with the NEP in the Soviet Union. NEP is not a new economic policy as compared to the old economic policy; it is simply the economic policy of the current period.

As I have already pointed out earlier, the guarantee of noncapitalist development is the revolutionary nature of the state. What will be the nature of the state in the period of noncapitalist development? As has already been pointed out in the theses and established with sufficient certainty during the discussions here, the nature of the state will be determined by a democratic dictatorship, as distinguished from the dictatorship of the proletariat. Here again we see a type of state which is intermediate between a democracy, that is, a capitalist democracy, and a dictatorship of the proletariat. It will be a democracy in the sense that its base will consist of not one class, but of a coalition of three classes. It will be a dictatorship in the sense that these three classes will form one whole on the basis of a program of overthrowing and destroying all classes outside of the bloc of these three classes. The democratic nature of this dictatorship assures the possibility of teamwork between the proletariat and the petty bourgeoisie. But since this democracy contains at the same time an element of dictatorship, the decisive factor will be the proletariat which will ward off the danger of democratic degeneration.

But this brings up a second question: Can this state lead directly to socialism by omitting the period of the dictatorship of the proletariat? There are serious doubts and misgivings on this question in the Kuomintang. One cannot, however, dodge the answer out of the consideration that it might frighten the Kuomintang.

At the same time, it is quite fair to say that this question does not require an immediate solution. At the given moment, this question is more theoretical than politically relevant. For this reason, I intentionally did not touch upon it in my first speech. But it was mentioned in the course of discussion. A few words should therefore be said about it.

The dictatorship of the proletariat is necessary for destroying the dictatorship of the bourgeoisie. If we could envisage in China a society without a bourgeoisie, then, perhaps, the necessity of the dictatorship of the proletariat would not arise. But this is the Menshevik viewpoint. The British Labor Party adheres to a theory such as this. They say: In Russia it was necessary to overthrow tsarist autocracy; in England, however, the government is democratic; in England there is no dictatorship of the bourgeoisie; therefore, there is no necessity for a dictatorship of the proletariat.

We would find ourselves prisoners [v plenu] of the Menshevik theory if we were to assimilate such a naïve conception of the essential nature of the petty bourgeoisie who are participating with the proletariat in the revolutionary bloc.

The bloc forming the social base of the state in which noncapitalist economic development is possible, is a coalition of classes and, incidentally, it contains social elements that are bound up with the institution of private property. Consequently, the noncapitalist structure will contain the germs of private property. The immediate program of the national revolution does not include outright abolition of private property. In view of the necessity of creating a bloc composed of the petty bourgeoisie, the peasantry, and the proletariat, a program for the immediate abolition of all forms of private property would prove premature and harmful to the revolution. As long as private property continues to exist, the base for the bourgeoisie and for the development of capitalism will be preserved. Elements of private property remain in the social structure. The classes sharing power with the proletariat are tied to the principles and the institution of private property.

In the period of noncapitalist development—which is assured by two factors: the international situation and the internal alignment of class forces—the possibility of capitalist development still continues to exist. Therefore, noncapitalist development will not proceed peacefully; and during this period, the class struggle will continue. But we have one more guarantee and a very real one. It consists in that the proletariat will have hegemony in this bloc, in this revolutionary state. Ahead of us lies a period of class struggle, but at the same time we have a guarantee that the struggle will end in our victory. The revolutionary program for the nearest future makes provision for the overthrow of imperialism and militarism, for the liquidation of the last vestiges of feudalism and for the destruction of the political and economic power of the large-scale bourgeoisie. All three classes participating in the bloc are united on this program. The economic and political program which the bloc will have to adopt in order to carry on a successful struggle against its four enemies will assure noncapitalist development. As long as the economic base of imperialism—large-scale industry, railroads, the merchant marine, the banks is not nationalized, imperialism will not be over- thrown, and the power of imperialism in China will not be destroyed.

In China, the large-scale bourgeoisie is almost nonexistent as an in- dependent force. It has extremely close ties with imperialist finance. As the revolution destroys imperialism, it will at once demolish the native, large-scale bourgeoisie.

The decisive struggle against imperialism which this bloc must wage and the political impotence of the large-scale, native bourgeoisie make it virtually impossible for capitalism to develop in the country.

A capitalist development of the country under the hegemony of imperialist finance capital and based on economic concessions to im- perialism would signify the defeat of the Chinese revolution and the vic- tory of imperialism. The revolutionary state is obliged to fight to pre- vent such an outcome of the revolution, thus increasing the possibility of noncapitalist development.

In its agrarian program, the revolutionary state will have to go even further than would the bourgeoisie. This reasoning is not of a sub- jective order. The revolutionary state is forced into this; were it to con- fine itself to the framework of a bourgeois revolution, it would perpetuate the base for capitalist development, it would leave the germs of its own destruction. The aim of the agrarian program of the revolutionary-democratic state in the period of noncapitalist de- velopment will not be one of creating conditions for capitalist de- velopment. The agrarian reforms of the revolutionary-democratic state will lead to an agrarian revolution which only the proletariat can carry to its conclusion.

There are, furthermore, considerations of a political nature. Without the support of the popular masses, this bloc will not be able to pursue the struggle against its enemies—imperialism, militarism, the bour- geoisie, and the feudal lords. Therefore, this state must be a genuinely democratic state, committed to granting power to the workers and peasant masses. In view of the revolutionary war, the state will have to arm the workers and the peasants. This revolutionary-democratic state, with the germs and elements of bourgeoisie and capitalism, will be compelled to create the conditions for a proletarian revolution. The power will pass into the hands of workers and peasants. Workers and peasants will be armed. Conditions, fully favorable to a direct struggle for socialism, will be created. The economic base of capitalist development will be undermined; the bourgeoisie will be politically annihilated.

The proletariat and the peasantry will be armed. This will occur under conditions of the hegemony of the proletariat. Thus, after the process of noncapitalist development has significantly expanded, the ruling power will be in the hands of the proletariat, while the petty bourgeoisie will find itself in a weakened and isolated position. Under such conditions, it is doubtful that the final class conflict will assume such violent forms as would be the case in the highly developed capitalist countries.

To sum up: A democratic dictatorship cannot be a substitute for the dictatorship of the proletariat. The establishment of a democratic dictatorship does not mean that a dictatorship of the proletariat, as a transition to socialism, will be superfluous. But the class conflict which will end in the establishment of a dictatorship of the proletariat will not assume such sharp and violent forms as those inherent to the class struggle in highly developed capitalist countries. Thus, in general terms, I have touched upon the two basic points of the theses.

In conclusion, I would like to reply to the three questions raised by the comrade from Shanghai. These questions are highly important. There is no need, however, to reply to each of them separately. Essentially speaking, I have already answered them, in general, in my speech. The questions are:

1. How will the two parties carry out the dictatorship?

2. How will the Communist Party's transition from an opposition party to a government party occur?

3. Is the Wuhan government really capable of taking the path of noncapitalist development by means of confiscating large-scale industry, land, railroads, etc.? [The answers are:]

1. In the course of my speech I explained how the Communist Party and the proletariat will act within this bloc. During this period the democratic dictatorship will be carried out not by two parties, but by a bloc of three classes; the dictatorship will not be carried out by one party.

2. The very formulation of the question on the transition of the Communist Party from the opposition to power is erroneous. The

Communist Party is not now an opposition party. The proletariat is a part of the ruling bloc, and the Communist Party is participating in all the organs of state.

The question is not one of how to come to power, but, rather, one of how to get out of this period of partial power. I have already explained how this process will occur. In realizing its hegemony, the proletariat will gradually achieve dictatorship.

3. The present Wuhan government will not, on its own initiative, decide to nationalize land, railroads, and factories. But the objective conditions of the revolutionary struggle will force it to do so. The subjective factor here will again be the proletariat which not only supports this program objectively, but must also put it into practice. Being a revolutionary bloc of three classes, the Wuhan government must therefore implement the program of nationalization. The guarantee of this is the proletariat. If the proletariat, under the leadership of the Communist Party, can achieve hegemony during the present stage [of the revolution], then there is full guarantee that the Wuhan government will be compelled to carry out a program of nationalization.

In concluding, I would like to express my satisfaction that the theses of the Comintern have provoked neither opposition nor serious doubts here. This means that the Fifth Congress of the Chinese Communist Party has accepted the theses of the Comintern and, by commencing work on the basis of these theses, it is opening a new chapter in the history of the Chinese revolution. The Chinese Communist Party is a young party, but it has a strong base—the workers and the peasant masses who have gained enormous revolutionary experience in the course of the past few years. Therefore, the Communist International is confident that its Chinese Section will be capable of leading the national revolution through its various stages to the goal outlined in the theses of the Communist International.

May 5, 1927

15

THESES ON THE POLITICAL SITUATION AND
THE TASKS OF THE CHINESE COMMUNIST PARTY

Adopted at the Fifth Congress of the
Chinese Communist Party, May 9, 1927

1. Since the last congress of our party, the development of the revolution has proceeded at a rapid pace. The growth of our party has been equally rapid. At the time of the Fourth Congress, the Party had 950 members; now it has more than 50,000. The political influence of the party has increased even more. Our Party is the recognized leader of the proletariat and the peasantry in the whole country. It has led the proletariat in its unceasing struggle and in the armed uprisings against imperialism and militarism during the past two years. In only four years under the leadership of our Party, organizations uniting two and a half million workers and ten million peasants have been created. Our Party has become a party of the masses.

The struggle of the Shanghai proletariat which began May 30, 1925; the Hong Kong strike; the anti-imperialist struggle of the Hankow workers—these are the historical landmarks of the Chinese revolution. During the past two years, the proletariat played a dominant role in the national-revolutionary movement, but now it has captured the hegemony in this struggle. This role of the working class in the Chinese revolution guarantees that the revolution will not usher in a period of capitalist development, but will lead directly to the struggle for socialist construction.

2. The development of the Chinese revolution has fully confirmed the prognosis given in the theses of the Seventh Enlarged Plenum of the Executive Committee of the Comintern. As the national revolution expanded, the class struggle intensified. The feudal-bourgeois elements

within the Kuomintang were trying to lead the revolution to a compromise with native reaction and foreign imperialism. Leaning on the petty bourgeoisie, the peasantry, and the proletariat, the Left Wing of the Kuomintang came out against the feudal-bourgeois policy of compromise. A crisis developed in the national movement. As it turned out, the feudal-bourgeois elements were unable to subordinate the movement to their class interests and they split the party. Not only did they abandon the national-revolutionary struggle, but they turned against it and became an instrument of imperialism. The heroic Shanghai proletariat rose up twice in revolt in order to help the national armies. In the struggle against foreign imperialism and the Northern reaction, it made the greatest sacrifices. And despite this, soon after Shanghai was captured by an army of Southerners, workers were being shot in the streets of Shanghai by order of the renegade Chiang Kai-shek.

The revolution entered its third stage. The feudal elements and the large-scale bourgeoisie turned against the revolution. The social base at this stage of the revolution is the revolutionary bloc of the proletariat, the peasantry, and the urban petty bourgeoisie. The proletariat will have hegemony in this revolutionary bloc.

3. The rapid development of the revolutionary movement and the growth of the proletariat's influence within it at the same time give birth to the crystallization of all the forces of the counterrevolution. This manifests itself in the establishment of a united front of imperialists for the purpose of direct military intervention and a bloc composed of militarists and the reactionary, large-scale bourgeoisie directed against the national revolution. Fearing that the consolidation of the revolutionary-democratic power under the hegemony of the proletariat would create the premises for a decisive struggle for the final destruction of the power of imperialism and its allies in China, imperialism is seeking to intimidate the national-revolutionary government and to force it into a policy of compromise. On the other hand, imperialism is using every means to promote the creation of a counterrevolutionary bloc composed of militarists and the large-scale bourgeoisie. The menacing alliance of imperialism, militarism, and the large-scale bourgeoisie creates the greatest danger for the revolution at the very beginning of its third stage. The subsequent development of the revolution will pass in a resolute struggle against this alliance. Only by mobilizing all the forces of the people's energy by establishing a democratic dictatorship of the proletariat, the peasantry, and the petty bourgeoisie, will the national revolution fend off and finally destroy this alliance.

4. May 30, 1925, marked the beginning of the proletariat's struggle for hegemony. This struggle led to temporary success in the crea-

tion of a revolutionary-national government in Canton. But when the feudal-bourgeois elements became aware of the fact that an anti-imperialist struggle under the hegemony of the proletariat could go too far, creating an objective threat to their class interests, they tried to subordinate the national-liberation movement to their control. The first expression of this struggle between the proletariat and the bourgeoisie for hegemony in the national revolution was the *coup* of March 20 when Chiang Kai-shek overthrew the Left national government.

The *coup* of March 20 marked the beginning of the second stage in the struggle for hegemony. At this stage, the balance was in favor of the camp of the bourgeoisie. It used the victory in Kwangtung to spread its influence to other provinces. In this period the policy of our party was incorrect. A united front with the bourgeoisie against imperialism was necessary as long as the bourgeoisie still remained in the ranks of the national-revolutionary movement. But after March 20, the future role of the bourgeoisie became clear. The party failed to understand that the bourgeoisie had once again seized the leadership of the national revolution only in order to liquidate it. In view of this incorrect appraisal of the role of the large-scale bourgeoisie at a new and higher stage of the revolution, our Party joined the united front without demanding sufficient guarantees to protect the interests of the laboring masses. In the period of reaction that followed the *coup* of March 20, the task was not one of overthrowing Chiang Kai-shek. The Party should have continued to struggle for hegemony, it should have created a revolutionary Left Wing bloc of the proletariat, the peasantry, and the petty bourgeoisie to counterbalance the feudal-bourgeois leadership which, objectively, could not but betray the revolution. This task did not contradict the tactic of a united front.

In the struggle for hegemony, the proletariat must have the peasantry for its ally. The proletariat must demand a radical agrarian reform in order to consolidate its alliance with the peasantry in the struggle against the feudal-bourgeois reaction. It turned out that the Party was unable to lead the proletariat to realize this aim. The united front was much too broad. It encompassed even the feudal-patriarchal forces of reaction in the village. The demands of the Kwangtung peasant movement, which was led by our Party, went no further than the organization of peasant unions and the reduction of rentals. The feudal-bourgeois bloc was already preparing to compromise and to liquidate the revolution, while our Party did not understand that it was necessary to strike at the very foundation of its power in the village. The feudal-bourgeois conspiracy against the revolution should have been answered by intensifying the social base of the revolution. This was not done. It was due to this very mistake that Kwangtung was so easily lost.

5. The subjective motive of the Northern Expedition was the desire of the bourgeoisie to expand its power; objectively, however, the North-

ern Expedition was a means of developing the revolution. Therefore, the policy of supporting the Northern Expedition was correct.

Here again our Party did not devote sufficient attention to the necessity of intensifying the social base of the revolution concomitantly with its territorial expansion. The source of this error was the overestimation of the role of the large-scale bourgeoisie. The policy of the Party was aimed at helping the bourgeoisie to complete the first stage (territorial expansion) of the revolution; the second stage (intensification of the revolution) was to have followed later. As a result of this erroneous policy, those revolutionary-democratic forces which could have organized a resistance against the feudal-bourgeois elements—whose aim was to use military victories for the purpose of expanding their own power—were not mobilized. In the end, the feudal-bourgeois elements were able to amass such strength that they began openly to proclaim their monopoly of the national-liberation movement and succeeded in splitting it. Thanks to the erroneous conception of the policy of a united front, the social base of the reaction in regions occupied by the national army was left untouched. As a result, it became impossible to isolate Chiang Kai-shek when he rose up against the Party. The feudal-bourgeois elements broke away from the national revolution, taking a considerable number of forces with them. Kwangtung would not have been lost so easily had the position of the reactionary classes been successfully weakened by intensifying the class struggle in the towns and villages (especially in the villages).

6. The overestimation of the role of the large-scale bourgeoisie led to an underestimation of the petty bourgeoisie. The petty bourgeoisie can never become an independent political force. When the large-scale bourgeoisie in alliance with the feudal reaction was preparing for a compromise and for the liquidation of the revolution, the proletariat should have devoted particular attention to the petty bourgeoisie to prevent it from going over to the side of the bourgeoisie. The principal cause of the defeat of the Shanghai uprising was that the proletariat did not provide itself with the support of the petty-bourgeois masses.

Chiang Kai-shek did not become a counterrevolutionary all of a sudden or on April 12 when he issued the order for the massacre of workers in the streets of Shanghai. He became an enemy of the revolution back on March 20, 1926. But our Party was unable to demonstrate that the bourgeoisie, in the person of Chiang Kai-shek, was seeking to liquidate the revolution; for this reason, our Party failed to mobilize the urban democratic masses around the proletariat for the purpose of preventing the establishment in Shanghai of the neomilitaristic dictatorship of Chiang Kai-shek.

7. The Fifth Congress of the Communist Party believes that the

February uprising of the Shanghai proletariat was premature. Our Party could not gain control of the masses in the instant of this revolutionary enthusiasm. Even more premature was the attempt to form in the city a government based on a disguised Soviet of Workers' Deputies. The large-scale bourgeoisie did not support the movement from the beginning. The white terror that started frightened the petty bourgeoisie. The proletariat found itself isolated. The time between the crushing of the February uprising and the March uprising should have been used for establishing a close alliance between the proletariat and the petty-bourgeois masses as a basis for a revolutionary-democratic government. But our Party, having met with failure in the first premature action, plunged to the other extreme; in its desire to enlist the participation of the large-scale bourgeoisie in city government, it completely forgot about the petty bourgeoisie. Another mistake of our Party was that it led the Shanghai movement completely uncoördinated with and independently of the general development of the national-revolutionary struggle.

8. The Fifth Congress does justice to the historical significance of the heroic struggle of the Shanghai proletariat. It asserts that in spite of the errors and defeats, the Shanghai uprisings are outstanding events in the proletariat's struggle for hegemony in the revolution. At the present stage, when the revolutionary-democratic bloc of the proletariat, the peasantry, and the petty bourgeoisie is becoming the social base of the revolution, the Shanghai proletariat will remain as the most important support of the revolution, and Shanghai—as one of the basic centers of the struggle. The Fifth Congress repudiates the view that compromise with imperialism is inevitable for anyone who occupies Shanghai. Chiang Kai-shek occupied Shanghai with the sanction of imperialism; but since the very uprising of May 30, the Shanghai proletariat has not ceased its struggle against imperialism and, in the end, it will overthrow the power of imperialism.

9. The Fifth Congress definitely subscribes to the view that the desertion of the feudal-bourgeois elements does not weaken the revolution. The movement is undergoing not a period of decline, but a period of intensified revolutionary struggle. In this period, the proletariat is becoming the motive power in the struggle for an agrarian revolution and a democratic political power. As long as the feudal-bourgeois elements remained in the national movement, they prevented the realization of the agrarian and democratic program of the revolution. This inhibited the revolutionary energy of the masses. Now all obstacles to the free development of the revolutionary-democratic forces are removed, and the movement is therefore gaining strength.

The rapid territorial expansion of the revolution must be accompanied by intensification of the revolutionary base in territories under Nationalist occupation. The loss of Kwangtung demonstrates the danger of expansion without a corresponding intensification of the revolution. At the present stage, the chief aim of the revolution is to destroy the very roots of the reaction in order to consolidate the victory. This will be achieved by carrying out a program of radical agrarian reform and by the establishment of revolutionary-democratic power in the village.

10. The development of the revolution has increased the danger of imperialist intervention. This creates a defeatist mood, especially among the petty bourgeoisie, and results in a tendency to move the base of the revolution further away from the strongholds of imperialism. The Fifth Congress cautions the party against inadmissible tendencies of this type. The danger of an imperialist intervention really exists. The Communist Party will rouse the worker and peasant masses to a resolute struggle for the defense of the revolution against imperialist attack. The basic aim—defense and intensification of the bases in the south and in the center—does not preclude the necessity or the possibility of expansion in all directions. But the Communist Party must fight against this tendency to abandon or weaken the existing base under the pretext of expansion.

The rich and economically developed southeastern and central regions must not be left to the complete disposal of the bourgeoisie.

The Fifth Congress entrusts the Communist Party with the subsequent task of intensifying and consolidating the bases of the revolution. If radical agrarian reform and the establishment of revolutionary-democratic power in the village is postponed until the final conclusion of the Northern Expedition, the bourgeoisie, screening behind a false banner of nationalism, will consolidate its power in the occupied regions. But this would only strengthen the position of imperialism, since the Chinese bourgeoisie is much too weak to exist as an independent force; China would then enter a period of economic development under the hegemony of the finance capital of imperialism which would contribute significantly to the stabilization of the world economy on a capitalist basis. China would remain under imperialist domination which, possibly, would alter somewhat its forms. This would signify the liquidation of the revolution.

In order to consolidate the gains of the revolution, the Communist Party must rouse the laboring masses against the feudal-bourgeois reaction. The base of the revolution must be consolidated in those provinces where there is a battle-hardened proletariat, where there are mass peasant organizations and highly developed organizations of the Kuomintang and the Communist Party. The Communist Party cannot conceive of a base for the revolution more rich in possibilities and more reliable than the Shanghai proletariat, the Canton working class, the revolutionary peasantry in the provinces of Kwangtung, Kiangsi, Hunan, and Hupeh. Without underestimating in the least the necessity of the further territorial expansion of the revolution and the annihilation of Chang Tso-lin, the Fifth Congress at the same time sets before the Communist Party as its principal task in the immediate future the ruthless struggle against the reaction in those provinces where the revolution has been partially achieved, namely, in Kwangtung, Fukien, Chekiang, Kiangsi, Hunan, Hupeh, and Kwangsi. The realization of this task will mean the establishment of a revolutionary-democratic power over a considerable area that is prepared for this in the social and economic respects. This will nullify all the efforts of the feudal-bourgeois elements to liquidate the revolution. All the objective conditions (national and international) favor the development of the Chinese revolution toward a democratic dictatorship of the proletariat, the peasantry and the urban petty bourgeoisie.

The Fifth Congress of the Chinese Communist Party censures any deviation from this perspective, indicated in the theses of the Communist International and flowing from the course of events, as a tendency to surrender the leadership of the revolution to the bourgeoisie, which would signify the liquidation of the revolution.

11. Four years ago, the Communist Party entered the Kuomintang on the two following conditions: (a) preservation of its organizational independence, and (b) the right of criticism for the purpose of pursuing its own policy as determined by the interests of the working class. In its relations with the Kuomintang, our Party has resolutely counteracted all efforts by the Right Wing of the Kuomintang to restrict its organizational independence. As a result of this policy, the number of members of our Party in the Kuomintang has grown.

However, our Party was not always able to pursue an independent proletarian policy in the Kuomintang. This was mainly the result of an inability properly to evaluate the class basis of the Kuomintang. The Fifth Congress believes that our mutual relations with the Kuomintang must be freed of the past traditions which had obstructed the implementation of our political line. During the present stage of the revolution, the interests and the influence of the working class must exert definite pressure on the policy of the Kuomintang and the national-revolutionary movement.

Relations between the Communist Party and the Kuomintang at the present stage of the revolution are becoming closer than ever before.

The withdrawal of the bourgeoisie transforms the Kuomintang into a revolutionary bloc of three oppressed classes—the proletariat, the peasantry, and the urban petty bourgeoisie; and the motive power of this bloc is the proletariat. Under these conditions, the Communist Party shares with the Kuomintang not only the responsibility, but also the power. The Communist Party must achieve [a situation where] the interests of workers and peasants are taken into account in decisions on all matters relating to the policy, the program, and the tactics of the revolution. The Communist Party can be neither a subservient appendage nor the opposition with respect to the Kuomintang. The revolutionary bloc must have a common platform of the national revolution.

Closer ties between the Communist Party and the Kuomintang are expressed in the participation of Communists in the national and provincial governments, as well as in the new procedure of discussing all major problems of the revolution in mixed committees. In this new situation, factional work has acquired extreme importance. The influence of the masses on various state and party organs will be realized through Communist factions. The Fifth Congress calls upon the Party to beware of liquidationist tendencies which might arise as a result of the new organizational forms of our relations with the Kuomintang. It must be remembered that a revolutionary bloc is not a party.

The radical solution of the agrarian problem is the basic task at the present stage of the revolution. This agrarian revolution, necessary for the consolidation of the revolutionary alliance of the proletariat, the peasantry, and the petty bourgeoisie, is to be led by the proletariat. The Fifth Congress repudiates the mechanistic theory that the Communist Party is a party of only the proletariat and that the Kuomintang has charge of the peasantry. The agrarian revolution, that is, the overthrow of feudalism, is accomplished by the most revolutionary class of a given epoch. Being the most revolutionary class in China in the given historical period, the proletariat is the leader of the peasantry in its struggle against feudal absolutism.

12. The characteristic feature of the present period of the revolution is the hegemony of the proletariat. But the proletariat will not be able to fulfill this important political function—the realization of hegemony—if its economic interests are not ensured. Poorly paid, badly fed, shabbily clothed, and exploited, the proletariat cannot, of course, attain that height of political development which is necessary for the vanguard of a gigantic revolutionary struggle. Therefore, the Communist Party must struggle vigorously for raising the living standards of the proletariat; this is the first condition of the preparation of the prole-

tariat for duly fulfilling its historical role. The Fifth Congress believes that no considerations must stand in the way of realizing the following demands of the proletariat: (a) an eight-hour working-day, (b) earnings that correspond to living wages, (c) legislation on the protection of labor, (d) provision of work or aid to the unemployed, (e) protection of women and child labor, (f) old-age insurance and pension.

13. Recognizing the tactical importance of using conflicts that arise between militarists' armies for the purpose of developing the revolution, the Fifth Congress at the same time sets before the Communist Party the task of reorganizing the army.

The development of the revolution demoralizes the ranks of the militarists, and their less reactionary elements join the revolutionary army. In the final account, however, the subsequent development of the revolution threatens the interests and the power of the Left militarists. As a result, they either thwart the development of the revolution, or turn against it. These unreliable elements cannot constitute the only armed force of the revolution. The revolution must create its own army. An agrarian revolution would create a social base for a genuine revolutionary army. The peasants will join the army to defend what they have gained thanks to the revolution.

The armies of Left militarists which join the revolution will be subject to centralized command and supply. Even after joining the revolutionary army, the Left militarists insist on preserving their own independent fighting units. Their soldiers do not dissolve in the ranks of the revolutionary army and, following the traditional feudal vassalage, they subordinate themselves first of all to their own militarist commanders. The land question should be brought out in the political work of revolutionizing these troops. The propaganda for an agrarian revolution will meet with warm response among these soldiers who are either landless or of the poorest peasantry, and they will put their trust in the national-revolutionary government which can resolve the land question in practice.

14. Thanks to the active hostility of the large-scale bourgeoisie and the establishment of a powerful counterrevolutionary alliance, thanks to the threat of an imperialist intervention and an economic blockade, the national-revolutionary government is experiencing grave financial difficulties. It is impossible to continue the revolutonary war, to reorganize the army, and to create a state machinery for realizing a democratic dictatorship, if the financial difficulties are not overcome.

The Communist Party must vigorously repel any attempts to solve the financial problem at the cost of increasing the economic burden of the laboring masses. This will not be a way out of the financial difficulties. On the contrary, it will only serve to weaken the base of the national government. The Fifth Congress declares that only an agrarian revolution can bring about a real solution to the financial difficulties. The confiscation of landlords' lands would draw into the state treasury, in the form of a land tax, a part of those enormous sums which the landowners receive as rent. For a temporary solution of the financial crisis, the following measures should be adopted: (a) the establishment of high property taxes and (b) the floating of a revolutionary war loan with compulsory negotiation of such loan allocated among classes living from unearned income (that is, capitalists and landlords).

15 Youth has played an important role in the development of the revolutionary movement in China. Under the leadership of the Communist Youth Association, the youth has been in the forefront of all sectors of the fight and has given the Party enormous support. At the present stage of the expansion and intensification of the revolutionary movement, the role of youth has grown even more, and the Party must devote serious attention to it. The Party has not devoted sufficient attention to the youth movement in the past. In the future, the Party must establish closer ties with the Communist Youth Association; it must provide it with true leadership and render real assistance in its work. The Communist Youth Association is one of the most important sectors of the Communist movement; through it the Party will exert its influence on the broad masses of working youth. To date, the growth of the Communist Youth Association has been inadequate in comparison to the opportunities that are present—which should be explained by the weakness of its work among the masses in the various spheres of its activities and by its inability organizationally to consolidate its political influence. In its future work, the Communist Youth Association must pay particular attention to the development of economic work among the masses, to the work in villages and in the army, making use of all legal avenues. The Party is confident that the Fourth Congress of the Communist Youth Association will be held in the spirit of these instructions.

16. Now, more than ever before, the Party must devote attention to work among the mass of exploited women.

The exploitation of women will undoubtedly become an important factor in the revolutionary bloc of the proletariat, the peasantry and the urban petty bourgeoisie. Being the most oppressed segment of the population, women will be the most loyal workers of the revolution.

17. The experience of the past year has shown that auxiliary organi-

zations, and especially the **MOPR** *, have played a big role in mobilizing the masses for the revolutionary front. The Party must continue to devote serious attention to these organizations in order to strengthen through them its influence among the broad masses of workers, peasants, and the intelligentsia.

* International Organization to Aid Revolutionary Fighters.—Eds.

16

RESOLUTION ON THE AGRARIAN QUESTION

Adopted at the Fifth Congress of the
Chinese Communist Party, May 9, 1927

I. ANALYSIS OF THE GENERAL SITUATION

1. The economic life of the Chinese village is still based to a considerable extent on feudal relations. A large part of all the land (approximately 66 per cent) belongs to landlords who grant the land on lease. The tenants and subtenants possess no property rights on the land they cultivate. The rental is not fixed, and even the right of tenure is not assured. The average rental goes up to 50 per cent of the value of the gross output. In addition, a series of other duties are imposed arbitrarily on peasants by the landlords and the military bureaucracy who have the political power in the village. Only 34 per cent (approximately) of the land belongs to the peasants who till it. Large farms of the capitalist type can hardly ever be found in China except in certain northern provinces (Shantung and Manchuria). Communal, ancestral, and temple lands make up a large part of the land under cultivation. Communal ownership of these lands has actually been long ago destroyed. Yet the system of management of these so-called communal properties even to this day forms the basis of patriarchal power in the village. The ownership of these lands was seized by the village elders and the peasants cultivating these lands were expropriated. Through appropriation, the village elders turned into landlords and, on the strength of the tradition of communal ownership of land, they still enjoy patriarchal rights and power. Thus, feudal-patriarchal relations are a characteristic feature of the economic structure and the political power of the Chinese village.

2. At the same time, primitive methods of capitalist exploitation have penetrated into the village economy. Thus, the peasantry is ex-

posed to the dual effect of the precapitalist and capitalist forms of exploitation. This results in the ever-growing pauperization of the peasantry and the extreme backwardness of the whole system of the national economy.

The rental levied by landlords forms such a large part of the gross output that the cultivator is left with no surplus. The peasant's share is even less than what is necessary to sustain the most abject existence. This represents the precapitalist form of exploitation. It does not permit the peasant to improve the means and methods of land cultivation. It is the cause of the primitive state of agricultural production. In practice —this is slavery. The peasant produces only for his own consumption; the surplus is appropriated by the landlord.

The system of capitalist exploitation was built on the basis of these feudal relations. As a rule, the rental is paid to the landlords in kind. (This, too, is one of the survivals of feudalism). In this way, agricultural surplus becomes accumulated in the hands of feudal landlords who, consequently, become simultaneously representatives of commercial capitalism. But their essentially feudal nature prevents them from developing in the direction of capitalism. The wealth that is accumulated from the precapitalist exploitation of the peasantry is not converted into industrial capital. It is used for land speculation and for usury.

Economic backwardness prevents the development of modern means of communication. This, in turn, causes the territorial division of the national economy. The country is broken up into a number of isolated local markets under the monopoly control of landlords who have charge over all the agricultural surplus. Under such conditions, the landowning class has the complete opportunity to inflate prices, thus exploiting not only the peasantry, but also both the proletariat and the urban petty bourgeoisie. The underpaid proletariat is forced to pay more and more for food products, while the small merchants become helpless victims of the monopolistic speculations of the landowner class.

This complex system of primitive exploitation has led to the lavish growth of usury. Usury is the only credit system and the only method of capital accumulation. But this usurious capital does not contribute to the development of commerce and industry. It is again diverted to land speculation. The exhorbitant rental fees and other feudal duties, combined with forcible requisitions by the military-bureaucratic state machinery, keep the peasantry on the brink of starvation.

The military-bureaucratic machinery which possesses supreme power in the majority of provinces exploits the peasant masses in the most diverse ways; the most brutal of these are: (a) exorbitant taxes levied both legally and illegally; (b) unremunerated orders for military supplies (rice, boots, horses, and so on, for the troops); (c) requisitions during military operations; (d) free labor (carriers for the army); (e) emission of paper currency devoid of any value; and (f) the *likin* [inland custom tax].

These predatory, semifeudal methods of exploitation have had a catastrophic effect on the productive capacity of the whole country. Deprived of the surplus of its production and constantly on the brink of starvation, the peasantry is incapable of improving its economy. The high rate of feudal rentals tie down the capital to the parasitic exploitation of land, thus hindering the development of capitalist farming. Even the capital of urban merchants is invested in land speculation to the detriment of the industrial development of the country.

3. Rural overpopulation makes impossible the continued existence of the feudal-militaristic system of exploitation. Rural overpopulation resulted from industrial backwardness. Imperialist domination deters economic progress. Thus, there is an organic connection between imperialism and the catastrophically acute agrarian problem.

Imperialism aims at colonial expansion in order to find a market for its goods and cheap raw material for the industry of its parent state. The most valuable raw material is the labor force. Countries in a colonial or a semicolonial position (like China) are turned into agricultural "hinterlands" for the industry of the parent states and into reserves of cheap labor. It is clear that imperialist rule leads to industrial backwardness of the colonies which, in turn, leads to their agrarization. Large-scale and free migration of work-hands from village to town cannot occur due to the absence of industrial development. This creates rural overpopulation and acts as an artificial support to the outmoded feudal economy which, under different conditions, would have been abolished through the development of higher forms of production. Rural overpopulation contributes to the perpetuation of feudal relations and exploitation in the village.

The ever-growing army of landless peasants cheapens labor almost completely, strengthening by the same token the base of imperialism. All these reasons taken together account for the extreme pauperization and destitution of the peasant masses. The millions of destitute peasants can find no productive application of their labor and turn into bandits and hired soldiers. Militarism—a unique social phenomenon in China, fostered by the deterioration of the national economy—becomes a military expression of the feudal reaction and an instrument of imperialism. The landlords and gentry, the usurers and militarists—all of them, as a whole, form a monstrous machinery of the feudal reaction and the primitive accumulation of capital. This machinery drains the vital energies of the peasantry and destroys to the end the very foundation of the national economy. Such are the conditions under which imperialism achieves the highly developed system of capitalist exploitation.

Economic bankruptcy is pushing the peasants into the arms of the usurer. The monstrous interest rates are increasing, and the peasant is no longer capable of extricating himself from debt. He is forced to sell his land which then becomes concentrated in the hands of the usurer. On the other hand, the army of landless peasants is growing and serves as an inexhaustible source of cheap labor and as a base for militarism and banditry. The expropriation of the peasantry is also brought about by the imperialists themselves buying up land in the maritime provinces and by their acquiring sections of Manchuria and Inner Mongolia for colonization purposes.

4. Both native militarism, draining the vital forces of the nation, and foreign imperialism, obstructing the economic and political development of the country, depend upon feudal relations in the village. For a successful struggle against these enemies of the Chinese masses, therefore, it is first necessary to clear the countryside of the survivals of feudal relations and patriarchal power. A radical change in the system of landownership is a cardinal principle of the national revolution without which the struggle for genuine democratic freedom cannot develop. In order to wipe out the militaristic and imperialist superstructure, it is necessary to undermine its foundation.

5. The peasantry constitutes the overwhelming majority of the population. Without the active and conscious participation of the peasant masses, the national revolution cannot succeed. When the sources of agrarian exploitation are removed, the energies of the peasant masses will be mobilized for the national revolution. The agrarian revolution —the destruction of feudalism—is an imperative condition for the establishment of democracy. In the normal evolution of society, the peasantry becomes emancipated from the feudal yoke of the bourgeoisie. But in China the normal process of social evolution was disrupted by the interference of imperialism. In China, the bourgeoisie did not develop as a social force hostile to feudalism. On the one hand, the bourgeoisie grew out of the feudal landowning class and continues to remain closely connected with it; on the other hand, it grew as a middleman (compradore) of imperialist exploitation. In both cases, the Chinese bourgeoisie is inseparably connected with the forces that exploit the peasantry. For this reason, the bourgeoisie cannot be the bearer of an agrarian revolution. In view of its hostile attitude toward the agrarian revolution, the bourgeoisie is not only incapable of leading the struggle

for democratic freedom, but it even becomes an enemy of the latter (the split of Chiang Kai-shek).

Objectively, the Chinese national bourgeoisie represents a factor that is hostile to imperialist monopoly of the national economy, to this most important cause of the perpetuation of feudal relations in the village. However, due to its organic ties with feudal relations, the bourgeoisie cannot accomplish the task of an agrarian revolution, even for the sake of its own class interests, and, consequently, it cannot create the conditions for a decisive struggle against imperialism.

In view of this, the leader and the defender of the peasantry in its historical struggle against feudalism will not be the bourgeoisie, but the proletariat, supported by its revolutionary ally—the urban petty bourgeoisie.

6. The economic consequences of precapitalist feudal exploitation are felt by the proletariat and the urban petty bourgeoisie in the form of high prices on foodstuffs and restrictions on the free development of commerce. For this reason, both of these classes are opposed to the feudal exploitation of the peasantry. A radical reform giving the peasant all rights to the harvest which he gathers from the land he cultivates will prove beneficial not only to the peasantry, but to the whole people. A higher standard of living for the peasant masses will bring about an enormous development of trade. If surplus production is not taken away from the cultivator, he will be able to free himself from the tenacious clutches of the usurer and save enough funds to improve the means and methods of land cultivation. This will result in extraordinary growth of the general agricultural production of the country. The rise in agriculture will assure work to the landless peasants who are now replenishing the ranks of the militarists' armies. The destruction of the monopoly of the feudal lord-usurer will create a free market and will cause a lowering of prices. Finally, the abolition of feudal rentals will open up a significant source of revenue to the state.

7. Only the transfer, without compensation, of rented land to the tenant-peasants cultivating it can wipe out feudal exploitation. In order to overthrow the patriarchal political power in the village, the gentry must be deprived of control over communal, ancestral, and temple lands which they have seized by fraudulent means. In order to assure the implementation of a radical agrarian reform, the peasantry must be vested with political power in the village. Command of the armed forces in the village must be wrested from the gentry and given to the peasantry. The country will be rid of the curse of militarism when its social roots are destroyed by the transfer of land and by the availability of productive employment for millions of landless peasants. Final

abolition of usury is possible only after the removal of the economic causes that foster it. A state agricultural bank, a credit coöperative society, and other higher forms of credit will put an end to usury. An immediate struggle against usurious extortions is even now one of the most important tasks of the revolution in the village. All these tasks are inseparable from one another. When the task of liberating the peasant masses from feudal-patriarchal exploitation is achieved, the victory of the national revolution will be guaranteed.

8. The Fifth Congress of the Chinese Communist Party believes that a radical solution of the agrarian problem requires a fundamental re-distribution of land based on the principle of equalization. This is not feasible as long as the land is not nationalized. The Communist Party will lead the peasantry in its struggle for an equalizing distribution of land, since this will bring the inevitable result of the nationalization of land and the abolition of private ownership of land, that is, the realiza-tion of the basic principles of the Communist agrarian program.

II. Trends of the Peasant Movement in China

9. The experience in Kwangtung, Hunan, Hupeh, and other provinces demonstrates that the principal participant in the peasant movement in China is the poor peasantry (tenants, semitenants and peasants who do not exploit hired labor). A base and a character of the movement of this sort sets before the poor peasantry the perspective of an agrarian revolution. The basic trend of the movement at the present stage is to destroy the patriarchal and feudal power and to establish a peasant power. Hence, the problem of arming the peasantry acquires special significance in this struggle. In some places, this general trend turns into a demand for a practical solution of the land question.

10. However, the peasant movement in different provinces has not yet reached a common level. In the North, where the oppression of the militarists is still strong, peasant unions are illegal; the peasant movement is not developed there. In the provinces of Kiangsi, Anhwei, Chekiang, and Fukien, the movement arose only very recently. There, the struggle began for the reduction of rentals, interest rates, and heavy taxes, and against the gentry and the bandits. But in these provinces the peasantry is under the oppression of Chiang Kai-shek himself. The cradle of the peasant movement is Kwangtung. But in this province, objectively the peasants have already gone beyond the stage of economic demands for the reduction of rentals and high interest rates and are now demand-ing arms, land, and participation in government. During the painful struggle of the past two years, however, we were unable to direct the

movement according to a correct, well thought-out policy. The recent reactionary demonstration of Li Ti-sin[?] once again leads to the oppression of the peasantry and encourages the gentry and the bandits to assume a counteroffensive. Kiangsi, Hunan, and Hupeh are under the control of the national government. Although in Kiangsi the peasants have, in fact, started the struggle for the reduction of rentals and interest rates, in general they are still in the stage of organizing and consolidating their forces. This is explained by the circumstance that Kiangsi is under the iron heel of Chiang Kai-shek. The peasant masses have twice risen to the struggle, seeking to overthrow his power. In Hupeh and especially in Hunan, the peasant movement, although not throughout, has reached the highest degree of development. The Hunan peasants have overthrown the power of the gentry and the bandits. They have shattered the very foundations of the old regime and are fighting to establish their own power. In some regions, the peasants are participating in local self-government. Furthermore, in Hupeh and Hunan the peasants are starting to resolve the land problem by confiscating and distributing lands belonging to the gentry and the bandits.

11. The peasant movement in China developed chiefly under the leadership of the proletariat. Without this leadership it could not have followed the correct revolutionary path and would not have had a clear perspective. A peculiar form of the peasant movement are the organizations of "The Red Spears" and "The Tightened Stomachs." They are medieval in their organizational structure and in their methods of struggle.

Where class differentiation has not developed to the extent that it has in Hunan, the movement is often organized under the leadership of large landowners and is used by the reactionaries. But even a movement such as that is revolutionary because it is aimed against militarism, heavy taxes, and local autocratic power.

12. The feudal-patriarchal elements of the reaction (bandits, gentry, corrupt officials), of course, strive to suppress the developing peasant movement. They employ their own armed forces (*min-t'uan* and bandits) and, in alliance with the militarists, attack the peasants, and organize blood baths in order to crush the movement. However, the peasant movement is developing with comparative freedom in areas under the control of the national government. The movement is attaining great heights and is becoming a strong force. In such cases, unable to fight the movement in the open, the gentry and the bandits resort to passive resistance and to heinous plots: they take the rice out of the provinces, they refuse loans to peasants, or they lay claim to the rights

exercised by peasants and create false peasant unions. In regions under the rule of Chiang Kai-shek, there can be only unions of the gentry and bandits. But even in the territory of the national government, the gentry and the bandits, in alliance with the feudal elements of the army, often attack the peasants. For this reason, the peasant struggle is now assuming the sharpest forms.

13. The peasant movement usually begins with the fight against high rentals and interest rates, against oppression by the gentry and the bandits, and then turns into an attack on the power of the bandits and the gentry. As the struggle develops, the peasants try to obtain arms and, finally, reach the point of armed conflict with their oppressors. In those regions where revolutionary battles are fought, the peasants support this struggle, overthrowing at the very outset the power of the gentry and the bandits.

This proves that the peasants need armed force and political power not only for solving the agrarian problem, but even for lowering the rental and the high interest rates. In the stage through which the peasant movement is now passing, it must clash with the patriarchal and feudal forces and defeat them. In this entire struggle, the principal and central force is the poor peasantry; from it the movement draws its revolutionary might. This movement against the feudal power objectively lays the beginning of the solution of the agrarian question. The Chinese peasants and, especially, the lowest stratum, acutely feel the shortage of land, the exploitation by landlords, and the monstrous taxes. In order to achieve their goal, they must fight for power, they must crush the gentry and the bandits who have seized, and taken charge of, the taxation machinery. They must fight for land and put an end to a regime of exploitation established by the landlords; in this struggle, they turn from demands for lower rentals to the slogan of "land to those who till it."

14. Although in the present period of the revolution the peasant movement has not reached the same level throughout the country, two basic features are common to all regions: the struggle for the overthrow of the feudal-patriarchal power has already begun, while the solution of the land question is only beginning. This constitutes an important peculiarity of the new stage of the revolution. The development of the class struggle in the village [and] the intensification of the agrarian revolution will not only defeat the weapons of imperialist rule in China, but will also seriously shatter the economic foundations of the reactionary feudal and large-scale bourgeoisie; imperialism will thus be deprived of the basis on which it could organize the reactionary elements

against the revolution. In other words: *the present purpose of the revolution consists in overthrowing the power of the gentry and the bandits, confiscating the land of the large landlords and counterrevolutionaries —the chief acting force here being the poor peasantry—in order to establish the power of the peasantry in the village, to improve in practice the economic position of the peasantry, and to lead it to the redistribution of land.*

III. The Agrarian Platform of the National Revolution

On the basis of an analysis of the objective conditions and the subjective forces of the peasant movement, as set forth above, the Fifth Congress of the Chinese Communist Party resolves that the following measures are necessary for the solution of the agrarian problem at the present stage of the revolution:

a) Confiscation of all communal, ancestral, temple, and school lands, and lands belonging to the Christian Church, as well as company-owned real estate, and the transfer of such lands to the peasants who till them. The management of all confiscated lands must be assigned to land committees which will decide whether to cultivate the confiscated lands on communal principles or to divide it among the laboring peasants.

b) Landlord estates which have been rented to tenants shall be confiscated without redemption and transferred, through the land committees, to the peasants who cultivate them.

Land belonging to small owners shall not be confiscated. Land belonging, as of this date, to officers of the revolutionary army is likewise not subject to confiscation.

Soldiers of the revolutionary army who do not own land shall be granted land for cultivation at the end of the revolutionary war.

c) Confiscated lands shall be exempt from all duties with the exception of the progressive land tax payable to the state. Rental on confiscated land shall be lowered to a level corresponding to the rates of the land tax on the confiscated land. A fixed rental and the right of permanent tenure shall be established for peasants cultivating unconfiscated lands and they shall be exempt from all other duties.

d) The landlords and the gentry shall be deprived of all political rights and power. Establishment of village self-government responsible to the village assembly which draws support from the oppressed classes of the village.

e) Disarmament of the military forces of the village reaction; organization of a peasant militia for the protection of the village government and the gains of the revolution.

f) Establishment of state agricultural banks and peasant credit coöperative societies, producers' and consumers' coöperatives, and the development of irrigation.

g) Struggle for the protection of the peasantry against usurers. Annulment of accumulated debts, and the establishment of limiting interest rates.

17

MANIFESTO OF THE FIFTH CONGRESS

OF THE CHINESE COMMUNIST PARTY

During the past two years, the national-liberation movement developed at an extremely rapid rate. The power of imperialism, acquired and consolidated by almost a hundred years of oppression, exploitation, plunder, and robbery, has become unsteady. In this period of the triumphant revolutionary struggle, the proletariat and the peasant masses were the determinant factors of the movement. Only thanks to the indivisible support of the laboring masses was the national-revolutionary movement able to establish a firm base for itself in Kwangtung. The national army carried the banner of the revolution right through to the very Yangtze River, likewise thanks to the assistance of workers and peasants. And when the guns of the imperialist fleet were trained at the soldiers of the national army to prevent their entrance into Shanghai, the proletariat once again breasted the fire. The revolutionary demonstration of the masses dealt a heavy blow to the power of the imperialists in the Yangtze Valley and helped the national-revolutionary government to establish its power in Wuhan. In the past, the proletarian and peasant masses fought in battle, struggled and sacrificed themselves for the sake of the revolution. The future of the revolution will depend upon their will to fight and their determination to win.

One of the peculiarities of this period of intensive, revolutionary development was the process of class differentiation within the ranks of the national movement. The anti-imperialist struggle could not be unleashed without a concurrent development of the struggle against capitalist and feudal exploitation. The class struggle developed side by side with the national struggle. This intensified the contradictions in the ranks of the nationalists and, finally, led to a split.

The anti-imperialist struggle is not new in China. Properly speaking, it has been under way from the very emergence of imperialist domination. The revolutionary movements of the past (the Opium War, the T'ai-p'ing revolt, the Boxer Rebellion, and so on) which are usually depicted as antiforeign in character were essentially a primitive expression of anti-imperialist sentiments.

Imperialist domination in China spread in two ways: first, by crude military force aided by modern implements of war and, second, by bribery of the ruling dynasty and the feudal-bureaucratic officials. The first factor played a decisive role in the period of penetration of the country; and the second factor assured the consolidation of imperialist domination. The rebellions of the past were crushed as a result of the superior military organization of the foreign powers which also had the support of the Chinese feudal dynasty and the military-bureaucratic state power. The anti-imperialist movement subsequently acquired a democratic character and, in 1911, overthrew the Manchurian dynasty. The coincidence of an anti-imperialist struggle with a struggle for the liquidation of feudalism and all other elements hindering the democratization of the country is a feature that is not only peculiar to the present period of the revolution. This has always been an essential feature of the national-liberation movement. This democratic, anti-feudal character of the movement has merely assumed a sharper form at the present time as a result of the development of the movement.

The revolution of 1911 overthrew the corrupt Manchurian dynasty, but it was unable to carry out the task of democratizing the country. The reason for this was the restricted social base of the revolution. Only a very narrow stratum of the population—the bourgeoisie and the liberal intelligentsia—took part in the revolution. They were not strong enough to cope with the reactionary elements supported by imperialism. The first republic turned out to be short-lived, and the revolution was virtually liquidated. Only the mutual rivalry of imperialist powers prevented Japan from restoring the monarchy under its own auspices.

When the national movement was revived after the war under a sign of protest against the Versailles treaty, it already possessed a broader democratic base.

In 1919, the urban democracy, led by the petty intelligentsia, mainly students, became the motive force of the movement. But even then, the social roots of the movement did not penetrate the thick of the masses. The laboring masses were not yet drawn into the movement for national liberation. The boycott movement was aimed against imperialism; but it still had not acquired a revolutionary-democratic character and did not demand the liquidation of feudalism and the reactionary forces associated with it which formed the base of imperialism in China.

The boycott movement has its limits. It cannot develop to the point of becoming a serious threat to imperialism without making an enemy out of the native merchants who deal in foreign goods. In this contradiction lay the weakness of the movement of 1919. Nevertheless, the boycott movement was a prelude to the genuine revolutionary training of the declassed intelligentsia which looked to the laboring masses for the source of revolutionary energy.

The fact that the pioneers of the workers' and peasants' movement following the movement of 1919 came out of this very movement speaks sufficiently of the social relations that tie the petty bourgeoisie with the working class in the struggle against foreign imperialism and native reaction. It is extremely important to recall this fact in the present period when the revolution is in need of a militant alliance with the urban petty bourgeoisie, the peasantry, and the proletariat.

The "urban democracy" (small-scale manufacturers, small merchants, artisans, the intelligentsia, salaried people) is oppressed both economically and politically. It demands political rights and opportunities for economic development. It participates in the anti-imperialist movement in order to express its dissatisfaction with the existing situation, but it cannot lead the movement too far without damaging its own immediate class interests. The breakdown of trade is the first consequence of an anti-imperialist struggle, and this not only brings losses to the large-scale bourgeoisie (the compradores, bankers, wholesalers-importers), but also affects the economic interests of the petty bourgeoisie. Through its membership and leadership, the anti-imperialist struggle is connected chiefly with the "urban democracy" and is therefore unable to go far on account of its internal contradictions. The urban democracy alone cannot fight even for political rights. The struggle for political rights cannot be intensified without intensifying economic contradictions. The movement of 1919 has proved this. The most progressive elements of the petty bourgeoisie, its declassed elements, began to search for a way of fighting that would be freer of contradictions. They discovered a new direction of the revolutionary struggle in the growing dissatisfaction of the working class. In order to fight successfully for its economic interests and to win democratic political rights, the urban petty bourgeoisie must necessarily unite with the proletariat in a simultaneous struggle against imperialism and its native allies (feudalism and militarism).

Obstacles preventing the economic development of the petty bourgeoisie are not a consequence of imperialist domination. On the contrary, under present Chinese conditions, the petty bourgeoisie is economically dependent to a large measure on the freedom and the flourishing of foreign trade. The economic interests of the petty bourgeoisie suffer most of all from the feudal character of the national economy and the incessant civil wars of the militarists. These two factors are in turn closely connected with imperialism, and they continue to exist as a disastrous result of imperialist domination. The feudal economy prevents the expansion of the internal market. The feudal nature of the Chinese state machinery places dozens of obstacles in the way of free trade development (heavy taxes and, especially, the *likin*) [inland custom tax]. Militarism imposes a heavy burden on the commercial segments of the population and frequently destroys trade almost altogether. The feudal-militaristic autocracy deprives the petty bourgeoisie of all its political rights. All these factors militate against the interests of the petty bourgeoisie, not to speak of the working class and the peasantry. The urban democracy with its anti-imperialist sentiments is beginning to rise against such a situation. It is rebelling against the oppression, but does not know where or how to assume the offensive against the enemy. A direct attack against imperialism would soon begin to tell on its own economic interests and, in despair, it gives up fighting. The interests of the petty bourgeoisie demand the removal of the factors that contribute directly to its own oppression, preventing the expansion of the market, disrupting trade and ruining the petty intelligentsia and the salaried people. On the other hand, the removal of these factors shatters the basis of imperialism. But the petty bourgeoisie is unable independently to find and pursue the path of revolution that will save it. It is capable of this only in collaboration with, and under the guidance of, the proletariat. The most important achievement of the movement of 1919 was that the petty bourgeoisie objectively, if not consciously, turned to the proletariat.

The Shanghai events of May 30, 1925, showed that the national-liberation movement became a mass movement. This was preceded by a period of organizing the working class which created a base for a new type of an anti-imperialist struggle. Demands for the abolition of unequal treaties, territorial rights, customs monopoly, and so forth were no longer empty words. They now had a powerful support—mass action. The revolutionary action of the Shanghai proletariat and the democratic masses was drowned in blood; but it had an impact on the whole country and affected the position of the imperialists. The large-scale bourgeoisie, closely connected with imperialist trade and finance, hastened to liquidate the strike movement of the Shanghai workers as soon as it acquired a revolutionary-political character. The large-scale bourgeoisie broke the united national front, thereby doing a service to imperialism. The conferences on customs and extraterritorial questions cannot be considered a concession by imperialism to the large-scale bourgeoisie in gratitude for its betrayal of the revolution. They were wrenched from imperialism by the revolutionary action of the working class and the democratic masses.

Another expression of the revolutionary awakening of the Chinese masses was the seamen's strike and the Hong Kong strike. The latter assumed a purely political character and will forever remain a bright event in the history of the Chinese revolution. These actions of the proletariat strengthened the social base of the Canton national government and turned it into a central organ of struggle against imperialism and for democratic freedom. The Canton government, supported by the working class and the democratic masses, repelled the counterrevolutionary movement of "The Paper Tigers," inspired and organized with the help of British imperialism. The compradores wanted to overthrow the Canton government. The working class stood up to its defense. Again, the heroism and sacrifices of the working class saved Canton from an imperialist attack from Hong Kong and dealt a heavy blow to imperialist trade by subjecting Hong Kong to a blockade that lasted a whole year.

These and many other memorable events testified to the expansion of the social base of the national-liberation movement.

The gigantic wave of the movement carried away even the bourgeoisie. But its motive power was the working class and the urban democracy who were creating a revolutionary bloc in the process of the struggle.

With this type of a social base, class contradictions could not completely disappear in the national movement. The anti-imperialist struggle could not have acquired a revolutionary character without at the same time developing into a class struggle. The task of the national revolution consisted of not only an attack against imperialism, but also the liquidation of feudal-patriarchal, socioeconomic relations which prevent the free development of the anti-imperialist struggle. The national revolution has outgrown the narrow program of the bourgeois democracy.

Such a transformation of the social aspect of the national-liberation movement alarmed not only the imperialists; the large-scale bourgeoisie was just as frightened. It perceived the growth of the revolutionary-democratic forces of the movement as a threat to its own class interests. It wanted the working class and the democratic masses to sacrifice themselves in the name of the interests of native capitalism. But the objective significance of the movement could not be destroyed by the subjective desires of the bourgeoisie.

The interests of the native bourgeoisie contradict the interests of the imperialist monopoly. As a consequence, the bourgeoisie participated in the anti-imperialist movement and, during the first stages, directed the movement. Much deeper, however, is the antagonism that exists between the interests of the Chinese masses and those of imperialism. The national bourgeoisie is seeking a compromise with imperialism. The interests of the laboring masses demand the final abolition of imperialist domination. With the exception of the compradore elements, the bourgeoisie is antagonistic to imperialism and would be glad to see China freed for native capitalist exploitation. However, final destruction of imperialist domination can be achieved only through a revolutionary struggle which, in the process of its development, will destroy the instruments of feudal-capitalist exploitation with the help of which imperialism acts in China. A revolutionary struggle for the complete overthrow of imperialism requires the intensification of the class struggle. This prospect has inspired the bourgeoisie with terror.

Unable to arrest the revolutionary development of the national movement owing to the influence of the laboring and democratic masses, the large-scale bourgeoisie split the united anti-imperialist front. By the *coup* of March 20, the bourgeoisie once again seized the leadership of the national movement and tried to swerve it to the narrow path of the interests of native capitalism—to the path which, under the given conditions, would lead inevitably to a compromise with imperialism. The program of bourgeois nationalism, headed by Chiang Kai-shek, consisted of uniting the country by military conquests and then coming to an agreement with imperialism on the right to exploit the Chinese masses.

As long as the bourgeoisie continued fighting against militarism, it retained objectively its anti-imperialist character. Therefore, the proletariat formed a united front with it and mobilized the peasant and democratic masses for the support of the Southern national army in its struggle against Northern militarism. It was only thanks to the enthusiastic support of the worker and peasant masses that the Southerners' army defeated the forces of Sun Ch'uan-fang with such ease. The bourgeois nationalists strove for military victory in order to increase the power of their class. But the development of the national-revolutionary movement is not determined by group interests; it develops in accordance with the objective conditions of the country. The interests of the Chinese people demand the liquidation of feudalism, the establishment of a democratic government, and the overthrow of imperialism. The Northern victories of the national army gave the masses an opportunity to develop the struggle for achieving this three-fold objective. For this reason the success of the Northern Expedition at once strengthened and weakened the position of the bourgeoisie.

The organized might of the proletarian and peasant masses which grew out of the Northern Expedition interfered with Chiang Kai-shek's attempt to subordinate the whole national movement to his personal military dictatorship and to make it dependent on the special interests of the bourgeoisie. But the bourgeoisie already possessed enough forces to split from the united national-revolutionary front. By this very action, the bourgeoisie became an ally of militarism and an instrument of imperialism, despite its nationalistic pretensions.

The feudal-bourgeois elements, headed by Chiang Kai-shek, turned against the national revolution and became an instrument of imperialism even before they formally left the ranks of the national movement. By the murder of labor leaders back in Kiangsi, Chiang Kai-shek already demonstrated his hatred of the working-class and peasant movement. In order to help the national army capture Shanghai, the proletariat organized an armed uprising, but Chiang Kai-shek was in no hurry to reach Shanghai. He rejected the powerful, friendly hand which the Shanghai proletariat extended to him, and remained unperturbed when Sun Ch'uan-fang organized a blood bath of the Shanghai workers. Soon after his arrival in Shanghai, Chiang Kai-shek, at the demand of imperialism, ruthlessly suppressed the proletarian uprising organized for the purpose of assisting the national army.

Chiang Kai-shek's struggle against the working-class movement and his violent hatred of the Communist Party reveals the whole fraud of his nationalistic pretensions. At the present stage of the national revolution, its motive force is the working-class and peasant masses. Only the revolutionary action of workers and peasants can assure the success of the struggle against imperialism. Anyone who comes forward against the revolutionary activity of the laboring masses and tries to crush the organizations of workers and peasants is an enemy not only of the working class, but of the national revolution as well. All the actions of Chiang Kai-shek and his supporters from the very moment of the *coup* of March 20 have been directed against the national revolution. And this cannot be regarded as actions by individual persons. Chiang Kai-shek and his supporters are representatives of a class; they are representatives of the large-scale bourgeoisie.

The triumphant march of the national army to the Yangtze River and the gigantic development of the revolution have inspired the imperialists with horror. Forces were moved into the Chinese waters. Measures were taken for the defense of Shanghai (the base of imperialism) in the event that the city is threatened by the revolutionary army.

However, imperialism did not dare take any open action to counteract the nationalist forces. It tried to penetrate the ranks of the nationalists and to demoralize them. The imperialists perceived the national bourgeoisie as their objective ally in the struggle against the Chinese revolution. While organizing impressive military demonstrations, imperialism at the same time let it be known that it agrees to consider the interests of the large-scale bourgeoisie, if the latter opposes the revolution. The bourgeoisie took note of this imperialist policy and decided in favor of betraying the revolution.

The betrayal of the bourgeoisie inspired imperialism with new hopes. The imperialist powers decided on active military intervention, making use of the split in the nationalist ranks. By its aggressive policy to the national-revolutionary government, imperialism in its turn gave moral support to the traitorous bourgeoisie which had established its center in Nanking under the false banner of nationalism.

Class differentiation and the danger of imperialist intervention—these are the two characteristic features of the present situation. These two factors are intimately connected. The danger of an imperialist intervention can not be successfully overcome without taking into account the lessons derived from the process of class differentiation. The class struggle has intensified. The anti-imperialist struggle can no longer be separated from the class struggle. The proletariat participated in a united front with the bourgeoisie as long as the latter, even if indirectly, fought against imperialism. Now the bourgeoisie has openly rejected the anti-imperialist struggle and has declared war on the working class. Feudal reaction, militarism, and imperialism stand behind the bourgeoisie. A counterrevolutionary bloc of all these forces has been formed against the national revolution. This bloc must be repulsed and crushed. In this lies the task of the revolution.

WORKERS AND PEASANTS OF CHINA!

Strengthen your organizations, create a revolutionary bloc with the urban democracy, and make the national-revolutionary government thereby invincible.

After the reaction is resolutely eradicated in all parts of the country, the revolution will move ahead, it will break up the counterrevolutionary bloc, wipe out militarism, and overthrow imperialism. The social base of the revolution must be intensified. The proletariat, the peasantry, and the urban democratic elements have fought and sacrificed themselves in the name of the revolution. The defense of their interests and the destruction of their enemies will promote the development of the revolution.

Events have shown that imperialism can fight with the Chinese revolution only through its native allies. The revolution must now assume the offensive against them in order to weaken the base of imperialism. The traitorous bourgeoisie strives to unite around itself all the forces of the reaction in the territory of the national government. A reactionary cordon—Nanking, Shanghai, Kwangtung, Kiangsi, Szechuan—has been formed in order to cut the national-revolutionary government off from the North and strangle it. The counterrevolution, of course, is calculating on the support of reactionary, feudal-patriarchal elements. In order to protect itself against this counterrevolutionary plot, the national-revolutionary government must destroy the base of the counterrevolution on its own territory. The proletariat and the peasantry must support the national-revolutionary government in carrying out this task. At the present stage, the national revolution coincides with the agrarian revolution.

Lands belonging to the large landlords must be confiscated. The *min-t'uan* must be disarmed. The power of the gentry must be crushed. The village power must be built on the basis of village democracy. A peasant militia must be organized for the defense of the revolution. The slogan "land to the peasants" will give to the revolution an army so enormous that it will make the revolution invincible.

The agrarian revolution in provinces under the control of the national government will assure the latter the sympathy and support of peasant masses in other parts of the country. This will undermine the position of militarism. The peasants will welcome the national army as its liberator. Militarism will be destroyed; it will be caught between two fires—the revolutionary army on the front and the peasant revolts in the rear.

The economic blockade organized by imperialism, the feudal obstacles to trade and the internecine wars of the militarists oppress the petty bourgeoisie. It must therefore enter the revolutionary-democratic bloc with the proletariat and the peasantry for the struggle against imperialism, feudal reaction, and militarism. The Communist Party will lead the proletariat to the defense of the interests of the petty bourgeoisie. The peasants will create a united front with the petty landowners in order to destroy feudal absolutism and the power of the gentry. The petty merchants must be freed from exorbitant taxes.

The proletariat is the vanguard of the revolutionary-democratic bloc. But it will not be able to fulfill its role without defending its own class interests. A higher standard of living will increase the fighting capacity of the proletariat. When it leads the peasantry into the struggle against feudalism and defends the interests of the petty bourgeoisie, the proletariat must not at the same time weaken its struggle with capitalism for higher wages, for a shorter working day, for improved working conditions, and so on. Further, in view of the fact that imperialism enjoys a monopoly position in all spheres of the Chinese economy since it owns the railroads, the heavy industry, and the banks, the proletariat must demand their nationalization. The proletariat is defending the interests of the petty bourgeoisie, while the petty bourgeoisie is supporting the struggle of the proletariat against capitalism. A revolutionary-democratic bloc of the proletariat, the peasantry, and the petty bourgeoisie will be created on the basis of this mutual support.

After the betrayal of the feudal-bourgeois elements, the Kuomintang becomes a revolutionary-democratic bloc of the proletariat, the peasantry, and the petty bourgeoisie. At the present stage of the revolution, the principal task of the proletariat consists of strengthening the Kuomintang, and rallying the democratic masses around its banner. The revolutionary-democratic bloc is the leader of the national revolution. In consolidating this bloc, the proletariat attains hegemony in the revolutionary struggle. The Communist Party is entering the Kuomintang and is taking part in the national government, but it does so not as a rival striving to seize power; it is doing this in order to consolidate the revolutionary elements, in order to assure the development of the revolution.

The democratic dictatorship of the petty bourgeoisie, the peasantry, and the proletariat will overcome the unavoidable threat of an imperialist intervention and the plot of the counterrevolutionary bloc. With respect to the mentioned three classes, the national-revolutionary state will be a democratic state; but it will be a dictatorship with respect to the other classes. Who is not with us is against us; all the enemies must be ruthlessly destroyed—this is the fundamental principle of the national revolution.

The moment the Chinese national revolution enters the higher stage of the decisive struggle, the objective conditions—national as well as international—will be favorable to it. It is entering this stage as a result of the objective conditions.

The desertion of the bourgeoisie frees the movement of factors which bring about internal contradictions and conflicts. The movement is becoming homogeneous and directed at a single goal. Class differentiation produces the necessity of intensifying the social base of the movement. This draws ever larger masses into the struggle, thus causing a gigantic development of the revolution.

The international situation is no less favorable. Imperialism is attempting to create a united front against the Chinese revolution, but the general decline of world capitalism is creating ever-growing contradictions between the imperialist powers. They cannot reach an agreement among themselves in regard to active military intervention in China. Even in one and the same country the bourgeoisie is not united on this question. Some demand aggressive measures for the defense of their investments; others want the establishment of peaceful conditions that would promote the development of trade. This circumstance reduces the danger of an immediate and united military intervention. The consolidation of the traitorous Chinese bourgeoisie will provide imperialism with new opportunities for intervention.

There is still another factor which makes a military intervention in China quite difficult. This factor is the opposition of the proletariat in the imperialist countries. The time has passed when China could be intimidated by a few gunboats and one or two hundred marines. Intervention in China at the present time will mean a protracted war. The proletariat in imperialist countries will staunchly revolt against a colonial war. It will not be easy to provide the necessary means (troops, equipment, and so on) for the intervention. War in China will cause serious political complications in the imperialist countries themselves. The Chinese revolution enjoys enormous sympathy and support throughout the world. The exploited classes and the oppressed peoples in the whole world are together with the Chinese masses in their struggle for liberation.

PROLETARIANS AND PEASANTS OF CHINA!

The revolution, at its present stage, demands more self-sacrifice, courage, and determination than ever before. On you depends the success of not only the Chinese revolution, but also the development of the world revolution. There is no reason to lose heart. Victory is close. You must fight and win in order to create a new, free China on the ruins of capitalism, militarism, and imperialism.

DOWN WITH THE COUNTERREVOLUTIONARY BLOC OF IMPERIALISM, MILITARISM, AND THE TRAITOROUS BOURGEOISIE!
LONG LIVE THE REVOLUTIONARY-DEMOCRATIC ALLIANCE OF THE PROLETARIAT, THE PEASANTRY, AND THE PETTY BOURGEOISIE!
LONG LIVE THE CHINESE REVOLUTION!
LONG LIVE THE WORLD REVOLUTION!

The Fifth Congress of the Chinese Communist Party

Hankow, May, 1927

18

THE BOLSHEVIK PARTY

Comrades, on behalf of the delegation of the Communist International, I welcome the new Central Committee of the Chinese Communist Party. The Fifth Congress of the Chinese Communist Party is a significant event in the history of the Chinese revolution. It has met at a most critical moment of the revolution. Before the congress lay a series of highly important questions on the correct solution of which depends the further development of the revolutionary movement. At the next stage of the revolution, the proletariat will have hegemony in the struggle for national liberation. Therefore, the party of the proletariat must have a clear, political line and strong and experienced leadership. We succeeded in solving both of these problems: the congress provided the Party with a correct policy and with the best possible leadership under the circumstances. The theses adopted by the Seventh Enlarged Plenum of the Executive Committee of the Comintern defined the general perspective and furnished the basic guiding policy of the Chinese Communist Party. The task of the Chinese Communist Party is to carry out these theses in practice.

The most important task of the Fifth Congress was to evaluate the the theses correctly and to find the right ways of realizing them. The discussion on the theses and on a number of other questions raised at the congress demonstrated that the historical importance of the theses has been understood by the Party. The Central Committee elected at the congress will be able to lead the Party in the spirit of the adopted theses. We are at a turning point in the history of the revolution and it is therefore necessary for the Party to analyze the past and to recognize its mistakes not only for purposes of criticism, but also for the sake of deriving lessons from the experience gained. This task, too, the congress has accomplished with success. It has defined the immediate tasks

M. N. Roy's address to the Central Committee of the Chinese Communist Party elected at its Fifth Congress.—Eds.

of the Party and has noted the weaknesses and mistakes of the past. It has derived priceless lessons from the accumulated experience, with benefit to the whole Party. In the future, the Party will be free of these weaknesses and will not repeat its mistakes.

This congress was Bolshevik; it showed that the Chinese Communist Party is on the way to becoming a genuine Bolshevik party. This is precisely what is necessary for the subsequent development of the Chinese revolution. Only under the leadership of a truly Bolshevik party can the future of the Chinese revolution be assured. And the Fifth Congress has shown that this subjective factor does exist. All objective conditions for the development of the revolution are present. From this objective situation arises a subjective factor—a genuine Bolshevik party. The delegates to the congress will leave for all parts of the country to participate in the struggle against reaction, imperialism, and militarism. The delegates' return to their localities will strengthen the revolutionary movement to a great extent, it will lend it the necessary leadership for the successful continuation of the revolutionary struggle, and will lead it, through a series of consecutive stages, to victory.

There were a number of questions which aroused doubts among the workers. All these doubts have been dispelled by the congress. First of all, there was the question of whether the revolution was entering a period of decline or rise. The congress declared clearly and explicitly that the revolution is continuing to develop. There are no signs of decline. Both the subjective and objective factors favor the further development of the revolution.

Second, there was a question concerning the forms and limits of the agrarian revolution. The agrarian problem is the most vital question of the present period. Here, too, the congress drew up the correct line for the Party. Rejecting an excessively radical policy which might injure a revolutionary bloc with the petty bourgeoisie, the congress declared explicitly that there is necessity for partial confiscation of land at the present stage of the revolution ([that is], confiscation of all lands except those belonging to small landowners and to the revolutionary officers' corps). Guiding themselves by this basic principle, the Communists will be able to develop the peasant movement. A gigantic development of the peasant movement on a general scale will be a heavy blow to the rural reaction and will weaken imperialism and militarism.

Third, there was a question concerning the role of the proletariat. Everyone was in agreement that at the present stage of the revolution the proletariat will have the hegemony. There was no clear conception, however, of the exact meaning of hegemony and of how it was to be achieved. Not only did the congress declare in absolutely unequivocal terms that the proletariat must play the dominant role at the present stage of the revolution, but it also provided clear directives as to how the proletariat should achieve this dominant role.

Fourth, there was a question concerning relations with the Kuomintang. There were misgivings that our relations with the Kuomintang would suffer from the revolutionary policy on the agrarian and other questions. The congress removed these doubts and showed that the revolutionary agrarian policy and the defense of the interests of the proletariat will not weaken our ties with the Kuomintang. On the contrary, only a policy of this kind would permit the establishment of a revolutionary alliance between the proletariat, the peasantry, and the petty bourgeoisie. At the present stage of the revolution, the Kuomintang must represent the politically organized form of this alliance.

To judge accurately the conditions that have arisen, to evaluate correctly the development of the revolution, and to obtain a clear picture of the situation it was necessary to analyze the Kuomintang's policy and to examine the various trends within it. But this critical analysis was in no way born of a desire to sever our relations with the Kuomintang. The congress merely acted according to one of the conditions on which the Communist Party entered the Kuomintang: [namely, that it be] an independent political factor and exercise the right of criticism at its own discretion. Not only did the congress not entertain the question of a break with the Kuomintang, but it furnished its critical analysis of the situation so as to determine the way to transform the Kuomintang during the next stage of the revolution into an organ of the democratic dictatorship of the proletariat, the peasantry, and the urban petty bourgeoisie. One of the basic tasks of the proletariat and its party at the given stage of the revolution consists not of weakening but of strengthening the Kuomintang, of converting it into a firm, revolutionary alliance of oppressed classes waging a struggle against imperialism, militarism, and the reactionary bourgeoisie.

The congress discussed these questions very thoroughly. It provided clear and explicit answers to them.

The Chinese Communist Party emerges from the Fifth Congress as the resolute and courageous leader of the proletariat.

The Fifth Congress of the Chinese Communist Party is an important event in the history of not only the Chinese revolution, but of the world revolution as well. The Bolshevik party in China will be able to develop the Chinese revolution along the lines indicated in the theses of the Comintern. The Fifth Congress has contributed to the consolidation of this Bolshevik party in China. The development of the Chinese revolution along the lines indicated in the theses of the Comintern speaks of the development of the world revolution in the most immediate sense. Therefore, the Fifth Congress will remain a memorable event in the history of the world revolution. It has contributed to the development of the world revolutionary movement and has done much toward its victory.

The congress concludes its work at a time when the revolution is being threatened from all sides by a series of powerful enemies. Under these conditions, the congress drew up a policy for the working class and for the entire revolutionary movement—a policy that will help the Chinese workers and peasants to repel the attack of the counterrevolutionary bloc and to lead the Chinese revolution to final victory.

The Fifth Congress of the Communist Party suggests the following slogans for the Chinese revolution:

The first slogan: "Down with Imperialism." This is not a slogan of agitation. It speaks of the determination to rouse all oppressed classes of China to a decisive struggle against imperialism under the hegemony of the proletariat at a moment when the national bourgeoisie is seeking to compromise with imperialism.

The second slogan: "Long Live the Revolutionary Alliance of the Proletariat, the Peasantry, and the Petty Bourgeoisie!" And from this slogan follows another one: "Long Live the Kuomintang—the Organ of the Democratic Dictatorship of These Three Classes!"

The decisions of the Fifth Congress of the Chinese Communist Party spell a challenge to imperialism, miltarism, and the bourgeoisie which has turned against the revolution. With this slogan, the proletariat will seize the leadership of the national-liberation movement.

Comrades, we wish you every success in the gigantic struggle which you will wage in all of China: your success will be the victory not only of the Chinese revolution, but of the whole world revolution as well.

LONG LIVE THE CHINESE PROLETARIAT AND ITS PARTY—THE CHINESE COMMUNIST PARTY!

May 9, 1927

19

THE FIFTH CONGRESS OF
THE CHINESE COMMUNIST PARTY

The preceding congress of the Chinese Communist Party was held two years and four months ago. At that time the Party was illegal and had 950 members. At the Fifth Congress, 50,000 members were represented. This phenomenal, numerical growth of the Party still does not fully reflect the growth of its political influence. The Communist Party, whose base is the proletarian and peasant organizations across the country, is the most important factor in the present political situation. (The All-Chinese Federation of Labor has 2,500,000 members, and the Federation of Peasant Unions—6,000,000; both of these organizations and others are under the leadership of the Communist Party.) Two months before the beginning of the Fifth Congress, the Kuomintang offered to the Communist Party that it take part in the national government. In accordance with the resolution of the Communist International, the Communists accepted the Ministry of Labor as well as the Ministries of Agriculture and Internal Affairs. At the given stage of the revolution, these ministries play an extremely important role. Not only has the Communist Party become a legal, mass party with decisive political influence, but it has also gained control of that sphere of the state machinery which concerns the working class and the peasantry.

Thanks to the class differentiation within the Kuomintang, its tie with the Communist Party has become closer than ever before. The withdrawal of the large-scale bourgeoisie has lessened the contradictions within the party of the Kuomintang and has turned it into a revolutionary bloc of the urban petty bourgeoisie, the peasantry and the proletariat, supported by some elements of the national bourgeoisie. Mutual relations between the Communist Party and the Kuomintang have

M. N. Roy's article; also in *International Press Correspondence,* Vol. XVII, No. 41, July 14, 1927, pp. 909–910.—Eds.

improved considerably since the proletariat is now the support and the motive power of the bloc. The improvement in the relations has expressed itself organizationally in the creation of mixed committees.

Nevertheless, the Fifth Congress of the Chinese Communist Party had to resolve a number of highly important questions. It was not easy to settle these questions. At the time that the congress convened, the Chinese national movement was threatened with an imperialist intervention; with the help and the inspiration of the imperialists, a counterrevolutionary cordon was created for strangling the revolution; consequently, this caused certain panic in the nationalist ranks and, in part, even among the urban masses.

The chief task of the Fifth Congress was to provide a correct evaluation of the situation. The Fifth Congress fulfilled this task and dispelled all doubts regarding the future of the revolution. After furnishing an analysis of the past and present political events from the point of view of the proletariat, the congress rejected the theory that the betrayal by the large-scale bourgeoisie and the threat of an imperialist intervention are retarding the development of the revolution. On the contrary, these facts indicate that the revolution has entered a period where its base is the exploited classes whose political and economic interests do not permit a compromise with imperialism and native reaction. The proletariat and the peasantry must wage a resolute struggle against imperialism and its native allies. In the process of this struggle, all the energies of the laboring masses will be mobilized, and this will intensify the social base of the revolution and will ensure its victory.

How was the imperialist attack to be resisted and how was the revolution to be defended against the counterrevolutionary bloc which was strengthened by the large-scale bourgeoisie—such was the second question that stood before the congress. The congress provided a very clear answer to this. Since all the reactionary classes have turned against the revolution, the task of the revolution at the given stage of its development consists of extirpating the reaction wherever possible and, especially, in territories occupied by the national government. The Fifth Congress declared therefore that the national revolution is first of all an agrarian revolution. Imperialist rule in China relies on militarism and the combined forces of the reaction. The social base of militarism and reaction must be sought in the feudal character of the Chinese national economy and political power. The congress proclaimed the necessity of leading the peasantry to a resolute struggle against feudalism. The slogan of this struggle is "Land to the Peasants"; in order to take possession of the lands belonging to large landowners, the peasants must have political and military power. In adopting this revolutionary decision, the congress showed that only the proletariat can lead the peasantry to an agrarian revolution which is a necessary condition not only for a successful struggle against imperialism, but also for the free, economic development of the country.

Peasant revolts constitute the most distinctive feature of the present stage of the revolution. A gigantic peasant movement is developing in provinces occupied by the national army. In a number of provinces, peasant unions represent the only form of organized power. Peasants are becoming armed and are disarming the forces of reaction. They are confiscating landlord estates. All this was reflected at the congress of the Communist Party. The peasant masses are inflamed with revolt. The proletariat must become its leader. This task defined the work of the congress.

The third important decision of the congress concerned the question of the nature of the state that will be created by the revolution. It is the opinion of the congress that the revolution, developing under the hegemony of the proletariat, must establish a democratic dictatorship of the proletariat, the peasantry, and the petty bourgeoisie. The present national-revolutionary government contains the germs of this democratic dictatorship. Communist participation in this government—in all of its organs—will further its development into an organ of democratic dictatorship. The congress noted the presence of timid and wavering elements among the petty bourgeoisie and pointed out that the struggle against these elements represents the most important condition for the consolidation of the revolutionary bloc of the proletariat, the peasantry, and the urban petty bourgeoisie.

Leading members of the Kuomintang participated in the opening of the congress and announced their determination to strengthen the bloc with the Communist Party. Comrade Wang Ching-wei was present at the report delivered by the Comintern representative regarding the perspectives and the character of the Chinese revolution. He expressed his complete agreement with the report and declared that the petty bourgeoisie must advance toward socialism jointly with the proletariat.

The historical significance of the Fifth Congress of the Chinese Communist Party is that it indicated to the proletariat and its allies how to develop the revolution further in order for it to become a mighty weapon in the destruction of capitalism. If the Chinese revolution were to develop under the leadership of the bourgeoisie, it would bring about in China conditions promoting the stabilization of capitalism in the whole world. The Fifth Congress of the Chinese Communist Party showed that the Chinese revolution must and can go further only under the hegemony of the proletariat who will prevent a capitalist development of China under the aegis of imperialist finance capital. Thus, the Congress bears international significance and represents a landmark in the history of the struggle for socialism.

May 10, 1927

20

RESOLUTION OF THE POLITICAL BUREAU
OF THE CHINESE COMMUNIST PARTY

Adopted on May 13, 1927

RELATIONS BETWEEN THE COMMUNIST PARTY AND THE
KUOMINTANG ON THE QUESTION OF THE PETTY BOURGEOISIE

The Fifth Congress of our Party established the basic principles which must guide the relations between the Communist Party and the Kuomintang. The principal objective of our collaboration with the Kuomintang at the present stage of the revolution is to strengthen and consolidate the revolutionary bloc of the petty bourgeoisie, the peasantry, and the proletariat in the decisive struggle against foreign imperialism and native reaction. The Communist Party remains in the Kuomintang, because the latter, with its present social composition, represents a revolutionary bloc directing a democratic revolution aimed at the destruction of feudalism, the annihilation of militarism, and the overthrow of imperialist rule.

The Communist Party is the party of the proletariat. The basic principle of its program and policy is the defense of the interests of the working class and the carrying through of the class struggle until the ultimate goal—the realization of socialism. The interests of the working class require the development of the revolution. The alliance of the proletariat, the peasantry, and the urban petty bourgeoisie is a requisite for the development of the revolution. Therefore, the task of the proletariat is to create and strengthen this alliance.

Being objectively the most revolutionary class, the proletariat becomes a force cementing this bloc and propelling it on the path of a steadfast, consistent revolutionary policy. At the present stage, the proletariat is not alone in assuming the leadership of the revolution. It guarantees a leadership of the revolution by the Left Kuomintang in accordance with the needs of the situation.

At the present stage of the revolution, relations between the Communist Party and the Kuomintang are based on the hegemony of the proletariat in the struggle. The Communist Party is entering the Kuomintang, collaborating with it, strengthening the Left Wing and assisting it in leading the national revolution, but it must not at the same time forfeit the character of an independent political factor which first of all represents the interests of the proletariat and acts accordingly. The proletariat cannot enter the bloc (with the Left Kuomintang) at the expense of its class independence. Only through the medium of its party—the Communist Party—can it carry out its role as a factor which cements this bloc and pushes it constantly forward.

Since the proletariat must enter the bloc (with the Left Kuomintang) in order to guarantee the further development of the revolution, the Party in its tactics must also take into account the interests of the non-proletarian classes participating in the bloc. The Fifth Congress quite clearly stated the way in which collaboration between the proletariat and the urban petty bourgeoisie and the small [land] owners [khoziaeva] of the village can be assured.

The development of the revolution makes it necessary for the Communist Party to have an explicit policy on the question of defending the interests of the petty bourgeoisie.

Proceeding from the resolution of the Fifth Congress, the Politbureau of the Central Committee adopts the following practical measures for removing any possible difficulties in the sphere of the relations between the Communist Party and the Kuomintang on the question of the urban petty bourgeoisie.

1. The Ministry of Labor shall establish a court of arbitration for resolving conflicts between petty entrepreneurs and their employees.

2. The Ministry of Labor shall establish laws covering the working day, minimum wages, pensions, social insurance, labor conditions, and so on. Special attention must be paid to the regulation of employees' working conditions in commercial enterprises.

3. The exhorbitant demands of commercial employees shall be restricted. Workers' control shall be regulated so as to provide against interference in the administration of enterprises. A special committee composed of representatives of the General Federation of Labor, the Ministry of Labor, the Union of Employees, and the Union of Merchants, shall examine all demands laid down by commercial employees and shall set reasonable limits for them according to the rise in prices.

4. There must be no obstacles to the commercial activity of imperialists at the present time.

5. All merchants, with the exception of those involved in or suspected of counterrevolutionary activity, must enjoy the common political and civil rights.

However, one can not eradicate by these measures the dissatisfaction that exists among the urban petty bourgeoisie and that reflects on the relations between the Communist Party and the Kuomintang. The urban petty bourgeoisie is suffering economically from the consequences of the economic blockade which imperialism and the counterrevolutionary large-scale bourgeoisie are trying to establish around the national territories. The continuous civil wars waged by the militarists, the high taxes and the *likin*—these are the other factors which create grave economic difficulties for the petty merchants. The Communist Party has supported and will [continue to] support the petty bourgeoisie in the struggle against these factors of oppression. The position of the urban petty bourgeoisie cannot be improved without destroying the economic blockade and removing these factors—which can only be achieved as a result of the victory of the revolution. In fighting against imperialism, militarism, and the counterrevolutionary large-scale bourgeoisie, the proletariat is defending the interests of the petty merchants and artisans.

(The concrete proposals were not carried out. [M.N.R.])

21

REVOLT OF HSIA TOU-YIN.

DECLARATION OF THE CHINESE

COMMUNIST PARTY

The revolt of Hsia Tou-yin has shown that there still exist reactionaries who are masked as revolutionaries. They support the revolution, always looking for an opportunity to turn against it and, if possible, to destroy it. But the revolution is too strong to be so easily destroyed. Based on the energy of the workers and peasants, on their will to self-sacrifice and their resolve to fight, the revolution has become invincible. It has survived the betrayal of Chiang Kai-shek. It will deal summarily with Hsia Tou-yin and his like.

Reactionaries like Hsia Tou-yin turn against the revolution and seek to overthrow the national government under the pretext of the necessity of fighting communism. They seek to unite the urban and rural petty bourgeoisie under the flag of the reaction ostensibly for the purpose of fighting the Communist Party. They stir up panic among the petty bourgeoisie by spreading a propaganda of lies to the effect that Communists want to exterminate the middle classes.

In view of this, the Communist Party must issue an explicit declaration regarding its attitude toward the petty bourgeoisie.

Strictly speaking, the Communist Party leaves no room for doubt on this question. It would not and could not have entered the Kuomintang and collaborated with it if its policy were directed at the extermination of the petty bourgeoisie. The Fifth Congress of the Communist Party pointed out that the only guarantee of the further development of the national revolution and its final victory is a revolutionary-democratic alliance of the petty bourgeoisie, the peasantry, and the proletariat. A militant and lasting alliance of these three classes can only be established on the basis of mutual security. The proletariat cannot seek an alliance with the petty bourgeoisie and, at the same time, make plans for its extermination. Such are the arguments demonstrating with absolute conviction the utter falsehood of the propaganda which seeks to destroy the democratic, anti-imperialist front. Nevertheless, the reactionaries are making a bugaboo of "Communist excesses" which must serve as a smoke screen for all their traitorous attacks against the national revolution.

In its resolutions, manifestos, and speeches, the Communist Party has repeatedly formulated its attitude toward the petty bourgeoisie in the most explicit terms. Let us briefly explain its position here.

In the villages—the Communist Party is against confiscation of lands belonging to petty landlords and to officers of the revolutionary army. It demands that all soldiers and officers of the national army who do not have land be endowed with it. The Communist Party considers that petty landlords who are not implicated in counterrevolutionary activity must exercise their political rights and participate in the democratic organs of village self-government.

In towns—the Communist Party demands the reduction of heavy taxes which weigh on the petty merchants. The destruction of transportation in the country as a result of the militarists' war among themselves and the various feudal duties, especially the *likin,* are ruining the merchants. The economic blockade instituted by the imperialists and the large-scale bourgeoisie is likewise harming the interests of merchants. By fighting against militarism, feudalism, imperialism, and the large-scale bourgeoisie, the Communist Party is defending not only the interests of the proletariat and the peasantry, but also the interests of the petty merchants. The Communist Party demands that all urban petty merchants, with the exception of those associated with the counterrevolution, be granted political and civil rights.

This position is quite clear. It refutes the malicious propaganda which is being conducted by reactionaries, such as Hsia Tou-yin. Imperialism hates the Communists. Chang Tso-lin shoots the Communists. Sun Ch'uan-fang, under the guise of suppressing a Communist plot, has drowned in blood the demonstration of the Shanghai proletariat which welcomed the arrival of the national army. Chiang Kai-shek is slaughtering the workers and persecuting the Communists. Li Chi-shên is killing the Communists. Everyone knows what these people represent and what their goals are. They are all counterrevolutionaries and hirelings of imperialism. And then there appears Hsia Tou-yin with his "laudable" program of "saving China from communism." Like all other anti-Communist heroes before him, he is not really seeking the salvation of

China, but, rather, the defense of imperialism, militarism, and feudal reaction against the mounting wave of the revolution.

Hsia Tou-yin and his brothers, the feudal-militarist bandits who suck the blood of the laboring masses, have every ground to hate Communists, to fear them, and to demand their heads as payment for their own questionable and traitorous support of the national government. But the exploited, indigent petty bourgeoisie must not succumb to their deception. The restoration of feudalism and militarism in the national territory will not help, but will seriously damage the interests of the small owners and merchants. Evidently, Hsia Tou-yin is counting on the absence of common sense among the democratic petty bourgeoisie when he claims to defend their interests and appeals for their support of his traitorous, militarist adventure.

The revolutionary demonstrations of the peasantry, especially in Hunan, are throwing the military circles into confusion. Hsia Tou-yin counts on using this confusion in the military circles to further his own counterrevolutionary goals. The Communist Party line in regard to the question of the property of small landowners shows quite clearly that the "excesses" are not caused by the Communist Party. They are inevitable. While regretting the ill-fated consequences of these "excesses," the Communist Party must point to their objective causes, the immediate removal of which would alleviate the situation and deprive the reactionaries of any pretexts whatsoever for their counterrevolutionary actions.

The peasantry enthusiastically welcomed the national revolution as the liberator from the centuries-old yoke which made slaves of the peasants. The agrarian program of the Kuomintang has opened to the oppressed peasantry an alluring picture of a new life. It was embraced with an enthusiasm that gave birth to a spontaneous revolutionary movement. The realization of the program, however, was delayed. The patience of the peasants was becoming exhausted. Under such conditions, rash, ill-considered actions were inevitable. If the peasant movement had received step by step the realization of its demands as expressed in the program of the Kuomintang, the lamentable incidents would have been avoided.

The revolution has promised land and freedom to the peasantry. The sooner these promises are fulfilled, the better. In stirring up the peasantry against feudal exploitation and patriarchal oppression, the Communist Party is acting in strict conformity with the program of the national revolution. The exploited peasantry rose to the struggle against he feudal-patriarchal lords of the village. As has been frequently declared before, the policy of the Communist Party is not directed against the petty bourgeoisie. On the contrary, its objective is an alliance with the petty bourgeoisie for a struggle aimed at overthrowing feudal-patriarchal absolutism and establishing a democratic regime in the village. The Communists have even demanded that, in exceptional cases, the national government guarantee the petty landlords a defined fixed rent from their land.

The destruction of the feudal-patriarchal regime in the village will benefit not only the peasantry. The merchants, the rural, and the urban population are also interested in this economically. Improvement of the economic position of the peasantry will stimulate trade. The destruction of the feudal regime will remove the obstacles to the development of trade. If the petty landowners are satisfied with a fixed rent, guaranteed by the government, and restrain themselves from counteracting the peasant movement which is the basis of the national revolution in China, then the peasantry will not touch them.

A promise by the Kuomintang promptly to carry out agrarian reforms is the only way to restrain some of the inevitable "excesses" of the spontaneous mass movement in the village. This will strengthen the revolution, unite the peasant masses around the national government, and the revolt of Hsia Tou-yin will be crushed immediately.

The Communist Party is exposing Hsia Tou-yin's claims to the role of a defender of small owners against "Communist excesses" and is calling upon the workers and peasant masses to stand firmly on the side of the national government in order to smash the revolt of Hsia Tou-yin. The lower middle classes in the town and the village will go against their own interests if they allow themselves to be deceived by reactionaries like Hsia Tou-yin. Their real interests lie with the victory of the national revolution, with the extermination of imperialism, militarism, and feudalism. They must not play into the hands of reactionary militarists and traitors of Hsia Tou-yin's type or oppose the revolution by attacking the Communist Party. On the contrary, they must unite with the proletarian and peasant masses for the defense of the revolution against reactionary traitors.

The Communist Party proclaims herewith its loyalty to the national government and declares its intention to support the revolutionary alliance with the lower middle classes and defend their interests.

The Communist Party believes that the false pretensions of Hsia Tou-yin will not find the slightest response in either the national army or among the petty bourgeoisie; it believes that his revolt will be quickly crushed and that he will be punished as an enemy of the revolution. On its part, the proletariat will defend the revolution with arms in hand and will help the national government to carry out the agrarian program of the Kuomintang.

DOWN WITH HSIA TOU-YIN—THE STANDARDBEARER OF REACTION!
DOWN WITH ALL FEUDAL-MILITARIST ENEMIES OF THE NATIONAL
    REVOLUTION!
LONG LIVE THE REVOLUTIONARY DEMOCRATIC ALLIANCE OF THE
    PETTY BOURGEOISIE, THE PEASANTRY AND THE PROLETARIAT!
LONG LIVE THE KUOMINTANG—THE LEADER OF THE NATIONAL
    REVOLUTION!
LONG LIVE THE NATIONAL GOVERNMENT!

The Chinese Communist Party

Hankow, May 18, 1927

NOTE: The revolt of Yang Shên in Szechuan and of Hsia Tou-yin in the southern part of Hupeh created a sharp conflict in the Kuomintang between the Left
Wing of the petty bourgeoisie and the generals. At that moment it was necessary
for tactical reasons to intensify this conflict. Certain concessions should have
been made to the petty bourgeoisie in order to alienate it from the openly reactionary officers who were raising the banner of revolt against the national revolution under the pretext of defending the interests of the middle classes. In those
circumstances, the "orientation toward T'ang Shêng-chih" prevailed in the Central
Committee of the Communist Party. The leading comrades considered him to be a
"100 percent revolutionary." The policy sought to create within the national government a combination of forces the center of which was to have been T'ang Shêng-
chih. This policy was, of course, completely erroneous. It aroused suspicions of
the Left Wing Kuomintang, and particularly of Wang Ching-wei. The latter believed that the Communists were planning a militarist plot to destroy the Left
Wing. It was in view of this strained situation, partly created in the Party by the
erroneous policy of certain Communists, that the declaration, presented above,
was issued; its aim was to win the confidence of the petty bourgeoisie and to incite
it against the reactionary officers.
    In carrying out this same tactic which sought to drive a wedge between the
militarists and the petty-bourgeois elements, the Central Committee of the Communist Party decided to induce Wang Ching-wei to submit to the Military
Council a resolution declaring Hsia Tou-yin an insurgent who arose against the
national government. This would have led to an open break between the revolutionary militarists and the petty-bourgeois Left. But the Communists, working in
the highest organs of the Kuomintang, did not carry out this decision of the
Central Committee.
    While the Military Council was hesitating to adopt measures against Hsia Tou-
yin who was already within twenty miles of Wuhan, the Communist general Yeh
T'ing took the initiative and crushed the revolt. He was supported by the Left
Wing of the Kuomintang. Students of the Whampoa Military Academy (for the
most part petty-bourgeois Left Wing supporters of the Kuomintang) fought heroically under the command of the Communist Yeh T'ing. Thus, this tactic, to the
extent that it was pursued, proved successful. If the Communists in the highest
organs of the Kuomintang had acted in accordance with the decisions of the
Central Committee, the revolt of Yang Shên and Hsia Tou-yin could have become
the turning-point of the revolution. [M.N.R.]

22

APPEAL TO THE SOLDIERS OF HSIA TOU-YIN

COMRADES! You are soldiers of the national revolution, the aim of which is to overthrow imperialism, annihilate militarism, give land to the peasants and bread to the workers.

Your general Hsia Tou-yin, has turned against the revolution, because it threatened the power of the feudal-militarist class of which he is a representative. Your brother-soldiers are fighting in the North against Chang Tso-lin. Hsia Tou-yin wants to cut them off from the rice supply. In this way he is helping Chang Tso-lin to rout your brothers—the fighters on the northern front.

COMRADES! You are all peasants. Need and destitution have driven you into the army. Feudal exploitation has torn you from the land which your forefathers owned and cultivated. You are fighting for the national revolution in order to have the land returned to you. Hsia Tou-yin wants to preserve the power of the landlords and the gentry. He and his like want to destroy your brother-peasants in Hunan, because they are taking the land away from the landlords and the gentry.

Hsia Tou-yin says that he is revolting not against the national government, [but] that he wants to kill the Communists. Why does he want to kill the Communists? Because the Communist Party is defending the interests of soldiers, workers, and peasants. The Communist Party is demanding that peasant land be exempted from rent and other feudal duties; that the soldiers be endowed with land. Hsia Tou-yin is against the Communists, because he is against peasants and soldiers. He is for the landlords and the gentry.

Hsia Tou-yin and reactionary generals like him receive large sums of money from the national government in order to pay salaries and provide food and clothing to the soldiers. They steal a large part of this money, and, therefore, the soldiers receive no salary, [and] are hungry and ragged.

COMRADES! Do not subordinate yourselves to reactionary officers—

enemies of soldiers and peasants. Be loyal to the Kuomintang and to the national government which is leading the struggle against imperialism and militarism and is defending the interests of soldiers, peasants, workers, and small merchants. Arrest Hsia Tou-yin and his reactionary officers as traitors. Be loyal soldiers of the revolution which is fighting for your country and for your class.

DOWN WITH HSIA TOU-YIN!
DOWN WITH THE LANDLORDS AND THE GENTRY!
LONG LIVE THE KUOMINTANG AND THE NATIONAL GOVERNMENT!
LAND TO THE PEASANTS AND SOLDIERS, BREAD TO THE WORKERS!

May 18, 1927   Chinese Communist Party

NOTE: It was decided to urge the Political Council of the Kuomintang to issue a similar appeal to the soldiers. But the Communists—members of the Political Council of the Kuomintang and those working in the highest organs of the Kuomintang—did not insist on this. Even the Political Bureau of the Central Committee of the Communist Party did not want to issue an appeal fearing that it may have a demoralizing effect not only on the army of Hsia Tou-yin, but also on the whole national army. [M.N.R.]

23

RELATIONS WITH THE KUOMINTANG AND THE
INDEPENDENCE OF THE COMMUNIST PARTY

There is no need of raising an alarm about the danger of a break each time we discuss the relations between the Communist Party and the Kuomintang. There is no question of a break now. Therefore, we will set this question aside in the present discussion. It is impossible to discuss our relations with the Kuomintang in an unprejudiced manner if one is at all times influenced by the thought of a break. At the present, our relations with the Kuomintang must be determined by the necessity of remaining in the Kuomintang. Any proposal for withdrawing from the Kuomintang in the immediate future must be rejected. The program on the basis of which Communists may and must participate in the Kuomintang has not yet been carried out. The Communist Party entered the Kuomintang to further the development of the national revolution. At the given stage of the national revolution, the Communist Party must remain in the Kuomintang for the purpose of consolidating the Left Wing—in order to assist it, in order to arouse it to the struggle against the feudal-bourgeois reaction.

Recognizing the necessity of collaborating with the Kuomintang, the Communists must not, however, shut their eyes on the difficulties that ensue from these relations, on the fact that there are within the Kuomintang elements definitely hostile to the Communist Party. These difficulties should have been foreseen. Chiang Kai-shek's separation did not completely rid the Kuomintang of elements of the feudal-bourgeois reaction. It was a mistake to regard the whole Wuhan group as the Left Wing. On the contrary, one of the aims which the Communist Party should have pursued while remaining in the Kuomintang after the split was to intensify the differentiation between the feudal-bourgeois reac-

Presumably M. N. Roy's address and proposals to The Politburo of the Chinese Communist Party.—Eds.

tion and petty-bourgeois radicalism. The Communists did not appreciate the importance of this tactical aim; for this very reason, our relations with the Kuomintang now appear to be fraught with such overwhelming difficulties.

The appraisal of the social character of the Kuomintang after the split was incorrect. Consequently, the difficulties that have now arisen could not have been anticipated. There was a mechanistic conviction that all the feudal-bourgeois elements had broken away and that the Kuomintang had become a revolutionary, democratic party whose base was the petty bourgeoisie, the peasantry, and the proletariat. As a result, it was calculated that everything would proceed smoothly. If the class composition of the Kuomintang were in fact so simple, then the Communist Party would have had much greater scope of work within it. The complete removal from the Kuomintang of representatives of feudal lords and the bourgeoisie would, of course, have ironed out the internal class contradictions. Facts have shown, however, that this was not the case. When the feudal lords and the bourgeoisie, as a class, turned against the revolution, their agents still remained in the ranks of the Kuomintang and continued to occupy leading posts. The majority of the Central Committee of the Kuomintang (Wuhan) consists of these agents of the feudal-bourgeois reaction who took a frankly hostile position toward the national revolution. The internal situation in the Kuomintang is extremely peculiar. Its ranks consist chiefly of petty bourgeois and proletarian elements. Its basis and its sphere of activities are the democratic masses. But the leadership of the Kuomintang, of the Central Committee, is comprised primarily of feudal-bourgeois leaders and, therefore, does not and can not represent the masses of its members and followers.

The difficulties which the Communist Party is experiencing are rooted in its relations not with the Kuomintang *per se,* but with the leadership of the Kuomintang. If this is borne in mind in determining the relations with the Kuomintang, the problem will be much easier to resolve. Our tactic under these circumstances must be determined not by the desire to maintain good relations with the leaders, but by the necessity of using the party as a whole as an instrument for developing the revolution.

I do not propose effecting an internal *coup* in the Kuomintang. The task lying before the Communist Party is one of freeing the Kuomintang from its present leadership; however, it is impossible to achieve this immediately.

The time is not yet ripe for the slogan "Down with the present Central Committee." Ultimately, the Kuomintang will either be freed of its present leadership or cease being the organ of the national revolutionary struggle. The Communist Party must help the Kuomintang to rid itself of reactionary leaders. This can be done by assisting and strengthening the reliable elements of the Left. The present Central Committee of the Kuomintang is an enemy not only of the Communist Party; it does not represent the interests of those classes which form the basis of the Left Wing Kuomintang. It is making preparations to betray these classes, to betray the national revolution. The Communist Party must stir up the masses represented in the Kuomintang and all its supporters against this danger. The participation of the Communist Party in the Kuomintang is expressed not only in the fact that Communists receive government posts and arrange joint conferences. Effective collaboration between the Communist Party and the Left Wing Kuomintang must be realized in local organizations among the masses. When the Left Wing elements find a vantage ground in the local organizations of the Party and are supported by the masses, then the pressure on the leaders will make itself felt. The Central Committee will have to deal with the opposition of the whole Party, bound up with the revolutionary masses and drawing its support from them. At such time it will be easy to overthrow the present gang of agents of feudal-bourgeois reaction who have usurped the power under the banner of the Left Wing Kuomintang. In short, the Kuomintang must be rebuilt not from above, but from below. It needs to be democratized. The task of the Communist Party in the present situation is not one of overthrowing the Central Committee of the Kuomintang; at present it is necessary to expose to the masses the counter-revolutionary tendencies of the leaders; it is necessary to help the lower strata [of the population] to rid themselves of agents of those classes which have already turned against the revolution.

All the difficulties in our relations with the Kuomintang lie in our relations with the leaders. We do not have these difficulties with the party masses. The biggest difficulties arise in solving the agrarian problem. For one month we have carried on endless negotiations on this subject with the leaders of the Kuomintang in an effort to find a common platform. In the end, the Central Committee of the Kuomintang actually refused to carry out those measures of agrarian reform which were promised in previous decisions. This led to a crisis in the relations between the two parties. But does this policy of the Central Committee reflect the position of the whole party? No. The Hupeh provincial peasant committee of the Kuomintang adopted a resolution on the agrarian question. This resolution was approved by the provincial committee of Hunan and Kiangsi. It was advanced by the local organizations of the Kuomintang as a common platform for both parties. The platform proposed by the Communists at the joint conference was even more radical than this resolution. This is proof of the solidarity of the Communist Party and the masses of the Kuomintang. This also proves that the conflict between the Communist Party and the present Central Committee of the Kuomintang is a reflection of the conflict between the leading and the rank-and-file members of the Kuomintang. The root of this evil lies in the fact that the present Central Committee does not represent the petty bourgeoisie which, at the given stage, constitutes the social base of the Kuomintang. If the Central Committee had honestly reflected the interests of the petty bourgeoisie, there would have been considerably less grounds for friction, for the withdrawal of the feudal bourgeoisie created a more favorable situation for collaboration between the proletariat and the petty bourgeoisie in the national-revolutionary struggle. There can be no doubt that even the petty bourgeoisie must be prepared to overcome some immediate difficulties and rid itself of a number of traditional class prejudices in order to remain loyal to the national revolution. If it is unable to do this, it must go over to the side of the feudal-bourgeois reaction which contradicts its own class interests. It is no accident that Wang Ching-wei is the only one of the major leaders of the Kuomintang who is trying to maintain friendly relations with the Communist Party. He is the only representative of the petty bourgeoisie in the leading organs of the Kuomintang (the Political Council and the Military Council). The majority of the Central Committee represents either the feudal reaction or the bourgeoisie which has already turned traitor. There is nothing surprising in the fact that, with the given composition of the Central Committee, very serious symptoms have begun to appear in the Kuomintang. The petty-bourgeois minority in the Central Committee is intimidated and is beginning to submit to the influence of the feudal-militarist bourgeois majority.

Under these conditions, the Communist Party must mobilize the Kuomintang masses to a struggle against the reactionary leadership. The situation has changed; consequently, the forms and methods of our collaboration with the Kuomintang, too, must change. Solidarity with the leaders can be maintained only at the price of betraying the rank-and-file masses. The tactic of the present moment is a united front of the masses against the reactionary leaders. Such a tactic will not lead to a break with the Kuomintang. On the contrary, it will consolidate the revolutionary-democratic alliance of the proletariat, the peasantry, and the urban petty bourgeoisie; and the Kuomintang can continue its existence only as a militant organ of this alliance.

Our relations with the Kuomintang do not represent an end in itself. They are only a means to an end. The main purpose of our collaboration with the Kuomintang at present is to draw the petty-bourgeois masses deeper into the revolutionary struggle, to liberate them of the reactionary influence of feudal lords and large-scale bourgeoisie. We shall not be able to lead the petty bourgeoisie to the revolutionary struggle if we have no organizational bond with it. The petty-bourgeois masses are in the Kuomintang, and in their majority they are under its influence. It is exactly for this reason that the proletariat stays in the Kuomintang; the Kuomintang must be used by it as an organ of the revolutionary democratic alliance.

Can the Communist Party have an independent political line under such conditions? Can it remain in the Kuomintang and draw the petty-bourgeois masses into the revolutionary struggle if it pursues an independent policy? The Communist Party entered the Kuomintang [on the condition that it] reserves the right of political independence, but owing to an erroneous conception of the united front, this right was not realized. As a result, the Party committed grave errors. A repetition of such errors at the critical moment of the present will prove fatal to our Party and to the revolution.

What is a political party? It is an organized and conscious vanguard of a certain class. Either the Communist Party is a political organ of the proletariat, or it is not. The political independence of the Communist Party means independence in defending the interests of the working class under all conditions and by any means. The defense of the interests of the working class is a basic principle of Communist policy. If the Communist Party compromises on this principle, it will cease to be a political organ of the proletariat. At the same time, it would be a mistake to think that the Communist Party can maintain its independence only when it is fighting directly for the dictatorship of the proletariat. The Communist Party does not stop being a 100 percent proletarian party even in the case where it does not demand the immediate realization of socialism. If the Communist Party leads the proletariat through successive stages, through partial demands, to the struggle whose ultimate aim is the realization of socialism, it is really defending the interests of the working class. The collaboration of the Communist Party with the Kuomintang is a stage in the proletariat's struggle for socialism. Therefore, by entering the Kuomintang and working within it, the Communist Party does not cease to be an independent political party of the proletariat. The Communist Party will cease to be an independent political party only in the event that it ignores the interests of the proletariat for the sake of easing frictions with the Kuomintang. The question now stands as follows: Can the Communist Party remain in the Kuomintang and at the same time defend the interests of the proletariat? If this has become impossible, our relations with the Kuomintang must evidently be changed.

What must be that policy which defends the interests of the proletariat as well as those of the whole laboring majority of China? It must be a policy of developing a revolution which will overthrow imperialism and extirpate native reaction. The Communists are staying in the Kuomintang and are participating in national government in order to make use of the Kuomintang and the national government as an instrument for developing the revolution.

By opposing the Communists' right to defend the interests of the working class under all conditions, the Kuomintang leaders intend to retard the development of the revolution, doing this not so much in the interest of the petty bourgeoisie as in the interest of the large-scale bourgoisie and the feudal landlords. They call the workers and peasants to bear sacrifices so that the interests of the capitalists and feudal lords are not disturbed. They want the peasantry to submit to the militant feudal reaction which is rearing its head against the national revolution. They are appealing to the working class to reject the struggle not only against the native bourgeoisie, but even against imperialism. They are ordering industrial workers in foreign enterprises not to strike, but to refer their demands to the minister of foreign affairs who will reach an agreement with the imperialists.

Whether or not workers and peasants will submit to these demands of the Kuomintang is a different question. But what is significant in the present situation is that the Kuomintang has issued a manifesto * which represents a declaration of its right to act as the defender of the feudal-bourgeois reaction in the face of the mounting wave of the revolution. One cannot disregard such a position of the Kuomintang. It must affect its relations with the Communist Party.

We can no longer ignore the fact that the Central Committee of the Kuomintang is pursuing an antiproletarian, antipeasant and anti-Communist policy. An explanation for this fact can be found. (There are comrades who consider the Communists responsible for this). Now, however, our task is not one of seeking an explanation for this fact, but of taking cognizance of it and adopting measures that are appropriate to the situation that has arisen.

---

*On May 19, the Central Committee of the Kuomintang issued a manifesto openly opposing the worker-peasant movement which is blamed for the split in the Kuomintang ranks. The manifesto states that anticapitalist and antifeudal movements weaken the struggle against imperialism. Workers must refuse to fight against capitalism. At the same time, strikes in foreign enterprises are prohibited. [M.N.R.]

In the given case, it would be useful to recall the mistakes committed by our Party after the *coup* of March 20, 1926. There is much in common between Chiang Kai-shek's *coup* a year ago and the present revolt of Hsia Tou-yin. The counterrevolutionary trend expressed in the revolt of Hsia Tou-yin was not liquidated after his defeat. This trend exists in the leading circles of the Kuomintang and is becoming more and more apparent with every day. The Hsiatouyinists who sit in the Kuomintang are urging it to adopt an antilabor, antipeasant, anti-Communist policy. The task of the Communists at the present moment is to free the Kuomintang from the danger of Hsiatouyinism. How can this be done? Not by compromising with the Kuomintang leaders the majority of whom are supporters of Hsiatouyinism. We can accomplish this task only by approaching closer the rank-and-file masses of the Kuomintang, by cautioning them against the danger of Hsiatouyinism and by helping them to wipe out this danger. Communists will accomplish nothing positive by remaining in the Kuomintang if they do not transform it into a militant organ of the revolutionary, democratic alliance of the proletariat, the peasantry, and the petty bourgeoisie. The Kuomintang leaders are not only betraying the interests of workers and peasants; they are pursuing a policy that is hostile even to the petty bourgeoisie which forms the social base of the Left Wing of the Kuomintang. If we adapt ourselves to the position of the leaders, it will simply mean that we endorse their antilabor, antipeasant, and anti-Communist policy. If the Communists do not counteract the development of counterrevolution in the leading circles of the Kuomintang for the sake of avoiding a break with them, then they will not only cease to represent the working class, but will also be helping those who want to destroy the Kuomintang as an organ of the national revolution.

I will touch on one more question before proposing a draft resolution on our relations with the Kuomintang. Two perspectives now lie before the revolution. One of them—the transformation of the Kuomintang into an organ of the feudal-bourgeois reaction—is sought by the [Kuomintang] leaders. It will lead inevitably to a reconciliation with the reactionary elements which have left the Kuomintang and have turned against the national revolution. The leadership of the national revolution will be returned to the bourgeoisie which seeks a compromise with imperialism and is tied to native reaction. A compromise with imperialism will mean the defeat of the revolution. Such is one perspective. The other is the perspective of a revolutionary struggle for the establishment of a democratic dictatorship of the proletariat, the peasantry, and the petty bourgeoisie. The Left Kuomintang and the national government in Wuhan should be regarded as a step in this direction; but there is still much to be done to reach this goal. The Wuhan government cannot develop peaceably into an organ of democratic dictatorship. Experience has shown that there are numerous difficulties along this path. Serious thought should be given to what must be the next steps on the path to democratic dictatorship. I am raising only one question at this point: how is the democratic dictatorship to be achieved? Until now, our tactics have amounted to helping the petty-bourgeois Left Kuomintang come to power, which power it would share with the proletariat and the peasantry, thus creating a democratic dictatorship of three oppressed classes. Experience has shown that there are sufficient grounds to doubt the correctness of this course. Do we not find ourselves now in a period when the revolution must develop new forms of struggle and new organs of power? The slogan of democratic dictatorship was advanced during the Russian Revolution of 1905. This slogan meant that power must be seized for the purpose of establishing not a dictatorship of the proletariat, but a democratic dictatorship of workers and peasants. But the objective did not consist of helping the peasantry win power. It is the proletariat that must take power—with the help of the peasantry—and build a state on the basis of the two classes. I believe that this likewise must be the present tactic in China. To begin a struggle of the working class for power—that is what must be the next step toward the establishment of a democratic dictatorship. We saw that when the working class puts the petty bourgeoisie in power, as it happened with the Left Wing Kuomintang in Wuhan, the petty bourgeoisie does not share the power with workers and peasants, but places it in the hands of the bourgeoisie and even in the hands of feudal militarists. I raise this question: Can a democratic dictatorship be achieved through the present petty-bourgeois organ of power which inclines toward capitulation, or must the proletariat seize power and retain it on the basis of an alliance of three classes? The course of events is such that this question will have to be answered in the near future. The continuing collaboration with the Kuomintang must parallel preparations of new forms of struggle and new organs of power, appropriate to the situation and necessary for achieving the goal. Collaboration with the Kuomintang must continue, because it will give us an opportunity to make the necessary preparations. If we collaborate with the Kuomintang for the sake of any other goals and nourish any illusions about the social character and the political aims of the Kuomintang leaders, we will lead our Party into liquidation and the revolution will be in jeopardy.

Some comrades say that if we demand more than what the Kuomintang and the national government are prepared to agree to, then we must leave the Kuomintang. The situation is not so simple. Between the two extremes of a compromise and a break lies a distance of considerable measure. The type of reforms that the national government can give to the workers and peasants is one matter, but that program toward the realization of which the Communist Party is leading the working class and the peasantry is an entirely different matter. The demands of the worker and peasant movement which is led by the Communists must not and can not be restricted by considerations of the length to which the Kuomintang and the national government are prepared to go. If the Communists were to direct the worker and peasant movement on the basis of demands that are approved by national leaders, they would lead it into liquidation. We do not foist our program on the Kuomintang, and the Kuomintang, in turn, should not demand that we stop being Communists in order to demonstrate our loyalty. Our relations must be determined by this principle.

This principle was established by the congress of our Party. The task now is to apply it to the concrete situation. The Fifth Congress set three basic tasks before the Party:

1) to develop the agrarian revolution,
2) to intensify the workers' movement,
3) to win over the petty bourgeoisie.

The Fifth Congress also pointed out that in fighting economically and politically against feudal reaction, one should at the same time neutralize the petty bourgeoisie. I propose that the Communist Party issue a declaration on the manner in which it will carry out this threefold task; the declaration must show how the development of the agrarian revolution and the workers' movement can be accomplished without violating the interests of the petty-bourgeois masses.

The Communist Party does not demand of the national government a decree on the confiscation of land. Our task is to organize and to lead the peasant masses ourselves to the seizure of land. In this way, we will test the Kuomintang. The leaders say that they are remaining faithful to the agrarian program of their party, but that they cannot carry it out at once in view of the objections of army officers who all originate from the feudal-landlord strata.

In developing the agrarian revolution, the Communists are acting against the feudal lords and militarists who seek to destroy the Kuomintang. If the Kuomintang leaders are really faithful to the program of their party, they can not oppose peasants who take upon themselves the task of carrying out this program; otherwise, they would merely expose themselves as traitors to their own party.

Such a policy by our Party will show that Communists are not acting against the interests of the petty bourgeoisie; [it will show], on the contrary, that they are striving for an alliance with the petty bourgeoisie, for a struggle against the enemies of the Kuomintang, against the enemies of the national revolution.

The Communist program of the national revolution does actually defend the interests of the petty bourgeoisie. If we formulate clearly our program and carry it out decisively, the small landowners will be neutralized, and the source of conflicts with the urban petty merchants will be eliminated. If the Communist Party acts in conformity with the resolution which I am going to propose, the support of the Kuomintang masses will be assured. The antagonism between the feudal-bourgeois leaders and the petty-bourgeois members [of the Kuomintang] will be intensified. In the consequence, the Kuomintang will be freed from the dominance of the agents of the feudal-bourgeois reaction, and it will become a militant organ of a revolutionary-democratic alliance of the proletariat, the peasantry, and the petty bourgeoisie. In carrying out such a policy, the Communist Party will not provoke a break with the Kuomintang: on the contrary, it will be saved from the clutches of the feudal-bourgeois reaction; it will become stronger than it has ever been before, it will prove capable of leadership in the national revolution.

There follows below the draft declaration which I propose should be issued on behalf of our Party on the question of our relations with the Kuomintang:

1. At the present stage of the revolution, collaboration of the Communist Party with the Kuomintang is still necessary.

2. The following conditions define our collaboration with the Kuomintang: (a) development of the democratic forces, (b) persevering struggle against reactionary elements in the Kuomintang in the aim of, first, isolating them, and then forcing them out of the party, (c) seizure of leadership by the Left Wing which is closely connected with the masses, (d) defense of the interests of the proletariat and the peasantry.

In the Realm of the Agrarian Question

1. The immediate establishment of democratic power in the villages and districts [okrugi]; power must belong to the delegates' assemblies. The delegates must be elected by peasant unions and other people's organizations. 70 percent of the assembly seats must belong to delegates of peasant unions. This is a highly democratic measure since the overwhelming majority of the rural population is made up of peasants.

The following elements must be removed from participation in these assemblies both in the capacity of members and in the capacity of electors: (a) large-scale landlords whose lands are subject to confiscation, (b) the gentry, (c) former officials.

2. Control of the armed forces (with the exception of the regular army) must belong to the village and district organs of power under the supervision of the Ministry of Internal Affairs.

3. Creation of military-political schools for peasant delegates to train officials for new government organs and officers for the rural militia.

4. Organization of land committees, attached to rural organs of power, composed of representatives of peasant unions, local organs of power, the militia, and local committees of the Kuomintang and the Communist Party. The functions of the land committees shall be: (a) to determine the land that is subject to confiscation, (b) to enforce confiscation of land belonging to large-scale landlords, temples, churches, capitalist companies, and so on, (c) to distribute the confiscated land, (d) to determine the size of land taxes and rental fees.

5. Reduction by 50 percent of the rental fee on unconfiscated land belonging to small landholders, and its reduction to the level of taxes collected by the state from confiscated land.

6. Legislation for curbing usury. Liquidation of peasant indebtedness.

7. Abolition of all duties and taxes, with the exception of a single land tax (on confiscated land), and the reduction of the rental fee (on unconfiscated land).

8. Establishment of agricultural credit banks. Confiscated public land and the ancestral and temple lands must provide a basis for credit operations.

9. Organization of producers' and consumers' coöperatives.

10. Regulation of fallow lands.

As concerns the workers' movement, here is our minimum program:

1. Legislation on: an eight-hour working-day; minimum wage rates; labor conditions; protection of women and child labor; factory inspection; workers' control; protection of health; and education.

2. Practical measures for aid to the unemployed.

3. Establishment of factory committees for the protection of labor. Factory committees will not have control over production.

4. The right of workers to strike. Abolition of compulsory arbitration.

5. The Federation of Labor shall undertake to prevent cessation of work on any [arbitrary] ground.

6. The national government must take possession of, and put into operation, factories closed down by entrepreneurs who refuse to satisfy the demands of the workers or to pay taxes to the state.

7. Unions shall not exercise the right to arrest the entrepreneurs. All complaints must be referred to the court of arbitration, attached to the Ministry of Labor *, which has the right to arrest and punish the entrepreneurs at fault.

8. Trade unions shall have the right to arrest and punish workers who have turned traitors.

9. Pickets of armed workers will form a part of the militia attached to the Ministry of Internal Affairs.† The director of the militia of a given locality has general charge over the armed pickets jointly and in collaboration with the trade union.

10. The organization of pioneers (factory-school students) [fabzavucheniki] shall be under the strict control of the Federation of Labor and will be restrained from interfering in the administration of enterprises.

With respect to the petty bourgeoisie, the Communist Party will be guided by its resolution of May 13.‡

May 24, 1927

NOTE: This resolution was neither adopted nor rejected by the Political Bureau. [M.N.R.]

* The minister of labor was a Communist, and he could determine the composition of the court of arbitration. [M.N.R.]

† The Minister of Internal Affairs, who at this moment was a Communist, had supreme control over the police forces and, in this capacity, had the right to appoint, employ or discharge directors of the militia. [M.N.R.]

‡ See Appendix III. [M.N.R. Page 283 in this book.—Eds.]

24

30TH OF MAY MANIFESTO OF
THE CHINESE COMMUNIST PARTY

Two years ago, the revolutionary action of the Shanghai proletariat laid the beginning to a new stage in the struggle for national liberation. During this stage of the revolutionary struggle, the dominant role was played by the working class of the entire country which followed the noble and heroic example of the Shanghai proletariat. All the events that have occurred in the time since May 30, 1920 [?1925] have shown that the proletariat is the deciding factor in the anti-imperialist struggle.

Two years ago, at the beginning of May, a strike flared up in the Japanese cotton factories in Tsingtao. Japanese imperialism ordered its agent, Chang Tsung-ch'ang, to crush the strike. The workers in the Japanese textile factories in Shanghai came to the aid of their comrades in Tsingtao and declared a sympathetic strike, demanding better treatment and regular payment of wages. The workers were attacked by the Japanese and Chinese police. Their leader, Ho Chun-hung [?] was killed. As it turned out, this shooting was not a simple incident in an economic struggle. The strike widened and assumed a political character.

The proletariat appealed to the whole population to join the struggle against imperialism. Students responded to this appeal with enthusiasm. A gigantic anti-imperialist movement developed under the leadership of the proletariat. A number of students and workers were arrested by the imperialist police. An enormous demonstration was staged demanding the release of the arrested leaders. The demonstration moved along Nanking Road, close to the British police station. It was fired upon, and then followed the blood bath of May 30.

A new era began in China. A new class stood in the vanguard of the national-liberation movement. This was the proletariat "who has nothing to lose but his chains, and who must conquer the whole world" in the revolutionary struggle. The atrocities of imperialism were answered by a general strike in which close to 300,000 workers took part. Students and merchants followed the proletariat. Schools and enterprises were closed down. The foreign quarters were subjected to an economic blockade. Under the leadership of the proletariat a new form of a movement developed; boldly it defied the power of imperialism, repelled it resolutely, and dealt a cruel blow to the position and prestige of imperialism in China.

The general strike continued, expanding and developing uninterruptedly in the direction of an armed struggle against imperialism. This gigantic struggle against the formidable might of imperialism demanded endless sacrifice and resolve. Events soon showed that not all classes of the Chinese people were equally prepared to undertake suffering, sacrifices, and the struggle for national liberations. The imperialists shut off the electricity in Chinese factories. The patriotism of the bourgeoisie was put to a test, and it did not pass it. As soon as matters concerned the pocket, the national bourgeoisie entered into negotiations with the imperialists on liquidating the general strike. The wealthy bourgeoisie was the first to betray the movement. It was followed by the petty bourgeoisie. Thus, the proletariat was forced to continue the anti-imperialist struggle alone. At the same time, Chang Tso-lin, at the request of his imperialist masters, sent his worthy son to establish "peace and order" in Shanghai.

Betrayed by the national bourgeoisie, abandoned by the petty bourgeoisie, threatened by imperialist guns and in the clutches of brutal repressions by Chang Tso-lin, the proletariat for three months led a heroic struggle.

The heroism, sacrifices, and determination of the Shanghai proletariat stirred the whole country. The gigantic wave of the anti-imperialist movement, whose fearless vanguard was the working class, began to rise everywhere.

May 30 is a memorable day in the history of the Chinese revolution. It is a red day also in the history of the Chinese proletariat.

Three important lessons can be derived from the May 30th movement:

1. Mass action is a powerful weapon which can defy the imperialists' guns and the militarists' hangmen.

2. The national bourgeoisie betrays the anti-imperialist struggle as soon as the latter acquires a revolutionary character.

3. The proletariat is the only class prepared to make the necessary sacrifices and possessing sufficient resolve to carry out the struggle regardless of the difficulties involved.

The two years which have elapsed since the day of May 30, 1925 have furnished sufficient proof that this is indeed the case! The future development of the revolution and its final victory will likewise depend upon our ability to act in accordance with these lessons.

The organized action of the working class paralyzed the economic life of Hong Kong for more than a year. The national power in Kwangtung consolidated despite all attacks and plots from the direction of Hong Kong, because it was supported by the action of the masses.

The national army succeeded in routing the armies of Wu P'ei-fu, Sun Ch'uan-fang, and Chang Tsung-ch'ang in spite of their superior armament, because the masses supported it with enthusiasm. The weakness of the militarists' armies lies in the dissatisfaction and the hostility on the part of the people. The strength of the national army is the sympathy and the support of the masses. The military actions of the Northern Expedition were fortified by the gigantic, revolutionary enthusiasm of the masses which swept out the reaction.

Similarly, in Wuhan, the imperialist power was challenged in consequence of mass action which, in turn, strengthened the position of the national government.

The result of these two years was not only the rapid growth of the initiative of the proletariat which pushed the revolution forward; the revolutionary activity of the proletariat had also an enormous influence on the expansion and intensification of the social base of the revolution resulting from the impetuous growth of the peasant movement in provinces that had passed to the control of the national government. An organized proletariat of two and a half million and its revolutionary ally of ten million organized peasants make up the fundamental base of the revolution.

The second lesson which we must extract from the movement of May 30 speaks of the unreliability of the bourgeoisie as a factor in the revolution. That this lesson is the most important one was shown by events that followed, namely, the *coup* of March 20, 1926, when the feudal-bourgeois elements in the Kuomintang, headed by Chiang Kaishek, overthrew the Left power in Canton, and the final betrayal of the revolution by the very same elements and their alliance with the counterrevolution.

The history of the national movement is replete with facts showing that there is no class other than the proletariat which would always be willing and able to make big sacrifices for the revolution. The proletariat has more than once taken the brunt of the blow in the struggle against imperialism. All the militarists, as far as this was possible, participated in the bloody massacres which have made famous the revolutionary self-sacrifice of the proletariat. Chiang Kai-shek became a hero who put to a final test the revolutionary staunchness of the proletariat. In order to obtain money from the national bourgeoisie and to ingratiate himself to the imperialists, he became a murderer of the Shanghai workers. But he now understands that his militarist dictatorship cannot continue to defend the interests of the feudal-bourgeois classes and serve as a new instrument of imperialism if he wages a relentless war against the Shanghai proletariat. The tactics have therefore changed. Brutal repressions proved unsuccessful. He did not succeed in crushing the workers' movement. Now Chiang Kai-shek is trying to demoralize it and to split it. But the fascist unions, organized under his leadership, were unable to attract the Shanghai proletariat. Even at the very center of the imperialist power, in the very hell [peklo] of bourgeois reaction, in the citadel of Chiang Kai-shek's neomilitarism, the proletariat remains the sustaining support of the revolution and inspires imperialism with terror.

By far the best way of commemorating May 30 and rendering homage to the memory of the fallen heroes would be to assimilate these three lessons:

1. Mass action is a powerful weapon in the revolutionary struggle.

2. The bourgeoisie deserted the revolution as soon as its pocket book was threatened.

3. The proletariat with its ally—the peasantry—is the loyal and valiant soldier of the revolution.

The proletariat must reserve for itself the historical role which it assumed two years ago—on May 30. The further the revolution develops, the more does the proletariat become its motive force. The proletariat held a united front with the national bourgeoisie as long as the latter participated in the anti-imperialist struggle. Now the bourgeoisie has deserted to the camp of the counterrevolution. In this period of the revolution, the task of the proletariat is to enlist the broad masses of the peasantry and the urban petty bourgeoisie into the revolutionary struggle. This task the proletariat will fulfill, leading the peasantry in its struggle for the abolition of feudalism, leading the urban petty bourgeoisie in its struggle against the imperialist blockade, militarist oppression, high taxes, and for democratic freedom.

The large-scale bourgeoisie, inspired and supported by imperialism, is trying to unite the reactionary forces throughout the country under the false banner of nationalism raised by the Nanking clique. In order to defend the revolution, the proletariat must develop and unite around itself the revolutionary forces of the entire working class, the peasantry, and the urban petty bourgeoisie. The Communist Party will lead the proletariat in the achievement of this historical task.

At the present stage of the revolutionary struggle, the soldiers are also an ally of the proletariat. They should be drawn into the worker-peasant movement. They are under the feudal influence of generals. This influence must be destroyed. Soldiers must become conscious allies of the proletariat in the revolutionary struggle. They are all poor peasants. The feudal exploitation of the village and the resulting economic backwardness of the country drive masses of destitute peasants into the army for merciless extermination in endless civil wars. The class interests of the soldiers are tied up with the struggle against feudal and capitalist exploitation. It is for this reason that they will respond with enthusiasm to the appeal for a revolutionary alliance of workers, peasants, and soldiers aimed at destroying feudalism, wiping out militarism, overthrowing imperialism, and undermining the foundations of class exploitation.

The Chinese proletariat marked the day of May 30, 1927, by laying down the demands for *democratic freedom, bread, land, and peace* as the slogans under the symbol of which the revolution must develop during the next stage.

Bread to those who work and produce riches for the foreign imperialists and the native bourgeoisie! Land to the peasants and soldiers. Peace to the country! An end to the extermination of landless peasants and the economic ruination of the country. Democratic freedom for the oppressed classes—the proletariat, the peasantry, and the urban petty bourgeoisie!

Such are the basic tasks of the revolution.

MAY THE MEMORY OF MAY 30, 1925 LIVE!

MAY THE MEMORY OF THE MARTYRS LIVE FOREVER!

DOWN WITH IMPERIALISM AND ITS ALLIES—MILITARISM, FEUDALISM, AND THE REACTIONARY BOURGEOSIE!

LONG LIVE THE REVOLUTIONARY-DEMOCRATIC ALLIANCE OF WORKERS, PEASANTS, SOLDIERS, AND THE PETTY BOURGEOISIE!

The Chinese Communist Party

Wuhan, May 30, 1927

25

REVOLUTION AND

COUNTERREVOLUTION IN CHINA

"It can be hoped that the extermination of communism and of future Communists in Hunan and Hupeh will be sufficiently impressive." So wrote with relish a Shanghai imperialist magazine on the subject of the last reactionary revolts in the territory of the national government. These cordial greetings from the imperialist camp reveal the true nature of the revolt of Hsia Tou-yin and the *coup* in Changsha. The reactionary-militarist elements in the national-revolutionary army have undertaken a mission whose fulfillment will be to the taste of imperialism; and imperialism is counting on the mission being fulfilled. It is perfectly obvious that the insurgent militarists in Hunan have some kind of strings of connections with imperialism. Otherwise, from where would the imperialists have so much confidence in the success of the insurgents if a way had not been found to assist the latter in their counterrevolutionary undertaking? It is as clear as day who stands behind these revolts and inspires them. Yang Shên, Hsia Tou-yin, Hsü, and other known and unknown heroes are marionettes who are brought into motion by strings which are pulled from Shanghai by way of Nanking. The network of these strings will strangle China; the ends of it lie far beyond Shanghai, beyond the ocean, in the ministries and bank offices of imperialist capitals.

Hsia Tou-yin, Hsü, and Yang Shên are shooting peasants and hungry workers not, as they are saying, in defense of the sacred rights of property. They are committing these murders in the capacity of agents of imperialism. Their mission, therefore, does not consist of making "the extermination of communism and of future Communists sufficiently impressive." Their mission is to crush the national revolution which is

An article by M. N. Roy; published also in *International Press Correspondence,* Vol. 7, No. 42, July 21, 1927, p. 926.—Eds.

challenging imperialist rule and which, by its essence, presents a constant threat to feudalism and to its violent (specifically Chinese) expression, [i.e.] militarism.

The imperialist masters have inadvertently given away the secret of the renegades. The crusade of these pathetic militarists is aimed not only against communism. "Future Communists" are also included in the list. The meaning of this is clear.

Who are these "future Communists"? They are the Chinese masses. They cannot, as a whole, be branded as Communists, but they are nevertheless hated by the imperialists and their native allies. Only one revolutionary class—the proletariat—is advocating communism. However, other revolutionary classes exist within the modern structure of the Chinese society. These classes are struggling not for communism. They are struggling for those political and economic conditions which can be established only when foreign imperialism is driven out of the country and when feudalism, with all its ramifications, is wiped out in its entirety. These nonproletarian, revolutionary classes are the peasantry and the petty bourgeoisie; they constitute the overwhelming majority of the population of China. It is precisely they who are being called "future Communists," and the holy mission of Hsia Tou-yin, Hsü, and Co. consists similarly in their "extermination."

These revolutionary classes are united with the proletariat under the banner of the Kuomintang in the historical struggle for the overthrow of imperialism and the liquidation of feudalism. The national government in Wuhan is the symbol of the anti-imperialist struggle of the Chinese people. Those who, on the orders of imperialism and to its greatest satisfaction, organize insurrections for the purpose of exterminating "communism" and "future Communists" are, consequently, enemies of the national revolution, traitors to the Kuomintang, insurgents against the national government. In other words, they are counterrevolutionaries.

The development of the revolution always entails the crystallization of the counterrevolution. Reactionary social elements, whose authority and privileges are threatened by the revolution, quite naturally organize a resistance. The first task of the revolution is to crush this resistance.

The victorious offensive of the national-revolutionary army has dwelt a shattering blow to the reaction which was personified by the militarism of Sun Ch'uan-fang, Chang Tsung-ch'ang and Wu P'ei-fu. The military forces of the reaction have retreated, but the social basis of the reaction, that is, feudalism, has continued to exist in the national territory. To expand the victory over reaction, to launch an offensive against its social base—such must be the next step of the revolutionary development.

Class differentiation was inevitable. The national bourgeoisie participated in the struggle against imperialism and militarism, since these were
factors which counteracted its economic interests in the broad sense of
the word. But from the moment that the anti-imperialist movement
entered the period of revolutionary struggle, the national bourgeoisie
began to search for ways to betray it. The more revolutionary classes
assumed the leadership of the movement and led it forward.

The national-revolutionary movement, based on the oppressed petty
bourgeoisie, the peasantry and the proletariat, is leading the offensive
against feudalism; and this is a sign of its growth. The Chinese revolution has entered upon a stage in which the national revolution is becoming essentially an agrarian revolution. At this stage, a new group of
counterrevolutionary forces is rearing its repulsive head. Heretofore,
the revolution was accomplished mainly in the towns. Revolutionary activities of the proletariat and military operations formed the chief features of the revolution. Now, the social meaning of the revolution is the
prime consideration. The revolution is spreading to the village and developing into a war against the old social order based on feudal relations.
For this reason, those classes which enjoyed well-being under the old
social order, who lived at the cost of a parasitic income from land, who
possessed the unlimited right of exploiting the semibondaged peasant
masses are now putting up a resistance to the revolution. Their resistance
is organically connected with the struggle of other counterrevolutionary
forces against the revolution, with the struggle of imperialism and the
traitorous national bourgeoisie. Thus arose the profane alliance of all
the reactionary forces for the purpose of counteracting the revolution.

An unmistakable sign of the organic unity of all these diverse, territorially dispersed forces of reaction is that they are all tainted by one
and the same anti-Communist color varying only in shade. Chang Tso-
lin and his allies are beheading the Communists and slaughtering workers and peasants; Chiang Kai-shek is killing Communists and suppressing the workers' movement; Li Chi-shên, the worthless militarist from
Kwangtung, is executing Communists and wants to crush the workers'
and peasants' organizations; Yang Sen started his campaign against
Wuhan by slaughtering Communists; imperialism has repeatedly declared its willingness to recognize a national government which is free
of Communist influence; and, finally, Hsia Tou-yin and Tsêng Kuo
[-fan] [Sun Fo] are undertaking the holy mission of defending the Kuomintang and the national government against "excesses" of the peasant
movement which is led by the Communists.

In all these cases, communism is merely a bugaboo. Essentially, the
struggle is directed against the national revolution. No one will believe

that imperialism or Chang Tso-lin can have better regard for the national revolution than for Communists. The same applies to all who act under a comparable flag. To wage a struggle against classes that form the social base of the national revolution means to wage a struggle against the organs of the national revolution, that is, against the Kuomintang and the national government.

The anti-imperialist struggle is not a thing in itself. It is not an abstract concept. The Chinese people are fighting against imperialism, because imperialism hinders the economic development of the country. Feudalism is a backward form of economy. The anti-imperialist struggle cannot, therefore, be separated from a struggle for the abolition of feudalism. Imperialism and feudalism go hand in hand to maintain the Chinese people in a state of political, economic, and cultural backwardness.

It is impossible to continue the war against imperialism without intensifying at the same time the struggle for the abolition of feudal relations in the village. The party that will lead the anti-imperialist struggle must also promote the liquidation of feudalism.

And if this is the case, then the revolts of the feudal-militarist elements, aimed against the peasantry, are at the same time also aimed against the Kuomintang and the national government. The bugaboo of communism and the so-called "excesses" will not help to conceal the real situation. The revolt of Hsia Tou-yin, just as the *coup* in Changsha, represents an open, patently counterrevolutionary action. Its aim is to exterminate the antifeudal movement in the village and thereby to undermine the revolutionary-democratic base of the Kuomintang and the national revolution.

Hankow, June 1, 1927

26

OPEN LETTER TO THE
CENTRAL COMMITTEE OF THE KUOMINTANG

The revolution is passing through a critical stage in which it will encounter and will have to solve many difficult problems. The basic task of the moment is to discover the means of carrying out a series of measures of agrarian reform in order to intensify the base of the revolution after having satisfied the demands of the awakening peasant masses. The revolutionary agrarian policy of the Kuomintang has incited the peasant masses to active demonstrations. The time has come to realize this policy. The Kuomintang is a revolutionary party of the democratic masses, and the realization of this policy represents its historical task. The future of the revolution—the destiny of the Chinese peoples—depends upon your resolute actions in the situation that has developed.

The beginning of the agrarian revolution at once impelled the reactionary elements to take counterrevolutionary action. The feudal-militarist elements, representing the interests of the class which lives at the price of a parasitic income from land, have come out against the peasantry with arms in hand. They are threatening to destroy the Kuomintang and to overthrow the national government should the latter, remaining true to its revolutionary principles, lead the peasantry into the historical struggle against feudalism. The aggressive position of the reactionary elements has engendered ambivalent attitudes among the leading circles of the revolutionary movement. It is believed in these circles that the national army as a whole will become hostile to the government if agrarian reforms are carried out.

Certain elements in the army are opposed to agrarian reform. This is true. But by no means is the entire army opposed to the peasantry; nor can it be opposed to it. All the soldiers are either landless or poor peas-

Also appeared in abridged form in *International Press Correspondence,* Vol. 7, No. 37, June 30, 1927, pp. 783–784.—Eds.

ants and, therefore, they cannot be conscious enemies of the peasant movement. Possible antagonism on their part to the agrarian reforms demanded by the peasantry is a result of their lack of awareness which will be used by the reactionary elements in the army. So far as the soldiers are concerned, the national army—objectively—is an army of the agrarian revolution. Furthermore, the majority of the lower-ranking officers is recruited from the petty bourgeoisie which is likewise oppressed and exploited. In view of the fact that the national revolution will not deprive them of their property, they will not allow themselves to be swayed into actions aimed at defending the power and privileges of the large-scale landlords and the autocratic gentry. The latter now have a monopoly on all posts connected with power and privileges. With their abolition, economic relations and political power will become democratized. For this reason, the agrarian revolution does not bring detriment to the petty bourgeoisie of the town or village. On the contrary, the revolution will liberate if from economic stagnation and will grant political rights to it. If the low-ranking officers of the national army understand this, they will devotedly support the Kuomintang and the national government in the implementation of the democratic policy of agrarian reform. Finally, the national armies are headed by old revolutionaries with high ideals of democratic freedom.

With such a composition, the national army cannot as a whole be hostile to agrarian reform. The majority of the army, its most important component parts (the soldiers, the low-ranking officers, and the leaders) will be loyal to the Kuomintang and the national government. As a result, the reactionary minority will be isolated and crushed in the event of any kind of counterrevolutionary action on its part.

The Kuomintang must not hesitate for a minute in choosing its path. The path of agrarian reform is the path of the revolution. The path of the reactionary militarist elements is the path of the counterrevolution. The Kuomintang now stands at the crossroads. The reactionary militarists have risen in open, counterrevolutionary revolt (the revolt of Hsia Tou-yin and the *coup* in Changsha signify just this). They have declared war on the workers' and peasants' movement. They are shooting workers and peasants in exactly the same way as this is being done by Chang Tso-lin, Sun Ch'uan-fang, Chang Tsung-ch'ang, Chiang Kai-shek, and Li Chi-shên. They demand of the Kuomintang a rejection of the policy of agrarian reform (i.e., a betrayal of the peasantry) in order to win the favor of the reactionary landlords and the gentry. They are defying the authority of the party and the national government. After the *coup* in Changsha, the provincial committee of the Kuomintang was dissolved and in its place a new committee was created without the sanction of the Central Committee. A special commission, dispatched by the national government, did not receive a permit for passage into Changsha.

These are patently counterrevolutionary acts. The band of reactionary militarists has risen against the party, the government, and the supreme command. It has usurped power in Wuhan. In the situation that has developed, the duties of the Kuomintang are clear. It must either crush this band of reactionaries and restore its own authority, or capitulate. The Kuomintang cannot select the latter course without betraying its traditions, principles, and program, without ruining itself politically. The counterrevolution in Wuhan must be crushed. Fast action is necessary. Hesitation at a moment like this is fatal.

The Central Committee of the Communist Party proposes that the following measures be taken for crushing the counterrevolution in Wuhan:

1. A decree of the national government declaring the insurrectional committee in Changsha counterrevolutionary and appealing to the soldiers to join the revolutionary masses for the overthrow of [this committee].

2. The dissolution of the insurrectional committee and the appointment of a legal, provincial government.

3. An immediate punitive expedition for suppressing the revolt. Authorize General T'ang Sheng-chih to dispatch to Wuhan the necessary troops for crushing the counterrevolution.

4. The dissolution of the self-appointed committee of the Kuomintang and the appointment of a new committee with full powers for settling the political situation.

5. A decree of the national government granting complete freedom to organizations of workers and peasants and to the Communist Party in Hunan.

6. An order by the national government for the return of arms confiscated from workers' and peasants' detachments.

7. The arming of peasants as a guarantee against future counterrevolutionary flare-ups.

The implementation of these measures against the counterrevolution will assure the Kuomintang the complete confidence of the peasant masses not only in Wuhan but in the entire country. The peasant masses will see the national banner as an emblem of their freedom. They will rise up against the forces that are fighting the national government.

When the large-scale bourgeoisie, the feudal reactionaries and their military representatives turn against the party of the national revolution, the latter must establish closer ties with the democratic masses, awaken their revolutionary awareness and lead them boldly in an offensive against the counterrevolution. The revolution will find itself in jeopardy if the Kuomintang and the national government fail to rouse the laboring masses to a decisive revolutionary struggle at a time when the reactionary elements are amassing their forces through open counterrevolutionary actions.

WITH REVOLUTIONARY GREETINGS,

CENTRAL COMMITTEE OF THE CHINESE COMMUNIST PARTY

Hankow, June 3, 1927

27

COMRADES! The national government is committed to liberating you from age-old exploitation. It must wipe out the oppression from which you suffer. It must give land to those who cultivate it.

Peasant masses in all of China are rebelling against the inhuman conditions of life. They want to put an end to imperialist rule. They want to throw off the militarism that is sucking all the lifeblood out of them. They want to take away the land from the large-scale landlords who do not cultivate it, but live in luxury and depravity extorting huge profits from the peasantry. They want to destroy the power of the gentry who are oppressing the rural population.

The rapid development of the national revolution has accelerated the spread of peasant revolts. The Hunan peasantry emerged as the vanguard of the movement. The reactionary classes, living at the expense of exploiting the destitution of the peasantry, were alarmed by the upsurge of the peasant movement. The peasant unions in Kwangtung have become victims of the terror of Li Chi-shên as they continue to put up a courageous resistance to him. Now the reaction has reared its head even in Hunan.

A gang of reactionary militarists seized power in Hunan and dissolved the committee of the Kuomintang and the provincial government which aided and encouraged the peasant movement. A massacre of workers and peasants is occurring in Changsha and in all parts of the province. The counterrevolutionary band in Changsha wants to crush the Hunan peasant movement. Peasant unions are resisting the onslaught of the counterrevolution. In this struggle they are defending not only the interests of peasants in the whole country, but also the ideals of the national revolution. The Hunan peasantry must therefore be supported by the Kuomintang and the national government.

The Hunan peasants, as the vanguard of the whole peasant move-ment, must continue the struggle against the large-scale landlords, the gentry and the counterrevolutionary militarists. They must confiscate the lands belonging to large-scale landlords, to capitalist companies and to Christian churches. They must destroy the power of the gentry. They must take from the corrupt gentry the management of communal, tem-ple, and ancestral lands and hand it over to the land committees of local rural governments. They must establish democratic self-govern-ment in the village. They must arm for the struggle against reaction and for the defense of the gains of the revolution. The counterrevolutionary militarist clique in Changsha must be overthrown.

In leading this revolutionary struggle, the Hunan peasantry must know how to win allies. The large-scale landlords and the gentry are enemies of the peasantry. They also oppress the petty landholders in the same way. For this reason the peasantry (tenants, cultivators of their own land, landless farm laborers, and others) must join forces with the petty landholders in the struggle against the power of the large-scale land-lords and the gentry. If we want to consolidate [this alliance], the prop-erty of the petty landholders must remain inviolable. Similarly, officers of the national army, fighting against imperialism and militarism, are allies of the peasant movement. Their land should not be confiscated; their families should not be mistreated. Soldiers are either poor or land-less peasants. To inflict any measure of damage to their families, to take anything away from them, means to harm the peasant movement. Such thoughtless acts provide the reactionary officers with an oppor-tunity to incite the soldiers against the peasant movement. Peasant unions must not permit such acts to occur.

COMRADES, the Hunan peasantry must be supported in every possible way in order to overthrow the counterrevolutionary gang in Changsha. It is necessary to support their revolt against the counterrevolution. If they are routed, not only would this throw back the peasant movement in the whole country, but it would be a crushing blow to the national revolution. The position of the reactionary elements would become more secure. The struggle against imperialism would be slowed down.

Peasants must not regard the soldiers as their enemies. On the con-trary, a close tie must be established between the peasant movement and the mass of soldiers who should be drawn into the peasant unions. Soldiers who for the most part are landless peasants are compelled by destitution and poverty to sell their lives to the militarists. There are tens of millions of such landless peasants in the country. They must be endowed with land. The national revolutionary government must ac-commodate these landless millions on free lands. The soldiers will join the peasant movement in order to achieve this task. It is in their interest to join the peasantry in the struggle against reaction and counterrevolution.

Fighters of the Hunan peasant movement! Demand the surrender of the counterrevolutionary gang in Changsha! Organize an armed uprising for overthrowing it! Help the national government to restore [its] power in Hunan! Support the Kuomintang against the counterrevolutionary militarists! *

DOWN WITH THE CLIQUE OF HSÜ K'Ê-HSIANG WHO SEIZED POWER IN CHANGSHA!

DOWN WITH THE WEALTHY [*krupnye*] LANDLORDS AND THE GENTRY!

LONG LIVE THE KUOMINTANG AND THE NATIONAL GOVERNMENT!

LAND TO THE PEASANTS AND THE SOLDIERS!

The Chinese Communist Party

Hankow, June 4, 1927

---

* At this instance, the Kuomintang and the national government as a whole had not as yet openly identified itself with the Hunan counterrevolution. Furthermore, the *coup* in Changsha was interpreted as an attempt by Chiang Kai-shek to deal a blow to Wuhan. For this reason, the revolution could still develop under the flag of the Left Kuomintang providing that the internal contradictions in the Kuomintang intensified under the pressure of the masses. After the *coup* in Changsha, the authority of the national government could be restored only by the transfer of all power to the peasant unions and by the democratization of the Kuomintang. [M.N.R.]

28

THE COUNTERREVOLUTION AND COMMUNIST

TACTICS: DEFENSE OR OFFENSE

Comrade Ch'ên Tu-hsiu informed us of the situation in encouraging tones; but we need no illusions.

It was not for the defense of the national government against the counterrevolution, nor was it for the struggle against the counterrevolution in Hunan that T'ang Shêng-chih decided to send his troops back to Hankow. We know that he was constantly in touch with Hsia Tou-yin when the latter rebelled against the national government, that he praised him as a "revolutionary who in the course of eight years has fought for the cause of the people." His wavering and indecisive position with respect to the *coup* in Changsha is also well known. His efforts to legalize the Hunan counterrevolution was a secret to no one. All his generals support the Chiang Kai-shek clique. He will not dare to oppose his generals. At the same time, he knows that the *coup* in Changsha was inspired from Nanking, that the majority of his generals are in sympathy with Chiang Kai-chek; therefore, he can not fully approve of measures which indirectly undermine his power and position. He is afraid to advance further to the north while the basis of his power and importance in Hunan itself is being threatened. His generals, too, do not want to continue the struggle with Chang Tso-lin while an agrarian revolution is developing at home in Hunan.

Apart from this, T'ang Shêng-chih did not want, from the very beginning, to advance to the north. Now the situation has become clear. He can move on Peking only under the command of Fêng Yü-hsiang. But he does not want to do this. He does not want to take the chestnuts out of the fire for Fêng. Hence, he recalled the army in order to strengthen his position in Hunan and Hupeh. He would have agreed to

Presumably M. N. Roy's statement in the Politburo of the Chinese Communist Party.—Eds.

a joint campaign against Peking, if only the Fourth and Eleventh armies would be sent there. But Fêng demanded more. The Fourth and Eleventh armies were so debilitated that they alone would not have been sufficient to satisfy Fêng's dreams, [namely], the conquest of Peking. When the Fourth and Eleventh armies decided to return to Wuhan in order to launch an immediate attack against Peking in accordance with the decisions adopted before the Northern Expedition, T'ang Shêng-chih began to act fast. He could not permit the Fourth and Eleventh armies to return to Wuhan while his units remained in the North. At that time, T'ang Shêng-chih was acting in the role of a "Leftist" which, however, should not mislead us. He found himself between the frying pan and the fire: on the one side was Fêng Yü-hsiang, on the other—Chiang Kai-shek. T'ang Shêng-chih belongs to neither of these groupings; therefore, he wants to play the role of a Leftist and head a third military combination in an attempt to become the master of the situation. T'ang Shêng-chih refused to participate in a joint campaign against Peking, because in that event he would have had to recognize the leadership of Fêng Yü-hsiang. A return to Hunan, however, preserves his independent political status and broadens his power in Hunan and Hupeh. The arrival of his army will not be a help to the revolution; rather, it would merely increase the danger of a counterrevolution.

Therefore, I cannot share Comrade Ch'ên's optimism that the return of the Eighth and Thirty-Sixth armies will create a balance of forces and destroy the monopoly position of the Thirty-Fifth Army in Hunan and Hupeh. We must not be deluded by T'ang Shêng-chih's public declarations on the *coup* in Changsha. The fact is that neither the national government nor T'ang Shêng-chih lifted a finger when Hsü K'ê-hsiang engineered his *coup* with a detachment of 1,700 men. The Leftist phraseology of T'ang Shêng-chih cannot conceal this fact. He merely wants to deceive the masses by these phrases. The Communist Party must see to it that the masses do not fall under the sway of the masked deception. T'ang Shêng-chih's involvement in Hsia Tou-yin's revolt and in the *coup* in Changsha must be exposed. He is no less responsible for the counterrevolutionary demonstrations in Hunan and Hupeh than are his generals. This must be told to the masses. Any optimism in regard to the present "calm situation" (Comrade Ch'ên's appraisal) will simply breed a conciliatory attitude within the Communist Party. To believe in the "Leftist" phrases of T'ang Shêng-chih means to betray the masses.

The return of T'ang Shêng-chih's army to Hankow and the decision to remain here for one month in order to make preparations is a highly dangerous sign at a time when the officers of this army are becoming so aggressively reactionary in Hunan and in Hupeh. We must not close our eyes to this. T'ang Shêng-chih himself admits that he cannot vouch for his officers. The present situation should be evaluated as follows: the reaction is becoming more active not only in the army, but also in the present Central Committee of the Kuomintang. The tactic of the Communist Party must follow from this perspective.

It would be a mistake to call the present Central Committee of the Kuomintang Leftist. A general attack on the workers' and peasants' movement is now the basic feature of its policy. It is preparing for an open struggle against the Communists. It is silently encouraging counterrevolutionary insurrections directed against the workers' and peasants' movement and against the Communist Party. The present Central Committee of the Kuomintang and the national government have completely surrendered their power in Hunan to counterrevolutionary officers. Only three-quarters of the Hupeh province remains under the control of the Wuhan government.

T'ang Shêng-chih's intention to attack Chiang Kai-shek is dictated solely by personal considerations. His officers do not want to fight Chiang Kai-shek. Their sympathies lie more with Nanking than with Wuhan. Some of them are, in fact, connected with the Nanking group. In political and social respects, the so-called Left-Wing group in Wuhan differs but little from Nanking. Today they both represent feudal-bourgeois interests. The petty-bourgeois Left Wing became frightened of the revolution and capitulated to the reactionary elements in the Central Committee. The recent resolutions and declarations of the Wuhan Central Committee of the Kuomintang are no less reactionary than the Nanking platform. Under these conditions, there has arisen, in the objective sense, a tendency toward agreement, if not personally with Chiang Kai-shek, then with Nanking. It is even possible that Chiang Kai-shek will have to be discarded in order to save face. But the essential meaning of the situation resides in the fact that the Central Committee of the Wuhan Kuomintang is moving in the direction of counterrevolution.

Wuhan wants to liquidate the split of Chiang Kai-shek. But this can have real political significance only in the event that the national revolution is raised to the higher stage of an agrarian revolution. The Wuhan group, however, will not go for this. Hence, it must either settle its political differences with Nanking or leave the political stage. The restoration of unity the Wuhanites wanted to celebrate in Peking. They have shouted too much against Chiang Kai-shek to be able now to rejoin his clique without a certain amount of advance preparations. The play had to be carefully staged. But the Peking plan was not realized. It was thwarted by T'ang Shêng-chih. Now the Wuhanites want to go to Nanking and Shanghai in order to restore the desired unity there. They are proposing to move on Nanking not in order to fight against Chiang Kai-shek, but in order to betray the revolution to the bourgeoisie. The plan for a military campaign against Nanking is simple fraud. Everyone knows that the generals of all the Wuhan armies, with the exception of the Fourth and Eleventh armies, are opposed to fighting Chiang Kai-shek. These generals are, in fact, negotiating with Chiang Kai-shek and the Nanking clique for the overthrow of the Wuhan government if it does not surrender completely to the counterrevolution.

Our "allies" are holding their plans secret from us. But they have transmitted them to the agents of Japanese imperialism. A few days ago, Hsü Ch'ien informed the Japanese telegraphic agency, *Rengo,* that there are no reasons preventing a reconciliation between the Wuhan government and the Nanking government after the occupation of Peking. Here it is not only a question of a reconciliation with Chiang Kai-shek, but also one of betraying the revolution, surrendering the power to the feudal-bourgeois reaction, and striking a bargain with imperialism.

The Wuhan Kuomintang cannot win the graces of the Shanghai bourgeoisie, nor can it come to an agreement with imperialism unless it opposes the workers' and peasants' movement and severs its relations with the Communist Party. The Wuhan Central Committee still can not bring itself to launch an open attack against the workers' and peasants' movement. It is seeking to demoralize it and to destroy its revolutionary character. It is trying to demoralize even the Communist Party. While conspiring against the Communist Party, while encouraging and participating in demonstrations of counterrevolutionary officers against the workers' and peasants' movement, the Wuhan Kuomintang is still inviting the Communists into its friendly embrace. If the Communists do not see through this and maintain a silence, the Kuomintang will allow them to become ministers, members of the Political Council, and so forth and so on. But if the Communists were to demand of the Kuomintang that it defend the interests of workers and peasants, that it curb the actions of the counterrevolutionary officers, that it fight against a betrayal of the national revolution—then the Wuhanites will treat the Communists in the same manner as do Chiang Kai-shek, Li Chi-shên and other militarists. There must be no illusions here. The situation is indeed such that a decision can not be postponed. What will be the policy of the Communist Party in this situation?

Two courses are open to the Communist Party: defense or offense, retreat or attack.

Can we retreat in the present position? Can we adopt a defensive policy? A defensive policy invariably means surrender to the mercy of the Kuomintang; it means that we will cease being Communists, if only in name. The Kuomintang demands nothing more and nothing less than the virtual liquidation of the Communist Party and the workers' and peasants' movement. It demands the "correction" of excesses and the more we "correct" the excesses, the more demands will it continue to make. Let me give an example of how far the Communist Party has gone on this question of "excesses." In order to preserve friendly relations with the Kuomintang, which has become an instrument of the counterrevolution, which totally supports the bloody acts of the militarists, the Communist Party is agreeing to liquidate the mass movement. Our Party is undertaking the task of "correcting" the excesses without even clarifying whether or not these excesses have, in fact, occurred. Under the present conditions, Communists must encourage and develop these excesses, and not "correct" them. What do these demonstrations represent which the Kuomintang brands as "excesses" of the workers' and peasants' movement, and which Comrade Ch'ên Tu-hsiu condemns as "an infantile disorder." They are, in fact, revolutionary actions of the working class and peasant masses. Must we restrain these actions, "correct" these "disorders" for the sake of winning the good graces of the feudal lords and militarists and their petty-bourgeois agents? Must the Communist Party betray the workers and peasants in the heat of the revolutionary struggle and seek to preserve the alliance with the petty-bourgeois Left-Kuomintang leaders who have become open counterrevolutionaries? No, comrades, the Communist Party cannot do this. The Communist Party must give full support to the peasants who are seizing the land and expropriating the landlords, the usurers, and the gentry. The Party must head the peasantry and create a regime of terror in order to extirpate the reaction in the village. The Communist Party must advance the slogan: "All power in the village to the peasant unions." The whole country must be inflamed with Jacquerie.* The reaction has declared war on the working class. The challenge must be accepted. Terror must be answered with terror. The basis of feudal reaction and its military expression—militarism—must be wiped out. The actions of the proletariat, censured by the Kuomintang as "excesses," are necessary to the struggle with counterrevolutionary plots against the national revolution.

The Kuomintang is accusing the peasant unions of confiscating land from petty landholders and from officers of the national army. It is complaining that the peasant unions are headed by bandits,† that there

* A revolt of French peasants against the nobles in 1358, named from the contemptuous title, Jacques Bonhomme, given by the nobles to the peasantry; hence, any revolt of the peasants.—Eds.

† The designation of "bandits" and "thieves" are given to landless and often unemployed villager paupers. Being the most exploited stratum of the rural popu-

are but few real peasants in these unions. It is spreading awesome tales about the destructive and lawless acts of peasant unions and is requesting the coöperation of the Communist Party in suppressing these acts in the name of the "defense" of the national government. Let us examine the facts. "A great stir" developed over the "excesses" in the district of Hwangkang (Hupeh), as a result of which the peasant union there was dissolved. The local committee of the Kuomintang which supported the actions of the peasant union was similarly dissolved for violating the instructions of the Central Committee. A representative of the provincial government (Communist) was sent there to carry out the decisions of the Central Committee of the Kuomintang on reorganizing the local committee of the Kuomintang and the peasant union. The Peasant Section of the Central Committee of the Communist Party also sent a comrade to investigate the situation on the spot. This comrade returned yesterday with the following report:

The whole story about excesses is a lie; not a single tobacco leaf was damaged.* The majority of the members of the peasant union consists of tenants. There are very few "bandits" in the union. Only forty confiscations occurred. But all these confiscations were carried out in strict accordance with the resolution of the Kuomintang. Lands belonging to officers and to petty landholders were not touched. Only lands of notorious counterrevolutionaries were subjected to confiscation.

When it was established that the Central Committee of the Kuomintang adopted its decision on the basis of false information, our agent proposed to the representative of the provincial government (a Communist) not to carry out the instructions on hand and to telegraph to Hankow that the entire report does not correspond to reality and that the decision must be changed. But the representative of the provincial

---

lation, they are the most active element of the peasant movement. The Kuomintang declared that it is not the peasants, but these very landless bandits who, at the instigation of Communists, are demanding the confiscation of land. The Central Committee of the Communist Party tended to accept such a depiction of the situation. In reality, matters stood differently. The majority of the members of the peasant union consists of tenants. In general, the composition of the peasant union is, approximately, as follows: 65 percent tenants (small and average peasantry), 15 percent peasants owning land which they cultivate, 15 percent landless paupers and 5 percent others (petty intelligentsia, petty merchants, handicraftsmen, etc.). [M.N.R.]

* In June, the Central Committee of the Kuomintang adopted a resolution on dissolving the party committee and the peasant union in the district of Hwangkang in view of the destruction of one hundred tobacco plantations by members of the peasant union and in view of the fact that the local committee of the Kuomintang, contrary to the instructions of the Central Committee, gave sanction to the confiscation by the peasant union of land belonging to officers of the national army and to petty landholders. [M.N.R.]

government refused to accept this advice. The order he received for carrying out the decision of the Kuomintang emanated not only from the government, but also from Comrade Ch'ên Tu-hsiu personally.

All these stories about "excesses" are usually deceitful fabrications. If the Communists begin to coöperate with the Kuomintang in correcting the nonexistent "excesses," they will only assist the counterrevolutionaries in liquidating the peasant movement. A liquidation tendency of this kind also exists with respect to the workers' movement. The Kuomintang is demanding that trade unions subject themselves to a so-called self-discipline that restrains the revolutionary activity of the proletarian masses.

There exists a theory that there is nothing we can do at the present moment; that our Party is incapable of counteracting and destroying the counterrevolution; that the Party must go underground for a few years to prepare for a future struggle for power. This is a pernicious theory—that only in the process of the struggle with reaction can the Party prepare itself for the struggle for power. Our Party is very young. Organizationally, it is weak. It does not have an illegal machinery. If it suddenly goes underground, without putting up a fight, it will be virtually destroyed. Conversely, a determined resistance by the counterrevolution will strengthen the Party both politically and organizationally. This theory of "preparation" is not new. It exists also in other countries. It is a social-democratic theory. If we seriously want to prepare the working class for victory, the Party must begin to fight. It is absolutely inevitable that the working class commits careless acts in the process of the movement. But without participation in the revolutionary struggle it is impossible to make the working class be 100 percent prepared. If the Communist Party now becomes a victim of the theory of retreat and if it adopts defensive tactics, the leadership of the revolution will be seized by the bourgeoisie. This will result in a compromise with imperialism and a temporary defeat of the national revolution. The defeat of the national revolution will be an event of international importance. It will reflect on the position of the Soviet Union. Therefore, the decision of the Communist Party at the critical moment of the present has international significance. The imperialist powers are preparing for war against the U.S.S.R. The policy of encircling the U.S.S.R. with hostile states has been pursued systematically in the course of two years, beginning with Locarno. Recently, the anti-Soviet policy has assumed openly provocative forms. Raids are being made on Soviet embassies and consulates; England is severing diplomatic relations; a Soviet ambassador was killed in Poland. Everything possible is done to provoke a war with the U.S.S.R. If imperialism succeeds in reëstablishing its position in China, the plan of encircling the Soviet Union will be completed.

In this critical situation, the task that lies before the Chinese Communist Party is clear. No two alternatives present themselves. One cannot pose the question: to retreat or to advance? There is only one course: we assume the offensive. We must fight and win. This is not a tactic of desperation. This tactic is prescribed to us by the objective situation. In view of the situation that has arisen in China and its connection with the international situation, the Communist International proposes to the Chinese Communist Party that it assume the offensive. The meaning of the directives of the Communist International is that the Chinese working class must fight and win, that the Chinese Communist Party must lead the workers and peasants in their revolutionary struggle. If we meet with failure in China, we may be smashed all over the world and the very existence of the first socialist country will be threatened.

Is the Communist International imposing an unfeasible task on the Chinese Communist Party? No. The new directives are merely the practical expression of those theses which the Chinese Communist Party adopted at the Fifth Congress. The basic tasks at the given stage of the revolution are the realization of the hegemony of the proletariat, the establishment of a state of democratic dictatorship, the destruction of feudalism by means of land confiscation and the subversion of the economic base of imperialist power by nationalizing railways and heavy industry. Can these tasks be fulfilled without a struggle? In adopting the theses of the Communist International, the Fifth Congress has committed the Party to this struggle. The development of events in the course of the past six months has shown that the Communist International gave a correct appraisal of the situation, that it furnished the correct perspectives for the development of the revolution, and that it set before the Communist Party revolutionary tasks which flow out of the existing conditions.

Can it be said that the victory of the working class will be absolutely assured if the Communist Party leads it into attack? This is another question. There can be no 100 percent guarantee. No revolutionary struggle has ever started with a 100 percent guarantee. Revolutionary tactics can not and must not be determined by the fear of defeat. Under the present conditions, we do not have 100 percent chances of victory. But our victory is not less probable than our defeat. The position in which the working class now finds itself is a result of the past mistakes of the Communist Party. Forces, antagonistic to us, are growing with each day; the auspicious conditions are changing more and more against our favor. Therefore, we must act immediately. The Party must break with the traditions of the past mistakes; it must accept without reservation the leadership of the International and lead the working class to the struggle so as not to lose the revolution.

The Fifth Congress censured the previous policy of the Party leadership. A policy of retreat under the pretext that the situation is not 100 percent in our favor would preserve in the Party the opportunism of old, but in a different and more dangerous form. The basic errors in our relations with the Kuomintang were committed in regard to the creation of a really revolutionary army and the question of Communist work in the national armies. If these errors are not corrected, our Party will perish. The position of the working class in the revolutionary struggle will improve and the chances of victory will increase as the Party departs from these mistakes not only in its resolutions, as was the case at the Fifth Congress, but in practice as well.

If, thanks to past mistakes, the position of our Party in the present revolutionary crisis is not entirely favorable, the present at the same time contains positive sides as well. Powerful objective factors are working in favor of our Party. All of them are contributing to the development of a revolutionary struggle and they will promote the final victory, if only the struggle will not be started too late. The masses throughout the territory of the national government are ready for the struggle. It is precisely this ever-growing readiness and will of the masses for a revolutionary struggle that has created the crisis in the Kuomintang. The continued development of this factor will push the feudal-bourgeois, petty-bourgeois, and intelligentsia leaders into the camp of counterrevolution, which is where they really belong, and will establish, as a genuinely revolutionary power, the democratic dictatorship of the proletarian, peasant, and petty-bourgeois urban masses. The masses want the struggle. The Communists must head them. The Hunan peasantry has raised the banner of agrarian revolution. The peasant masses in Hupeh, Kwangtung, and Kiangsi are behind us. The reaction is descending on the peasantry with vehemence. Can there still be any hesitation as to what the Communists must do? No! The Communist Party must stand at the head of the agrarian revolution. The problem of an alliance with the petty bourgeoisie loses its political significance at this point.

The Communist Party must not doubt the necessity of a break with the Kuomintang if the latter turns against the revolution. The break is becoming more and more unavoidable each day. The working class is under fire by the counterrevolution. Can the Communist Party betray the workers for the sake of preserving its ties with the Kuomintang?

But the change to an offensive not only in Hunan, but also on the whole front, must not necessarily mean an immediate break with the Kuomintang. At the present stage of the revolution, the Communist Party collaborates with the Kuomintang only to the extent that it is the representative of the petty-bourgeois urban masses, exploited and oppressed by imperialism, feudalism, militarism, capitalism. The present Central Committee of the Kuomintang no longer reflects the interests of the petty bourgeoisie. For this reason, friendly relations with the present Central Committee of the Kuomintang can no longer serve as an organizational expression of an alliance with the petty bourgeoisie. On the contrary, the petty-bourgeois masses should be delivered of leaders who betray their interests in order to do a service to the feudal-bourgeois reaction. This task must be fulfilled by the proletariat. The necessity of driving out the gang which heads the Kuomintang is growing with each day. This gang is in the service of the reactionary feudal bourgeoisie; it has usurped the leadership of the petty-bourgeois masses, taking advantage of their political backwardness. The proletariat must expose the surrender of the Central Committee of the Kuomintang to the mercy of the feudal-militarist reaction and seize the leadership of the petty-bourgeois masses; future collaboration with them will then proceed on the basis of these new relations. This means that the Kuomintang must be reorganized. The Communist Party may only continue to collaborate with a reorganized Kuomintang—a Kuomintang that genuinely represents the petty-bourgeois masses. The International indicates to the Communist Party the necessity of the reorganization of the Kuomintang.

In the given situation, what are the immediate tasks of the Communist Party?

1. The military sphere. Fêng Yü-hsiang's plan for the participation of the Wuhan armies in a joint (Fêng Yü-hsiang, Chiang Kai-shek, and T'ang Shêng-chih) campaign against Peking must be rejected. The Communist Party must agitate for a struggle against Nanking. Immediate steps must be taken for the reconquest of Kwangtung.

2. Creation of a truly revolutionary army under our control. The so-called national-revolutionary armies are neither national nor revolutionary. The method of Communist work in the armies should be changed. They have become an instrument of the counterrevolution; therefore, we must demoralize them. This must become the aim of Communist activity in the national armies. Revolutionary propaganda, associated with slogans of agrarian revolution, must be conducted among the soldiers in order to incite them to revolt against the feudal officers corps. Tactics of this kind will necessarily alter the character of the national armies. At the same time as this is being done, it is necessary to create a revolutionary army in the process of the struggle against the counterrevolution in Hunan and in other provinces. The arming of workers and peasants must be carried out on a broad scale.

3. Communist capture of the peasant insurrection in Hunan. The counterrevolutionary officers' clique in Changsha must be overthrown. The land must be confiscated. The power of the gentry must be destroyed. The *min-t'uan* must be disarmed. The agrarian revolution must shift from Hunan to the surrounding provinces, especially to Hupeh, Kwangtung, and Kiangsi.

4. Reorganization of the Kuomintang. The campaign for reorganization must not begin with the demand for the overthrow of the present Central Committee. We must begin from below. Local organizations must be mobilized for the struggle with the Central Committee. This is not a difficult task, since the majority of the local committees of the Kuomintang are under Communist control. The working class and peasant masses which follow the Communists must be poured into the local organizations of the Kuomintang; this will create a broad, revolutionary, social base for the struggle to overthrow the present Central Committee and to oust counterrevolutionary feudal-bourgeois-militarist elements from the Kuomintang. The Communist Party must openly criticize the antilabor class policy of the Central Committee without advancing the slogan for its overthrow until it has made the organizational preparations. When the preparatory work is completed (this will require approximately three months), it is necessary to demand the convocation of a congress. The congress will have to dismiss the counterrevolutionary Central Committee and transform the Kuomintang into an active organ of a democratic dictatorship.

5. Immediate conquest of Kwangtung. The influence of the counterrevolution in Wuhan has become much too strong; the most reliable forces will have to be withdrawn from there. The troops under our control and under the control of revolutionary officers sympathetic to us must be dispatched to the south for their return to Kwangtung. The Fourth and Eleventh armies will become reactionary in this atmosphere of counterrevolution. They must be sent to the south. In the process of conquering Kwangtung, a conscious revolutionary army will be developed and, if we are defeated in Wuhan, Kwangtung will become the territorial base of the revolution.

Such are the main tasks of the Communist Party. If we are able to fulfill them, the revolution will be saved. Otherwise, it will suffer a defeat which will be catastrophic not only for China, but will reflect unfavorably on our position in the whole world.

The Communist International is a world proletariat party. The Executive Committee of the Comintern directs the Communist parties in all countries. In a critical situation such as this, the directives of the International must be followed strictly. No time can be lost on discussion. The Comintern determines the actions of its national sections not only on the basis of its appraisals of the internal conditions of any given country, but also from the point of view of the world situation. The Chinese Communist Party, as a member of the world proletarian party, must act in accordance with the directives of the Comintern.

The Comintern issues its instructions not without reason. They are based not on false information *, as certain comrades assert, but are the result of a thorough study of the Chinese and international conditions. Comrade Ch'ên Tu-hsiu telegraphed to the Comintern his doubts concerning the correctness of the leadership. In reply to this, the Comintern repeated the very same instructions with even greater insistence: the Communist Party must lead the agrarian revolution forward; any attempt to restrain the forces of the agrarian revolution will bring defeat: we will lose everything.

If this is the case, any further discussions as to the correctness or incorrectness of the Comintern's directives are superfluous. Its instructions are correct. As a loyal and disciplined member of the world proletarian party, the Chinese Communist Party must act in accordance with them. Such is the order from the General Staff of the world revolution. The revolutionary proletarian forces of China must execute the order of the General Staff. This requires that the Party be militarized. At a moment when the counterrevolutionary forces are vehemently attacking the working class, the Politbureau must not remain a discussion circle preoccupied with endless arguments. The Political Bureau must become an army headquarters on the field of battle. Such are the concrete tasks before us. We have received an order. All our forces must be mobilized for the execution of this order, for the realization of this task.

Now I will pass to the concrete plan which will guide us in our immediate actions.

The Communist Party has addressed the Kuomintang in an open letter in which six demands were set forth. These demands were moderate. They created the possibility of continued collaboration on the basis of

---

* Certain members of the Politbureau did not agree with the directives of the Comintern on the pretext that these directives were allegedly based on an incorrect appraisal of the situation as presented in the reports of the Comintern representative in China. On behalf of the Politbureau, comrade Ch'ên Tu-hsiu sent a telegram to the Comintern in which he gave "the correct appraisal" of the situation. (See Appendix IV.) [M.N.R. Page 338 in this book.—Eds.]

a definite national-revolutionary platform. A week has passed. The Kuomintang did not even reply to the letter.* Such a situation can no longer be tolerated. We must immediately begin to agitate for the mass support of these demands. We must show the Kuomintang that the Communist Party is not a group of individuals, but a political organ of an entire class. These demands were laid down on behalf of toilers (the proletariat and the peasantry). We must bring into motion the revolutionary energy of the entire working class in order to fortify these demands and we must insist on them being carried out. This campaign will expose to the masses the conciliatory, counterrevolutionary, anti-labor policy of the Kuomintang. The leadership of the national revolution will change hands from the disloyal petty bourgeoisie to the proletariat.

A number of events have occurred in Kiangsi since the open letter was written. The demands associated with them must similarly be included in our agitation. I propose concretely:

1. To declare a general strike on Monday. I have already submitted this proposal several days ago; it can no longer be postponed.† The slogan "immediate fulfillment of the six demands contained in the open letter" must be supplemented by the following demands in connection with Kiangsi: (a) the immediate return of the exiled Communists and

* On receiving the open letter of the Communist Party, the Political Council of the Kuomintang decided to ignore it completely. Only Wang Ching-wei felt that the demands of the masses were formulated in the letter and that the Kuomintang should satisfy these demands. Wang Ching-wei's point of view was accepted; T'an P'ing-shan (a Communist) and Ch'en Kung-po (a former Communist) were entrusted with composing a reply. At the same time, it was decided that the press may only publish the letter of the Communist Party in conjunction with the Kuomintang's reply. The Communist Party's letter, however, was printed in the party organ, while the Kuomintang's reply was received and published on June 15. It was not possible to establish the identity of the author of the reply (See Appendix V). [M.N.R. Page 356 in this book.—Eds.]

† At the suggestion of the Comintern representative, the Politbureau decided to declare a general strike for the support of demands contained in the letter to the Kuomintang. But the decision was not carried out. The question was referred to the Politbureau for reëxamination. The consensus—not only of the members of the Politbureau, but also of those present at the meeting of the responsible trade-union workers—was against a general strike. The principal argument was that in a critical situation such as the present, a general strike would mean a declaration of war on the Kuomintang and the national government. In the end, the General Secretary of the All-Chinese Federation of Labor and member of the Politbureau, Comrade Li Li-san, proposed that a mass demonstration be staged to welcome the national leaders returning from the front, and that this demonstration be used in the aims of supporting the demands contained in the open letter. This proposal was supported and adopted unanimously, with the Comintern representative opposing. The proposal of the latter—to stage a mass demonstration before the arrival of the national leaders and to declare a general strike on the day of their arrival—was similarly rejected. Mass meetings for welcoming the national leaders, "the heroes of the national armies," were organized. But neither the general strike nor a strike in the arsenal took place. [M.N.R.]

Left-Wing members of the Kuomintang; (b) complete freedom for the workers' and peasants' movement; (c) recall of Chu P'ei-tê.

2. The convocation on Monday, in Hankow, Wuhan, and Hanyang, of mass meetings for adopting a resolution on the immediate satisfaction by the Kuomintang and the national government of the aforesaid demands.

3. The Party must appoint speakers to these meetings and give them thorough instructions on the general content of their speeches. It is likewise necessary to have as many speakers as possible from workers and peasants without party affiliation.

4. To threaten a strike in the Hanyang arsenal, if these demands are not immediately satisfied. Workers in the arsenal must openly declare: why should we work for supplying munitions to the national army when this army everywhere is massacring our brother workers and peasants; the Kuomintang and the national government are appealing to workers for sacrifices, but we do not want to sacrifice ourselves for the counter-revolution.

5. The All-Chinese Federation of Labor and the All-Chinese Peasant Union must pass energetic resolutions on full support of the demands and must insist on their immediate fulfillment. Similar resolutions must come from local workers' and peasants' unions all over the country.

6. Fifty comrades should be sent immediately to Kiangsi to occupy the posts of the expelled Communists. They must encourage and organize peasant revolts wherever possible. They must not be afraid of "excesses." These "excesses" should not be "corrected," but encouraged. Revolutionary agitation and propaganda should be conducted among the soldiers of Chu P'ei-tê's army.

7. In Hunan, the Communist Party must stand at the head of the peasant revolt. Many decisions have been passed in this regard, but, in practice, the work has not even been begun. The adopted decisions must be carried out.

In answer to a series of questions and objections to my proposals, I make the following additional comment: Arsenal workers must take part in the one-day general strike; at the same time, they must threaten to continue the strike in the event of a refusal to carry out the demands laid down by the strikers. A general strike under the present conditions can not last long in view of the vast unemployment. But there are qualified workers in the arsenal. It will not be easy to replace them. The government cannot accept that the arsenal not work in the heat of war. The threat of a strike in the arsenal will be most effective.

Comrade Ch'ên Tu-hsiu said that one must approach the question of a general strike and a strike of arsenal workers with great caution. He is prepared to accept mass meetings. In his opinion, we need neither retreat nor advance. He considers that a middle road can be found. This is once again the past policy of diplomatic maneuvers. Comrade Ch'ên fears that a general strike, and especially a strike in the arsenal, would develop into an open fight and that workers are liable to be shot. But the attack on the working class has already begun. Masses of peasants are being shot. Workers are being disarmed. They are also being shot. If the working class does not put up a resistance to the attack of the counterrevolution and if it does not develop this resistance into a counterattack, it will be crushed. I submit a proposal for a general strike and for a strike of workers in the arsenal not only as a demonstration of protest; strikes must become the beginning of an open struggle against the counterrevolution. Under the conditions that have arisen, the Communist Party must lead the proletariat to revolt.

Comrade Ch'ên considers that the adoption of offensive tactics should not necessarily mean that we must go to the end. In part, he is right. The offensive must unfold gradually. First of all, we must begin by mobilizing the working class for a resistance against the attacks of the reaction. But we can not and must not stop at the very beginning. This resistance must be developed into an offensive. The general political line adopted by our party leads to an open struggle. We insist on a struggle against Chiang Kai-shek. What does this mean? Is this a struggle against an individual person or a clique? No! This means that we are entering into a decisive battle against the bourgeoisie and the feudal militarists who are represented by Chiang Kai-shek and the Nanking group. At this stage of the revolution, the proletariat is undertaking the task of a struggle against the reactionary bourgeoisie and the feudal lords and militarists; the struggle against the Wuhan Kuomintang, therefore, becomes unavoidable, because its present policy is directed at a reconciliation with the counterrevolutionary classes. We cannot compromise with the Kuomintang without terminating the struggle against the bourgeoisie and the feudal reaction. The objective necessity of a struggle with the feudal-bourgeois reaction has inevitably pushed the proletariat into a clash with the agents of this reaction in the Wuhan Kuomintang who have seized power and are still holding it. There is therefore no middle road between retreat and advance. The Communist Party must either follow through to the logical conclusion of the general political line which it has adopted, or reject it entirely.

Comrade Li Li-san still harbors many illusions: (1) he proposes that revolutionary conditions be created with the help of the very same merchants' union under whose pressure the Kuomintang is attacking employees, disarming pickets, and dissolving pioneer organizations;

(2) he believes that the Kuomintang can be forced to become more Leftist by means of persuasion; (3) he hopes that Chu P'ei-tê * will become a revolutionary under the pressure of the masses. Revolutionary conditions are not created by arguments. They arise only as a result of the development of a revolutionary struggle. It is true that the revolutionary wave is receding: the reason for this must be sought in the incorrect policy which has restrained mass actions in the hope of creating an opportunity for further negotiations with the Kuomintang. Agitation and propaganda must be intensified; we must find allies for ourselves; certain social elements should be neutralized. All this it is necessary to do and all this can be done at the same time as we lead the masses into a revolutionary struggle.

The thoroughly opportunistic proposal of Li Li-san [calls for] postponing the general strike until the Kuomintang leaders return from Changchow and for announcing it on the day of their arrival in order to welcome them and to support the demands set forth in the open letter. This proposal flows from the assumption that the masses must not act otherwise than with the consent of the Kuomintang. The national government departed for Changchow to organize a counterrevolutionary plot. The generals are encouraging and arranging massacres of workers and peasants. It would be a big mistake under these conditions to stage a mass demonstration as a welcome to the national leaders. It might be interpreted that the proletariat is supporting the reactionary policy of the national government.

The proletariat must not ask, but demand. We formulated our demands openly over a week ago. The Kuomintang paid no attention to them. The Communist Party will discredit itself if it continues to take

---

* Chu P'ei-tê was a governor of Kiangsi. He always took a position intermediate between Nanking and Wuhan. Back in March, when the international workers' delegation traveled through Kiangsi, Chu P'ei-tê's officers were already massacring trade-union workers and peasants there. Subsequently, he acted as a mediator between Nanking and the most reactionary elements in Wuhan (Hsü Ch'ien, Ho Mêng-liu, Sun-Fo, Chên Ch'êng, and others) who, in May, already favored a reconciliation with the feudal-bourgeois rightwing Kuomintang and an open attack against the Communist Party. At the same time, he was participating in a struggle within the Nanking group; he supported the feudal-militarist faction of Pai Ch'ung-hsi (who, in the capacity of chief of the Shanghai garrison, shot workers there) and the Canton dictator Li Chi-shên against the comparadore bourgeois group of Chiang Kai-shek, Hu Han-min, and C. C. Wu. Those leaders in Wuhan (Wang Ching-wei, T'ang Shêng-chih, and others) who still wanted to fight Chiang Kai-shek, were seeking an alliance with the faction of Pai Ch'ung-hsi through the mediation of Chu P'ei-tê. The leading circles of the Communist Party similarly favored the policy of supporting a "third force." And as a result of this policy, the Politbureau rejected the demand for the recall of Chu P'ei-tê when he began to drive out of Kiangsi not only Communists, but also Left-Wing members of the Kuomintang. [M.N.R.]

no action. It must be shown that the Communist Party has laid down the demands on behalf of the working class. The proletariat must confirm this by its demonstration. It does not care in the slightest about the arrival of the generals and their allies from the national government. Do you believe that they will support our demands? The aim of the general strike is to intimidate the Kuomintang, to show it that it is losing the confidence of the masses thanks to its reactionary policy. It must choose between the reactionary generals and the revolutionary masses. One cannot at one and the same time welcome the generals as heroes and the Kuomintang as the leader of the revolution.

You propose that we wait for the return of the generals; but they do not wait. Every day they organize massacres of workers and peasants. Yesterday the entire committee of the Komsomol in Changsha (seven comrades including two girls) was shot. In such a situation, can we afford a delay any longer without discrediting the Communist Party as the leader of the working class? The Communist Party has already made far too great concessions. The more it conceded, the more the Kuomintang demanded; now it is demanding nothing more nor less than the liquidation of our Party. We must declare openly and clearly that the Communist Party is the party of the proletariat and that it will defend the interests of the working class at any cost.

June 9, 1927

29

At the Seventh Plenum, the Chinese Communist Party submitted a proposal on the confiscation of lands belonging to the reactionaries, the large-scale landlords and the gentry. The Comintern theses propose the confiscation of land belonging to the reactionaries. The Chinese Communist Party pursued the policy of confiscating land more energetically than before. The Agrarian Commission had discussed this question repeatedly. At the beginning it proposed confiscation of all land. [But] at the end it was decided to confiscate only the land of the large landholders. Upon the return of Wang Ching-wei, the Kuomintang began to discuss the agrarian question. The Agrarian Commission of the Kuomintang passed a decision on the confiscation of all land with the exception of lands [belonging] to petty landholders. This resolution was approved by the Politbureau of the Kuomintang. But in view of the opposition from the military, the resolution could not be published. Most of the officers come from the class of middle and petty landholders and are therefore antagonistic to the agrarian revolution. However, it is not the confiscation of land that serves as a pretext for the military, but, rather, "excesses" of the peasant movement, such as: the land and property of officers' families are confiscated, their relatives are arrested, the civilians are subjected to arrests and penalties; transport of rice is forbidden; compulsory contributions are imposed on merchants; the peasants appropriate the rice and eat it in the homes of rich people; small sums of money, sent by soldiers to their birthplace, are confiscated and distributed among the peasants. These excesses impel military men of the petty and middle landholder class by origin to create a united anti-Communist, anti-peasant front with the gentry and the bandits. Particularly embittered are those military men whose families have been subjected to assaults.

The peasant movement showed a particularly rapid development in Hunan. Ninety percent of the national army comes from Hunan. The whole army is hostile toward the excesses of the peasant movement. The revolt of Hsia Tou-yin and the *coup* in Changsha are an expression of this general hostility. In such a situation, not only the Kuomintang, but the Communist Party, too, must decide on a policy of concessions. It is necessary to regularize the excesses and to moderate the practices in the confiscation of land. A combined attack on the gentry and the bandits, supported by the small and average landholders, should be prevented in order to make possible a concentration of our forces for resisting the reaction. At the same time, this will accelerate the establishment of self-government in the villages and the arming of the peasantry as preparatory measures to the carrying out of land confiscation based on well-formulated plans and backed by sufficient organized strength. Otherwise, an immediate conflict with most of the reactionary armies will arise, a split with the Kuomintang will occur, and we will turn into an opposition party. The general mood in the Kuomintang [favors] a struggle with Chiang Kai-shek and the simultaneous suppression of the Communist Party. It is probable that it will be objectively impossible to remain in the Kuomintang in the nearest future. The opening address of T'an P'ing-shan is vague. It was delivered immediately following the revolt of Hsia Tou-yin. The Kuomintang decided to postpone the solution of the agrarian question and first to rout Hsia Tou-yin. As a member of the government, T'an P'ing-shan could not publicly defend a view divergent from the opinion of the national government. Your instructions are correct and important. We express our full agreement; the Chinese Communist Party seeks a democratic dictatorship, but it is impossible to achieve this in a short time. It is especially difficult to dislodge Wang Ching-wei by means of reorganization. Until we find ourselves in a position to fulfill these tasks, it is necessary to maintain good relations between the Kuomintang and the leaders of the national army. We must attract their Left-[Wing] leaders and find a common platform. If we split with them, it would make it difficult and even impossible to create our own military forces. The policy of confiscating lands from the large-scale landlords and counterrevolutionaries does not cease. The confiscation of land by the peasants themselves is not prohibited. Our immediate task is to correct the "excesses," then confiscate the land and expose the exaggerated reactionary propaganda in order to stop the panic among officers and the Left-[Wing] Kuomintang, and thus overcome the obstacles standing in the way of the peasant movement. The unemployed, landless peasants are the motive force in the Hunan peasant movement. They demand not only an equalizing distribution of land, but also the distribution of all property; this inevitably creates a conflict with the lease holders and the independent peasants. This must be changed, and the poor peasants must be made the center of the movement.

30

OPEN LETTER TO FÊNG YÜ-HSIANG

By the instructions of the Communist International, I send you warm congratulations on your brilliant victories and express confidence that these victories will be followed by new ones. The Chinese national armies are fighting for the freedom not only of China, but also of all mankind. Therefore, the sympathy, support, and enthusiasm of the oppressed peoples and exploited classes of the whole world are on their side.

The foremost military-political leaders of the revolution have gathered at the front to discuss the future course of military operations. This important decision will be taken after a mature and detailed discussion of the political situation. The attack against the Fêngtien clique must continue until Peking is taken and Chang Tso-lin is driven back to his Manchurian lair. But a new and more dangerous enemy of the national revolution has emerged. To crush this enemy is a matter of even greater necessity for the development and safety of the revolution. The new enemy is the neomilitarism of Chiang Kai-shek, supported by imperialism and the counterrevolutionary national bourgeoisie. The defeat of Wu Pei-fu, Sun Ch'uan-fang, and Chang Tsung-ch'ang and the imminent downfall of Mukden are making it necessary for imperialism to find a new and more reliable ally within China. Imperialism must have allies other than the demoralized feudal militarists. In the Nanking group which goes under the false banner of nationalism, imperialism can find an instrument that is suited to the new conditions. Screening themselves with the mask of nationalism, Chiang Kai-shek and his supporters might deceive a considerable part of the population. They are therefore more dangerous to the revolution than the reactionary Chang Tso-lin about whom few illusions exist.

The difference between Chang Tso-lin and Chiang Kai-shek, between the Fêngtien and the Nanking cliques, is not great. Both are persecuting Communists with savage fury; both are persecuting those

Kuomintang members who remain true to the revolutionary principles and traditions of their party; both are sworn enemies of workers and peasants; and both have their hands steeped with the blood of the laboring masses. Both these cliques are instruments of imperialism; both represent the narrow interests of the highest reactionary strata, and both want to overthrow the revolutionary national government of Wuhan.

The heroic uprising of the Shanghai proletariat in welcoming the national army was drowned in blood by the Northern militarists acting on imperialists' orders. Chiang Kai-shek did not rush to come to the aid of the Shanghai workers. But three weeks later, he commemorated his entrance into Shanghai by a massacre of workers who only recently had gone to such heroic sacrifices to assist the national army. Chiang Kai-shek established in Shanghai a regime no less bloody than the regime of Chang Hsüeh-liang, Chang Tsung-ch'ang, or Sun Ch'uan-fang. The actions of his agent, Li Chi-shên in Canton, are just as brutal and bloodthirsty as the actions of Chang Tso-lin in Peking.

Chiang Kai-shek will not delude anyone with his mask of nationalism. He says that he is not against the Kuomintang and the Wuhan government. He demands only that they rid themselves of Communist influence. Whether the Kuomintang and the Wuhan government are under the influence of the Communist Party is another question. But it is typical of Chiang Kai-shek to make the same demands as do the imperialists. The imperialists are also saying that they are ready to reconcile with a "genuine" national government which is not under Communist influence. Since they want one and the same thing, an alliance between them is inevitable. A few days ago, the British minister of foreign affairs, Chamberlain, declared in Parliament that the Nanking "national" government represents a new factor in the Chinese situation and that the policy of British imperialism must be oriented toward this new factor. The stormy development of the national revolution has destroyed the former instrument of imperialism. Imperialism now wants to use as a base for its further domination in China the reactionary, feudal-bourgeois military strata, represented by the Nanking group. Therefore, the immediate and most urgent task of the national-revolutionary armies is to wipe out the renegade, self-appointed group in Nanking. Chiang Kai-shek is waging a relentless war against Wuhan. He is aiding and abetting reactionary elements in territories under the control of Wuhan to incite open counterrevolutionary revolts. In his statement to a representative of the Japanese press, he admitted that Hsia Tou-yin and the counterrevolutionary officers in Changsha were acting under his orders. The counterrevolutionary influence of Nanking has displaced Wuhan's authority in Kiangsi. Now Chiang Kai-shek is distributing a circular telegram among officers and soldiers of the national army, calling upon them to subordinate to Nanking, to rise up against Wuhan and to shoot the Communists.

The split in the national ranks deserves every regret; but responsible for it is Chiang Kai-shek and his followers. They must be punished as enemies of the revolution. It is not a question of separate individuals. The Nanking group and its policy represent the interests of entire strata which have betrayed the anti-imperialist struggle and have turned against the revolution.

The aim of the national revolution is to liberate the people not only from the domination of imperialists, but also from feudal exploitation. Feudalism and its military expression—militarism—constitute the social basis of imperialism in China. Imperialism cannot be overthrown as long as its social base is not destroyed. Feudalism, combined with primitive capitalist exploitation, carries with it the pauperization of the peasantry. Millions upon millions of expropriated and destitute peasants provide cannon fodder for militarism. The national revolution cannot, therefore, realize its program of the annihilation of imperialism, the liquidation of militarism, and the democratization of the country without resolving the agrarian problem. The national revolution is essentially an agrarian revolution.

The peasant movement has been developing at an extraordinarily rapid date during the past year, threatening the interests of power and the privileges of classes whose prosperity derives directly or indirectly from the exploitation of the peasantry. China is an economically backward country. Agriculture constitutes the main branch of its production. The peasantry is the chief producer of goods. Imperialists, militarists, landlords, compradores, the gentry, the bourgeoisie—they all are interested in exploiting the peasantry. They all are opposed to any change whatsoever in the existing property relations thanks to which the peasantry finds itself virtually in a state of serfdom.

Imperialism entails the unlimited exploitation of Chinese labor. In struggling for a higher standard of living, the working class is thereby struggling against imperialist rule. This struggle strengthens the national movement. But the native bourgeoisie likewise exists at the expense of the exploitation of cheap labor. It is hostile to the aspirations of the working class to liberate itself from the present pitiful living conditions. As a result, imperialism and the native bourgeoisie unite against the working class.

The bloc of imperialism, feudalism, and the bourgeoisie against the national revolution is created by the coincidence of class interests. The center of this counterrevolutionary bloc is in Nanking, whereas Wuhan represents the other pole. It expresses the interests of the oppressed and exploited majority which consists of the proletariat, the peasantry, and the middle classes. These poles will never come together. The victory of the Nanking group will be the victory of the counterrevolution, [the victory] of imperialism. The victory of Wuhan will become the victory of the national revolution and will signify the downfall of imperialism, the abolition of militarism, the liquidation of feudalism, and the democratization of the country.

Such are the considerations which must determine the direction of military operations.

The task of occupying Peking, of driving Chang Tso-lin back into Manchuria, must not interfere with the more important and more urgent revolution task—that of liquidating the center of the counterrevolution in Nanking. Concentration of all national forces against Peking will allow imperialism to organize an attack from the rear with the help of the native reaction. The cradle of the revolution—Kwangtung—is lost. Workers and peasants who have created there the citadel of revolution are now moaning under the bloody heel of Li Chi-shên. Thanks to the intrigues of Chiang Kai-shek, the counterrevolution is triumphing in Hunan. Kiangsi has also been given away to the reaction. There is no guarantee that Wuhan, too, will not become, in its turn, the victim of reaction if the headquarters of the counterrevolution in Nanking are not destroyed. To send the entire national army to Peking means leaving the revolutionary South at the mercy of the reaction which is supported by imperialism. If the reaction is not hit from the rear, the successes on the northern front will be useless—the loss of thousands of heroes will prove to be in vain.

The destruction of the counterrevolutionary center in Nanking, the recapture of Kwangtung, the extirpation of the reaction in regions which were first conquered for the national revolution—such are the immediate tasks that lie before the national armies. I hope that the revolutionary leaders who have gathered at the front will find a way of coördinating these tasks with the task of conquering Peking.

WITH REVOLUTIONARY GREETINGS,

M. N. Roy

Representative of the Executive Committee of the
Communist International in China.

Hankow, June 10, 1927

31

DRAFT OF THE CHINESE (THE COMMUNIST PARTY AND THE KUOMINTANG) PLATFORM OF THE NATIONAL REVOLUTION

Submitted to the Politbureau of the Chinese Communist Party on June 15, 1927

1. In the military realm.

a) Struggle against the center of the feudal-bourgeois counterrevolution in Nanking: The enemy of the revolution is not Chiang Kai-shek personally, but the feudal-bourgeois military bloc he heads which is supported by reactionary forces all over the national territory and countenanced by imperialism. The Nanking group is once again seeking to subordinate the national revolution to the leadership of the feudal lords and bourgeoisie. This would mean the defeat of the revolution, for under such leadership the national liberation movement will end in a compromise between foreign imperialism and the native bourgeoisie. Therefore, the destruction of the counterrevolutionary center in Nanking is the immediate military-political task of the revolution.

b) The immediate reconquest of Kwangtung: The counterrevolutionary power in Kwangtung serves as a connecting link between the Nanking center and the reactionary, militarist elements in the southwestern provinces; this is creating a counterrevolutionary cordon

---

NOTE: See [Document 20] for the preceding resolution of the Politbureau (dated May 13) on policy with respect to the petty bourgeoisie.

The platform was adopted with the changes indicated. However, no decision was made on insisting on it before the Kuomintang.

The proposal of the Comintern representative to bring up the question of land confiscation for discussion by the whole party was rejected. [M.N.R.]

which, if it is not destroyed, will be tightening so as to strangle Wuhan. The workers and peasant masses of Kwangtung who have fought for the revolution in the course of four years must not be left under the bloody heel of Li Chi-shen. The restitution of Kwangtung will also alleviate the financial situation.

c) Support of Fêng Yü-hsiang in the campaign against Peking.

2. In the political realm.

a) To liquidate the counterrevolution in Hunan.

b) To arrest the development of the counterrevolution in Kiangsi.

c) To strengthen the authority of the Kuomintang as the leader of the national revolution.

d) To subordinate the army and the provincial administration to the complete control of the national government.

e) To establish provincial assemblies to which the provincial governments shall be responsible.

f) To establish local self-government. The power of the landlords and the gentry must be destroyed.

g) To pursue a determined struggle against imperialism.

3. In the realm of the agrarian question.

a) Confiscation of land, as specified in the resolutions of the Kuomintang and the Tenth [? Fifth] Congress of the Communist Party.*

b) Reduction of land taxes; creation of agricultural banks; state assistance to agricultural coöperatives; establishment of irrigation works; organization of the resettlement of peasants; utilization of fallow land with assistance from the state.

c) Creation of a peasant militia under the control of the Ministry of Internal Affairs.†

d) Complete freedom for the peasant movement.

4. In the realm of the labor question.

a) Freedom of assembly, speech, and press. The right to strike.

b) An eight-hour working day; the establishment of minimum wages and the creation of labor legislation.‡

---

* This was rejected with one opposing vote by the Komsomol representative. It was decided instead "to refer the solution of the land question to a joint commission of both parties." [M.N.R.]

† The words "under the control of the Ministry of Internal Affairs" were deleted. [M.N.R.]

‡ The following additional words were adopted: "an eight-hour working day for industrial workers only." The length of the working day for other categories of workers was not specified. [M.N.R.]

c) Creation of armed workers' detachments as an urban militia under the control of the Ministry of Internal Affairs.*

5. *In the realm of foreign relations.*

a) Alliance with U.S.S.R.

b) Tactical maneuvers for splitting the united imperialist front; rejection of concessions to imperialism, as such.

c) A united front with the exploited classes and the revolutionary peoples of the whole world.

---

* The words "under the control of the Ministry of Internal Affairs" were deleted. [M.N.R.]

32

PLATFORM OF THE NATIONAL REVOLUTION

At the critical stage of the present, it is necessary to have criteria for determining the extent to which a given class, party or individual is national-revolutionary. There is much that is unclear on this question. Reactionary feudal lords and militarists who shoot workers and peasants call themselves nationalist-revolutionaries and assert that their bloody acts are committed in the name of the defense of the national revolution. The national government is seeking a bargain with imperialism; it is placing itself entirely at the disposal of counterrevolutionary generals; it is sanctioning the massacres of working people. Nonetheless, it calls itself revolutionary. The Kuomintang openly opposes agrarian reform (contrary to its own program); it inclines toward a reunion with the Nanking renegades; it is conspiring with counterrevolutionary militarists against the worker and peasant movement and it still lays claim to the title of leader of the national revolution. The time has come to separate the goats from the sheep. We have to know—and we must do it in such a way that the masses, too, would know—who is against the national revolution and who is for it.

The platform of the national revolution which I am proposing can serve as such a criterion. The classes, parties, or individual persons who will not accept this platform, who will not wage a decisive struggle on its basis, can no longer be considered adherents of the national revolution. It is quite obvious that this platform is not a program of the Communist Party. It is a revolutionary-democratic platform. It contains the elementary demands of the working class. If the Communist Party does not insist that the Kuomintang adopt this platform, it will cease being the political party of the proletariat; it will betray the working class; it will commit political suicide.

Presumably M. N. Roy's address to the Politburo of the Chinese Communist Party. He notes: "See 'Draft Platform of the National Revolution'" [Document 31].—Eds.

Our relations with the Kuomintang cannot be an end in itself. The Communist Party entered the Kuomintang and collaborated with it in the interest of developing the national revolution. If the Kuomintang is no longer an instrument of the national revolution, our position and tactics with respect to it should be radically changed. We must therefore pose a clear question to the Kuomintang and the masses: is the Kuomintang prepared to accept the platform of the national revolution? The development of the movement has raised a number of socioeconomic problems on the solution of which depends the victory of the national revolution. We must know, and the masses must know once and for all, whether or not the Kuomintang wants to consider and to solve these problems. If it wants to do this, then the Communist Party will continue to collaborate with it, it will support it. If it does not want this, then there no longer exists the objective necessity of our collaboration with the Kuomintang. In such a case, we must no longer regard the Kuomintang as an ally in the revolutionary struggle, but, rather, as an enemy—as an instrument of the counterrevolution. In this case, the task of the Communist Party is to open the eyes of the masses to the counterrevolutionary transformation of the Kuomintang.

Collaboration between the two parties must continue not on the conditions laid down by the Kuomintang, but on those created by the national revolution. If the Kuomintang seeks collaboration with the Communist Party, if it seeks the support of the masses, it must accept at the very least the minimum-program of the national revolution. On no other conditions can the Communist Party remain in the Kuomintang and enlist for it the support of the masses. The minimum-program has been formulated in the platform. We must ask the Kuomintang: is it prepared to adopt this platform? And we must declare to the Kuomintang: if it is prepared, we will stay with it; and if not—we will part.

The development of the revolution creates class differentiation within the Kuomintang. This has now led to a crisis. Class interests are alienating the leaders from the masses. We must accelerate this process of class differentiation. Undoubtedly the present Central Committee of the Kuomintang will not adopt the platform we propose. Its policy of the past few weeks lends conviction to this. Nonetheless, it still lays claims to being revolutionary in character and thereby deceives the masses. We must throw off its mask. We must force this reactionary clique to come out in the open against the minimum demands of the national revolution. When the Central Committee refuses to collaborate with us on the basis of this platform of the national revolution, the Communist Party will address the members of the Kuomintang over the heads of its leaders, exposing them and branding them as betrayers of the party program and of the cause of the national revolution.

The crisis in the relations between the Kuomintang and the Communist Party is closely connected with the crisis within the Kuomintang —with the crisis in the relations between the leaders and the party masses. The question has been raised as to whether the Communist Party can remain in the Kuomintang. But there is a yet more important question: do the present leaders of the Kuomintang have the right to act on behalf of the party and its followers? We know that it does not. The leaders are pushing the Kuomintang in the direction of the counterrevolution. The masses must know about this. If the reactionary leaders are ousted, if the party is democratized, if it fully accepts and fights for the program of the national revolution, then the Communist Party will remain in the Kuomintang. If the alarm concerning the possible rift in our relations with the Kuomintang stands in the way of the necessary struggle against the reactionary leaders, then the very meaning of the entry of the Communist Party into the Kuomintang becomes destroyed.

I will now turn to the criticism leveled against the platform I proposed. Both Comrade Borodin and Comrade Ch'ên Tu-hsiu consider that this program lays down the maximum demands of the working class. In their opinion, this is what we want. They consider that our task is to ascertain what the Kuomintang wants and to find a way to reach an agreement with it. Borodin says that the future of our relations with the Kuomintang depends on our answer to the questions raised by the Kuomintang in regard to: (1) diarchy (two parties); (2) control over the mass movement; and (3) industry and commerce. Borodin believes that if we do not make concessions on all these issues, a break with the Kuomintang is inevitable; he asserts further that a break at the present time is both undesirable and harmful. In his opinion, our break from the Kuomintang will throw it into the arms of the counterrevolution. He evidently thinks that the Kuomintang is still devoted to the revolution. He definitely maintains that it is a mistake to consider the present Central Committee of the Kuomintang as counterrevolutionary. He draws no distinction between the leaders and the masses of the Kuomintang. From his point of view such a distinction "has no practical significance." Proceeding from these assumptions, Borodin proposes that the Communist Party concede on all the three questions for the sake of improving its relations with the Kuomintang.

What are the implications of this complaint in regard to "diarchy"?

The Kuomintang is hurling defiance at the Communist Party and demanding its liquidation. Can we yield on this question? The Kuomintang agrees to the existence of the Communist Party on the condition that it cease to be an independent political factor. Is any compromise possible on the question of the political independence of our party? For Borodin, this question is solved simply. He does not believe that in the present situation the Communist Party can preserve its political independence. In his opinion, the Communist Party cannot exercise full political independence while remaining in the Kuomintang. But the Communist Party cannot be 50 to 80 percent independent. Either it is an independent political factor, or it is not. There can be no compromise here. Therefore, any agreement with the counterrevolutionary Central Committee of the Kuomintang on the question of "diarchy" is possible only on the condition of the liquidation of the Communist Party, and this is precisely what Borodin is proposing. Let him understand what follows from his proposal.

The second demand, that of control over the mass movement, is a practical formulation of the demand in regard to the existence of the Communist Party. The Kuomintang is demanding that the Communist Party organize no mass demonstrations without its sanction; furthermore, that it "lead" the mass movement jointly with the Kuomintang. It is suggested to the Communist Party that it reject its role of the revolutionary leader of the working class and become a gendarme of the Kuomintang. On these conditions, the Communist Party may come to an agreement both with the counterrevolutionary generals and the ideologists of the feudal-bourgeois reaction. Even here Borodin looks for a compromise. He proposes that in the economic struggle the leadership of the working class should belong to the Communist Party; in the political sphere, however, it should give up the masses to the Kuomintang! In the heat of the revolutionary struggle, one can not draw a line between economic and political activity. Every strike bears a political character and develops in the direction of revolt. Borodin palliates his proposal by pointing out that the Communist Party will reserve the right of propaganda and agitation. This palliative does not alter the Menshevik character of his proposal. To separate, in the heat of revolutionary struggle, agitation, and propaganda from action—this is not Bolshevik policy. The Communist Party is conducting propaganda for an agrarian revolution; it is agitating for the confiscation of land. When, as a result of this propaganda and agitation, the masses are prepared for action, the Communist Party will have to go to the Kuomintang to receive sanction of this action. Such is the practical meaning of Borodin's proposal. Experience speaks against this proposal. Political dependence will tie the hands of the Communist Party in the realm of propaganda and agitation as well.

The Kuomintang knows that the Communist Party is the leader of the masses. It knows that the masses are ready for a revolutionary struggle. It has launched an attack on the masses. But it also knows that the masses can only achieve victory under the leadership of the Communist Party. It is therefore seeking to discredit and demoralize the Communist Party. By adopting Borodin's proposal, the Communist Party will play into the hands of the counterrevolution. Our bond with the Kuomintang which in its time contributed to the development of the revolution would in the present situation and on the conditions proposed by Borodin and Ch'ên Tu-hsiu merely assist the counterrevolution.

The question of commerce and industry was quite clearly explained by Borodin. He said that here it is a question of relations between the Kuomintang and the large-scale bourgeoisie. Two weeks ago, the Party advised the trade unions to subject the workers to "revolutionary self-discipline" in order to stop the complaint on the part of the petty bourgeoisie. This was done under the pretext that the Kuomintang represents the petty bourgeoisie, and that if we do not make certain concessions to it, our relations with the Kuomintang will be broken off. Now they are suggesting to the working class that it make concessions in order that the Kuomintang could return to the camp of the big bourgeoisie. Next, they will demand concessions to imperialism, and, probably, this will be similarly justified by the necessity of preserving our relations with the Kuomintang! The Kuomintang wants to come to an agreement with Nanking. It wants to win the graces of the Shanghai bourgeoisie. And so the working class must support it in these counterrevolutionary aims. What must the working class do for this? Make sacrifices. The workers must not demand higher wages; they must agree to a longer working day; they must not strike—in a word, they must declare civil peace. All this must be done in order to preserve our relations with the Kuomintang which is deserting to the counterrevolution!

No, comrades, agreements with the Kuomintang on the question of the counterrevolution do not enter into the tasks of the Communist Party. Its task is to oust the traitorous leaders, to expose them to the masses as enemies of the national revolution and thus transform the Kuomintang into a revolutionary-democratic mass party which would conduct a really national-revolutionary struggle under the hegemony of the proletariat. We will achieve this goal once we compel the Kuomintang leaders to define their attitude toward the platform of the national revolution at the present stage.

There have been submitted a number of amendments to the platform proposed by me. The correction on the agrarian question cannot be accepted. Borodin proposes that the entire question of the confiscation of land be dropped. He points out that here we must make concessions to the Kuomintang. But, after all, this is the question of all questions at the present moment. To yield on this point would mean to surrender the position on the whole front. Besides, the Kuomintang has adopted the agrarian platform of the national revolution which was proposed by the Communist Party even before it appeared in the Fifth Congress resolution on the agrarian question. Now the Kuomintang wants to reject it under the pressure of the reactionary feudal lords and militarists who have seized power. To yield on the question of confiscation does not mean "to give the Kuomintang a certain amount of leeway," as Borodin believes; such a concession would leave the peasantry to the mercy of the feudal-militarist counterrevolution. We must help the Kuomintang, but only if it fights against the reaction. We must not help its aspirations to satisfy the counterrevolutionary generals.

Comrade Ch'ên's proposal to refer the agrarian question to a mixed commission of both parties is a step backward. An agreement on the question of partial confiscation was reached at a joint conference. The Kuomintang now wants to annul the decision of the joint conferences. To refer this question back to the joint commission would imply our agreement to a reëxamination of the earlier decision.

Borodin's formulation "to strive for the confiscation of land belonging to large-scale landlords" shifts the entire question to a future time, while this is the most burning question of the day. The peasants are already carrying out confiscation. Should the Communist Party support them or not? This is the way the question stands. There can be no doubt as to what our answer should be. The Communist Party must support the peasants. We must also seek to obtain the Kuomintang's support of the peasantry. If it does not give this support, the Communist Party will not hesitate in its choice between the Kuomintang which is under the control of feudal militarists, on the one hand, and the revolutionary peasantry, on the other.

It is truly astonishing that the Communist Party can consider as exorbitant those demands of the proletariat which have been entered in the platform. These are the most elementary demands that the proletariat can lay down at the given moment. The question of the right to strike arouses objection. The Kuomintang and the national government question this right. But the proletariat must, after all, defend itself. The Kuomintang cannot object to the rest of the demands and at the same time lay claims to the title of a revolutionary-democratic party. In all "respectable" democratic countries, the proletariat enjoys these rights. Can the proletariat support the Kuomintang, can the Communist Party collaborate with it, if the Kuomintang is opposed even to such elementary rights of the working class? The central question at the moment is the arming of workers. The reaction is attacking the revolution from all sides. The petty bourgeoisie is hesitating at this critical moment. Most of the military forces are under the control of feudal lords and reactionaries. The task of defending the revolution falls on the proletariat. The arming of workers, therefore, becomes an urgent necessity. The unwillingness of the Kuomintang to reach an agreement on this question will prove that it wants to betray the revolution.

Comrade Ch'ên Tu-hsiu is opposed to the subordination of the peasant militia to the Ministry of Agriculture. Why? He points out that the Kuomintang will interpret this as a threat to its power. Any effective preparation of the working class for the inevitable revolutionary struggle is a threat to the bourgeoisie, and it will always interpret it in just this way. Must the working class, therefore, forever relinquish preparations for the struggle? This would be simple capitulation.

The Communists entered the national government at the invitation of the Kuomintang. They accepted this invitation not out of politeness. They entered the national government in order to transform it into an organ of democratic dictatorship. Only on this condition can they remain in the government. The organization and leadership of the urban and rural militia is the function of the Ministry of Agriculture which is at the same time the Ministry of Internal Affairs. Why should the Kuomintang be opposed to the Ministry of Agriculture and Internal Affairs fulfilling its function? Why did it turn out that a Communist heads this ministry? [Because] this would place the Communist Party in an awkward position. The Kuomintang invites the Communists to enter the government; but it does not give them any power, it does not trust them. It is perfectly evident that the Kuomintang wants to use the Communist ministers as policemen, it wants to use them to control the workers' and peasants' movement so as to discredit the Communist Party. Are we going to get caught on this bait? The Communist Party must make it clear to the masses that it entered the government to defend the interests of the working class, to develop the revolution, and that it would not for a minute hesitate to leave the government and to declare war on it if its stay in the government pours water on the mill of reaction.

We must place the Kuomintang in a position where it must of necessity give a direct answer. We must force it to make an explicit declaration before the masses as to whether it is prepared to lead the national revolution forward or wants to betray it. Our relations with the Kuomintang will be determined by its reply to this question. If it does not break with the feudal counterrevolution and the bourgeois reaction, the Communist Party must break with it. More than that: the Communist Party must launch a struggle against it as an agent of the counterrevolution.

June 15, 1927

33

THE KUOMINTANG'S REPLY TO

THE OPEN LETTER OF THE CHINESE

COMMUNIST PARTY, JUNE 15, 1927

DEAR COMRADES!

Your letter of June 4 has been received and studied. Our party's policy on peasants and workers has been formulated by our leader. The peasant and worker masses represent the staunch and steadfast foundation of our party. Ever since our party was reorganized in 1924, this idea has received more and more definite expression. In the past, whether it was in Canton or during the Northern Expedition, our party has always fought for the interests of the masses, for the principles of our leader. This is understood not only by members of our own party, but also by the broad masses of China. The Chinese national revolution is a revolution by means of which the broad masses and, especially, the unfortunate, destitute peasants are seeking liberation. From the time of the Second Congress of our party and right up to the plenum of the Central Committee in March of the current year, our comrades did not refuse to devote their full attention to the resolving of the peasant question. The agrarian problem was a subject of lengthy, painstaking and profound discussion. But as long as a solution is not found to the agrarian problem, the peasant problem will also remain unresolved which, in turn, delays the consummation of the revolution. This is completely clear to the comrades of our party.

After the revolt of Chiang Kai-shek, reactionary forces from all parts of the territory under the national government have gathered around him. The Yangtze Valley is under the control of the old militarist regime. The revolutionary forces are not secure. Hence, numerous reactionary

Translation from the Chinese. [M.N.R.]

demonstrations occurred following the betrayal of Chiang Kai-shek. In spite of the efforts of our comrades, these reactionary elements were not suppressed. Oh, how serious is the present situation! Such events are inevitable in every stage of revolutionary history; they are likewise inevitable in any revolutionary party. Our party believes it to be a usual thing. We cannot be responsible for the change of policy of the leader and of our party. We consider, however, that we should have intensified our work. At the same time, we admit that many of our comrades have committed careless acts in the past and that they do not have a correct understanding of our task. Often, in directing the workers' and peasants' movement, our comrades do not base their actions on the party's resolutions; sometimes, they even misinterpret them. Such faulty leadership not only weakens the organization of the party, but even harms the interests of peasants and workers. Bearing this principle of the revolution in mind, the party frankly admits the carelessness of some of our comrades in the past and is doing everything in its power to correct this.

Since the time of the reorganization of our party, your party has constantly been doing its maximum to participate in the national revolution. Many members of your party have entered our party in order to help in the accomplishment of the historical task. Therefore, we hope that in the serious situation of the present, your party, on the one hand, will help our party to correct the careless acts committed in the past and that, on the other hand, you will instruct your comrades that at the present critical moment both parties must be aware of their responsibility.

Now concerning the *coup* in Hunan. Our party has on two occasions sent responsible comrades to Hunan to investigate and settle this matter. It is true that there is still no detailed account. Nevertheless, two principles, which have already been adopted, can be reported to your party: (1) improper actions of the military must be curbed, and (2) careless actions on the part of the peasant movement must be corrected. As concerns the first principle, it has already been explained in our resolution of last Friday, and there is no need to repeat it here.

With revolutionary greetings.

THE CENTRAL EXECUTIVE COMMITTEE OF THE CHINESE KUOMINTANG

34

THE CRISIS OF THE NATIONAL REVOLUTION

AND THE TASKS OF THE PROLETARIAT

COMRADES!

On behalf of the Communist International, I welcome the Fourth Congress of the All-China Federation of Labor and through it the proletarian masses of China.

The Fourth Congress of the All-China Federation of Labor is an event of great importance not only for the Chinese federation, but for the whole world of revolution as well. At preceding congresses, the All-China Federation of Labor was faced with the tasks of agitation, propaganda, and organization. The present congress must resolve the questions of the leadership of the proletarian army in the decisive revolutionary struggle of the present. In a relatively short period of time, the All-China Federation of Labor has united under its banner two and a half million workers. This is the revolutionary vanguard of the entire working class of China. Your task now is to lead this organized proletarian force forward so that it could occupy its proper place in the foremost ranks of the national revolution and assist the revolution in overcoming the present crisis. During the past four or five years, the proletariat played a most important role in the national-revolutionary movement. In the present period, its role in the national revolution must become decisive.

After a period of very rapid development, the national movement now finds itself in an extremely dangerous crisis. Resolute actions on the part of the proletariat will make it possible to overcome this crisis and to move ahead to final victory. As a result of the development of the revolution, the bourgeoisie left the national-revolutionary front and

---

M. N. Roy's speech at the Fourth Congress of the All-China Federation of Labor.—Eds.

turned against it. It has joined the ranks of the counterrevolutionary front.

The proletariat accepted suffering, brought sacrifices and fought with self-denial for the cause of the national revolution. Wherever the bourgeoisie is now in power, still screening behind the false banner of nationalism, the working class is subjected to persecutions just as brutal as in territories under [the control of] Chang Tso-lin and other militarists.

Twice did the Shanghai proletariat rise in heroic revolts to facilitate the arrival of the national revolutionary army in Shanghai. But now Shanghai has been occupied by it. Chang Kai-shek has become the ruler of the town, and already, a few days later, the leaders of the so-called national army are organizing bloodbaths of the Shanghai workers who had fought so heroically for the revolution. The bourgeoisie has left the ranks of the revolution and is compromising with imperialism. Imperialism is exploiting and oppressing the petty-bourgeois masses. The economic progress of the petty bourgeoisie is hampered by imperialist rule, on the one hand, and the feudal lords' control over the economic and political life of the country, on the other. But even in the ranks of the petty bourgeoisie, whose interests are bound up with the victory of the national revolution, there is hesitation and vacillation. The petty bourgeoisie alone is incapable of carrying the revolution further. Taking advantage of this vacillation of the petty bourgeoisie, the large-scale bourgeoisie is trying to win it over to the side of the counterrevolution in order to create a united front of all reactionary forces against workers and peasants.

As a result, the responsibility for the future development of the national revolution falls on the proletariat. The proletariat must come forward as the leader of the revolution. It must lead the petty bourgeoisie into a struggle against imperialism, for national liberation. On the other hand, the reactionary feudal elements and their representatives in the national army have assumed the offensive throughout the whole national territory. Peasant organizations are subjected to brutal persecutions not only in Kwangtung, but also in Hunan, Kiangsi, and even in Hupeh. The very existence of peasants' and workers' organizations is being threatened. The petty-bourgeois Left Wing leaders of the Kuomintang are vacillating. They are looking on helplessly at the events. They do not dare step forward to start a revolutionary struggle against the reaction.

The development of the agrarian revolution, that is, the development of the peasants' struggle against the landlords, the gentry, and all the reactionary strata, is the only guarantee of a successful outcome of the national revolution. The bourgeoisie, aided and abetted by imperialism, is trying to mobilize all the forces of reaction and all the forces in the whole country to create a united front against the revolution. The task of the revolution at the present moment is to attack the reactionary forces, to destroy their roots wherever they exist, and to smash them once and for all. If this is not done, there is no guarantee of the success of the revolution. At present, this is the most important question of the Chinese revolution.

This question also confronts the Fourth Congress of the All-China Federation of Labor, because only the proletariat can lead the peasantry in a struggle against feudal reaction, in a struggle for agrarian revolution.

Therefore, comrades, the tasks before the Fourth Congress cover the interests not only of the proletariat, but of the whole revolution as well. This congress must decide not only on how to defend the interests of the proletariat, but also on how the proletariat is to assume the leadership of the revolution. The trade unions must become militant organs of the proletariat, organs of the revolutionary struggle.

Without an agrarian revolution, the national revolution cannot be successful. The proletariat must stand at the head of the agrarian revolution. It must demand of the petty-bourgeois national leaders that they put an end to their hesitations and join the struggle against the reaction. Your congress must demand of the Kuomintang and the national government that they recognize the danger of a revolt in Changsha and of the events in Kiangsi. The proletariat, in the capacity of the leader of the agrarian revolution, must demand resolute actions from the national government to crush the counterrevolution in Hunan and Kiangsi. Only by such actions can the proletariat become the actual leader of the agrarian revolution.

The Fourth Congress of the All-China Federation of Labor is of great significance to the cause of world revolution, because the outcome of the Chinese revolution will determine the development of the world revolution. The Fourth Congress must provide the whole working class with a militant program, it must show the working class how to lead the democratic bloc in a struggle for national liberation.

All the proletarian organizations of the world are convinced that the vanguard of the Chinese proletariat will prove capable of fulfilling its historical task and of providing the national-revolutionary movement with the leadership it needs at the critical moment of the present.

June 20, 1927

35

LETTER TO THE SHANGHAI COMMITTEE

Proposed by the Secretariat on June 23, 1927

The dispatch of imperialist forces to the north of China should be protested. A militant anti-imperialist movement in Shanghai must be prepared in the course of one month. Students, merchants, and workers must declare a general strike. The demonstration must go into the foreign quarters. The movement must be broader and deeper than that of May 30, 1925. If necessary, the following slogans must be advanced: "Confiscate the property of the imperialists of China!" "Take back the concessions!" "Confiscate the Japanese textile factories!" and so on. Thorough preparations should be made before the movement is begun. Anti-Japanese agitation must be conducted among various classes. A mood must be created against the landing of imperialist forces. The atmosphere must become more and more charged with every day. Similar preparations must be conducted in Chekiang, Nanking, Ningpo, Chinkiang, Wusih, and so on. Agitation must penetrate deeply into the army, into the lower-ranking officers; it must inflame the soldiers and the masses. Agitation must also deeply inflame the peasants along the railway lines and the big towns. Soldiers and peasants did not join the movement of May 30. This was its shortcoming. This time, the coöperation of soldiers and peasants must be assured. As a result of these measures, Chiang Kai-shek's armies will be demoralized at their base. Underground work among foreign seamen and city policemen must be started in good time. This movement will force the imperialists to occupy Nanking and Shanghai. Such an action on the part of the imperialist powers can once again lead to a big wave of agitation against imperialism all over China, to the destruction of the very roots of Chiang Kai-shek, and *to the smashing of the danger from the Right in the Wuhan government.*

The goal of the movement is to confiscate the properties of imperialists and large landlords' estates, to overcome the present, dangerous crisis of the revolution and to destroy the hegemony of the large-scale bourgeoisie. This movement must burst like an explosion just at the moment when either Chiang Kai-shek attacks Wuhan, or Wuhan attacks Chiang Kai-shek. Exert all your energies toward this. Agitation should be conducted among the petty bourgeoisie against Chiang Kai-shek's plans to float a domestic loan for twenty million dollars in the form of banknotes.

In order that you understand the meaning of this resolution, we present the following explanation:

1. Since the time of May 30, especially after the victorious Northern Expedition, imperialism donned a mask of gentleness in the aims of attracting the bourgeoisie and assisting the new Right Wing of the Kuomintang. The success of the first Northern Expedition gave Chiang Kai-shek and the large-scale bourgeoisie grounds to think that the national revolution could be easily accomplished. They raised the banner of anticommunism. The Communist Party focused all the people's attention on the peasants' and workers' movement. Under this pretext, Chiang Kai-shek and the bourgeoisie used the anti-imperialist mood of the petty bourgeoisie to turn it against the peasants' and workers' movement and against the Communist Party.

2. This policy of Chiang Kai-shek enjoys a certain amount of influence in the Wuhan government. The vacillations of the petty bourgeoisie and the middle officers corps, the betrayal of Hsia Tou-yin and Hsü K'ê-hsiang—such are the manifestations of the influence of Chiang Kai-shek's slogans.

3. In the course of the past several months, the anti-imperialist movement has weakened. The imperialist intervention became more brutal, especially during the events in Nanking. In the face of imperialist intervention, the Wuhan government is compelled to pursue a policy of concessions. The proletarian masses must submit to so-called revolutionary discipline. As a result, the anti-imperialist movement in the territory of Wuhan is becoming quieter than in other places. If we are going to continue this policy of making concessions and maintaining an inert position, the situation will become extremely dangerous. The peculiarity of the Chinese revolution is its anti-imperialist character. Lately, it seems that this task is being forgotten. All the efforts have been concentrated on the struggle with feudalism. On the other hand, Chiang Kai-shek and Li Chi-shên in Shanghai and Kwangtung, screening themselves behind the false banner of the national revolution and at the same time opposing a class revolution, resort to all manner of subterfuge—they are creating a deceptive anti-imperialist movement in order to delude the masses.

4. On the one hand, the anti-imperialist movement is quieting down, but on the other hand, from the point of view of the petty bourgeoisie, the peasant-worker movement has become "too red." In addition, the slogans: "Arm the peasants and workers," "Confiscate the land," "Noncapitalist development" and so forth arouse the suspicion of the petty bourgeoisie and force it to think that the Communist Party will soon incite a revolt against the Kuomintang, that the Communist Party wants a class revolution, and not a national revolution. Under the conditions of armed imperialist intervention and the terror of Hsia Tou-yin, the petty bourgeoisie easily succumbs to the influence of the propaganda of Chiang Kai-shek's group; it is rejecting the three points * of political activity and is falling into the arms of Chiang Kai-shek. The objective reason for this tendency to the Right is the decline of the anti-imperialist movement.

5. The petty bourgeoisie does not recognize that confiscation of land is necessary for the national revolution. It believes that only the Communist Party is interested in this. It thinks that this is necessary for the Communist Party in order to carry out an October revolution and to establish the dictatorship of peasants and workers. Therefore, not only does it not advance this task now, but it wants to overthrow the worker and peasant movement and to sever relations with the Communist Party.

If the Communist Party retreats under these conditions and if it accepts these propositions, the result will be the liquidation of our forces, the relinquishing of the hegemony of the proletariat, and the surrender to the mercy of Chiang Kai-shek! This will mean the victory of capitalism! *If we continue to insist on the confiscation of land and on the arming of workers and peasants, the result will be an immediate break with the Kuomintang, and the immediate break with the Kuomintang will mean the immediate liquidation of our party.* If we do not act cautiously in this situation, the result will be the immediate defeat of the bourgeoisie.

[Paragraph 6 is missing.—Eds.]

7. Can we temporarily relinquish the policy of arming workers and peasants and the confiscation of land? One could do what we are now

---

* The three points of the political line of Sun Yat-sen are: alliance with the U.S.S.R., aid to the workers' and peasants' movement and collaboration with the Communist Party. In his political will, Sun Yat-sen set down these three points as the basis for directing the policy of the Kuomintang. It should be remembered that these three points are different from the "three national principles," formulated by Sun Yat-sen long before his death. Those three principles were: nationalism, democracy, and the people's livelihood (subsequently this was usually interpreted as socialism). [M.N.R.]

doing in settling the Hunan problem (it was decided that in the struggle against Hsü K'ê-hsiang, we ourselves would confiscate the land from the large landlords and give arms to the peasants). This is an independent policy. But it is *fraught with danger*. If we act independently, *our relations with the Kuomintang will be broken, and then we will have to perish—a glorious way to perish.* This is not a way out of the crisis. We must discover a new way. The new policy will not only lead us out of the dangerous crisis; it will expand and intensify the revolution and lead us to final victory. What is this new path? It is indicated in the resolution cited above; it is a second May 30; this is not a subjective theory, but an objective necessity and possibility.

8. *We must not fear imperialist conquest and intervention in the territory of Chiang Kai-shek. The outright seizure of Shanghai, Fuchow, Nanking, and so on, by imperialists is more advantageous than seizure by Chiang Kai-shek or Li Chi-shên, for, in the event of an imperialist seizure, we can raise a new anti-imperialist war.* This war will lead directly to the necessity of arming peasants and workers and to the confiscation of land. With this high wave, the internal reaction will not dare rear its head. The tendency toward a split * will be thwarted. There can be no doubt that this high wave will crush the forces of Chiang Kai-shek, will destroy the hegemony of the bourgeoisie and will restore and strengthen our hegemony. Consequently, this tactic is most correct and necessary.

You must prepare this movement quickly and well. You must not consider that this movement concerns workers alone; different classes must be drawn into it. This movement must come as an explosion of the people's wrath. It must be general and national in character. Do not be afraid of Nanking, Shanghai, Ningpo, and so forth, being occupied by foreign troops. You must expand and intensify the movement in the presence of foreign power. The more this movement develops, the easier will it be to organize our forces; and the forces of the bloc (the proletariat, the peasantry, and the petty bourgeoisie) will crush the forces of Chiang Kai-shek.

On the basis of this resolution, the military section must draw up a careful plan and put it through everywhere (among the armies of Chiang Kai-shek and among foreign troops). Expand the existing anti-Japanese movement. Agitate among the petty merchants and peasants against the twenty million domestic loan. Strengthen the basis of workers' unions; provide for the invincible strength of workers' organizations. Try to draw the students and the Left-[Wing members of the] Kuomintang into this struggle.

---

* Between the Kuomintang and the Communist Party. [M.N.R.]

One more question. It concerns our relations with the imperialists. From the international point of view, we should have joined forces with Japan. From the internal-national point of view, it is necessary to destroy the Anglo-Japanese alliance. In the territory of Chiang Kai-shek and Chang Tso-lin we must definitely be *against Japan. In Wuhan we must have a friendly attitude toward Japan.* Bearing these principles in mind, select the most concrete tactics and slogans. But do not give way to too great misgivings lest this interfere in the development of the movement.

36

THE ANTI-IMPERIALIST STRUGGLE

AND THE CLASS STRUGGLE

The document * submitted by the Secretariat is extremely dangerous. It speaks of organizing an anti-imperialist struggle in the place of a class struggle; by emphasizing the national aspect of the revolution, they want to blur its class character. The anti-imperialist struggle is extremely important. It constitutes the basic feature of the Chinese revolution. At present this struggle is suffering a depression. Not only in Shanghai, but even in Wuhan itself, it is virtually prohibited by the national government. For the Communist Party, the unfolding, the expansion and the intensification of the anti-imperialist struggle constitutes an important task.

But in the document submitted to us, the stick is bent in the opposite direction. It is proposed that the class struggle be replaced by an anti-imperialist struggle which must form the basis of the revolution. This proposal speaks of the desire to oppose reality. While the anti-imperialist struggle constitutes the basic feature of the Chinese revolution, it should be remembered that at the present stage its motive power is the class struggle. The one cannot be replaced by the other. The class struggle has intensified in the process of the national-revolutionary movement; civil peace can be restored only on the condition that all the gains of the revolutionary struggle are destroyed. At the present stage of the revo-

Presumably M. N. Roy's statement in the Politbureau.—Eds.

* This document (see Appendix VII [page 361 in this book.—Eds.]) was supposed to have been sent to the Shanghai district committee in the form of a letter of instructions from the Central Committee. When it was decided, after a lengthy discussion in the Politbureau, to substitute for this letter a resolution on the anti-imperialist struggle, the Secretariat declared that the letter had already been sent to Shanghai. [M.N.R.]

lution, an effective struggle against imperialism can be waged only by unleashing the class struggle.

It says in the document that as a result of intensifying the class struggle we have become involved in a terrible crisis. Therefore, so the document states, we must find the way out in our abandoning the class struggle and in enlisting the masses in a new anti-imperialist movement. Such was the tactic of Manchurian absolutism during the Boxer rebellion. It is really hard to believe that the tactics of Manchu absolutism can find defenders in the ranks of the Communist Party! The essence of the proposal amounts to the fact that the Communist Party must divert the attention of the masses from the burning questions of the agrarian revolution in the aim of establishing civil peace with the feudal warlords and their representatives from the petty-bourgeois intelligentsia.

The document advances the following two theses:

1. Such slogans as "Arm workers and peasants," "Confiscate the land," "Noncapitalist development" and so on only [serve to] push the petty bourgeoisie into the camp of the counterrevolution. The conclusions that are drawn from this correct evaluation of the situation are completely erroneous, capitulationist, liquidationist. The conclusion is drawn that these slogans must be discarded and the old, worn-out slogan of agitation, "Down with imperialism!" be advanced in their place—a slogan which is being used by all the counterrevolutionary generals, including Chang Tso-lin himself. The comrades who worked out this document do not understand that the anti-imperialist struggle has assumed in the process of its development the more concrete forms of class struggle. Their thesis contradicts the theses of the Comintern. It repudiates the resolution of the Fifth Congress of the Party. The proposal to discard the above-mentioned slogans on the class struggle presupposes that they do not correspond to the present conditions.

2. The second fundamental idea of the [above] thesis is that if the Communist Party will adopt an independent political line, a split with the Kuomintang is inevitable. Proceeding from this assumption, the suggestion is made that the Communist Party has no independent political line of its own. The idea of collaboration with the Kuomintang is being converted into a real fetish to which everything must be sacrificed. If the class struggle carries the threat of a split with the Kuomintang, the Communist Party must put an end to the class struggle—that is what the Secretariat is proposing!

Next, the proposed plan for developing a new wave of the anti-imperialist struggle is, mildly speaking, quite dangerous. Essentially, this is provocation. Strictly speaking, it is proposed that we provoke the imperialists into occupying Shanghai, Nanking, Canton, and other ports!

This is really unheard of. Next, the document asserts that as a result of such occupation, a united national front will once again be formed in the anti-imperialist struggle. It is hard to understand how the occupation of Shanghai, Nanking, Canton, and so on would lead to the overthrow of the bourgeoisie and place the proletariat at the head of the revolution. Nonetheless, such is one of the arguments advanced in defense of the proposal. The Communist Party must liquidate the class struggle and provoke the imperialists into occupying the principal economic centers of the country in order that the proletariat could find itself at the head of the revolution! This is a highly complicated tactic of sheerest opportunism. Such a tactic is absolutely inadmissible for the Communist Party.

This document proposes to the Shanghai Committee that it stir up a new wave of an anti-imperialist movement whch must begin in one month under the slogan: "Confiscate the concessions!" Who is going to participate in this movement? Neither the large-scale nor the petty bourgeoisie. In the present period of depression, one can not count on the success of the anti-imperialist movement in enlisting the petty bourgeoisie into such a revolutionary movement without the necessary preparation. The proletariat will have to go by itself, it will have to throw itself on the imperialist guns. This is adventure. You refuse to lead the proletariat into a revolutionary struggle against reaction in an area where there are considerable chances for success; you refuse to head a revolt of the Hunan peasantry against the decaying feudal reaction, yet you make plans for sending the Shanghai proletariat, debilitated by three revolts, tortured by the White terror, to certain defeat at the hands of imperialists who are considerably stronger than are our enemies here! To reconcile your differences with the wavering petty bourgeoisie and the counterrevolutionary feudal war lords, you propose to make martyrs of the Shanghai proletariat who has already brought heavy sacrifices. This means leading the proletariat not to victory, but to slaughter. The Shanghai proletariat is too valuable an acquisition for the Chinese revolution to sacrifice it so lightly.

It is absolutely necessary to develop an anti-imperialist movement on a national scale. This would hamper the formation of a single counterrevolutionary front. The Communist Party must take this task upon itself. But it must not be advanced as an alternative to the class struggle, as the present document proposes. The attention and the energy of the masses must not be diverted from the internal problem of class struggle for the sake of the external problems of the struggle against imperialism. The one and the other must be developed at the same time. In practice, the one complements the other. They are inseparable.

I make a motion * to reject the letter and I propose that another plan be drawn up for an anti-imperialist campaign.

June 28, 1927

---

* See Appendix VII, page 195. [M.N.R. Page 361 in this book.—Eds.]

37

The collapse of the Kuomintang marked a sharp turning point in the development of the Chinese revolution. The process of class differentiation within the national movement—a process that was occurring simultaneously with the development of the revolution—reached its peak. The role of the Kuomintang, unifying all anti-imperialist and democratic forces over a period of several years, proved to be played out to the end. The class struggle, in its most acute form, became intertwined with the national struggle and, in the end, the Kuomintang betrayed the national revolution. Not only did it renounce the principles of freedom and democracy which it upheld over a period of several years; in the brutal encounter of class conflicts, the Kuomintang itself fell apart.

In the transitional periods between its individual stages, the revolution suffered a number of rather serious defeats. These defeats gave rise to doubts as to the correctness of the Kuomintang's policy during the first stages of the revolution. The opposition in the All-Russian Communist Party (B) and its adherents in other countries were saying that the defeats of the Chinese revolution were caused by the erroneous and "opportunistic" policy of the Communist International. These doubts can be dispelled and the groundlessness of this charge can be demonstrated by answering the following questions:

1. Was the policy of supporting the Kuomintang correct, [i.e.,] the policy of the Communist Party's entry into the Kuomintang and its collaboration with it during the first stages of the revolution?

2. Was the Communist International able to anticipate the situation created by the development of the revolution, and did it possess a correct policy in this situation?

This was originally M. N. Roy's introduction to the volume of documents and materials presented on the preceding pages.—Eds.

This book provides the answer to the second question. By the end of 1926, the Communist International was already fully cognizant of the situation that had arisen in China as a result of the Northern Expedition. The Communist International took into account the fact that the national armies, having routed the Northern militarists, dealt a cruel blow to the might and prestige of imperialism in the entire South of the country, but at the same time it clearly foresaw the turning point in the process of the development of the revolution that followed from this military victory. The Comintern foresaw that the bourgeoisie would betray the national revolution and it advanced the policy of mobilizing the revolutionary-democratic forces as bases of the revolution in its new stage of development. The general practical instructions for the new situation, outlined in the theses of the Seventh Enlarged Plenum of the Executive Committee of the Communist International, were later set down in more concrete form in subsequent resolutions of the Communist International. However, it is not enough to have a clear perspective and a correct policy. It is equally important to possess the instrument for putting this policy into practice. The documents cited in this book furnish exhaustive proof that the defeat was promoted to a considerable extent by the defects of the instrument through which the Communist International was forced to act in China.

In any given country, the Communist International can influence the situation first of all through the instrumentality of its section in that country. The Chinese Communist Party did not understand the full meaning of the resolutions of the Communist International and was unable to act in accordance with them. Furthermore, at the crucial moment its leaders refused to accept the instructions of the Communist International. The defeat was also brought about by many other objective factors; the decisive factor, however, is the role that the Party plays in a revolutionary crisis. The inability of the Chinese Communist Party to rise to the occasion is lamentable, but there were historical reasons for this. The Party was too young to accomplish without errors the gigantic task that lay before it. It lacked the necessary political development and experience. If one ignores—as does, in fact, Comrade Trotsky—the youth, the ideological immaturity, and the weakness of the Party's direction of vital factors in a revolutionary crisis, it would mean simply that one underestimates the Party's role in the revolution. This book shows the degree to which the stated factors influenced the situation. After barely two years of existence as a Party in the real sense of the word, the Chinese Communist Party was confronted squarely with the task of leading a revolution that involved hundreds of millions of people; its enemies were world imperialism and native reaction which included the bourgeoisie, united in a strong bloc. Founded in 1920, the Chinese Communist Party nevertheless remained right up to 1924 a small organization exerting little influence on the political life of the country. Similarly, this small group played no appreciable role in the ideological preparation of the great revolutionary movement. Until recently, the Marxist theory of revolution was virtually unknown in China, if one does not count the narrow circle of the intelligentsia which had no ties whatsoever with the masses. Such were the traditions of the Chinese Communist Party. The years 1925 and 1926 marked a tremendous gain in the numerical strength of the Party and its political influence increased to an even greater measure. At the beginning of 1927, it had 55,000 members; 33,000 belonged to the Komsomol. The workers' movement in the whole country and the peasant movement in the southern provinces were completely under Communist leadership. The Communists were the most active factor in all spheres of the political life of the country. The Party leadership, however, could not keep in step with this sudden growth of the organization. This was quite natural. In view of its extreme youth and the absence of ideological traditions, the Party did not possess cadres that could yield new leaders capable of rising to the occasion. The Party developed in a period of stormy revolutionary struggle. It recruited new members and acquired political influence under the conditions of such struggles as the May 30 movement in Shanghai; the Hong Kong seamen's strike; the strike and the blockade of Hong Kong which lasted for years; the Northern Expedition; the Shanghai uprisings; the capture of Hankow; and so on. As a result, the Party underwent a veritable metamorphosis. From a small organization, consisting chiefly of intellectuals, it was suddenly converted into a mass proletarian Party, leading 2,500,000 organized workers and approximately 9,000,000 organized peasants who were drawn into the gigantic revolutionary struggle. The Party leadership, however, remained predominantly intellectual; it was stunned by the development of events and was unable to take command of the situation. It should be borne in mind that almost all the first leaders of the Communist Party came from the ranks of the Kuomintang and brought with them the reformist traditions of the Kuomintang. At the same time, the party was too young to put forward new leaders from its rank and file for replacing the old.

Such was the instrument through which the Communist International had to work in China. The difficulties which had to be confronted have been clearly shown in this book. A perfectly correct policy, conforming fully to the successive changes in the situation, could not be implemented due to stubborn opposition from the opportunistic leaders of the Party. On the other hand, the intrinsically healthy Party and the masses' will to struggle were likewise unable to influence the situation to any decisive extent—once again due to the interference of the reform-minded leadership. The counterrevolutionary *coup* in Changsha roused the peasants at once, and they advanced on the town from all sides. Around 2,000 soldiers under the command of counterrevolutionary officers were stationed in the town; against it, marched around 22,000 peasants, partly armed. In this situation, the provincial committee of the Party received a secret order from the Central Committee prohibiting the attack on Changsha and proposing that the peasants retreat and disperse in view of the fact that General T'ang Shêng-chih could handle the situation by himself. The minister of internal affairs—the Communist T'an P'ing-shan—refused to issue the necessary documents legalizing the movement of the 8,000 armed peasants. The Political Bureau of the Central Committee did not insist that T'an P'ing-shan take this action. One could cite numerous equally tragic examples to prove that the leadership was weak, opportunistic and semi-Kuomintang [in character], that it did not give the Party the possibility to act in accordance with the directives of the Communist International, and that this contributed greatly to the defeat.

The objection might be raised that the opportunism of the Communist Party leaders was a result of the International's preceding policy in China. Let us, therefore, reply to the question: Was the policy of supporting the Kuomintang correct, that is, the policy of the Communist Party's entry into the Kuomintang and its collaboration with it during the first stages of the revolution?

All the results of this policy demonstrate the necessity of a categorical reply in the affirmative. The task of the Communist International in China, as in all other colonial countries, is to mobilize all the available forces that can be led into the struggle against imperialism. It is perfectly evident that the classes which make up these forces cannot all be mobilized on the Communist platform. A much broader basis must be found for this purpose. In China, such a basis could be created by the Kuomintang. For this reason, the starting point of the policy of the Communist International in China consisted in the support of the Kuomintang, in giving it strength and assistance for the purpose of developing the anti-imperialist struggle.

For many long years the Kuomintang existed in name only. It was an [unofficial], amorphous association of scattered groups and political intellectuals' clubs enjoying the moral and material support of rich merchants, mainly from abroad. The Kuomintang was not a political party. Its program was vague to the utmost; its organization was extremely diffuse. Its activities were chiefly conspiratorial in character and relied on favorable military combinations and on taking advantage of contradictions between the imperialist powers. The movement had no roots in the masses. However, thanks to the important role that the Kuomintang played in the revolution of 1911 and in subsequent events, it had democratic traditions behind it. In general, the Kuomintang's platform was national independence of the democracy and social progress. The national sentiments of the whole people and the indignation at the foreign yoke sought fitting and effective expression in the Kuomintang.

Under the influence and with the support of the Communist International, the Kuomintang turned into a political party with a revolutionary democratic program and with organizational forms necessary for conducting an effective struggle against imperialism. The Kuomintang outgrew the traditions of conspiratorial diplomacy and military actions. It began to orient itself toward the masses. It understood that the active participation of the masses is the prime condition for the success of the anti-imperialist struggle. It was precisely in this period of its reorganization that the Communist Party entered the Kuomintang at the suggestion of the Communist International. Before this, the Communist Party was a small group that consisted primarily of radical intellectuals possessing no organic ties of significance with the political life of the country. In order for the Communist Party to develop, it was first of all necessary to do away with this isolation. By entering the Kuomintang, the Communist Party was acquiring organic ties with the national-revolutionary movement and was receiving an opportunity to exert influence on it.

As a result of such a tactic, the national movement became a mass movement developing under the flag of the Kuomintang. At the very same time, the Communist Party penetrated the proletarian and peasant masses and became their leader. The laboring masses could not have been mobilized so quickly into the anti-imperialist struggle had not the Communist Party participated in the national-revolutionary movement as a component part of the Kuomintang. Such was the first stage of the revolution—the Kwangtung stage. The national-revolutionary party became organized. The party won the confidence of the masses. The Communist Party received the opportunity freely and legally to build powerful workers' and peasants' organizations over a considerable extent of the territory. A national-revolutionary state was created which, with the support of the masses, repelled imperialist attacks from Hong Kong and crushed the military actions of the native reaction inspired and supported by the self-same imperialism. A national army was also created. In short, the national revolution found a sufficiently strong base and was prepared to spread to other parts of the country. Then the

Northern Expedition started. On the second stage of the revolution, the policy of the Comintern was still to support the Kuomintang in order to carry the banner of the national revolution to other provinces in order to rout the Northern militarists who, in the capacity of agents of imperialism, ruled over Shanghai and the whole Yangtze Valley. The Northern Expedition gave the Communist Party a brilliant opportunity to conduct revolutionary agitation among the masses of a number of provinces. Many millions of peasants and workers, not as yet touched by the revolution, were not only drawn into the movement, but became organized under the exclusive leadership of the Communist Party. The military expansion increased the power of those feudal-bourgeois elements in the Kuomintang which were subsequently to betray the revolution, but at the same time the mass base of the revolution expanded to such enormous proportions that a guarantee was being created against any danger from the Right. The victories gained by the army under feudal-bourgeois leadership were of themselves of great revolutionary significance. The success of the Northern Expedition was indeed a big revolutionary victory. The crushing defeat inflicted on the northern militarists in the Yangtze Valley was a cruel blow to the power and prestige of imperialism not only in China, but in the entire Far East. The seizure by the masses of the British concession in Hankow and the uprising of the Shanghai proletariat who discerned the menacing forces of world imperialism poised for armed intervention, were the culminating point of the revolutionary development.

The Right feudal-bourgeois elements of the Kuomintang understood that the revolution was proceeding over their heads and that the Communists were supporting them only in the interests of developing the revolution. This betrayal by the feudal-bourgeois elements which in effect occurred in March, 1927 was, however, anticipated by the Communist International back in November, 1926 when it foresaw the third stage in the development of the revolution. [See *Document 1:* Theses on the Chinese Situation by the Seventh Extraordinary Plenum of the Executive Committee of the Communist International, Sections 5 and 6.] It was assumed that in the third stage the revolution would be abandoned by the feudal-bourgeois elements and that it would be based on a coalition of three classes: the proletariat, the peasantry, and the urban petty bourgeoisie. In this period, the revolution was to develop under the slogans of land confiscation and democratic dictatorship. This course of development for the Chinese revolution was outlined by the Communist International in November, 1926.

Support of the Left-Wing Kuomintang as an organ of struggle against imperialism and national reaction, including the traitorous bourgeoisie, became all the more necessary when the feudal-bourgeois elements turned against the revolution. The petty bourgeoisie, frequently constituting the majority of the population in Chinese towns, represents a highly important social factor in China. These petty-bourgeois masses were imbued with resolute anti-imperialist sentiments and they stood behind the Kuomintang. The peasant movement was spreading under the protection of the Kuomintang which commanded considerable authority among the peasantry. Even among the working-class masses, the Kuomintang still enjoyed great popularity. Under such circumstances, the Communist Party had to remain in the ranks of the Kuomintang and use it as the center around which all revolutionary-democratic forces were grouping themselves. Such were the tactics of the Wuhan period. The Kuomintang was still the party of the national revolution. The Communist Party could not break with the Kuomintang, subjected as it was to attack by imperialism and native reaction; it would have resulted in confusion among the masses who still trusted the Kuomintang.

The purpose of collaboration with the Kuomintang during the Wuhan period was to free it once and for all from the influence of the feudal-bourgeois elements that had turned against the revolution and to convert it into an organ of democratic dictatorship under the hegemony of the proletariat. The leaders of the Communist Party could not understand this. For collaboration they substituted capitulation. Their opportunism hampered the development of mass revolutionary action and, especially, the agrarian revolution which could crush the forces of reaction. In this case, defeat could have been avoided, and the revolution would have continued to develop uninterruptedly until it achieved final victory.

As it happened, however, the revolution suffered a series of defeats at the very moment when it should have outgrown the Kuomintang period. The basic reasons for the defeat lay in the objective conditions—the unequal alignment of forces. But the Bolshevik policy, pursued by the Communist International in the course of the subsequent stages of the revolution, had created for it such a firm mass base that had there been available at the critical moment a genuine Bolshevik leadership, the forces would have turned out to have been equal. In this event, the revolution, developing in a constantly rising movement, would have achieved final victory.

BIBLIOGRAPHY

BIBLIOGRAPHY

NOTE: Except for a few items marked with an asterisk (*), the sources listed below are in the Hoover Library, Stanford, California.

BOOKS, ARTICLES, POLITICAL DOCUMENTS

Aikhenvald, A. "O takticheskoi linii Kominterna v Kitae" (On the tactical line of the Comintern in China), *Pravda,* Nos. 102, 103, 104, May 8, 10, 11, 1927. Also appeared in book form under the same title.

*Bakulin, A. B. *Zapiski ob ukhanskom periode kitaiskoi revoliutsii* (*Iz istorii kitaiskoi revoliutsii 1925–1927 g.g.*) (Notes on the Wuhan period of the Chinese revolution, 1925–1927). Moscow and Leningrad, 1930.

Borodin, M. M. "Krestianskoe dvizhenie v pr. Khubei: Rech t. Borodina proiznesennaia na krestianskom sezde v U-chan" (The peasant movement in Hupei province: Speech of Comrade Borodin at the peasant congress at Wuhan). *Materialy po Kitaiskomu Voprosu,* No. 9, 1927, pp. 4–44.

———. "Prichiny porazheniia kitaiskoi revoliutsii" (Reasons for the defeat of the Chinese revolution), *Izvestiia Ulan-Bator-Khoto,* No. 73 (417), September 28, 1927, pp. 3–4.

Brandt, Conrad. "Bibliographical Sketch. Ch'ên Tu-hsiu, Pre-Communist Phase." Harvard University Library. Papers on China from Regional Studies Seminar, Vol. II.

———. *Stalin's Failure in China.* Cambridge, Mass., 1958.

Brandt, Conrad, John K. Fairbank, and Benjamin Schwartz. *A Documentary History of Chinese Communism.* Cambridge, Mass.: Harvard University Press, 1952.

Bubnov, A. "O kitaiskoi revoliutsii" (On the Chinese revolution), *Kommunisticheskaia Revoliutsiia,* No. 8, April 1927, pp. 3–10.

Bukharin, N. I. "An Abrupt Turn in the Chinese Revolution," *International Press Correspondence,* VII:41 (July 14, 1927), 897–899 and VII:42 (July 21, 1927), 927–930.

———. "Development in the Chinese Revolution," *The Communist International,* July 30, 1927, pp. 219–222.

———. "Na krutom perevale kitaiskoi revoliutsii" (At a steep pass of the Chinese revolution), *Pravda*, No. 154, July 10, 1927, pp. 2–3.

———. "Perspektivy kitaiskoi revoliutsii: doklad . . . Ianvar 1927" (Prospects of the Chinese revolution: Report . . . January, 1927), *Revoliutsionnyi Vostok*, No. 1, 1927, pp. 3–21. Address to the students of the Communist University of the Toilers of the Far East.

———. "Problemy kitaiskoi revoliutsii" (Problems of the Chinese revolution), *Pravda*, Nos. 88 and 89, April 19 and 20, 1927. Also in a separate publication: *Les problèmes de la révolution Chinoise*, Paris, 192–.

———. "Tekushchii moment kitaiskoi revoliutsii" (The present stage of the Chinese revolution), *Pravda*, No. 145, June 30, 1927, pp. 2–3. Also in English: "The Position of the Chinese Revolution," *International Press Correspondence*, VII:39 (July 7, 1927), 874–876.

———. "Results of the [Eighth] Plenary Session of the ECCI on the Chinese Revolution," *International Press Correspondence*, VII:39 (July 7, 1927), 879–884.

Ch'ên Pan-tsu [Ch'en T'an-ch'iu]. "Reminiscences of the First Congress of the Communist Party of China," *The Communist International*, October, 1936, pp. 1361–1363.

Ch'ên Tu-hsiu. "Kuo-min-tang tang-nei chiu fen yü chung-kuo ko-ming" (Internal conflict of the Kuomintang and the Chinese revolution), *Hsiang-tao-chou-pao*, No. 190, March 6, 1927, pp. 2045–2046.

———. *Kao ch'üan-tang t'ung-chih-shu* (Letter to the Comrades of the Communist Party), [n.p.] December 10, 1929. Also: "Pismo tov. Chen Du-siu ko vsem chlenam kitaiskoi kommunisticheskoi partii" (Letter of Comrade Ch'en Tu-hsiu to all members of the Chinese Communist Party), *Biulleten Oppozitsii*, No. 15–16, September–October, 1930, pp. 19–33.

———. "Rech tov. Chen Du-siu" (Speech of Comrade Ch'ên Tu-hsiu), *Pravda*, May 15, 1927, p. 2. Abridged translation of Ch'ên Tu-hsiu's speech at the Fifth Congress of the Chinese Communist Party, April 29, 1927. Also "Political Report at the Fifth Congress of the Chinese Communist Party," *International Press Correspondence*, VII:34 (June 9, 1927), 716–717 (abridged).

———. "Shih-yüeh ko-ming yü tung-fang" (The October Revolution and the East), *Hsiang-tao chou-pao*, November 15, 1926, pp. 1849–1850.

Chinese Communist Party. "Letter to the Kuomintang, June 16, 1927," *International Press Correspondence*, VII:37 (June 30, 1927), 783–784.

Ch'ü Ch'iu-pai. *Chung-kuo ko-ming chung chih cheng-lun wen-t'i* (Controversial problems in the Chinese revolution). [n.p.] 1928.

Chu Hsin-fan [also known as Chu Ch'i-hua]. *Chung-kuo ko-ming yü chung-kuo she-hui ko-chieh-chi* (The Chinese revolution and China's social classes). 2 vols., Shanghai, 1930.

Chung-kuo hsien-tai-shih yen-chiu-hui (Modern Chinese History Research Association). *Chung-kuo hsien-tai ko-ming yün-tung shih* (History of the contemporary revolutionary movements in China). 2 vols., Yenan, 1941.

Communist International. *Piatyi Vsemirnyi Kongress Kommunisticheskogo Internatsionala, 17 iiunia–8 iiulia 1924 g: Stenograficheskii otchet* (Fifth Congress of the Communist International, June 17–July 8, 1924: Stenographic report). Moscow-Leningrad, 1925.

———. *Protokoll des Vierten Kongresses der Kommunistischen Internationale, Petrograd-Moskau vom 5. November bis 5. Dezember 1922.* Hamburg, 1923.

———. *Kommunisticheskii Internatsional v dokumentakh: Resheniia, tezisy i vozvaniia kongressov Kominterna i plenumov IKKI, 1919–1932* (The Communist International in Documents: Decisions, theses, and appeals of the Congress of the Comintern and Plenums of the ECCI, 1919–1932). Moscow, 1933.

———. *Vtoroi Kongress Kominterna, iiul-avgust, 1920 g.* (Second Congress of the Comintern, July–August, 1920). Moscow, 1934.

Communist International. Executive Committee. *Die chinesische Frage auf dem 8. Plenum der Exekutive der Kommunistischen Internationale, Mai 1927.* Hamburg–Berlin, 1928.

———. *Puti mirovoi revoliutsii: Sedmoi rasshirennyi plenum Ispolnitelnogo Komiteta Kommunisticheskogo Internatsionala, 22 noiabria–16 dekabria 1926. Stenograficheskii otchet* (The ways of world revolution: Seventh Plenum of the Executive Committee of the Communist International, November 22–December 16, 1926. Stenographic report). Moscow, 1927.

"Declaration of the Executive Committee of the Kuomintang." *Pravda*, No. 76, April 5, 1927, p. 2.

"Declaration of the First Congress of the Kuomintang," in Hsü, *Sun Yatsen: His Political and Social Ideas*, pp. 119–141.

"Deklaratsiia priniataia na avgustovskoi konferentsii KKP" (Declaration passed at the August [1927] conference of the Chinese Communist Party) in Mif, *Kitaiskaia Kommunisticheskaia Partiia v kriticheskie dni*, pp. 200–239; also *Materialy po Kitaiskomu Voprosu*, No. 8, 1927, pp. 13–26; see also Brandt, et. al. *A Documentary History of Chinese Communism*, pp. 109–114.

"Dispatch from Consul General Lockhart, Hankow, to Secretary of State, January 22, 1927." State Department Archives, 893.00/8342, as cited in Wilbur and How, *Documents on Communism*, pp. 400–401.

"Discours du Général Tsiang kie-cheu à Nan-tch'ang, le 7 mars 1927 contre la faction communiste de Ou-Hang . . . Abrégé" in Wieger, *Chine moderne*, VIII, 133–134.

Dridzo, S. A. [A. Lozovsky]. *Revoliutsiia i kontr-revoliutsiia v Kitae* (Revolution and counterrevolution in China). Moscow, 1927; also *Revolution und Konterrevolution in China*. Moscow, 1928; also *Pravda*, Nos. 204, 205, 206, 207, 209, 210, September 8, 10, 11, 14, 15, 1927.

Ercoli, M. [Palmiro Togliatti]. "Report on the Chinese Commission [of the Eighth Plenum of the ECCI, May 1927]" in Communist International. Executive Committee. *Die chinesische Frage auf dem 8. Plenum der*

Exekutive der Kommunistischen Internationale, Mai 1927, pp. 145–151.

Fischer, Louis. *The Soviets in World Affairs.* 2d ed., 2 vols. Princeton, 1951.

Grossman, Richard (ed.). *The God That Failed.* New York, 1949. [pp. 106 ff.: Eighth Plenum of the ECCI, May 1927.]

Hatano, Ken-ichi. "Chūgoku Kyōsan-tō-shi" (History of the Chinese Communist Party). *Ajia Mondai Koza.* Tokyo and Osaka, 1939, II, 23–46.

Holcomb, Arthur N. *The Chinese Revolution: A Phase in the Regeneration of World Power.* Cambridge, Mass., 1930.

How, Julie Lien-ying. *See* Wilbur.

Hsü, Leonard Shih-lien. *Sun Yat-sen: His Political and Social Ideas.* Los Angeles, 1933.

Hsueh, Chun-tu. *The Chinese Communist Movement, 1921–1937: An Annotated Bibliography of Selected Materials in the Chinese Collection of the Hoover Institution on War, Revolution, and Peace.* Stanford University, The Hoover Institution, 1960. 131 pp.

Hua Kang. *I-chiu-erh-wu-nien chih-i-chiu-erh-ch'i-nien-te chung-kuo ta ko-ming shih.* (History of the great Chinese revolution, 1925–1927). Shanghai, 1931.

Huston Collection of Miscellaneous Materials dealing with cultural, political, and economic conditions in China, 1917–1931. Hoover Institution, Stanford, California.

Huston, Jay Calvin. "Sun Yat-sen, the Kuomintang and the Chinese–Russian Political Economic Alliance." An unpublished manuscript in the Huston Collection, Hoover Institution, Stanford, California.

*India, Government of. *Judgment in the Meerut Communist Conspiracy Case. Judgment delivered by R. L. Yorke, Esq., I. C. S., Additional Sessions Judge, Meerut, on January 16, 1933 in the Meerut Communist Conspiracy Case. Sessions Trial No. 2 of 1930. King Emperor versus P. Spratt and Others. Charge under Section 121-A, I. P. C.* 2 vols. Simla: Government of India Press, 1932–1933.

Isaacs, Harold. *The Tragedy of the Chinese Revolution.* 2d. rev. ed. Stanford University Press, California, 1961.

"Istoricheskie korni Chen'dusiuizma: Doklad t. Kommunara i rechi tt. Chang Biao [?], V. Strakhova, G. Voitinskogo i dr." (Historical roots of Ch'en Tu-hsu-ism: Report by Comrade Kommunar and speeches by Comrades Chang Biao [?], V. Strakhov, G. Voitinsky and others), *Problemy Kitaia,* No. 3, 1930, pp. 189–231.

Kommunisticheskii Internatsional (Communist International). 1919–1943. Periodical. Moscow. Organ of the ECCI. Also appeared in English, French, and German.

"Krestianskoe dvizhenie v Khunane" (The peasant movement in Hunan), *Kommunisticheskii Internatsional,* No. 21 (95), May 27, 1927, pp. 22–29. Also published in the Chinese Communist Party's organ, *Guide Weekly,* March 12, 1927.

"Krizis levogo Gomindana" (Crisis of the Left Kuomintang), *Pravda,* No. 167, July 28, 1927, p. 1. (Editorial.)

Kun-ch'an kuo-chi tui chung-kuo ko-ming chüch-i-an (Resolutions of the Comintern on the Chinese revolution). With an introductory article by Po-shan (pseud. of Li Li-san) entitled "The Lessons of China's great revolution, 1925–1927." Shanghai, 1950.

Kuo-min-tang chung-yang chien-ch'a wei-yüan-hui (The Central Committee of the Kuomintang), "T'an-ho Kung-ch'an-tang liang ta yao-an" (Two proposals for the impeachment of the Communist Party), as cited in Schwartz, *Chinese Communism and the Rise of Mao,* p. 51.

Lenin, V. I. *Sochineniia* (Works), 2d ed., 30 vols. Moscow and Leningrad, 1926–1932.

Lentsner, N. "Ideologicheskie istochniki oshibok rukovodstva Kitkompartii" (Ideological origins of mistakes in the leadership of the Chinese Communist Party), *Kommunisticheskii Internatsional,* No. 32 (106), August 12, 1927, pp. 6–11.

"The Letter from Shanghai, March 17, 1927." Signed by N. Nazonov [Nassonov], N. Fokine, and A. Albrecht and reproduced in Trotsky, *Problems of the Chinese Revolution,* pp. 387–432. Also in a separate issue: N. Nazonov, *La lettre de Shanghai, document inédit cashé par Staline.* Paris, 1927.

"Lettre du général Tsiang kie-cheu aux Camrades du Parti révolutionnaire, le 16 mai 1927" in Wieger, *Chine moderne,* VIII, 151–154.

Liau Han-sun (Li Han-chün). "The Betrayer of the People, Chiang Kai-shek and the Revolutionary Kuomintang," *International Press Correspondence,* VII:26 (April 21, 1927), 527–528.

Li Chi-hu. "Natsionalnaia revoliutsionnaia armiia Kitaia i politrabota v nei" (The National Revolutionary Army of China and political work in it), *Revoliutsionnyi Vostok,* No. 2, 1927, pp. 122–133.

Li Min-hun (comp.). *Ch'ih se tang an* (Materials on Red activities in China). Peking, 1929.

Lozovsky. *See* Dridzo.

Madiar, L. (Magyar, L. I.). "Ob izuchenii agrarnogo voprosa v Kitae" (On the study of the agrarian problem in China), *Revoliutsionnyi Vostok,* Nos. 4–5, 1928, pp. 77–99.

Mandalian, T. "Pochemu obankrotilos rukovodstvo kitaiskoi kompartii" (Why did the leadership of the Chinese Communist Party fail?), *Pravda,* No. 159, July 16, 1927, pp. 2–3; also trans. in Chinese: Mandalyan, *Wei shen-ma chung-ko kung ch'an-tang ti ling-tao p'o-ch'an,* Moscow, Sun Yat-sen University, 1927, as listed in Wilbur and How, *Documents on Communism,* p. 583.

Mao Tse-tung. "Krestianskoe dvizhenie v Khunani: Pismo s Chansha ot 18 fevralia s.g." (The peasant covement in Hunan: A letter from Changsha, February 18, 1927). *Revoliutsionnyi Vostok,* No. 2, 1927, pp. 107–122.

Maring, G. (Hendricus Sneevliet). "Revoliutsionno-natsionalisticheskoe dvizhenie v iuzhnom Kitae" (Revolutionary-nationalist movement in South China), *Kommunisticheskii Internatsional,* No. 22, 1922, pp. 5803–5815.

Martynov, A. "K peregruppirovke sil kitaiskoi revoliutsii" (On the regrouping of the forces of the Chinese revolution), *Kommunisticheskii Internatsional*, No. 8 (82), February 25, 1927, pp. 9–18.

———. "A New Stage of the Victorious Revolution," *The Communist International*, No. 7, May 1, 1927, pp. 131–133. (On the seizure of Shanghai by the workers.)

———. "Problema kitaiskoi revoliutsii" (The problem of the Chinese revolution), *Pravda*, No. 81, April 10, 1927, pp. 4–5.

Mif, P. A. *Kitaiskaia Kommunisticheskaia Partiia v kriticheskie dni* (The Chinese Communist Party in critical days). Moscow, Gosizdat 1928; also *Bolshevik*, Nos. 21, 23–24, November 15 and December 31, 1927; No. 5, March 15, 1928.

———. "Kharakter i dvizhushchie sily kitaiskoi revoliutsii" (The nature and the moving forces of the Chinese revolution), *Bolshevik*, No. 1, January 1, 1927, pp. 12–26.

———. "Krestianskii vopros v Kitae" (The peasant problem in China), *Kommunisticheskii Internatsional*, No. 10–11 (68–69), November 22, 1926, pp. 26–36; No. 13 (71), December 10, 1926, pp. 20–28.

*———. *Kitaiskaia revoliutsiia* (The Chinese Revolution). Moscow, 1932.

———. "Spornye voprosy kitaiskoi revoliutsii" (Debatable problems of the Chinese revolution), *Bolshevik*, No. 3–4, February 29, 1928, pp. 108–122.

"Minutes of the Chinese Subcommittee of the ECCI," *The New Militant*. New York, February 8, 1936.

Mitarevsky, N. *World-Wide Soviet Plots as Disclosed by Hitherto Unpublished Documents Seized at the U.S.S.R. Embassy in Peking*. Tientsin, 1927.

Nazonov, N. (Nassonov). *See* "The Letter from Shanghai."

North, Robert C. *Moscow and Chinese Communists*. Stanford, California, rev. ed. 1962.

*Nose, Torazō. *Shina ni okeru Kominterun Seisaku no Tokusei ni kansuru Ippanteki Kenkyū* (General studies of the characteristics of Comintern policies in China). Tokyo, 1941.

"The Parting of the Ways in China," *The Communist International*, No. 11, July 30, 1927, pp. 210–213. (Editorial.)

"V [Piatyi] sezd Kompartii Kitaia i Gomindan" (The Fifth Congress of the Chinese Communist Party and the Kuomintang), *Kommunisticheskii Internatsional*, No. 11 (85), March 18, 1927, pp. 3–8.

Pick, Eugene (pseud.). *China in the Grip of the Reds*. Shanghai, 1927.

"Plans on the Organization of Party Cells," as trans. in Wilbur and How, *Documents on Communism*, pp. 104–109.

"Pobeda shankhaiskikh rabochikh" (Victory of the Shanghai workers), *Pravda*, No. 65, March 22, 1927, p. 1. (Editorial.)

"Political Report of the Central Committee of the Chinese Communist Party," January 26, 1927, as trans. in Wilbur and How, *Documents on Communism*, pp. 421–434.

Popov, K. "Marks i Engels o krestianstve v proletarskoi revoliutsii" (Marx and Engels on peasantry in the proletarian revolution), *Kommunistiche-skaia Revoliutsiia,* No. 8, April 1927, pp. 11–25.

"Postanovlenie IKKI o tekushchem momente kitaiskoi revoliutsii" (Resolution of the ECCI on the present situation in the Chinese revolution), *Pravda,* No. 157, July 14, 1927, p. 2; also *International Press Correspondence,* VII:44 (July 28, 1927), 983–985.

"Problema kitaiskoi revoliutsii" (The problem of the Chinese revolution), *Pravda,* No. 180, August 10, 1927, p. 3. Section 3 of the Resolution on the International Situation by the Joint Plenum of the Central Committee and Central Control Commission of the All-Russian Communist Party (B), August 9, 1927.

Rafes, M. G. *Kitaiskaia revoliutsiia na perelome* (The Chinese revolution at a turning point). Moscow, 1927.

"Resolution of the ECCI on the Present Situation of the Chinese Revolution." *International Press Correspondence,* VII:44 (July 28, 1927), 983–985.

"Resolution [of the Eighth Plenum ECCI, May 1927] on the Chinese Question," *International Press Correspondence,* VII:35 (June 16, 1927), 737–741; also *Kommunisticheskii Internatsional v dokumentakh,* pp. 717–729.

"Resolutions on the Peasant Movement," as trans. in Wilbur and How, *Documents on Communism,* pp. 296–302.

"Resolutions on the Problem of the KMT Left Wing . . . ," as cited in Wilbur and How, *Documents on Communism,* pp. 376, 378.

"Resolutions on the Question of Organization," as trans. in Wilbur and How, *Documents on Communism,* pp. 100–103.

"Resolutions on Relations Between the Chinese Communist Party and the Kuomintang," as trans. in Wilbur and How, *Documents on Communism,* pp. 278–281.

"Revoliutsiia i kontr-revoliutsiia v Kitae" (Revolution and counterrevolution in China). *Bolshevik,* No. 7–8, April 15, 1927, pp. 3–12. (Editorial.)

"Revoliutsiia v Kitae i Gomindan" (Revolution in China and the Kuomintang). *Pravda,* No. 61, March 16, 1927, p. 1. (Editorial.)

Roy, M. N. "The Fifth Congress of the Communist Party of China," *International Press Correspondence,* VII:41 (July 14, 1927), 909–910. Also in French edition on July 13, 1927.

————. *India in Transition.* With collaboration of Abani Mukherji. Geneva, 1922.

————. *Kitaiskaia revoliutsiia i Kommunisticheskii Internatsional. Sbornik statei i materialov* (The Chinese revolution and the Communist International). Moscow-Leningrad, 1929.

————. *My Experience in China.* 2d ed. Calcutta, 1945.

————. "New Economic Policy of British Imperialism," *The Communist International,* No. 21, 1926, pp. 70–91.

————. "Polozhenie vnutri Kommunisticheskoi Partii Kitaia ko vremeni V sezda" (The situation within the Chinese Communist Party at the time of the Fifth Congress), *Kommunisticheskii Internatsional,* No. 41, October 14, 1927, pp. 46–47.

———. *Political Letters.* Zürich, 1924.

———. "Revolution and Counter-Revolution in China," *International Press Correspondence,* VII:42 (July 21, 1927), 926.

———. *Revolution and Counter-Revolution in China.* Calcutta: Renaissance Publishers, 1946.

———. "Social Democracy and the Chinese Revolution," *International Press Correspondence,* VI:93 (December 31, 1926), 1643–1645.

Schwartz, Benjamin. *Chinese Communism and the Rise of Mao.* Cambridge, Mass., 1951.

Sia Ting. "The Peasant Movement in China," *International Press Correspondence,* VII:36 (June 23, 1927), 760–761.

Sokolsky, George E. "The Kuomintang," *The China Year Book.* Tientsin, 1928, pp. 1309–1402.

"The Significance of the Plenum of the Executive Committee of the Kuomintang," *Pravda,* No. 76, April 5, 1927, p. 2. (In Russian.)

"Soviet Intrigues in China." Huston Collection, Hoover Institution, Stanford, California.

"Soviet Report on the Split Between Chiang Kai-shek and T'ang Sheng-chih," as trans. in Wilbur and How, *Documents on Communism,* pp. 435–436.

Stalin, J. *Works,* I– . Moscow, 1946– .

———. "Concerning Questions of the Chinese Revolution: Reply to comrade Marchulin," *Works,* IX, 236–242.

———. *Marxism and the National and Colonial Question; A Collection of Articles and Speeches.* New York, 1935; also in Russian: *Marksizm i natsionalno-kolonialnyi vopros* [Moscow], 1935.

———. "Notes on Contemporary Themes," *Works,* IX, 328–369; also *Pravda,* No. 169, July 28, 1927, pp. 5–6.

———. "The Prospects of the Revolution in China: A Speech delivered in the Chinese Commission [of the Seventh Plenum] of the ECCI, November 30, 1926," *Works,* VIII, 373–391; also *Bolshevik,* No. 23–24, December 31, 1926, pp. 13–21; also *Kommunisticheskii Internatsional,* No. 13 (71), December 10, 1926, pp. 9–19.

———. "Questions of the Chinese Revolution: Theses for Propagandists, Approved by the CC [of the] CPSU (B)." *Works,* IX, 224–234; also *Pravda,* No. 90, April 21, 1927, p. 3.

———. "The Revolution in China and the Tasks of the Comintern: Speech delivered at the Tenth Sitting, Eighth Plenum of the ECCI, May 24, 1927," *Works,* IX, 288–318.

———. "Talk with Students of the Sun Yat-sen University, May 13, 1927," *Works,* IX, 243–273.

Sten, Ia. "Kitaiskaia revoliutsiia i taktika Kominterna" (The Chinese revolution and the tactics of the Comintern), *Kommunisticheskaia Revoliutsiia,* No. 13–14, July 1927, pp. 28–43.

———. "Voprosy kitaiskoi revoliutsii" (Problems of the Chinese revolution),

Kommunisticheskaia Revoliutsiia, No. 16–17, August–September, 1927, pp. 34–43.

"Stepanov's Report at a Meeting of the Communist Party Branch," as trans. in Wilbur and How, *Documents on Communism*, pp. 248–253.

"Stepanov's Report on the Present Situation of the Russians in Kwangtung Following Conflict between Chiang Kai-shek and the Russians," as trans. in Wilbur and How, *Documents on Communism*, pp. 254–265.

Stetsky, A. "Kriticheskii punkt kitaiskoi revoliutsii" (Critical point in the Chinese revolution), *Pravda*, No. 85, April 15, 1927, p. 2; also in the *China Weekly Review*, July 30, 1927 (Huston Collection).

*Su-lien yin-mou wen-cheng hui-pien (Collection of documentary evidence of the Soviet Russian conspiracy). 10 vols., ed. and trans. by Peking Metropolitan Police Headquarters, Inspection Bureau, Commission for Translation and Compilation. Peking, 1928.

"Supplementary Theses." Russian text in Communist International, *Vtoroi Kongress Kominterna, iiul–avgust 1920 g.*, pp. 496–499.

Tan Ping-shan. *Entwicklungswege der chinesischen Revolution*. Hamburg–Berlin, 1927.

Tang Shin She [T'ang Sheng-chih]. "The Advance on Peking," *International Press Correspondence*, VII:34 (June 9, 1927), 711.

———. "The Canton Government and the Revolutionary Movement in China," *International Press Correspondence*, VI:27 (April 8, 1926), 415–416.

———. "The Victory of the Shanghai Workers," *International Press Correspondence*, VII:22 (March 31, 1927), 445–446.

T'ang Leang-li. *The Inner History of the Chinese Revolution*. London, 1930.

Teruni. "A Report to Borodin from Teruni, a Red Military Adviser [October 30, 1926], Following the Occupation of Wuhan by the Revolutionary Army," as trans. in Wilbur and How, *Documents on Communism*, pp. 413–421.

*"Ti-erh-tz'u ch'üan-kuo tai-piao ta hui hsüan-yen" (Manifesto of the Second Congress of the Chinese Communist Party [1922]) in Chu Hsin-fan. *Chung-kuo ko-ming yü chung-kuo she-hui ko-chieh-chih*, I, 259–280.

"Theses on the National and Colonial Questions." Russian text in Communist International, *Vtoroi Kongress Kominterna, iiul–avgust 1920 g.*, pp. 490–496.

Trotsky, L. D. "First Speech on the Chinese Question, Delivered at the Eighth Plenum of the ECCI" in *Problems of the Chinese Revolution*, pp. 83–101.

*———. "Kitaiskaya Kompartiya i Gomindan" (The Chinese Communist Party and the Kuomintang). Trotsky Archives, Harvard University Library, dated September 27, 1926.

———. *Problems of the Chinese Revolution*. Trans. with an introduction by Max Shachtman. New York: 1932.

———. *The Stalin School of Falsification*. New York, 1937.

*———. "Voprosy nashei politiki v otnoshenii Kitaya i Yaponii" (The prob-

lems of our policy in regard to China and Japan). Trotsky Archives. Harvard University Library.

Ts'ai Ho-sen. "Istoriia opportunizma v Kommunisticheskoi Partii Kitaia" (An account of opportunism in the Chinese Communist Party), *Problemy Kitaia,* No. 1, 1929, pp. 1–77. Original appears in Li Min-hun (comp.), *Ch'ih setang an.*

Voitinsky, G. N. "K voprosu ob oshibkakh Kitaiskoi Kompartii v revoliutsii 1925–1927 gg." (On the question of the Chinese Communist Party's mistakes in the revolution of 1925–1927), *Problemy Kitaia,* No. 4–5, 1930, pp. 84–104.

————. "The Situation in China and the Plans of the Imperialists," *International Press Correspondence,* VI:39 (May 6, 1926), 599–601.

"Vozvanie Ispolkoma Gomindana" (Appeal of the Executive Committee of the Kuomintang), *Pravda,* No. 76, April 5, 1927, p. 2.

Vuyo Vuyovich. Speech at the Eighth Plenum of the ECCI in May 1927, as reproduced in Trotsky, *Problems of the Chinese Revolution,* pp. 382–396.

Wan, Yah-kang. *The Rise of Communism in China, 1920–1950.* Hongkong, 1952.

Wang Ching-wei. "Politicheskii otchet Van Tin-veia na II kongresse Gomindana (v Ianvare 1926 g.)" (Political report by Wang Chiang-wei to the Second Congress of the Kuomintang, January 1926), *Novyi Vostok,* No. 18, 1927, pp. 4–39. (Including the peasant question and the Kuomintang.)

————. "Razlichie mezhdu kommunizmon i Suniantsenizmom" (The difference between Communism and Sun Yat-sen-ism), *Materialy po Kitaiskomu Voprosu,* No. 1 (10), 1928, pp. 23–28. Speech to the students of Shanghai College, December 1927, trans. from Chinese.

Wieger, P. Leon, et. al. (compilers and translators). *Chine moderne.* 2d ed., 10 vols. [n.p.], 1920–1934.

Wilbur, C. Martin. *Chinese Sources on the History of the Chinese Communist Movement: An Annotated Bibliography.* New York: East Asian Institute of Columbia University, 1950.

Wilbur, C. Martin and Julie Lien-ying How (eds. and comps.). *Documents on Communism: Nationalism and Soviet Advisers in China 1918–1927. Papers Seized in the 1927 Peking Raid.* New York, 1956. With introductory essays by the editors.

Woo, T. C. *The Kuomintang and the Future of the Chinese Revolution.* London, 1928.

Wu Chih-hui. *Ko-ming yü fan-ko-ming* (Revolution and counterrevolution). Comp. by Lang Hsing-shih. Shanghai, 1928.

Yakhontoff, Victor. *The Chinese Soviets.* New York, 1934.

Zeitlin, E. "The New Stage of the Chinese Revolution," *International Press Correspondence,* VII:37 (June 30, 1927), 782–783.

*Zinoview, G. E. "Zaiavlenie k stenogramme ob'edinnennogo plenuma Ts. K.

i Ts. K. K." (A statement attached to the minutes of the joint plenum of the CC and CCC). Trotsky Archives, Harvard University Library.

NEWSPAPERS AND PERIODICALS

Biulleten Oppozitsii (Bolshevikov-Lenintsev) (Bulletin of the Bolshevik-Leninist Opposition). Frequency varies. Paris, Berlin, New York. July 1929–1941 (Nos. 1–87). Trotskyite organ.

Bolshevik. Semimonthly. Moscow. April 1924——. Organ of the Central Executive Committee of the All-Russian Communist Party (B). Changed to *Kommunist* with No. 20, 1952. 18 issues yearly beginning with 1952.

The Communist. Monthly. London. Feb. 1927–Dec. 1928. Preceded and succeeded by *Communist Review,* 1921–1927 and Jan. 1929——.

The Communist International. Monthly. New York, London, and Leningrad. May 1919–Dec. 1940. Official organ of the Executive Committee of the Communist International. Appears also in Russian, German, French, Spanish, and Chinese.

International Press Correspondence. Weekly. Vienna, Berlin, London. 1921——. Superseded by *World News and Views* in 1938. Superseded by *World News,* January 1, 1954. Appears in English, French, German, and Spanish.

Izvestiia Ulan-Bator-Khoto (News of Ulan-Bator-Khoto). Daily. Ulan-Bator-Khoto (formerly Urga), Mongolia. 1924——?. A Russian-language newspaper for the Soviet Russian colony in Ulan-Bator-Khoto.

Kommunisticheskaia Revoliutsiia (Communist Revolution). Frequency varies. Moscow, 1920–1935. Organ of the Central Committee of the All-Russian Communist Party (B).

Kommunisticheskii Internatsional (Communist International). Frequency varies. Moscow, 1919–1943. Organ of the Executive Committee of the Communist International. Also appeared in English, French, Spanish, Chinese, and German.

Materialy po Kitaiskomu Voprosu (Materials on Chinese Problems). Sixteen issues per year. Moscow, 1927–1928. Organ of the Scientific Research Institute for the Study of China, attached to the Sun Yat-sen University of the Toilers of the Far East.

The New Militant. Weekly. New York, 1934–1936. Continued as *Militant,* 1937——. Organ of the Workers' Party of America.

New York Herald Tribune. Daily. New York, 1841——.

New York Times. Daily. New York, 1851——.

North China Herald. Weekly. Shanghai, 1850–1941.

Novyi Vostok (The New East). Frequency varies. Moscow, 1922–1930 (Vols. 1–28). Organ of the All-Russian Association for Eastern Studies.

Pan-Pacific Worker. Frequency varies. Hankow, 1927–1930. Organ of the Pan-Pacific Trade Union Secretariat.

The People's Tribune. Daily Hankow, 1926–1927.

Pravda (Truth). Daily. Moscow, March 1917—. Organ of the All-Russian Communist Party (B).

Problemy Kitaia (Chinese Problems). Frequency varies. Moscow, 1929–1935 (Vols. 1–14). Organ of the Scientific Research Association for the Study of the National and Colonial Problems.

Revoliutsionnyi Vostok (The Revolutionary East). Frequency varies. Moscow, 1927–1937. Organ of the Scientific Research Association for the Study of the National and Colonial Problems.

World News and Views. See *International Press Correspondence.*

INDEX